THE CLAIRMONT FAMILY
JOURNALS: 1855–1885

THE CLAIRMONT FAMILY JOURNALS: 1855–1885

Edited by Sharon L. Joffe

LONDON AND NEW YORK

First published 2021
by Routledge
2 Park Square, Milton Park, Abingdon, Oxon OX14 4RN

and by Routledge
52 Vanderbilt Avenue, New York, NY 10017

Routledge is an imprint of the Taylor & Francis Group, an informa business

© 2021 selection and editorial matter, Sharon L. Joffe; individual owners retain copyright in their own material.

The right of Sharon L. Joffe to be identified as the author of the editorial material, and of the authors for their individual chapters, has been asserted in accordance with sections 77 and 78 of the Copyright, Designs and Patents Act 1988.

All rights reserved. No part of this book may be reprinted or reproduced or utilised in any form or by any electronic, mechanical, or other means, now known or hereafter invented, including photocopying and recording, or in any information storage or retrieval system, without permission in writing from the publishers.

Trademark notice: Product or corporate names may be trademarks or registered trademarks, and are used only for identification and explanation without intent to infringe.

British Library Cataloguing-in-Publication Data
A catalogue record for this book is available from the British Library

Library of Congress Cataloging-in-Publication Data
A catalog record for this book has been requested

ISBN: 978-0-367-20550-8
eISBN: 978-0-429-26275-3

Typeset in Times New Roman
by Apex CoVantage, LLC

CONTENTS

Acknowledgments vii
Editorial Standards and Practices x
List of Abbreviations and Identification xiii
List of Illustrations xiv
Editorial Symbols xvi
Chronology of Pauline Maria Clairmont xvii
Chronology of Wilhelm Charles Gaulis Clairmont xviii

1 Introduction: The History of the Shelley and Clairmont Families — 1

2 Pauline Clairmont's Australian Journal (1855–1857) — 33

3 Wilhelm Clairmont's Journal (1861) — 236

4 "Meine Fussreise im Juli 1885": Walter Clairmont's Journal (German transcription and English translation; 1885) — 298

5 Pauline Clairmont, the Governess Occupation, and the Genre of Life Writing — 332

Appendix A: The Godwin-Shelley-Clairmont Family Genealogical Table — 355
Appendix B: Historicizing the Journals: Austria, Australia, and the Banat — 356
Appendix C: Wilhelm Clairmont as an Appraiser — 362
Appendix D: Pauline Clairmont's Death Certificate — 366

Appendix E: Notarized Marriage Certificate of William Godwin and Mary Jane Clairmont 368
Appendix F: The Testimonies of Alma Crüwell-Clairmont and Walter Clairmont 371
Appendix G: Rosalie, Lady Mander's Letters to Alma Crüwell-Clairmont 376
Index 398

ACKNOWLEDGMENTS

The Carl H. Pforzheimer Collection of Shelley and His Circle, New York Public Library, Astor, Lenox, and Tilden Foundations remains the source of all three journals, letters, documents, and most photographs contained in this collection. Dr. Elizabeth Denlinger, the curator of the Carl H. Pforzheimer Collection of Shelley and His Circle, as well as Dr. Claus Bally, Mr. Peter Bally, and Ms. Sylvia Bally, Clairmont family heirs, granted me permission to publish in full the journals and manuscripts from the later generations of the Clairmont family held in the Carl H. Pforzheimer Collection of Shelley and His Circle.

I am profoundly grateful to the following people who provided me with assistance as I worked on this edition:

Dr. Elizabeth Campbell Denlinger, the Curator of the Carl H. Pforzheimer Collection of Shelley and His Circle at the New York Public Library. Dr. Denlinger gave me permission to transcribe, edit, and publish the journals, letters, and manuscripts belonging to the later generations of the Clairmont family and housed in the Carl H. Pforzheimer Collection of Shelley and His Circle.

Mr. Charles Cuykendall Carter, the Assistant Curator of the Carl H. Pforzheimer Collection of Shelley and His Circle at the New York Public Library.

Before I published *The Clairmont Family Letters: 1839–1889* in 2017, Mr. Hans-Jörg Bally (1918–2015), husband of the late Mary Claire Bally-Clairmont, and Mr. Peter Bally and Dr. Claus Bally, his second cousins, granted me permission to publish all documents, letters, and photographs from the later generations of the Clairmont family held in the Carl H. Pforzheimer Collection of Shelley and His Circle. Dr. Claus Bally shared information about the Clairmont family, and Mr. Peter Bally provided me with documents, photographs, and information pertaining to the Clairmont and Bally families. For this current edition, Dr. Bally, Mr. Bally, and Ms. Sylvia Bally granted me permission to publish the journals, letters, documents, and photographs from the later generations of the Clairmont family. I am immensely grateful to Dr. Bally, Mr. Bally, and Ms. Bally for their kindness. The Bally family also provided photographic images for this edition.

Mr. Christopher David Lahr, the grandson of Rosalie, Lady Mander, granted me permission to transcribe, edit, and publish his grandmother's letters to Alma Crüwell-Clairmont.

ACKNOWLEDGMENTS

Mr. Simon Alexander, Senior Development Editor, Routledge Publishers.

Additionally, I express my gratitude to the following individuals:

Sir Nicholas Mander, distant cousin of Sir Geoffrey Mander, put me in contact with Christopher Lahr, grandson of Rosalie, Lady Mander.

Mayor Michael Ludwig, Mayor of Vienna, declared the Clairmont Family Tomb in the Evangelischer Friedhof Matzleinsdorf an "honorary grave" ("Ehrengräber"), thereby saving the tomb from destruction.

Ms. Astrid Ryper of the Cultural Heritage Unit of Municipal Department – 7 for Culture in Vienna helped in preserving the Clairmont Family Tomb in the Evangelischer Friedhof Matzleinsdorf. Ms. Ryper was instrumental in presenting my argument for preserving the tomb to the office of the Mayor of Vienna.

Mr. Wolfgang Peter, Evangelischer Friedhof Matzleinsdorf, showed me the Clairmont family tomb in both 2018 and 2019, and assisted in providing me with access to information about the tomb.

Dr. Stephen Wagner, former Curator of the Carl H. Pforzheimer Collection of Shelley and His Circle, allowed me to see the Clairmont family materials during my 2004 visit to the New York Public Library.

Ms. Pernille Valentin, Ballyana Stiftung für Familien- und Industriegeschichte, Switzerland, put me in contact in 2015 with Mr. Peter Bally and Dr. Claus Bally.

Mr. William Oates, University Archivist, University of New England, Armidale, New South Wales, Australia, researched documents from Wilhelm Clairmont's time in Australia and granted me access to, and permission to publish from, the Dangar papers in the archive of the University of New England.

The Office of the Provost at Lamar University awarded me a Summer Research Fellowship in 2018. The Summer Research Fellowship supported my travel to the Carl H. Pforzheimer Collection of Shelley and His Circle at the New York Public Library and allowed me to spend an extended period in 2018 working in the collection.

Dr. James Sanderson, Chair of the Department of English and Modern Languages at Lamar University.

I am grateful to Arlo Pignotti for his work on the initial transcriptions, and for the editing work of Ann C. Sherwin, American Translators Association–Certified Translator from German to English, who transcribed and translated the German sections of the journals.

I also wish to acknowledge the assistance of the following individuals:

> Dr. Bruce Barker-Benfield, former Senior Assistant Librarian at the Bodleian Library, Oxford, United Kingdom; Stephen Hebron, Bodleian Library, Oxford, United Kingdom; Kimberley Smith, Senior Editor at Routledge Taylor & Francis Group, History of the Americas; Rachel Douglas, Editor, Routledge Historical Resources; Sarajayne Smith, Production Editor, Taylor & Francis Books; Marie Roberts, Deputy Account Manager, Apex CoVantage; Dr. Doucet Devin Fischer, editor of Shelley

ACKNOWLEDGMENTS

and His Circle; Dr. Jeanne Moskal, University of North Carolina at Chapel Hill; Dr. Amy Smith, Lamar University Center for Teaching and Learning Enhancement; Casey Lea Ford; Kate Epstein; Eileen Hudson (Nottingham City Museums and Galleries); Simon Brown (Curator, Newstead Abbey); Tom Price (Nottingham Museums); Thomas Lisanti (Permissions and Reproductions Services, New York Public Library); Frau Fuhs, Evangelischer Friedhof Matzleinsdorf; Frau Proll, Evangelischer Friedhof Matzleinsdorf.

The following people and organizations provided me with information as I worked on *The Clairmont Family Letters: 1839–1889* (2017). Their previous contributions enabled me to continue my work for this current edition, so I extend my thanks to them again (I repeat here their academic or institutional affiliations as they were in 2017): Leopold Mikec Avberšec, Archival Adviser and Senior Librarian, Pokrajinski arhiv Maribor (Regional Archives Maribor, Slovenia); Herbert Fischer; Margaret Woods, Armidale Family History Group, Armidale, New South Wales, Australia; The Heraldic-Genealogical Society Adler, Vienna; Dr. Mohan Ramaswamy, Associate Head for Research and Graduate Services, North Carolina State University Libraries; Dr. Endre Domiczi, Head of the Dean's Office, Faculty of Agricultural and Food Sciences, University of West Hungary; Dr. László Varga, University of West Hungary, Sopron, Hungary; Mr. Attila Németh, Secretary, University of West Hungary Alumni Association; John Dangar; Anthony (Bill) Dangar; Dr. Ulrike Denk, Academic Staff, Archiv der Universität Wien, Austria; Professor Dr. Ulrich Fellmeth, Archiv der Universität, Universität Hohenheim, Stuttgart, Germany; David Suttor; Carol Churches, Bathurst Family History Group and Bathurst Historical Society, Bathurst, New South Wales, Australia; Dr. Ekaterina Obuchova, The Byron Society in Australia; Dr. Ruth Koblizek, Curator, Picture Archive, Medizinische Universität Wien, Austria; Dr. Steven Tötösy de Zepetnek, Purdue University; Martina Pelz, Bibliothek der Gesellschaft der Ärzte (Library of the Society of Physicians), Vienna, Austria.

I thank my late father, Philip Joffe, my mother Dr. Ada Joffe, my brother Dr. Ian Joffe, and my sister-in-law Leila Joffe for their encouragement.

Finally, I dedicate this book to my daughters, Amanda and Ashley, whose support for my work is invaluable. Their commitment to the projects they undertake inspires me and I am profoundly grateful for their guidance and love.

EDITORIAL STANDARDS AND PRACTICES

This volume consists of three journals. The first two belong to Pauline and Wilhelm Clairmont and are transcribed and edited here for the first time since they were written in 1855–1857 and 1861, respectively. The third journal transcribed here likely belongs to Walter Gaulis Clairmont, Wilhelm's son (the journal writer's identity is fully discussed elsewhere in this edition). These three journals are housed in the Carl H. Pforzheimer Collection of Shelley and His Circle in the New York Public Library, which is also the repository for the extant letters Pauline and Wilhelm wrote to family members and friends, available since 2017 in *The Clairmont Family Letters: 1839–1889*. Mary Claire Bally-Clairmont and her brother, Christoph Clairmont (the grandchildren of Wilhelm Clairmont), bequeathed the documents to the Carl H. Pforzheimer Collection in 1997 and 1998.

Pauline wrote at least sixteen journals, but I have not been able to find any of the other fifteen. After Hans-Jörg Bally, the surviving spouse of Mary Claire Bally-Clairmont, died in 2015, I requested any additional journals from his survivors, but there were none in their possession. I will continue to search for any remaining journals and hope to publish them in a future edition should they become available.

I copy here the editorial principles that I followed in my edited collection, *The Clairmont Family Letters: 1839–1889*, and I continue to follow the principles that Betty Bennett and Marion Kingston Stocking set out in their respective editions of Mary Shelley's letters, *The Letters of Mary Wollstonecraft Shelley* (Bennett, ed. The Johns Hopkins University Press), and the Clairmont family's correspondence, *The Clairmont Correspondence* (Stocking, ed. The Johns Hopkins University Press).

Each of the three journals in this edition has a unique identifying call number. When Christoph Clairmont and Mary Claire Bally-Clairmont bequeathed the family papers to the Carl H. Pforzheimer Collection of Shelley and His Circle, the documents were named "Clairmontana," a call number system that identified documents about Claire Clairmont. Every journal has been given a reference number that begins with the letters CL'ANA. As in *The Clairmont Family Letters: 1839–1889*, the words "Unpublished. Text: M. S. Pf. Coll." follow each CL'ANA number. With this reference, each of the three journals is designated as unpublished and a manuscript in the Carl H. Pforzheimer Collection of Shelley

EDITORIAL STANDARDS AND PRACTICES

and His Circle, New York Public Library, Astor, Lenox, and Tilden Foundations. The CL'ANA call numbers of each of the journals in this edition are as follows:

Pauline Clairmont's 1855–1857 Australian Journal: CL'ANA 0176, unpublished manuscript, Carl H. Pforzheimer Collection of Shelley and His Circle, New York Public Library, Astor, Lenox, and Tilden Foundations

Wilhelm Clairmont's 1861 Journal: CL'ANA 0177, unpublished manuscript, Carl H. Pforzheimer Collection of Shelley and His Circle, New York Public Library, Astor, Lenox, and Tilden Foundations

(Possibly) Walter Clairmont's 1885 "Meine Fussreise im Juli, 1885:" CL'ANA 0063, unpublished manuscript, Carl H. Pforzheimer Collection of Shelley and His Circle, New York Public Library, Astor, Lenox, and Tilden Foundations

All other unpublished documents belonging to the Carl H. Pforzheimer Collection of Shelley and His Circle and referenced in this edition are also indicated by their unique CL'ANA numbers.

My standards and practices follow these precepts:

1. I have transcribed all journal entries exactly as their authors wrote them. I have not corrected any grammatical, spelling, or syntactical errors. I have not guessed as to the spelling or meaning of illegible words and have retained all orthographic faults. I have provided endnotes to explain anything that seems questionable in terms of spelling.
2. Illegible words are represented by the abbreviation "illeg." in square brackets.
3. I have not corrected any syntactical errors and have retained any punctuation flaws. I have not capitalized letters at the beginning of sentences when the writers did not. I have also retained capital letters where the writers chose to use them.
4. The writers sometimes used dashes instead of periods at the end of their sentences and I reproduce these forms, although I have regularized the size of the dashes and any spaces. Nineteenth-century writers frequently ended sentences with dashes.
5. Any additions to a journal entry such as a word or sentence added above the text have been silently incorporated into the text, and an endnote explaining the addition follows.
6. I have retained all abbreviations but have included an endnote if further clarity is required.
7. I have followed the paragraph breaks employed by each journal writer but have regularized the size of each paragraph's indentation. Paragraph breaks in this edition follow the publisher's style for indentation.
8. Most of the journal entries have endnotes to explain references alluded to in the primary documents.
9. I have included translations of any foreign language phrases or words in the endnotes. For a longer German or French page, or for a German or French paragraph included within a journal entry, I provide the German or French text followed by an English translation. Ann Sherwin, American Translators

Association–Certified German-English Translator, transcribed and translated the German entries while I transcribed and translated the French entries.

For Pauline's journal, whenever she code-switched (a practice to which she resorted fairly frequently), I have provided the English translation immediately following the German or French text. I have not incorporated these translations into the endnotes but have included them in the body of each journal entry for ease of reading.

10. All legible deletions have been included but struck through. Illegible deletions are noted by the abbreviation "illeg." in square brackets.
11. I used Google Maps to calculate all distances between towns and cities in the endnotes, but the dates of access vary. As I did in *The Clairmont Family Letters*, I have cited Google Maps one time in this edition's bibliography to cover all information retrieved from Google Maps on these different dates: www.google.com/maps/.
12. I have provided a bibliography of sources consulted after the introductory chapter, the chapter on nineteenth-century life writing, and Appendix B. I have also included additional bibliographic information in the endnotes for sources not cited in the list of citations for these two chapters and Appendix B.
13. For Pauline's journal, numbers included within each printed page in this volume (written at either the right- or left-hand margins) indicate where Pauline started a new page in her journal. As she handwrote her entries, the pages do not correspond to longer printed pages. I have chosen to create page breaks at the beginning of each journal entry, which I identify by a change in date rather than to divide the pages according to the way Pauline structured her journal.
14. Wilhelm's journal follows the pagination and format of his printed *Sands and Kenny's Diary and Almanac* (see his journal for more information about Sands and Kenny). Each page of the journal has either the month, the date, and the year printed at the top of the page, or the year, the date, and the month printed on the adjacent side (the order varies). On a double page, there are ruled lines for four entries (Sunday through Wednesday) and then for Thursday through Saturday on the following double page. Therefore, for this edition of Wilhelm's journal and for ease of publication, I have divided the journal's pages into clusters of dates. Whenever the journal begins a new section of dates with 1861 on the left-hand side of the page, I have started a new section for editorial purposes.

ABBREVIATIONS AND IDENTIFICATION

Abbreviations

CC   *The Clairmont Correspondence*
CFL   *The Clairmont Family Letters: 1839–1889*
LMWS *The Letters of Mary Wollstonecraft Shelley*

Identification

Each of the three previously unpublished journals in this collection is a manuscript within the Carl H. Pforzheimer Collection of Shelley and His Circle, New York Public Library, Astor, Lenox, and Tilden Foundations.

ILLUSTRATIONS

1 Portrait of Claire Clairmont by Amelia Curran (Accession Number: NA 271).
   Source: Newstead Abbey.
   Credit: By permission of Nottingham City Museums and Galleries (Newstead Abbey).
2 Clairmont family tomb, Evangelischer Friedhof Matzleinsdorf, Vienna, Austria, 2019.
   Source: Dr. Sharon L. Joffe.
   Credit: Dr. Sharon L. Joffe.
3 Photographic portrait of Pauline Clairmont, c. 1875.
   Source: Visual materials from the Carl H. Pforzheimer Collection. c. 1875. Photograph.
   Credit: The Carl H. Pforzheimer Collection of Shelley and His Circle, New York Public Library, Astor, Lenox, and Tilden Foundations.
4 Photographic portrait of Wilhelm Clairmont by Dr. Székely (photographer). Unknown date.
   Source: Visual materials from the Carl H. Pforzheimer Collection. Photograph.
   Credit: The Carl H. Pforzheimer Collection of Shelley and His Circle, New York Public Library, Astor, Lenox, and Tilden Foundations.
5 Photographic portrait of Ottilia Clairmont by Dr. Székely (photographer). Unknown date.
   Source: Visual materials from the Carl H. Pforzheimer Collection. Photograph.
   Credit: The Carl H. Pforzheimer Collection of Shelley and His Circle, New York Public Library, Astor, Lenox, and Tilden Foundations.

ILLUSTRATIONS

6   Photographic portrait of Walter Gaulis Clairmont. Unknown date.
    Source: Visual materials from the Carl H. Pforzheimer
        Collection. Photograph.
    Credit: The Carl H. Pforzheimer Collection of Shelley and His
        Circle, New York Public Library, Astor, Lenox, and
        Tilden Foundations.

7   Photographic portrait of Mary Claire Bally-Clairmont, 1987.
    Source: Mr. Peter Bally.
    Credit: Mr. Peter Bally.

EDITORIAL SYMBOLS

~~word~~   Deleted legible word
[illeg.]   Illegible word
[~~illeg.~~]   An illegible word that has been deleted
c.   Editorial conjecture, typically used for a date
/   Line changes

CHRONOLOGY OF PAULINE MARIA CLAIRMONT

1825	Birth in Vienna, Austria, of Pauline Clairmont to Charles Gaulis Clairmont (1795–1850) and Antonia Ghylain von Hembyze (1800–1868).
1850 (February)	Death of Charles Gaulis Clairmont.
1850	Pauline visits her aunt, Claire Clairmont (1798–1879), in England. Interactions with Mary Shelley, Sir Percy Florence Shelley, and Lady Jane Shelley.
1851	Death of Mary Wollstonecraft Shelley (1797–1851).
1853	Departure for Australia with her brother, Wilhelm Gaulis Clairmont. Assumes a position as governess in Bathurst, New South Wales, Australia, to the family of William Henry and Charlotte Suttor. Affair with her employers' son, William Henry Suttor, Junior, during her Australian stay.
1857	Returns to Vienna via England where she visits Claire Clairmont.
1863–1865	Resides in the Banat with Wilhelm Gaulis Clairmont. Pregnant in 1863–1864, but does not name the father of her child.
1864	Birth of Johanna Maria Georgina Hanghegyi. She is sent to live with Countess Károly in Hungary.
1865	Returns to Baden, Austria, to live with Antonia Clairmont.
1868	Death of Pauline's mother, Antonia Clairmont, from cancer.
1870	Move to Florence, Italy, to live with Claire Clairmont.
1871	Georgina Hanghegyi joins Pauline and Claire in Florence.
1879	Death of Claire Clairmont.
1885	Death of Georgina Hanghegyi.
1889	Death of Sir Percy Florence Shelley.
1891	Death of Pauline while hiking in Öblarn, Styria, with her nephew, Johann Paul Clairmont (son of Wilhelm and Ottilia Clairmont).
1895	Death of Wilhelm Clairmont in Vienna.

CHRONOLOGY OF WILHELM CHARLES GAULIS CLAIRMONT

1831	Birth in Vienna, Austria, of Wilhelm Clairmont to Charles Gaulis Clairmont (1795–1850) and Antonia Ghylain von Hembyze (1800–1868).
1849–1850	Wilhelm attends school at Queenwood, near Stockbridge in West Hampshire, some 112 kilometers southwest of London. Stays with his aunt, Claire Clairmont (1798–1879) in England. Interactions with Mary Shelley, Sir Percy Florence Shelley, and Lady Jane Shelley.
1850 (February)	Death of Charles Gaulis Clairmont.
1850 (April–August)	Attends Hohenheim Agricultural College (Koeniglich Württembergischen land- und forstwirthschaftlichen Academie Hohenheim) in Stuttgart, Germany.
1850–1852	Attends school at k.k. höheren landwirthschaftlichen Lehranstalt in Ungarisch-Altenburg (in Altenburg, Hungary).
1851	Death of Mary Wollstonecraft Shelley (1797–1851).
1853	Departure for Australia with his sister, Pauline Clairmont. Works on a variety of Australian farms.
1855	Ill-fated purchase with Julius Duboc of Kangaroo Hills. Sale of the farm by 1856.
1861	Return to Vienna.
1862	Begins working as a tenant farmer in Bobda in the Banat.
1866	Begins working as a tenant farmer near Ciakova in the Banat.
1866	Marriage to Ottilia von Pichler (1843–1913).
1868 (August)	Birth of Walter Gaulis Clairmont.
1868 (November)	Death of Wilhelm's mother, Antonia Clairmont, from cancer.
1869	Birth of Alma Pauline Clairmont.
1870–1871	Purchase of Nikolaihof in Marburg (today's Maribor, Slovenia). Purchase financed by Claire Clairmont.
c. 1874	Returns to Vienna to become an appraiser.

1875	Birth of Johann Paul Clairmont.
1879	Death of Claire Clairmont.
1889	Death of Sir Percy Florence Shelley.
1891	Death of Pauline in Öblarn, Styria, while hiking with her nephew, Johann Paul Clairmont.
1895	Death of Wilhelm Clairmont in Vienna.
1913	Death of Ottilia Clairmont.

1

INTRODUCTION

The History of the Shelley and Clairmont Families

This edited collection brings to light the extant journals of siblings Pauline Maria Clairmont (1825–1891) and Wilhelm Charles Gaulis Clairmont (1831–1895), the niece and nephew of Clara Mary Jane Clairmont (she styled herself as Claire; 1798–1879), thereby providing researchers with access to the greater Shelley family circle of which they were all participants to varying degrees. In 2017, I published the collected correspondence of Antonia (née Ghylain von Hembyze) Clairmont (1800–1868) and her children, Pauline and Wilhelm, to Antonia's sister-in-law and her children's aunt, Claire Clairmont. In the two-volume collection entitled *The Clairmont Family Letters: 1839–1889* (Pickering Masters Imprint of Routledge, Taylor and Francis) the 250 English-language letters (including letters from Clara Knox [1826–1855], Charles Gaulis "Charley" Clairmont [1835–1856], and Ottilia von Pichler[1] [1843–1913]) all tell a remarkable story of life in Austria, of interactions with the Shelley family with whom they were connected, and of a family's search for wealth and security in Australia and in the Banat region of the Austro-Hungarian empire. The letters also recount a family's struggles with issues such as an out-of-wedlock birth, various deaths, some of them of children before their parents, with a desire to be accepted in society, and with a lack of success financially to which Claire's generosity gave some substantial relief. These 250 letters link the children of Charles Gaulis Clairmont (1795–1850) who was the half-brother of Claire and the stepbrother of Mary Shelley (1797–1851), and his widow, Antonia, to the Shelley circle and provide us with a way to understand the relationships of these extended family members to the more well-known circle participants. As I argued in the Introduction to *The Clairmont Family Letters: 1839–1889*, Antonia, Pauline, Wilhelm, Clara, Charley, and Ottilia extend the original kinship circle of William Godwin (1756–1836), Mary Wollstonecraft (1759–1797), Mary Shelley, Percy Bysshe Shelley (1792–1822), and Claire Clairmont. My earnest hope is that both the earlier edition of the family letters and this current volume of the journals will be read together, as complements to one another, thus extending our understanding of what it meant to be a nineteenth-century family with significant literary roots whose lives in far-flung locations illuminate nineteenth-century concerns, living practices, mores, and modes of writing. This introductory chapter provides

INTRODUCTION

information about the Shelley-Clairmont circle and I retell here (but in different form) some of the information from my introductory chapter to *The Clairmont Family Letters: 1839–1889*. The story of this remarkable family bears repeating to contextualize the journals and the appendixes found in this edition.

The three journals that constitute this new edition are housed in the Carl H. Pforzheimer Collection of Shelley and His Circle in the New York Public Library. Wilhelm's only grandchildren, Mary Claire Bally-Clairmont (1922–2009) and Johann Christoph Clairmont ("Christoph"; 1924–2004) gave the family journals, letters, and photographs to the Carl H. Pforzheimer Collection of Shelley and His Circle between 1997 and 1998. Mary Claire Bally-Clairmont and her spouse, Hans-Jörg Bally, lived in Switzerland at the time of her death. She was instrumental in working with Marion Kingston Stocking, editor of *The Journals of Claire Clairmont* (1968) and *The Clairmont Correspondence: Letters of Claire Clairmont, Charles Clairmont, and Fanny Imlay Godwin* (1995), and was determined to preserve the Clairmont family papers. Mary Claire's brother, Christoph Clairmont, was a professor at Rutgers, The State University of New Jersey, United States of America, in the Department of Classics. He participated in numerous archaeological excavations with his wife, scholar Victorine Clairmont-von Gonzenbach (1922–2016), and which culminated in the publication of many books about his expeditions around the world. While they are of primary interest to archaeological experts, comparing his books to the work of his great great-aunt, Claire Clairmont, shows a similar sense of creativity and brilliance. *The Clairmont Family Letters: 1839–1889* gives full details about how the documents came to the collection: Donald H. Reiman (editor of *Shelley and his Circle* from 1965 to 1992, and later co-editor with Doucet Devin Fischer) was instrumental in securing the fate of these documents. Christoph Clairmont knew Reiman from a conference arranged by the Society for Textual Scholarship at City University of New York. He proposed that the Clairmont papers owned by himself and his sister, Mary Claire Bally-Clairmont, be donated to the Carl H. Pforzheimer Collection of Shelley and His Circle. The documents were consequently deposited in the Pforzheimer Collection between 1997 and 1998, where they remain today (*CFL* I: xix; and a conversation with Elizabeth Denlinger [Curator of the Carl H. Pforzheimer Collection of Shelley and His Circle], 2015). As of the date of publication of this edition, no further letters or journals have been discovered. The 2009 death of Mary Claire Bally-Clairmont was the end of the family line. The death in 2015 of Mary Claire Bally-Clairmont's spouse, Hans-Jörg Bally, yielded a few artifacts from his home which his second cousins, Dr. Claus Bally and Mr. Peter Bally, donated to the Carl H. Pforzheimer Collection of Shelley and His Circle. The 2016 death of Christoph's wife Victorine brought no such revelations. Unfortunately, none of Pauline's missing journals (discussed later in this chapter) were amongst that more recent cache of documents. This present edition reproduces Pauline's and Wilhelm's extant journals for the first time since they were written in the nineteenth century. I include here also a third journal, long believed to be Pauline's, but which likely was the work of Wilhelm's son, Walter Gaulis Clairmont.

INTRODUCTION

As extended family of the Shelleys to whom they were connected through Charles and Claire Clairmont, Pauline's, Wilhelm's and Walter's journals enable researchers to learn more about subsequent generations of this important literary family, broadening thereby researchers' understanding of the primary circle.

Many critical texts (including my own, *The Clairmont Family Letters: 1839–1889*) tell the story of the Shelley family and its association with the Clairmont family. In this introduction to the extant family journals, I reiterate some of what I discussed in *The Clairmont Family Letters* to provide background to the three writers represented in this edition. Following other texts, and as I did in *The Clairmont Family Letters*, I trace the circle to Mary Shelley's parents, Mary Wollstonecraft and William Godwin. Wollstonecraft's educational philosophy (which Mary Shelley would later emulate in *Frankenstein* to educate her creature who learned to speak French from the De Lacey family in much the same way Wollstonecraft suggested children learn how to read in her *Lessons. The first book of a series which I intended to have written for my unfortunate girl* [published posthumously in 1798],[2] her firm female friendships with Jane Arden and Fanny Blood (friendships that influenced the strong sororal bonds in her novels, *Mary, A Fiction* [1788] and *Maria, Or The Wrongs of Woman*, [1798]), her famous treatise *A Vindication of the Rights of Woman* (1792) in which she recognized the wrongs perpetuated against women, and her embrace of the French Revolution and Girondist politics all point to the strong sense of feminism that would pervade her works. Her affair with Gilbert Imlay (possibly 1754–1828), the birth of their daughter, Frances (Fanny; 1794–1816), in May 1794, and her two failed suicide attempts – which Godwin enumerated in his *Memoirs of the Author of a Vindication of the Rights of Woman* (1798) doing grave damage to her reputation – would brand her for centuries, causing the public and her critics to mark her as an outcast. Godwin was partially to blame for the public's reaction to Wollstonecraft's life story. In his *Memoirs of the Author of a Vindication of the Rights of Woman*, he bluntly elucidated her actions, including her suicide attempts. He called *A Vindication of the Rights of Woman* "a very bold and original production" and praised "the strength and firmness with which the author repels the opinions of Rousseau, Dr Gregory, and Dr James Fordyce, respecting the condition of woman" (Godwin, in Holmes [ed], 1987: 231). Godwin intended as a compliment his statement, "Yet, along with this rigid, and somewhat amazonian temper, which characterized some parts of the book, it is impossible not to remark a luxuriance of imagination, and a trembling delicacy of sentiment" (231–232). While he characterized her temper in this manner, critics of Wollstonecraft excoriated her for being worthy of the term "amazonian," a description Godwin intended to be positive. The writer Horace Walpole called her "a hyena in petticoats" and a review of her *Letters Written during a Short Residence in Sweden, Norway, and Denmark* (1795) and published in the *British Critic* of 1796 declared: "But when a woman so far outsteps her proper sphere, as to deride facts which she cannot disprove, and avow opinions which it is dangerous to disseminate, we cannot, consistently with our duty, permit her to pursue triumphantly her Phaeton-like career" (*Letters Written during a Short Residence in Sweden, Norway, and Denmark*, Horrocks [ed], 2013: 247–48). As Richard Holmes has shown, Godwin's *Memoirs* "appalled" "most" who read it with "horrid fascination" (*Memoirs of The Author of 'The Rights of Woman'*, Holmes [ed], 1987: 43). He likewise cites Robert Southey's accusation that Godwin displayed "a want of all feeling in stripping his dead wife naked" (*Memoirs of The Author of 'The Rights of Woman'*, quoted in Holmes [ed], 1987: 43). If there is any doubt of the misogyny involved in these criticisms, Holmes cites a *European Magazine* critic who described Godwin's *Memoirs* as "the history of a philosophical wanton" and saw Wollstonecraft as an "unhappy woman, whose frailties should have been buried in oblivion" (quoted in Holmes [ed.], 1987: 43). Naturally, such responses did little to ameliorate Wollstonecraft's "notorious reputation" both at the time and later as a "fallen woman in Victorian Britain" which Eileen Botting, Christine Wilkerson, and Elizabeth Kozlow attribute to "several biographies beginning with William Godwin's 1798 *Memoirs of the Author of A Vindication of the Rights of Woman* that chronicled his wife's romantic life prior to marriage" (Botting et al. 2014: 18). Her standing, now restored, remained in shreds until more recently. As Botting, Wilkerson, and Kozlow confirm: "The past decade of scholarly attention to the historical reception of Wollstonecraft has overturned the influential yet inaccurate tradition of historiography, shaped by the British Victorian view of the political philosopher William Godwin and his circle, that situated the sexual radical Wollstonecraft as publicly ignored or even unread for the bulk of the nineteenth century" (2014: 18).

Researchers such as William St. Clair and Emily Sunstein have documented in detail the relationship and subsequent marriage of Godwin and Wollstonecraft. St. Clair even provides information addressing the sexual nature of Godwin and Wollstonecraft's relationship while Godwin's journals, more recently made available, corroborate much of what researchers have previously surmised. Godwin famously noted his growing affection in his 13 July 1796 letter to Wollstonecraft, his initial dislike having ceded to sheer love and affection:

> Shall I write a love letter? . . . No, when I make love, it shall be with the eloquent tones of my voice, with dying accents, with speaking glances . . . with all the witching of that irresistible, universal passion. . . . Shall I send you a eulogium of your beauty, your talents and your virtues? Ah! That is an old subject; beside, if I were to begin, instead of a sheet of paper, I should want a ream.
>
> (Clemit 2011: 171)

The Wollstonecraft-Godwin relationship culminated in marriage in March 1797, but Wollstonecraft died that year from puerperal fever on 10 September following the 30 August birth of their daughter, Mary Wollstonecraft Godwin (later Shelley). In 1801, Godwin married Mary Jane Vial (1768–1841), who brought her two children, Charles Gaulis Clairmont and Clara Mary Jane (known as Claire) into the home. Godwin and his second wife had a son, William, in 1803. William Godwin,

Junior, died of cholera in 1832, leaving his wife, Mary Louisa Eldred, known as Emily, but no children. Although not much correspondence exists between Emily Godwin and Mary Shelley, we know that Emily continued to visit her in-laws from 1834 until 1836 (*LMWS* III: 136), and on 8 June 1844, Mary Shelley noted the resumption of correspondence with Emily and expressed her desire to support her sister-in-law financially: "I was glad to hear from you, as I had no idea where you were – nor could Claire tell me" (*LMWS* III: 135). As the letters show, Mary Shelley promised Emily a monthly stipend of £50 a year for her upkeep.

Identifying the father of Mary Jane Vial's two children, Mary Shelley's stepsiblings Charles and Claire, born before Vial's marriage to Godwin has been a topic of considerable debate. Charles Clairmont's father's identity has remained elusive, even though St. Clair suggests that Charles Abram Gaulis was probably Charles Clairmont's father (1989: 250). St. Clair recorded, however, that Claire's father was not able to be identified. Fortunately, recent discoveries have debunked previous theories about Claire's paternal origins. Vicki Parslow Stafford proved in 2010 that Sir John Lethbridge fathered Claire Clairmont (see "Claire Clairmont, Mary Jane's Daughter: New Correspondence With Claire's Father," https://sites.google.com/site/maryjanesdaughter/home). Stafford was investigating her own genealogy when she found evidence of Claire's father in the Somerset Archive and Record Service Office. Documents from 1797 to 1814 show that Lethbridge sent Mary Jane Vial money for the care of her daughter, Claire. Stafford includes the following from the catalogue of the Somerset Archive and Record Service, Dodson and Pulman, Solicitors Box 17: Lethbridge family legal papers, DD\DP/17/11 1797–1814, Correspondence concerning Mary Jane Vial: "Daughter of Mary Jane Vial. widow, alias St. Julian, fathered by John (later Sir John) Lethbridge of Sandhill Park and born at Brislington, c. 1797. The mother was committed to Ilchester gaol for debt in 1799 and 1800 and by 1811 had married – Godwin and moved to London" (https://sites.google.com/site/maryjanesdaughter/home/claire-s-father). As Stafford asserts, "The letters confirm without doubt that both Mary Jane Vial and Sir John Lethbridge accepted that he was the father of Mary Jane's daughter, born in Brislington, Somerset in 1798" (https://sites.google.com/site/maryjanesdaughter/home/claire-s-father). She further states, "The papers kept by attorney Beadon[3] establish beyond doubt that Sir John Lethbridge accepted (albeit grudgingly) that he was Claire's father, her birth being the result of a liaison with Miss Vial during some undetermined period in 1797" (https://sites.google.com/site/maryjanesdaughter/home).

Perhaps reflecting her jealousy over Godwin's first wife, Mary Jane Godwin treated her stepdaughter, Mary, poorly. The future Mary Shelley felt unloved by her stepmother, who clearly favored her own children. Mary's idolization of her father may not have improved their relationship; indeed, as Janet Todd remarks, "Mary made it clear she disliked her stepmother from the moment she arrived as rival for her father's love" (Todd 2007: 65). Mary Shelley noted in her letter to Percy Shelley on the 28 October 1814, "I detest Mrs. G. she plagues my father out of his life" (*LMWS* I: 3). Damning her stepmother, she told Marianne

Hunt on 5 March 1817, "Shelley [Percy] mentions Mrs. G's favour is she not an odious woman" (I: 34). Her letter to Percy Shelley of 26 September 1817 stated that Mary felt "something very analogous to disgust" towards Mrs. Godwin (I: 43). Todd elucidates the impact of disliking Mrs. Godwin for both of her stepdaughters: "where Mary turned her desolation outwards, openly hating Mary Jane as 'odious' and 'filthy', Fanny turned hers inwards.... Both girls escaped into reading" (Todd 2007: 65). Betty Bennett and Charles Robinson believe that Shelley received "immediate lessons in complex politics" in her home which housed "above the mantle, the ever present portrait of Mary Wollstonecraft reminding her of her own special heritage" (Bennett and Robinson 1990: 6). While Mary Shelley escaped her homelife through her relationship with Percy Shelley, Fanny Imlay was unable to avoid it. She would ultimately commit suicide in 1816, an event attributed by many critics to the abuse she suffered at the hands of her stepmother and her unreciprocated love for Percy Shelley.

Mary Godwin met Percy Bysshe Shelley at her father's home in 1812, an event which would later alter the trajectory of her life. Married to Harriet Westbrook (1796–1816), Percy Shelley had a daughter with her, Eliza Ianthe (married name Esdaile, 1813–1876) and then a son, Charles Bysshe (1814–1826). The mythology of Mary and Percy's love affair theorizes that they solidified their relationship a few years later at the grave of Wollstonecraft, an event to which Mary Shelley's daughter-in-law, Lady Jane Shelley (1820–1899), alludes in her 1859 *Shelley Memorials*: "To her [Mary], as they met one eventful day in St. Pancras Churchyard, by her mother's grave, Bysshe, in burning words, poured forth the tale of his wild past – how he had suffered, how he had been misled, and how, if supported by her love, he hoped in future years to enroll his name with the wise and good who had done battle for their fellow-men, and been true through all adverse storms to the cause of humanity. Unhesitatingly, she placed her hand in his, and linked her fortune with his own" (1859: 77–78). On 28 July 1814, and much to the chagrin of Mrs. Godwin, Percy and Mary left Europe accompanied by Claire. Their travels led to the publication of co-written work, *History of a Six Weeks' Tour* (1817), a text that Heather Bozant Witcher sees as being linked to the collaboration between Percy and Mary in their journals which, she believes, is evidence of their "attempt to redefine themselves from singular individualism to a radical pluralism. In this way, we see the beginnings of a sympathetic collaboration occurring within these shared pages, a collaboration that ultimately lends itself to narrative form in the published *History of a Six Weeks' Tour*" (Witcher 2016: 147). Mary's groundbreaking novel, *Frankenstein, Or the Modern Prometheus* (1818), owes its genesis to the couple's 1816 European sojourn. The year 1816 was marred by the suicides of Fanny Imlay and Harriet Westbrook. Critics have propounded that unrequited love for Percy Shelley and a family history of depression may have prompted Fanny's suicide. Todd, for example, records that with Mary and Percy's "elopement," Fanny "had lost two people she deeply cared for, one of whom she may have loved with passion" (Todd 2007: 139), and that Percy Shelley was "the man who in one way or another had stirred her passions" (2007: 141). Todd explains the 1816 meeting between Fanny and Percy Shelley in Bath where Fanny had hoped to see Mary and Percy. Todd opines that "now six month's pregnant, Claire must not be glimpsed" and that Mary "may not have wanted to deal with another sister or to share Shelley further.... To save Claire's reputation Fanny had to be rejected" (2007: 225). This meeting in which Percy Shelley "put her off somehow" (2007: 225) propelled Fanny towards suicide later that day and resulted in Percy Shelley's "poetic fragments" subsequent to this event as he probably came to the realization that Fanny had loved him: "Her voice did quiver as we parted, / Yet knew I not that heart was broken / From which it came – and I departed – / Heeding not the words then spoken. / Misery – oh misery / This world is all too wide to thee! / (2007: 225–226). Claire and the Godwins corroborated the assertion that Fanny had loved Percy Shelley and that "Fanny had killed herself because she loved Shelley and Shelley had always loved Mary and not her... Claire too assumed that Fanny loved Shelley" (2007: 243). Maurice Hindle believes that the reluctance of Wollstonecraft's sisters to accept Fanny as a teacher at their school in 1815 because of the notoriety associated with Percy and Mary's continental travels and because the Godwins hoped that Claire would still return to the family home shaped Fanny's "eventual destiny": "They were afraid that if Claire did return, Fanny would be morally tainted by the contact, and had no wish to endure the kind of damaged reputation (and reduced incomes) they had suffered 16 years before when Godwin published his revelations about Fanny's mother in the more than candid *Memoirs* of Wollstonecraft. Fanny's one escape route to independence was thus blocked" (Hindle 2006: 339–340). Hindle further asserts that Fanny's "displaced status, her disputed name, the pressures of poverty that were beyond her powers to resolve, and her abandonment to an unknown pauper's grave by those more concerned with reputation than respect" make one consider her "a potent embodiment of [Hazlitt's] 'the People'" (2006: 344). Following Fanny's tragic death, Harriet Westbrook's suicide enabled Mary and Percy to marry in December 1816 in a futile attempt to gain custody of the couple's children. Mary and Percy would have four children: a daughter who died in 1815 after living for a mere fifteen days, William (1816–1819), Clara (1817–1818), and Percy Florence (1819–1889). Percy Shelley drowned in 1822 while the family was sojourning in Italy, leaving a bereft Mary who raised her son, Percy Florence (the only one of her children to reach adulthood), in England. She died in 1851 of what her death certificate issued by the General Register Office in London termed a "Supposed Tumour in left hemisphere, of long standing" (*LMWS* III: Appendix I, 389).

Claire and Mary maintained a significant connection for most of their lives, although the later years were tempered with strife. Claire spent many key years with Mary, including the summer of 1816 which resulted in the ghost-writing competition where Mary "saw – with shut eyes, but acute mental vision, ... the pale student of unhallowed arts kneeling beside the thing he had put together" (Introduction to the 1831 edition of *Frankenstein* 2012: 350). After the 1817 birth of Claire's daughter, Clara Allegra (1817–1822) with Lord Byron (George

Gordon Byron, 6th Baron Byron; 1788–1824), Mary may well have been a source of support for Claire, to whom Byron was extremely harsh as he successfully worked to exclude Claire from Allegra's life. Ironically, even Lady Jane Shelley would erase Claire's presence completely in her *Shelley Memorials*, stating that "Mrs. Shelley [Mary] resided at Marlow, in company with her children, and with a little daughter of Lord Byron, called Allegra, and sometimes Alba" (Shelley, J., 1859: 88), thereby negating Claire's existence. Byron refused to allow Claire access to Allegra, moving her to Venice, Italy, and then to a convent in Bagnacavallo, a town in the province of Ravenna, Italy, where she died from typhoid fever in 1822. As I recount in *The Kinship Coterie and the Literary Endeavors of the Women in the Shelley Circle*, this death forced Claire to search for replacements amongst the young women she taught as a governess in Russia where she fled. Undeniably, Byron's cruelty to Claire extended after Allegra's death. He refused to tell her where their daughter was buried and he ordered a memorial plaque, omitting Claire's name. The plaque was to read: "In memory of Allegra, daughter of G. G. Lord Byron, who died at Bagnacavallo, in Italy, April 20, 1822, aged five years and three months" (Hall 1975: 21). Frances Trollope confirms Byron's actions in her poem, "Lines Written by a Celebrated Authoress on the Burial of the Daughter of a Celebrated Author" (1834):

> A simple shrine memorial of her name
> The mourning father wished erected near.
> No line of his from whom a word is fame
> Was on the humble tablet to appear.
> 'Twas but to mark, when near the spot he came
> To dew her grave with a paternal tear,
> That there his lovely Allegra was laid,
> That there his heart's fond tribute must be paid.
> (Hall 1975: 63)

Claire was spared seeing this elimination as the plaque was never constructed. In fact, it took Claire until 1869 to discover where her daughter was buried. Indeed, both the loss of Allegra and Byron's earlier betrayal seemed to have shaped Claire's destiny as she sought the affection of her nieces and nephews as compensation. Claire's support of Charles and Antonia's children, and her care of her great-niece, Georgina Hanghegyi (1864–1885) who came to live with her and Pauline Clairmont (Georgina's mother) in Florence in the 1870s, illuminates Claire's loyalty and ongoing commitment to her family. It was this closeness that ultimately divided Claire from Mary, because of the marriage of Claire's niece, Clara Clairmont, to Alexander Knox (1818–1891).

Fully understanding the journals presented here also requires comprehending the relationships between the various Clairmont relatives.[4] Pauline and Wilhelm's father, Charles, was the son of Mary Jane Vial and possibly Charles Abram

INTRODUCTION

Gaulis. Charles was born in 1795 and, as a young man, he relocated to Vienna in 1819 to teach English. He subsequently became a tutor to the aristocracy, notably the children of Archduke Franz Karl and Archduchess Sophie of Bavaria. Their two younger sons, Archduke Ferdinand Maximilian (1832–1867) and Archduke Karl Ludwig (1833–1896), were amongst Charles's students. Their brother, Franz Joseph (1830–1916) would be crowned emperor in 1848 (Kaiser Franz Joseph 1). Archduke Ferdinand Maximilian would become Emperor of Mexico in 1864, while Archduke Karl Ludwig's son, Franz Ferdinand (1863–1914) who was the heir to the Austro-Hungarian throne, would be assassinated in 1914 in Sarajevo, an act that would culminate in the First World War (1914–1918). In 1822, the Viennese authorities attempted to cast both Charles and Claire – who resided with him in Vienna for some time – as "subversive" (see Marion Kingston Stocking's footnote 2 in which she explains in detail how "Charles and Claire were unwittingly up against a powerful system" which Stocking characterizes as a "formidable system of censorship and police espionage" [*CC* 1: 209]) in an episode that could have resulted in their removal from Austria. Documents of support suggested that Charles was an upstanding citizen. Testimonies endorsing his character in 1822 came from aristocratic notables such as Count Dietrichstien-Prosekau-Lestic, Baron Gump, Baron Eskeles, and Princess Grassaltowitsch née Esterhazy (*CC* I: 206). Charles and Claire were thus allowed to remain in Vienna. Indeed, Ernst Joseph Görlich documents Charles's accomplishments and connections: "Einer der ersten, der in Österreich englische Sprache und englisches Wesen vertrat, war Charles Gaulis Clairmont, der dem Kreis um den großen englischen Lyriker Shelley angehörte" ("One of the first to represent the English language and the English essence in Austria was Charles Gaulis Clairmont, who belonged to the set around the great English lyricist Shelley" [Görlich 1970: 124, translation provided by Anja Reiner for *The Clairmont Family Letters*]). Charles was also an English teacher at the Theresianum Ritterakademie (see *CFL* I: 92–94) and he joined the faculty at the Universität Wien (University of Vienna) in 1839. As writers and teachers, both Charles and his wife, Antonia, wrote English-language instruction manuals. Antonia published a book, *Erste Schritte zur Erlernung der englischen Sprache, für Kinder von sechs bis zehn Jahren* in 1845 ("First Steps to Learning the English Language, for Children ages Six to Ten") and Charles was a prolific writer of English-instruction books. In 1845, his book, *First Poetical-Reading Book, Being an Impressive Collection of the Most Interesting Pieces in Verse in the English Language*, noted his academic affiliations by recording that he was a "Professor Extraordinary of the English Language and Literature at the Impl. and Rl. University of Vienna and at the Impl. and R. Ter. Academy of Nobles."[5] His other works (of which there were many) include: *Reine Grundlehre der Englischen Sprache* ("Basics of English Language," published in 1831 and updated in five subsequent editions), and *Vollständige Englische Sprachlehre: die Syntaxis in 30 Lectionen eingetheilt* ("Complete English Grammar: Syntax in 30 Lessons" which went through twelve editions starting in 1848). Politically,

INTRODUCTION

Charles expressed sympathy for those participating in the 1848–9 revolution, but as Stocking suggests he remained faithful to the crown who paid his salary, "uniting his liberalism with a loyalty to the Habsburgs, on whom he was dependent" (*CC* II: 493). Görlich also reflected on Charles's sense of allegiance: "So bleibt er selbst in den größten Stürmen der Revolution 'habsburgisch' gesinnt, was wohl mit dem Kreis zusammenhängt, in dem er verkehrte" ("Thus, even in the greatest storms of revolution, he stays Habsburg-minded, which probably correlated with the set he socialized with" [1970: 124, translation provided by Anja Reiner for *The Clairmont Family Letters*]).

Charles spent his adult life in Vienna and, in 1824, he married Viennese teacher, Antonia Ghylain von Hembyze.[6] Her parents were Georg von Hembyze, listed as a "Zollamts Oberbeamter" (customs office official) on Charles and Antonia's wedding certificate, and Anna Schönbigler. A copy (dated 1938) of Charles and Antonia's marriage certificate from 17 October 1824 records that Charles was from "Bristoll in England" (German for "Bristol in England"; see CL'ANA 0425, unpublished manuscript, Pforzheimer Collection). As their granddaughter, Alma Crüwell-Clairmont, stated in her memo dating from the 1930s (see the full translation of the German document in Appendix F of this book): "I have in my possession the authentic copy of a renewal letter signed by Empress Maria Theresia in 1764 affirming the nobility of the Ghislain d'Hembyse family, which had been temporarily forgotten after the family's emigration to Austria in 1650 but is proven as far back as the 14th century" (Crüwell-Clairmont's spelling for Ghylain von Hembyze; translation provided by Ann Sherwin). Furthermore, Konstantin Bouhelier Beaulier of Belgium signed a document in the eighteenth century that displays the von Hembyze family and its Belgian roots (see CL'ANA 0415, unpublished manuscript, Pforzheimer Collection). Charles and Antonia had seven children: Pauline, Clara, Wilhelm, Hermine (known as Mina, 1832–1847), Emily (Emmy, 1833–1856), Charles Gaulis (Charley), and Sidonia (Sidi, 1836–1856). Only two of the children would live long lives: Hermine died of consumption at age fourteen, Clara died in 1855, and Emily, Charley, and Sidonia all died in 1856 from various illnesses. While Charles predeceased the latter four children, his sorrow over Hermine's early death is palpably felt in his letter to Claire of 29 June 1847: "Up to the very moment of her dissolution she had not the smallest idea of her danger; and I am glad it was so; I would not allow a priest to come near her; can such a spotless being be better prepared for her passage into eternity [than] in the pure state of her own unconscious innocence. . . . She was frank and sincere almost to a fault, she was gentle, kindhearted and affectionate" (*CC* II: 482). In addition to providing the emotional support of being a sympathetic reader of such missives, Claire eventually became a source of financial support for Charles and Antonia, who were frequently impoverished. This support intensified after 1844 when Claire received the legacy that Percy Shelley had promised her in his will (his father, Sir Timothy Shelley, died that year, thereby making the legacy available to Claire). As Elizabeth Denlinger confirms, "Clairmont's situation became easier in 1841 when she was able to raise an income on her modest expectations; the legacy, when it finally came, put her in a position to help her brother, his wife, and their seven children" (Denlinger 2018: 9).

Claire likely felt her niece Clara Knox's death in 1855 particularly keenly as Clara's marriage to Alexander Knox had come between both Clara and Claire and also Claire and Mary Shelley. Clara visited Claire in England in 1849, then visited Mary Shelley, Percy Florence Shelley, and Jane Shelley. Claire was unable to accompany her niece on that occasion, but she clearly assumed that Clara would be well taken care of in the Shelley home. However, Clara entered into a romantic relationship with Knox, Percy Florence's friend with whom he attended Trinity College, Cambridge. A few weeks later, and without her parents' or Claire's consent, Clara married Knox. While Pauline's journal describes the marriage in positive terms (see her journal entry in this edition for 8 July 1855), Claire blamed Mary Shelley for not taking care of Clara adequately and the two stepsisters ceased corresponding in a rift that lasted until Mary Shelley's death in 1851. Furthermore, when Pauline went to stay with Claire in England in 1850, Claire solicited her niece as an ally in her feud with Clara and the Shelleys which caused Antonia to express concern in a letter to Claire from 18 September 1850 that Pauline would be harmed by Mary Shelley: "and, if Mrs. S. chose she might do Pauline serious injury in public opinion, just when she must try to find a footing and make or establish her character in the world" (*CFL* I: 97). Subsequent to the discovery of her stepsister's untimely death, Claire wrote to Percy Florence Shelley in a letter dated 2–5 February 1851: "I have heard to-day that your Mother is dead. I have no wish to add any thing to your affliction, but indeed it was most unkind in you never to let me know she was ill. Most unkind. Now I can never see her more! . . . the loss of an old friend has afflicted me most sensibly" (*CC* II: 536). Wilhelm reacted more positively to Mary Shelley's death, hoping that it would lead to reconciliation between his sister and his aunt. He wrote to Claire in a letter dated 2 March 1851: "The news of Mrs. Shelley's death I had first from the papers and afterwards learnt it from Mama but I do not know any of the particulars nor what was the cause of her sudden death. . . . At any rate Mrs S's [Shelley's] death must be considered as a favourable omen by those who take any interest in Clara for it can not but tend to loosen the connection between K. [Knox] and the S's [Shelleys]" (*CFL* I: 107). However, there was no reconciliation between aunt and niece, and Clara Knox died in 1855.

The Clairmont family faced many deaths in the 1850s, and Clara's was not the only one that likely created complicated feelings for Claire. In the year after Clara's 1855 death, Emily, Sidonia, and Charley all died from illness. These losses followed Charles's 1850 death after dining at the Archduke's home. Wilhelm explains the details in his letter to Claire of 12 February 1850: "Pauline writes that he was dining at the Arshduke's and accordingly not expected home that day (2 February) when between 8 and 9 in the evening, a stranger was announced at Mama's bearing the onepage that Papa had dropped down senseless in the room during a visit. Mama immediately set out with Pauline but it was too late. They had taken him to the hospital and bled him [and] he expired in half an hour; and was no more when Mama arrived" ([Wilhelm's spelling] *CFL* I: 72). Contradicting this account, Herbert Huscher notes that Charles "am 2 Februar 1850 in Wien auf der Strasse einem Schlaganfall erlag" ("Charles died of a stroke in the streets of Vienna," in "Charles und Claire Clairmont," p. 65). Charles's death notice ("Die Parte") records that he "died blest in the Lord on February 2, 1850, at 8 o'clock in the evening, in his 55th year of life, of a stroke" (*CFL* I: 140, image provided by Heraldic-Genealogical Society Adler, Vienna and reproduced in *CFL*; translation by Ann Sherwin). Archduchess Sophie, the mother of the future Emperor Maximilian, recorded in her journal her son's sorrow over Charles's sudden death: "Je dis à Maxi la mort du bon Clairmont qui l'affligea beaucoup" ("I told Maxi about the death of good Clairmont which distressed him a lot": Translation by Sharon Joffe. The original French sentence was initially quoted in Herbert Huscher, "Charles und Claire Clairmont," p. 65). Charles was buried in the General Währing Cemetery in Vienna (Allgemeiner Währinger Friedhof), but his remains were moved to the Matzleinsdorf cemetery once Währing cemetery closed some years later (see Appendix F for Alma Crüwell-Clairmont's and Walter Clairmont's remarks about the Clairmont family tomb, and the photograph in this edition of the family tombstone in the Matzleinsdorf Cemetery in Vienna, Austria). In the wake of his death his widow was debt-ridden and in emotional turmoil due to her discovery that he had been conducting an extra-marital affair with a woman Claire identified as Mrs. Kollonitz in her 1 August 1850 letter to Antonia. Antonia's letters to Claire describe her feelings. For example, in May 1850 she wrote, "if Charles had lived to know his secret discovered to me, how miserable would he have been, and could I have preserved even outward peace, or could I have remained quiet knowing these shameful transactions – or would he ever have broken off his old ways?" (*CFL* I: 82–83). In June 1850 she wrote: "I have written to [Alexander] Knox . . . and I let him into the secret of poor Charles' errors" (*CFL* I: 87). On 1 August 1850 Claire remonstrated, "I regret your having exposed my Brother's errors to Mr. Knox. . . . I conclude with asking you, what you would think of me if I wrote to Madame Kollonitz after the injuries she has inflicted upon our family" (*CC* II: 533), thereby naming Charles's mistress.

In the ensuing years, Claire constantly sent money to her brother's widow for her upkeep, and she was instrumental in providing financial assistance for Wilhelm's attempts to purchase a farm. Her ongoing funding of Pauline and Wilhelm is well-documented in their letters to her. Furthermore, she opened her home in England to the siblings, as the letters reflect. For example, as mentioned, Pauline visited her aunt in 1850. Additionally, Wilhelm initially stayed with Claire when he moved to England in December 1848 to study farming at Queenwood College in Hampshire, an enterprise she supported. He then moved to Hohenheim in Germany and then to Altenburg in Hungary to study agriculture, and Claire provided financial help for both these ventures. Later, in 1853, in search of better economic opportunities and supported in part by Knox who continued to provide financially for his wife's family, Wilhelm and Pauline went to Australia. Pauline took on the position as governess to the Suttor family, an account that she describes in the journal in this edition, while Wilhelm worked on different farms. Upon their return to Europe (Pauline in 1857 and Wilhelm in 1861, as their journals show), Wilhelm moved to the Banat region of the Austro-Hungarian empire to farm.

Wilhelm's letters to Claire and to his mother from Australia, as well as his letters to Pauline and Claire from his years in the Banat, appear *The Clairmont Family Letters*.[7] His journal in this present edition documents his departure from Australia on 22 January 1861 on the vessel, the *Behar*, for Suez, Cairo, and then to Alexandria. From Alexandria, he traveled to Nubia, Malta, and Messina on his way to Florence where he met up with Claire on 28 March 1861. As he told his surprised aunt in his letter: "I beg you to be prepared for the awful calamity of seeing me walk into your apartment in ten minutes from this" (*CFL* II: 7). The journal reproduced in this edition notes his encounter with Claire (see Wilhelm's journal entries for 28–29 March 1861). It also documents his attempts at finding a property to farm in Habsburg-controlled lands, an area spanning parts of present-day Croatia, Slovenia, and the Czech Republic. Wilhelm's friendship with the Hungarian magnate class at his college in Altenburg, Hungary, gave him access to important social contacts who provided him with accommodation and help in his travels.

Wilhelm initially worked as a tenant farmer in Bobda, a small town located in today's Western Romania in the commune of Cenei in Timiş County. Timişoara is Romania's third largest city and the capital city of the county. Pauline lived with him there for two years from 1863 to 1865, then went to Austria to take care of Antonia who was suffering from fatal cancer. During 1866, Wilhelm went to work on a farm called Tuzokrét, near Ciacova (in Romania today, about 34 kilometers from Timişoara). Later sometime after 1870, Wilhelm would become a tenant farmer in today's Belec, Croatia, 86 kilometers from Maribor, Slovenia. His letters give the farm's name as Belici or Beleci. By 1871, he and Claire then jointly bought a farm called Nikolaihof, from a man he referred to as Dr. Dominkusch. Located near Maribor (in today's Slovenia), the town was known by its German name, Marburg, when Wilhelm farmed there. As I indicated in *The Clairmont Family Letters*, Nikolaihof today is called Miklavski dvorec and it is situated on the left bank of the River Drau/Drava canal in the municipality of Miklavž na Dravskem polju (Source: Leopold Mikec Avberšec, Pokrajinski arhiv Maribor [Regional Archives in Maribor], personal correspondence, 3 November 2014). From footnoted information in *The Clairmont Family Letters*, "Records from the Pokrajinski arhiv Maribor show the register of the farm dating back to its purchase by Claire. In the document, Mary Jean Clairmont (instead of Mary Jane Clairmont) was recorded as the purchaser of the Walcker estate. Dr. Dominikusch's name was also included" (*CFL* II: 153). The German-language document of sale states: "Clairmont Mary Jean als Ersteh. der Walcker'schen /: D. Dominikus:/ [illeg.]" (Source: Pokrajinski arhiv Maribor). The English translation, provided by Ann Sherwin reads: "Clairmont Mary Jean as purchaser of the Walcker (D. Dominikus)." As explained, "The register depicts a negotiation deed. The property was apparently put up for sale in 1869 (sign C 1135 of the image) and the sale was concluded in 1871 (sign C 20506). Wilhelm's letter of 18 March 1871 documented that Dr. Dominkusch had purchased Nikolaihof from Mr. Walcker in order to recoup the money he had originally lent to Walcker. Walcker subsequently went insolvent" (*CFL* II: 153). Sadly, after the sojourn at Nikolaihof proved unsustainable, Wilhelm returned to Vienna by 1874 to become a surveyor of crown properties (see Appendix C for the translation of the document attesting to his appointment).

In 1866, Wilhelm married Ottilia[8] von Pichler (1843–1913) of Vienna, Austria. The bride was one of six children of a privy councilor, Johann Franz Hofrath von Pichler (1799–1892), and his wife Fanny Horstig d'Aubigny (1805–1874). Mary Claire Bally-Clairmont constructed a genealogical table of Ottilia's family and she provided birth and death information for Ottilia's parents (see CL'ANA 0425, unpublished manuscript, Pforzheimer Collection). Of her siblings, Ottilia references in her various letters her sister, Alma, and brother, Moritz. The couple likely met through another of Ottilia's sisters, Emily, who was married to Rudolf von Hauer, a friend of Wilhelm's from the k.k. höheren landwirthschaftlichen Lehranstalt in Ungarisch-Altenburg. Professor Hugo Hippolyt Hitschmann compiled a list of the school's alumni in his 1865 *Verzeichniss der Lehrer und Studirenden der erzherzoglichen landwirthschaftlichen Bildungsanstalt und der k. k. höheren landwirthschaftlichen Lehranstalt zu Ungarisch-Altenburg 1818–1848 und 1858–1864* ("Register of Teachers and Students of the Archducal Agricultural Academy and the k. k. Higher Agricultural Academy of Altenburg-Hungary 1818–1848 and 1858–1864"). He identified Wilhelm as a "Gutspächter bei Temesvár in Ungarn" ("an estate tenant near Temesvár in Hungary") after studying in Altenburg (Hitschmann 1865: 10–11) and von Hauer as a "Gutsbesitzer" ("landowner") (1865: 24–25). The Pforzheimer Collection has a photograph of a painting of Ottilia and Emily von Pichler as children about which Mary Claire Bally-Clairmont recorded: "links in weiss/Emily von Pichler/rechts in Blau mit Katze unsere Grossmutter/ Ottilie v. Pichler/ verh. Clairmont/ Bild aus Velden im Besitz von Marianne Fieber, Wien. (Photo von Henna Fieber erhalten)" (Translation from the German: "Left in white/ Emily von Pichler/ right in blue with cat our grandmother Ottilie v. Pichler/ married Clairmont/ Picture from Velden[9] owned by Marianne Fieber, Vienna (Photo obtained from Henna Fieber)." Wilhelm and Ottilia had three children: Walter Gaulis (1868–1958), Alma Pauline (1869–1946), and Johann Paul (1877–1942, "Paul"), all of whom would live through the years of National Socialism in Europe. Christoph Clairmont and Mary Claire Bally-Clairmont, whose donation of the family papers made the present volume possible, were the children of Paul and his wife Emmie Koller (1893–1986). New evidence shows that the third journal published in this edition, long thought to be Pauline's journal of a European excursion, probably belongs to Walter Clairmont (see "Meine Fussreise im Juli 1885" for more information about the journal writer's identity). Wilhelm and Ottilia are both buried in the family tomb in the Matzleinsdorf cemetery, along with Walter and Alma and their respective spouses.

INTRODUCTION

Wilhelm and Ottilia had two grandchildren, Mary Claire and Christoph. Christoph Clairmont died in 2004 and was survived by his wife, Victorine Clairmont-von Gonzenbach, who died in 2016. Their ashes are buried in Ernen, Switzerland. Mary Claire Bally-Clairmont died in Switzerland in 2009. She was survived by her husband, Hans-Jörg Bally, who died in 2015. Their ashes rest in Basel, Switzerland. Hans-Jörg Bally is survived by his second cousins, Dr. Claus Bally, Mr. Peter Bally, and Ms. Sylvia Bally.

Pauline's story is probably the most interesting within the context of these journals, particularly for the way in which descendant family members became responsible for the whereabouts of the journals themselves. Pauline predeceased her brother Wilhelm by four years, and she was buried in Öblarn, Styria, where she died. Though she likely did not write the journal of the European excursion ("Meine Fussreise im Juli 1885"), she was a prolific journal writer. Stocking recorded in "Miss Tina and Miss Plin: The Papers Behind *The Aspern Papers*" that Herbert Huscher had seen the family documents and that Pauline left sixteen or possibly more journals. Evidence in the form of letters to the American and British authorities after the Second World War suggests that Pauline's niece, Alma Crüwell-Clairmont, was the original curator of the journals and that her brother Walter Clairmont took over after her death in 1946. Alma was born in 1869 and married Gottlieb August Crüwell (1866–1931) who was an author, historian, and director of the library at the University of Vienna. The couple had no children. Walter, the oldest of the three siblings, was born in Tuzokrét when his parents were tenant farmers in the area. He wrote himself a succinct biography in 1933 to satisfy the authorities in Austria that he was not Jewish and therefore not subject to the anti-Jewish restrictions that Austrian Jews faced:

> I studied in Vienna at the Franz Josef Gymnasium and University of Agricultural Sciences, was assistant in the Archducal Dominion of Bellye for two years, but then changed careers; studied chemistry at the University of Basel, received my doctorate there on the basis of a dissertation on "Cretone" in 1893, worked for Agfa in Berlin as a chemist two years, then in a [textile-]printing factory in Russia seven years. Since 1903 I have been manager of the Neue Augsburger Kattunfabrik [New Augsburg Cotton Mill]. I acquired Bavarian citizenship in 1910 and was mustered out to the militia in 1911. On June 5, 1913, I married my wife, Frida née Zucker, in the Budapest Protestant church.
> (See Appendix F in this edition for the German translation of the document by Ann Sherwin)

Walter and Frida had no children together. In 1938, when the National Socialist agenda was reaching its apogée in Austria, the state demanded that Walter and Alma document their family origins to prove the absence of Jewish blood. Two documents they submitted, one by each of them, survive and form part of the Carl H. Pforzheimer Collection's holdings. While Walter's account explains the different denominations of Christianity to which his ancestors subscribed, Alma's concludes: "Thus our family stock represents a strong mix of good German, Roman, and English blood and contains not a drop of Semitic blood, as malevolent rumors would have it. The brunette features that Paul Clairmont, his brother Walter, and I share are first and foremost dominant traits inherited from the Walloon-Belgian stock, family characteristics that can also be observed in the last female representatives of this family, two Ghislain d'Hembyse ladies living in Linz" (English translation provided by Ann Sherwin; the entire transcription and translation of Alma's account can be found in Appendix F of this volume). The Pforzheimer Collection also has a document stamped with a Reichsadler (the Imperial Eagle, the symbol of the Nazi party) that proves the location, date, and by default the religion of Godwin and his wife on their marriage (see Appendix E), thereby confirming that the family was not of Jewish origin. It appears that not only was the family under surveillance for the possibility of a Jewish connection, but also that Godwin, as a British philosopher, was investigated. Nor was Alma's expression of anti-Semitism idle; she actively sympathized with National Socialism. Walter opposed the regime and they did not speak for years due to their political beliefs: "He had opposed the Nazi regime, and profound political differences had caused him some years before to cease communication with his sister Alma" ("Miss Tina and Miss Plin," p. 373).

The whereabouts of Pauline's other journals continue to remain a mystery. In "Miss Tina and Miss Plin: The Papers Behind *The Aspern Papers*," Stocking explains that Alma, as "custodian of the family archive" (Stocking 1978: 372), had sent away some of the documents "'to the country' for safekeeping" (p. 373). Alma's death in 1946 meant that her brother Walter assumed guardianship of the family documents. As a result, "the bulk of the papers . . . collected by the American military authorities" came into Walter Clairmont's possession after the Second World War (p. 373). Unfortunately, some of the documents have gone missing, "the material . . . has proved impossible to trace" (p. 373). Stocking notes that, by 1949, nine of Pauline's sixteen volumes had already been lost (volumes one through seven, and volumes nine and ten). At that time, she saw the remaining seven, which Walter described as "the rubbish my good old Aunt wrote down so volubly in her journals" (p. 374). When Stocking visited Mary Claire Bally-Clairmont in 1967, she discovered that volumes eleven through fifteen were missing, leaving only volume eight (transcribed in this journal) and volume sixteen extant. The subsequent loss of volume sixteen in the intervening time is unexplained. Of the nature of the journals examined by Stocking, she noted: "In her journals, Plin[10] [Pauline] moves almost unconsciously from one language to another, as though the European languages were all one to her. Like Claire [Clairmont], she appeared to be writing as an aid to her own memory, not for other readers. Unlike Claire, she seems to have used her journal as an outlet for the expression of opinions she could not freely air to her more conservative friends and relations" (p. 375). Stocking also provides us with dates and locations for each of the seven volumes she perused. They are as follows: volume eight is transcribed in this edition; volume eleven ("6 August 1859 to September 1866. In Rakicsan, near Mura in Hungary; travels in Italy, Germany, the Netherlands, and England; some periods with her mother and brother in Austria"); volume twelve (30 September 1866 until January 1868) records events in Germany and Vienna; volume thirteen (10 January 1868 to September 1868) is centered in Baden; volume fourteen (4 October 1868 to February 1870) describes Pauline "in Baden, with a visit to Hungary"; volume fifteen (2 March 1870 to October 1872) takes place in Italy; volume sixteen (17 May 1873 to October 1880) presents events in Florence and Vienna ("Miss Tina and Miss Plin," p. 375). Pauline's travels to Hungary were clearly to visit her daughter. In Baden she would have been visiting Antonia until the latter's death in 1868.

Declassified records from after the Second World War show that Stocking (then named Marion Kingston) and Walter Gaulis Clairmont attempted to locate the journals and family papers that went missing in 1948. Walter Clairmont wrote to James Garrison, Chief of the Reparations, Deliveries, and Restitution Division, Vienna Area Command, United States Forces Austria (USFA) for assistance with the "search." His letter dated 15 July 1948 mentioned Alma's death, noting she had been "in charge of our family papers." He identified Alma's niece living in Graz, Austria, Frau von Eissner, as "executrix" of his sister's will. Von Eissner, he explained, "has succeeded in securing part of these papers and . . . is asking me for the safest way how to send them to me" (Clairmont W., Fold Image, p. 136). Garrison wrote to Colonel Lorie of the Reparations, Deliveries and Restitution Division (RD and R Division), British Element, in Vienna, on the 27 July 1948, requesting that his office retrieve the papers from von Eissner so that Evelyn Tucker of the RD and R Division, United States Forces Austria, could collect the documents from the British Element in Vienna and deliver them to the British Consulate in Munich (Garrison, Fold Image, p. 137). Walter Clairmont, Garrison stated, "appears to be a British subject living in Bavaria." On 13 August 1948, Mr. P. Husband, Chief of the RD and R Division, British Element ACA, wrote to the Chief of the RD and R division of the United States Army noting that the Division had received a box from von Eissner "purporting to contain . . . 9 diary books of Life from Ms. P. Clairmont" as well as "diary books" and "little books" written by Ottilia Clairmont and several Clairmont family letters. Husband titled the memo "Original Correspondence – Shelley and Byron" (Husband, Fold Image, p. 134). On 27 September 1948 Tucker wrote a memo confirming that she had "delivered . . . 9 diary books of Life from Ms. P. Clairmont," on 23 September 1948 to Walter's wife (misspelling her name as Frieda; Tucker, Fold Image, p. 131). The memo also stated that the papers "were recovered by the RD&R Division . . . from Mrs. Alm. Cruwell, sister of Mr. Clairmont living in Graz, Steiermark" (Tucker's spelling for Alma; p. 131). Tucker was mistaken as Alma died in 1946. A signed receipt dated 22 September 1948 from Frida Clairmont in Munich confirmed acceptance of the diaries (Clairmont, F., Fold Image, p. 132). Tucker noted too in her memo of 27 September 1948 that Deputy Chief Ray E. Lee of the United States Forces in Austria, RD and R Division had photographed "about 40 papers – or sheets of one (or some) of the diaries – I do not know which" (Tucker, Fold Image, p. 131) before she delivered them to Frida Clairmont. Lee sent the photographs he had taken to a former professor of his son in Texas whom Tucker identified as "a Byron scholar." Tucker explained that she had not examined the "sealed cardboard box" before delivering it to Frida Clairmont (Fold Image, p. 131). On 21 March 1949, Stocking wrote to Garrison confirming that Walter Clairmont had received about "300 letters, three portraits, and a great many diaries" which she had seen and found to be in "excellent condition." She further mentioned the "undiscovered remainder of the papers" and provided two addresses for Alma prior to her 1946 death in case a further search yielded more information (Kingston, Fold Image, p. 129). On 30 March 1949, Garrison wrote back to Stocking referring her to Husband, Chief of the RD and R Division, British Element ACA, given that the two addresses Stocking had provided for Alma were now located in the British zone of Vienna (Garrison, Fold Image, p. 130). On that same day, 30 March 1949, Garrison recorded in a memo to Husband that "one case of the Clairmont papers" that the latter's office had delivered to the U.S. Element in summer, 1948 had been delivered to Walter Clairmont, who was at the time in U.S.-occupied Germany (Garrison, Fold Image, p. 128). He included Stocking's letter (Kingston, Fold Image, p. 129) asking for assistance (he stated that she was someone "who appears to have knowledge concerning the so-called 'Clairmont diaries'"[Garrison, Fold Image, p. 128]) saying he was bringing the matter to Husband's attention as the addresses referenced in the letter were in the British zone (Fold Image, p. 128). The matter came to rest in a 28 April 1949 letter from the British Element of the Allied Commission for Austria to the R D and R Division of the U.S. Army saying that Lee had received all extant documents on 26 August 1948: "It would appear, therefore, that such original correspondence of Shelley and Byron (Clairmont diaries) as is available has already been passed on to you" (Fold Image, p. 127). Walter's search for additional documents had proven unsuccessful.

However, Stocking records that she made "twelve pages of rough notes" from Pauline's journals ("Miss Tina and Miss Plin," Stocking 1978: 374), including some of the missing volumes, and she provides details in "Miss Tina and Miss Plin." Stocking describes Pauline as

> an emancipated woman – freedom-loving, high-spirited, and exuberantly sexual. More liberated and "romantic" than the Romantics, she recorded her intimate adventures with one man after another. Her journals show her as devoted to her brother and his children, deeply responsive to music . . . fond of horseback riding, drinking and smoking, traveling and (her father would have been pleased) literature. Almost perversely she seems to have enjoyed Byron most [Stocking alludes to Byron's ill-treatment of Pauline's Aunt Claire]. . . . In 1859 she writes of planning an article, thinks of making her living by her pen, and visualizes herself as already a writer and famous. . . . Her journals reveal an almost unflagging

gusto for life. . . . "Au fond," she wrote in 1859, "je suis née pour être courtisane, mais non levée à ce métier".

(pp. 376–377)

French translation by Sharon Joffe:

Fundamentally, I was born to be a courtesan, but I was not raised to this profession.

Stocking explains that the journals cover Pauline's years as a governess in Rakicsan, her pregnancy in 1863, her 29 January 1894 walk "through a snow storm" to "offer" her newborn daughter to Countess Károly (who took the child into her home), her various travels, and her visits to see her daughter (p. 377). Of her time with Claire in Italy, Stocking states that Pauline and Claire quarreled as Claire "lectured Plin that cold baths and strenuous exercise were bad for her, and she forbade her to marry a rather unsavory young man named Pasquale" (p. 378). Stocking also recounts that Pauline recorded the arrival in 1871 in Florence of her daughter, Georgina Hanghegyi, by then seven years old. Stocking remarks: "on 16 June the little girl arrived in Florence, disappointingly vulgar and snobbish, speaking horrible German with a Hungarian accent, interested only in Plin's clothes and rings, 'in short [Pauline wrote in her journal] not what any child of mine & free America ought to be'" (p. 378). Yet a "tug-of war" for the child's attention ensued between mother and great-aunt (p. 379). Stocking quotes the 3 March 1874 entry of Pauline's now-lost journal charging that with respect to Georgina Claire was treating Pauline much as Byron had treated Claire in the matter of their daughter: "*I* am the one on whom Aunt concentrates all her hatred – & strange to say – the very instrument she hoped to torture me with – à la Byron – escapes her – because the good little thing [Georgina] loves *me* – & obeys *me* for every feeling & sentiment & idea" (Pauline's emphasis; p. 379). Claire appears to have used Georgina as a pawn, vying for her attention and pitting her against her own mother. Another detail Stocking provides from Pauline's journals has to do with Edward Augustus Silsbee (1826–1900), the man who attempted to purchase the Shelley papers Claire had at the time and who wooed both Claire and Pauline in his endeavor. Stocking explains that Silsbee was adept at "flirting, according to Plin, with every female in Florence. Plin became increasingly jealous. With unconscious irony she wrote on 18 July 1875: 'I cannot help wondering at the longevity of Envy & Jealously in the human heart – There is Aunt [Claire] at 77 so jealous that no man dare come into the house but what must be exclusively occupied with her – This morning Mr. Silsbee came at 11 ½ and she talked with him until dinner time as soon as that was over she talked again until 4'" (p. 380). Stocking states that when Silsbee left Florence after failing to marry Pauline and thereby obtain the Shelley papers, "Plin mourned for him in her journal as though for a lost husband" (p. 380). Stocking also shows that Pauline's journals corroborate some of what Henry James wrote about in his 1888 work, *The Aspern Papers*, a novella he modeled on the story of Claire and Pauline[11]: "Through the medium of Plin's journal we now know some of the factual background to the gossip that Henry James was to transform into his exquisite novel" (p. 381). James tells a fictional account of two women, Juliana Bordereau and her niece Miss Tina (Miss Tita in the original publication) who live in Venice, and the unnamed narrator who attempts to get access to the love letters from American poet, Jeffrey Aspern (possibly a composite of Byron and Percy Shelley), written to Juliana. In James's telling of the story, Miss Tina offers the narrator the letters she inherits after her aunt's death in exchange for marriage. Initially, he rebuffs her but when he returns to fulfil Miss Tina's request and thereby get access to the letters, he finds that she has burned the letters, "she takes a bold step, obliterating the literary remains of her unacknowledged father and forfeiting the name to which she is entitled, just as she now refrains from pursuing the narrator as her prospective husband [there is a suggestion that Aspern is her father]. Escaping both the domination of Juliana and the patriarchal assignment of her ambiguous role . . . she earns her freedom from the past" (Scholl 2013: 87). The parallels between Silsbee's attempt to gain access to the Shelley papers in Claire's possession and James's narrator's quest are evident, even though Diane Long Hoeveler asserts that the narrator has other intentions: "The papers – the literal remains of Aspern – were never the real object of the narrator's quest. He has been from the beginning obsessed with vicariously experiencing on an artistic or visual level the relationship that Byron and Shelley had with Claire" (Hoeveler 2008: 29–30). Pauline's diaries are thus important artefacts as they confirm significant nineteenth-century literary and historical events. The journals, Stocking concludes, chronicle "a secret life, it was the life she lived and loved and wished to record" (p. 383). Pauline's extant Journal 8, published here, provides evidence of her extraordinary life.

Pauline was an accomplished pianist and linguist who first went to England in 1850 to find a position as a teacher and then, later, in 1853, to Australia where she would take on the role as a governess. Her letter to Claire of 19 February 1850 reveals her desire to earn money through assuming a job as an educator: "If therefore I come to England to give music or German lessons, or look for some place in a family I shall only beg you dear aunt to introduce me to some families. . . . I should be very glad to go to England" (*CFL* I: 74). Her subsequent move to Australia with Wilhelm in 1853 is indicative of her wish to provide financially for herself and her mother. Australia was a place in which people were supposed to make their fortunes and Wilhelm noted two people connected to Mary Shelley, her friend Mr. Charles Robinson and her cousin (by his marriage to Elizabeth Wollstonecraft, the daughter of Mary Wollstonecraft's brother, Edward), Alexander Berry, in his letter to his parents of 2 November 1849. He described Robinson's success in Australia: "A Mr Charles Robinson friend of Mrs. Shelley's spent up to his thirtieth year the whole of his little fortune in London without being able to succeed; he went out with no more than £5 in his pocket, and returned after 8 years stay a wealthy man." He portrayed Berry as "a common Yorkshire farmer who married Miss a cousin of

Mrs. Shelley's" and who "emigrated and I understand without a farthing to help him self with". Berry, he wrote, "now so far ammeliorated his condition that he possesses an income of no less than £10,000 a year and maintains by pensions several of his poor relations whom he had left in England when compared to himself rich. He has now retired to Sydney but farmes all his estates by stewards and bailiffs" (Wilhelm's spelling: *CFL* I: 51). It is also possible that Pauline and Wilhelm left England to avoid contagion, as various illnesses were rampant in Europe at the time. Indeed their sisters Emmy and Sidi, and brother, Charley, would all succumb to infectious disease in 1856. Pauline's letters record her appointment in Australia as a governess to the younger children of William Henry Suttor (1805–1877) and Charlotte Francis Suttor (1817–1879), but do not mention the love affair with her employers' eldest son, William Henry Suttor, Junior (1834–1905), which is documented in the journal presented in this volume.

The Suttors were a prominent Australian family. Ruth Teale explains that George Suttor (1774–1859) immigrated to Australia in 1800 and that his son, William Henry Suttor (1805–1877), worked on his father's farm, Brucedale, from 1834 onwards. William Suttor later owned more than 600,000 acres of land in the area.[12] Brucedale remains in the possession of members of the Suttor family, who raise sheep in the area today. William Henry and Charlotte Suttor's son, William Henry, Junior, and Pauline would have an affair, but even though Pauline acknowledged her desire to wed William, he would ultimately marry Adelaide Agnes Henrietta Bowler (1837–1920). As we will see, Pauline writes contemptuously about Adelaide in her journal. William (Junior) provides us with a description of Pauline in his *Memoirs*: "I was a boy of eighteen and she a woman of twenty-eight. . . . She was a short dark woman with jet black silky hair, dark brown eyes and very pretty hands and arms and a certain spice of devilry in her that made her (undeciphered word) to a raw country lad with all his passions just ripening unto manhood strength. I think she left us in 1857 having just taught me what it was to feel what love of a woman was like" (quoted in Voignier-Marshall 1983: 29). William was also a writer. He published a collection of short stories, *Australian Stories Retold; and, Sketches of Country Life* (1887), which includes a character (as I show in *The Clairmont Family Letters*) he appears to have modelled after Pauline. In "A Cattle Muster on the Plains," he describes "[a] late arrival from England, but has lived much on the Continent, and being somewhat self-willed, would defy conventionalities and make one of the party" (Suttor W., 1887: 82). Another story in William's collection, "The Van Dieman's Land Ghouls," states: "Tennyson must surely have seen Tasmania in a dream when he wrote the 'Lotus Eaters'" (p. 53). This statement may have reflected Pauline's influence, as she favored the poetry of Alfred, Lord Tennyson and whose poem, "The Lotos-Eaters," was published in 1832. William explained in his *Memoirs* that Pauline had introduced him to "the beauties of English literature" (Voignier-Marshall 1983: 29) and Pauline told Claire

INTRODUCTION

Clairmont in her 8 July 1853 letter of her relationship with a young man she called Mr. Blair and who had read Tennyson's poetry to her (*CFL* I: 154): "& when we come to hear about love in a cottage we shut up the book & sigh – Is that not a pleasant little passe tems!" (Pauline's spelling for "passe-temps," the French for "diversion"; p. 154). Here, Pauline references Tennyson's poem, "The Lord of Burleigh" in which the poet wrote: "love will make our cottage pleasant." The Pforzheimer Collection also has a copy of Tennyson's "The Charge of the Light Brigade" and parts of the poem, "Two Pictures,"[13] penned possibly in Pauline's hand (see CL'ANA 0423, unpublished manuscript, Pforzheimer Collection).

After her disappointment over the end of her relationship with William Suttor, Pauline returned to Europe in 1857, and her journal explains her adventures aboard the *Waterloo*. These adventures included a love affair and numerous flirtations, all of which she documents in her journal. From 1863 until 1865, Pauline resided with Wilhelm as he farmed in the Banat. She gave birth to her daughter, Georgina Hanghegyi (full name Johanna Maria Georgina), in 1864. Pauline never named the father of her child and Herbert Huscher proposes that Pauline gave her daughter the last name of Hanghegyi in "an attempt at a translation of the name Clairmont into Hungarian" (Huscher 1955: 47). Pauline then chose to send her child to live with Countess Károly in Hungary. While Pauline resided in Baden, Austria, with Antonia, she would visit her daughter on a regular basis. Stocking quotes Pauline's journal entry after visiting her daughter in 1870: "Altogether my heart is at peace about the child but the whole education the treatment is far from what I would wish to give her – she is too pale too tame too finnikin too timid too bourgeoisie in short. . . . but she has the English blood in her – slow of development. She is so primly dressed. . . . She speaks in a soft & low voice almost a whisper, & all her little wishes are modest & gentle. How unlike my wild gypsy nature" (Stocking "Miss Tina and Miss Plin" Stocking 1978: 377). It was after Antonia's death that Pauline moved to Florence to live with Claire and brought Georgina to live with them. Pauline continued to work to support herself and her family, as her letter to Wilhelm of 27 February 1877 illustrates. She described her "new duties" as "hard work" and herself as "Reader, secretary, housekeeper, companion, housemaid, ironer, needlewoman, in short Jack of all trades, if there are any visits I must do the lady & play on the Piano" (*CFL* II: 227). She outlived both her aunt and her daughter, as they died in 1878 and in 1885 respectively. Georgina's death certificate issued in Florence listed her name as "Giovanna Maria Giorgina Hanghegyi" and recorded that she was a "donna da casa" (Italian for a "woman who resides at home") whose parents were not known (see CL'ANA 0318, unpublished manuscript, Pforzheimer Collection). Pauline's sojourn for work and later travels in Europe in 1887 and 1889 are recorded in *The Clairmont Family Letters*. Writing to her niece Alma Clairmont on 20 July 1887, Pauline explained her chores while working

INTRODUCTION

at Zdounek in Moravia (probably her misspelling for Zdaunek) which included tea-making and piano playing. She also taught English while residing there (see *CFL* II: 251). In 1889, she vacationed in Europe, writing letters to her brother from Nice, Corsica, and Elba. Pauline died in 1891 after she fell from a mountain while walking with her nephew, Paul Clairmont, in Öblarn, Steiermark (Styria). She was buried there, and her death recorded in the *Das Vaterland* (see Page 5, http://anno.onb.ac.at/cgi-content/anno?aid=vtl&datum=18910715&seite=5&zoom=33). William Suttor also wrote poignantly to Wilhelm after he learned of the death of his former lover. He was, he wrote, "terribly shocked today to see in one of our papers here an account of the death by accident while ascending the Sonnenberg at Oblarn the account is as follows. 'A mountain accident in Upper Styria cost an English lady her life. Miss Pauline Clairmont was ascending the Sonnenberg at Oblarn only the day after her arrival when she slipped & rolled down the mountain side. Her lifeless body was found next day Is this true. I am you with much sympathy W. H Suttor" (William's spelling and emphasis; see CL'ANA 0199, unpublished manuscript, Pforzheimer Collection).

The Clairmont Family Letters: 1839–1889 and now *The Clairmont Family Journals: 1855–1885* enable researchers to have access to the documents of a remarkable family whose story exemplifies family dynamics over many generations. Sadly, today, there are no direct living descendants of the Clairmont family. The deaths of Christoph Clairmont and Mary Claire Bally-Clairmont in 2004 and 2009 respectively ended the family line, making it even more critical for researchers to preserve the family's letters, journals, and documents, as well as resting places. Editions such as *The Clairmont Family Letters: 1839–1889* and *The Clairmont Family Journals: 1855–1885* will assist in preserving the family documents. Additionally, conservation of the family tomb has also been accomplished. In 2018, I visited the Clairmont family tomb in the Evangelischer Friedhof Matzleinsdorf in Vienna, Austria, and saw that it was going to be rented and the Clairmont family bones buried in a communal grave ("Sammelgruft"). I thus wrote to Astrid Ryper of the Cultural Heritage Unit of Municipal Department – 7 for Culture in Vienna. I provided her with information about Charles Clairmont and his family as part of my request to have the city of Vienna spare the tomb from destruction. Ryper then sought the assistance of Michael Ludwig, the mayor of Vienna. In 2019, Ludwig's office declared the tomb an honorary grave ("Ehrengräber"), to be maintained forever by the City of Vienna (or until the working cemetery no longer functions; see the photograph of the Clairmont family tomb in this edition).[14] The history that links the Godwin-Shelley circle to the Clairmont family is extraordinary. It is the earnest hope of this editor that further journals and/or letters will be discovered in future years, enabling researchers to shed more light on this exceptional family whose connections to the extended Shelley family augment our understanding of that primary circle.

INTRODUCTION

Notes

1. Clara Knox and Charles Gaulis Clairmont were Charles and Antonia Clairmont's children. Ottilia von Pichler was Wilhelm Clairmont's wife.
2. In *Frankenstein*, the creature learns through observing the De Lacey family: "By great application . . . I discovered the names that were given to some of the most familiar objects of discourse: I learned and applied the words *fire, milk, bread*, and *wood*" (*Frankenstein* 2012: 129). In her *Lessons*, Wollstonecraft suggests in Lesson 1 that Fanny Imlay (for whom her book was intended) learn nouns only: "Bread. Milk. Tea. Meat. Drink. Cake" (in *Frankenstein*, Macdonald [ed], 2012: 269).
3. Attorney Robert Beadon practiced in Taunton, Somerset.
4. As already noted, while I originally discussed many of these events in *The Clairmont Family Letters, 1839–1889*, I reiterate some of the information here.
5. Impl and Rl are acronyms for Imperial and Royal (k.k. in German, kaiserlich-königlich), while the R. Ter Academy stands for the Ritterakademie Theresianum.
6. Antonia's book, *Erste Schritte zur Erlernung der englischen Sprache, für Kinder von sechs bis zehn Jahren*, records her name as "Antonia Clairmont, geb. Ghylain v. Hembyze" (English translation: Antonia Clairmont, born Ghylain v. Hembyze). Charles Clairmont's death notice ("Die Parte") also identifies her as Antonia Clairmont, born Ghylain von Hembyze (*CFL* I: 140). In Mary Claire Bally-Clairmont's family tree, Antonia's name is spelled "Antonia Ghilain d'Hambyze." Bally-Clairmont lists Charles Clairmont from Devonshire (death date, 1799) and Mary Jane Devereux as Charles's parents. She documents that Mary Jane Devereux married William Godwin in 1801. She spells Antonia's mother's name as Anna Schönbichler (see CL'ANA 0425, unpublished manuscript, Pforzheimer Collection).
7. Marion Stocking informed Mary Claire Bally-Clairmont in her letter of 25 April 1987 that she had perused the Clairmont family papers at "leisure," noting that "for someone who could read the old German, I think there would be a fascinating study of farm-life in Australia!" (see CL'ANA 0425, unpublished manuscript, Pforzheimer Collection).
8. The Clairmont family tomb in the Evangelischer Friedhof Matzleinsdorf records her name as Ottilia (see the photograph in this edition). Paul Clairmont's birth certificate also spells her name as Ottilia (see CL'ANA 0425, unpublished manuscript, Pforzheimer Collection). However, Wilhelm and Ottilia's wedding certificate reflects her name as "Ottilie" (see the photograph in this edition) as does the family's 1913 notice of her death (unpublished manuscript, Heraldic-Genealogical Society Adler, Vienna). Mary Claire Bally-Clairmont's family tree designates her name as Ottilie (see CL'ANA 0425, unpublished manuscript, Pforzheimer Collection). When Ottilia wrote to Pauline Clairmont in 1865 before her 1866 marriage to Wilhelm, she signed her name as Ottilia (*CFL* II: 76). Wilhelm first told Claire Clairmont about his engagement in a letter dated 6 February 1866 in which he recorded his fiancée's name as Ottilia (*CFL* II: 88). Wilhelm addressed his wife as "Tilly" or "Titsy" in his letters. She called him "Willy."
9. In a letter from Mary Claire Bally-Clairmont to Marion Stocking, dated 12 April 2005, Bally-Claimont explains: "That Mortiz (brother of Ottilie) is my great uncle and great-great father of my cousin in Paris. – Fanny [von Pichler; Ottilia's mother and Mary Claire's great-grandmother] made many trips and was enchanted by the Wörthersee (Lake of Wörther) Austria, about 70 km west Graz, bought there a farm house, later changed in a villa (still existing!): her son Moritz took it over. The Clairmonts were often there, as well as Christoph and I for summer holidays. the name of the village is Velden. Not many hotels on the border of the lake, really a beautiful spot; private estates on the lake, since years a jetset destination! – The villa sold about 26 years ago" (see CL'ANA 0425, unpublished manuscript, Pforzheimer Collection). Velden am

INTRODUCTION

Wörthersee is located in the state of Carinthia in the south Austria. The town lies on the lake (Wörthersee).

10 Pauline was known as "Plin" to her family. Stocking notes that Huscher said that Pauline was called "'die Ampel' (i.e. a hanging lamp), a further contraction of 'Aunt Plin'" ("Miss Tina and Miss Plin," p. 383).

11 In a letter dated 25 April 1987 to Mary Claire Bally-Clairmont, Stocking observes that James's "little novel" is "a very highly fictionalized account of Claire and Pauline's late years in Florence (which he makes into Venice)" (see CL'ANA 0425, unpublished manuscript, Pforzheimer Collection).

12 Ruth Teale, "Suttor, William Henry (1805–1877)," *Australian Dictionary of Biography*, National Centre of Biography, Australian National University, http://adb.anu.edu.au/biography/suttor-william-henry-1269/text7733, published first in hardcopy 1976 (accessed 10 July 2020).

13 The poet's identity is not known.

14 Wilhelm and Ottilia Clairmont and two of their children – Walter Gaulis Clairmont and Alma Crüwell-Clairmont and their respective spouses, Frida Clairmont (née Zucker) and Gottlieb August Crüwell – are all interred together. The stone also records Charles Gaulis Clairmont's name and the names of two of his daughters, Emily and Sidonia Clairmont. However, no cemetery records exist to prove conclusively that these three Clairmont family members are buried together with the others.

Image 1 Portrait of Claire Clairmont by Amelia Curran (Accession Number: NA 271).

Source: Newstead Abbey.

Credit: By Permission of Nottingham City Museums and Galleries (Newstead Abbey).

Image 2 Clairmont Family Tomb, Evangelischer Friedhof Matzleinsdorf, Vienna, Austria, 2019.
Source: Sharon L. Joffe.
Credit: Sharon L. Joffe.

Bibliography

Aberle, G., *From the Steppes to the Prairies* (Bismarck, N.D.: Tumbleweed Press, 1981).
Anonymous, Letter to the Director, RD and R Division. 28 April 1949. Records of the Reparations and Restitutions Branch of the U.S. Allied Commission for Austria (USACA) Section, 1945–1950, www.fold3.com/image/274319547, page 127, 21 July 2020.
———, *Picture of Vienna Containing a Historical Sketch of the Metropolis of Austria, a Complete Notice of all the Public Institutions, Buildings, Galleries, Collections, Gardens, Walks, and Other Objects of Interest Or Utility, and a Short Description of the most Picturesque Spots in the Vicinity, with a Map of the Town and Suburbs*. (Vienna: Braumüller & Seidel, 1844).
Austrian Newspapers Online. Österreichische Nationalbibliothek (Austrian National Library). http://anno.onb.ac.at/
Barker, T., *A History of Bathurst* (Bathurst, NSW: Crawford House Press, 1992).

INTRODUCTION

Bartley, N., *Opals and Agates, Or, Scenes Under the Southern Cross and the Magellans: Being Memories of Fifty Years of Australia and Polynesia* (Brisbane: Gordon and Gotch, 1892).
Bayley, W. A., *Behind Broulee: History of Eurobodalla Shire, Central South Coast, New South Wales* (Moruya, NSW: Eurobodalla Shire Council, 1973).
Bennett, B. T., and C. Robinson (eds.), *The Mary Shelley Reader: Containing Frankenstein, Mathilda, Tales and Stories, Essays and Reviews, and Letters* (New York: Oxford University Press, 1990).
Bennett, B. T., *Mary Wollstonecraft Shelley: An Introduction* (Baltimore: Johns Hopkins University Press, 1998).
Botting, E., C. Wilkerson, and E. Kozlow, "Wollstonecraft as an International Feminist Meme," *Journal of Women's History*, 26:2 (2014), pp. 13–38.
Čerin, B. and F. Vogelnik, *Maribor* (Ljubljana: Cankarjeva zal., 1988).
Clairmont, A., *Erste Schritte zur Erlernung der englischen Sprache, für Kinder von sechs bis zehn jahren.* (Vienna: Braümuller & Seidel, 1845).
Clairmont, C., "Eine Abendsgessellschaft in Berlin im Jahre 1895," *Navigare*, 1999, www.navigare.de/hofmannsthal/abend.htm#dulong2, 9 July 2020.
Clairmont, C. G., *First Poetical Reading-Book: Being a Progressive Collection of the most Interesting Pieces in Verse in the English Language; Beginning with the Simplest Poems – Poetisches Lesebuch für Anfänger* (Vienna: Braumüller & Seidel, 1845).
Clairmont, C. M. J., "The Pole," in C. E. Robinson (ed.), *Mary Shelley: Collected Tales and Stories* (Baltimore, MD: Johns Hopkins University Press, 1990), pp. 347–372.
Clairmont, F., Receipt of Clairmont Correspondence. 22 September 1948. Records of the Reparations and Restitutions Branch of the U.S. Allied Commission for Austria (USACA) Section, 1945–1950, www.fold3.com/image/274319558/, page 132, 9 July 2020.
Clairmont, W. G., Letter to James Garrison. 15 July 1948. Records of the Reparations and Restitutions Branch of the U.S. Allied Commission for Austria (USACA) Section, 1945–1950, www.fold3.com/image/274319568, p. 136, 11 July 2020.
Clarke, P., *A Colonial Woman: The Life and Times of Mary Braidwood Mowle, 1827–1857* (Sydney and Boston, MA: Allen & Unwin, 1986).
Clemit, P., M. Hindle, and M.Philp (eds.), *The Collected Novels and Memoirs of William Godwin* (London: Pickering and Chatto, 1992).
Conger, C. M., F. S. Frank, and G. O'Dea (eds.), *Iconoclastic Departures: Mary Shelley After Frankenstein* (Madison, NJ and London: Fairleigh Dickinson University Press, 1997).
Dabundo, L. (ed.), *Jane Austen and Mary Shelley, and their Sisters* (Lanham, MD: University Press of America, 2000).
Davidoff, L., and C. Hall, *Family Fortunes* (London and New York: Routledge, 2002).
Denlinger, E. C., "Horrid Mysteries of Cl Cl 26: A Tale of Mothers and Daughters," *19: Interdisciplinary Studies in the Long Nineteenth Century*, 27 (2018), https://doi.org/10.16995/ntn.817, 24 July 2020.
Dowden, E., R. Garnett, and W. Rossetti, *Letters about Shelley Interchanged by Three Friends – Edward Dowden, Richard Garnett and Wm. Michael Rossetti* (London: Hodder and Stoughton, 1917).
Eberle-Sinatra, M. (ed.), *Mary Shelley's Fictions: From Frankenstein to Falkner* (Basingstoke and New York: Macmillan Press, 2000).
Engelmann, N. and J. Michels, *The Banat Germans: Die Banater Schwaben* (Bismarck, ND: University of Mary Press, 1987).
Farwell, G., *Squatters' Castle: The Saga of a Pastoral Dynasty* (London and Sydney: Angus & Robertson, 1983).

Favret, M. A., *Romantic Correspondence: Women, Politics, and the Fiction of Letters* (Cambridge and New York: Cambridge University Press, 1993).
Ferry, J., *Colonial Armidale* (St. Lucia: University of Queensland Press, 1999).
Fitzgerald, J., *Big White Lie: Chinese Australians in White Australia* (Sydney, NSW: University of New South Wales Press, 2007).
Fisch, A. A., A. K. Mellor, and E. H. Schor (eds.), *The Other Mary Shelley: Beyond Frankenstein* (New York: Oxford University Press, 1993).
Frey, K. S., *The Danube Swabians: A People with Portable Roots* (Belleville, ON: Mika Pub. Co., 1982).
Frost, L., *No Place for a Nervous Lady: Voices from the Australian Bush* (Melbourne: McPhee Gribble/Penguin, 1984).
Garrett, M., *A Mary Shelley Chronology* (New York: Palgrave, 2002).
Garrison, J., Letter to Colonel Lorie. 27 July 1948. Records of the Reparations and Restitutions Branch of the U.S. Allied Commission for Austria (USACA) Section, 1945–1950, www.fold3.com/image/274319570/, p. 137, 9 July 2020.
———, Letter about Clairmont Diaries. 30 March 1949. Records of the Reparations and Restitutions Branch of the U.S. Allied Commission for Austria (USACA) Section, 1945–1950, www.fold3.com/image/274319550/, p. 128, 9 July 2020.
———, Letter to Marion Kingston. 30 March 1949. Records of the Reparations and Restitutions Branch of the U.S. Allied Commission for Austria (USACA) Section, 1945–1950, www.fold3.com/image/274319555/, p. 130, 9 July 2020.
Goerlich, E., "Charles Gaulis Clairmont," *Wiener Geschichtsblatter*, 25 (1970), pp. 124–125.
Google Maps. 2019–2020. Web. Various dates. www.google.com/maps/
Great Britain Foreign Office, Historical Section, *Transylvania and the Banat* (Wilmington, DE: Scholarly Resources, 1973).
Grylls, R. G., *Claire Clairmont, Mother of Byron's Allegra* (London: John Murray, 1939).
Hall, N., *Salmagundi: Byron, Allegra, and the Trollope Family* (Pittsburgh, PA: Beta Phi Mu, 1975).
Hay, D., *Young Romantics: The Shelleys, Byron and Other Tangled Lives* (London: Bloomsbury, 2010).
Hebron, S., and E. Denlinger, *Shelley's Ghost: Reshaping the Image of a Literary Family* (Oxford: Bodleian Library, 2010).
Hindle, M., "Victim of Romance: The Life and Death of Fanny Godwin," *Women's Writing*, 13:3 (2006), pp. 331–347.
Hirst, T. A., and J. Tyndall, *Introductory Lecture to the Course on Natural Philosophy: At Queenwood College, Hampshire* (Romsey: C.L. Lordan, 1853).
Hitchins, K., *Studies in East European Social History* (Leiden: Brill, 1977).
———, *A Concise History of Romania* (New York: Cambridge University Press, 2014).
Hitschmann, H., *Verzeichniss der Lehrer und Studirenden der erzherzoglichen landwirthschaftlichen Bildungsanstalt und der k. k. höheren landwirthschaftlichen Lehranstalt zu Ungarisch–Altenburg 1818–1848 und 1858–1864* (Ung. Altenberg: Alexander Czéh, 1865).
Hoeveler, D., "The Literal and Literary Circulation of Amelia Curran's Portrait of Percy Shelley," *The Wordsworth Circle*, 39:1–2 (2008), pp. 27–30.
Husband, R., Letter Confirming Receipt of Clairmont Materials. 13 August 1948. Records of the Reparations and Restitutions Branch of the U.S. Allied Commission for Austria (USACA) Section, 1945–1950, www.fold3.com/image/274319564/, p. 134, 11 July 2020.
Huscher, H., "Charles Und Claire Clairmont," *Englische Studien*, 76 (1944), pp. 53–117.

———, "Claire Clairmont's Lost Russian Journal and some further Glimpses of Her Later Life," *Keats – Shelley Memorial Bulletin*, 6 (1955), pp. 35–47.

———, "Charles Gaulis Clairmont," *Keats – Shelley Memorial Bulletin*, 8 (1957), pp. 9–18.

———, "The Clairmont Enigma," *Keats – Shelley Memorial Bulletin*, 11 (1960), pp. 13–20.

James, H., *The Aspern Papers and Other Stories* (Oxford [Oxfordshire]; New York: Oxford University Press, 1983).

Joffe, S. L., *The Kinship Coterie and the Literary Endeavors of the Women in the Shelley Circle* (New York: Peter Lang, 2007).

Joffe, S. L. (ed.), *The Clairmont Family Letters, 1839–1889* (London and New York: Routledge, 2017).

Jones, F. (ed.), *Maria Gisborne & Edward E. Williams, Shelley's Friends* (Norman: University of Oklahoma Press, 1951).

Jones, F. L., "Mary Shelley and Claire Clairmont," *South Atlantic Quarterly*, 42 (1943), pp. 406–412.

———, "A Shelley and Mary Letter to Claire," *Modern Language Notes*, 65:2 (1950), pp. 121–123.

Kelly, G., *Revolutionary Feminism: The Mind and Career of Mary Wollstonecraft* (New York: St. Martin's Press, 1992).

Kingston, M., Letter to Mr. Garrison. 21 March 1949. Records of the Reparations and Restitutions Branch of the U. S. Allied Commission for Austria (USACA) Section, 1945–1950, www.fold3.com/image/274319552, p. 129, 11 July 2020.

Lee, R., Letter to Walter Clairmont. 7 September 1948. Records of the Reparations and Restitutions Branch of the U.S. Allied Commission for Austria (USACA) Section, 1945–1950, www.fold3.com/image/274319561/, p. 133, 21 July 2020.

Leslie, L., "The Fact that is in Fiction: Autobiography in Claire Clairmont's 'The Pole'," *Keats–Shelley Review*, 20 (2006), pp. 69–88.

Levine, G., and U. C. Knoepflmacher (eds.), *The Endurance of Frankenstein: Essays on Mary Shelley's Novel* (Berkeley: University of California Press, 1979).

Luthar, O., *The Land Between: A History of Slovenia* (Frankfurt am Main: Peter Lang GmbH, 2013).

McInherny, F. and T. Schaeffer, *Our Grandchildren Won't Believe it: A Local History of the Wongwibinda, Aberfoyle and Ward's Mistake Areas* (Armidale, N.S.W.: Historical Group, 2004).

Mackaness, G., *Fourteen Journeys Over the Blue Mountains of New South Wales, 1813–1841* (Sydney and Melbourne: Horwitz-Grahame, 1965).

Mathewson, G., "Claire Clairmont on Shelley's Circle," *Notes and Queries*, 20 (1973), pp. 48–49.

Mellor, A., *Mary Shelley: Her Life, Her Fiction, Her Monsters* (New York: Methuen, 1988).

———, *Mothers of the Nation: Women's Political Writing in England* (Bloomington: Indiana University Press, 2000).

Morrison, L., S. Stone, and P. Feldman, *A Mary Shelley Encyclopedia* (Westport, CT: Greenwood Press, 2003).

National Archives. Web. www.archives.gov/

National Center of Biography. *Australian Dictionary of Biography*. Web. http://adb.anu.edu.au/

National Library of Australia. Trove. Newspapers Online. https://trove.nla.gov.au/newspaper/

Neuer Nekrolog Der Deutschen: 26 Jahrgang (Weimar: B.Fr. Voigt, 1850).

Norton, J., and H. Norton, *Dear William: The Suttors of Brucedale: Principally the Life and Times of William Henry Suttor Senior ("Dear William"), 1805–1877* (Sydney: Suttor Pub. Committee, 1993).

Paikert, G. C., *The Danube Swabians* (The Hague: Martinus Nijhoff, 1967).

Pearson, M., *Pastoral Australia: Fortunes, Failures and Hard Yakka: A Historical Overview 1788–1967*, Australia, Department of the Environment, Water, Heritage, and the Arts, Australian Heritage Council. and J. Lennon (eds), (Collingwood, Vic.: CSIRO Publishing in association with the Dept. of the Environment, Water, Heritage and the Arts and the Australian Heritage Council, 2010).

Poovey, M., *The Proper Lady and the Woman Writer: Ideology as Style in the Works of Mary Wollstonecraft, Mary Shelley, and Jane Austen* (Chicago: University of Chicago Press, 1984).

Prunk, J., *A Brief History of Slovenia* (Ljubljana: Založba Grad, 2000).

Reiman, D. H., K. N. Cameron, D. D. Fischer, et al., *Shelley and his Circle, 1773–1822* (Cambridge, MA: Harvard University Press, 1961–).

Ritter, E., "Über Hofmannsthals Besuch der Mozart-Centenarfeier in Salzburg im Juli 1891," *Navigare*. 1999, www.navigare.de/hofmannsthal/mozart.html, 11 July 2020.

Ryan, B., "Kameruka Estate, New South Wales, 1864–1964," *New Zealand Geographer*, 20:2 (1964), pp. 103–121.

Scholl, D., "Secret Paternity in James's *The Aspern Papers*: Whose Letters?" *Modern Philology*, 111:1 (2013), pp. 72–87.

Seymour, M., *Mary Shelley* (New York: Grove Press, 2000).

Shelley, J., *Shelley Memorials: From Authentic Sources* (Boston, MA: Ticknor and Fields, 1859).

Shelley, M. W., *The Letters of Mary Wollstonecraft Shelley*, ed. B. T. Bennett (Baltimore, MD: Johns Hopkins University Press, 1980).

———, *The Journals of Mary Shelley, 1814–1844*, eds. P. R. Feldman and D. Scott-Kilvert (Oxford and New York: Clarendon Press and Oxford University Press, 1987).

———, *The Novels and Selected Works of Mary Shelley*, eds. P. Clemit and N. Crook (Brookfield, VT: Pickering & Chatto, 1996).

———, *Maurice, Or, the Fisher's Cot: A Tale*, ed. C. Tomalin (Chicago: University of Chicago Press, 1998).

———, *Frankenstein Or, The Modern Prometheus*, eds. D. L. Macdonald and K. Scherf (Peterborough, ON: Broadview Press, 2012).

Small, V., *Kameruka* (Bega, NSW: Kameruka Estates, 1989).

Smith, G., *100 Years Peel and District* (Bathurst, NSW: Geoffrey A. Smith, 1998).

Snape, W. H., *Queenwood College, Near Stockbridge, Hampshire* (etching) (Wellcome Library: London, 1891).

St. Clair, W., *The Godwins and the Shelleys* (New York: Norton, 1989).

Stafford, V. P., "Claire Clairmont, Mary Jane's Daughter," https://sites.google.com/site/maryjanesdaughter/home, 11 July 2020.

Steigerwald, J., *Tracing Romania's Heterogeneous German Minority from its Origins to the Diaspora* (Winona, MN: Translation and Interpretation Service, 1985).

Stocking, M. K., "Miss Tina and Miss Plin: The Papers Behind *The Aspern Papers*," in D. Reiman (ed.), *The Evidence of the Imagination* (New York: New York University Press, 1978), pp. 372–384.

Stocking, M. K. (ed.), *The Journals of Claire Clairmont* (Cambridge, MA: Harvard University Press, 1968).

———, *The Clairmont Correspondence: Letters of Claire Clairmont, Charles Clairmont, and Fanny Imlay Godwin* (Baltimore: Johns Hopkins University Press, 1995).

Sunstein, E. W., *Mary Shelley: Romance and Reality* (Boston, MA: Little, Brown, 1989).

Suttor, C., *Charlotte Augusta Anne Suttor Diaries, 1848–1853* (Bathurst, NSW: State Library New South Wales, 1848–1853).
Suttor, W. H., *Australian Stories Retold; and, Sketches of Country Life* (Bathurst, NSW: G. Whalan, 1887).
Taylor, J. G., *The Social World of Batavia: European and Eurasian in Dutch Asia* (Madison: University of Wisconsin Press, 1983).
Todd, J., *Death and the Maidens: Fanny Wollstonecraft and the Shelley Circle* (Berkeley, CA: Counterpoint, 2007).
Todd, J., (ed.), *The Collected Letters of Mary Wollstonecraft* (New York: Columbia University Press, 2003).
Tóth, I. G., *A Concise History of Hungary: The History of Hungary from the Early Middle Ages to the Present* (Budapest: Corvina, 2005).
Tötösy de Zepetnek, S., *The Records of the Tötösy De Zepetnek Family* (West Lafayette, IN: Purdue University, 1993).
Tötösy de Zepetnek, S. (ed.), *Nobilitashungariae: List of Historical Surnames of the Hungarian Nobility* (West Lafayette, IN: Purdue University, 2010).
Trelawney, E. J., *Letters of Edward John Trelawny* (New York: AMS Press, 1910).
Tucker, E., Memo Confirming Delivery of Clairmont Materials to Frieda Clairmont. 27 September 1948. Records of the Reparations and Restitutions Branch of the U.S. Allied Commission for Austria (USACA) Section, 1945–1950, www.fold3.com/image/274319557/, p. 131, 8 July 2020.
Tullius, N., A. Leeb, and J. Pharr., "Banat," www.dvhh.org/banat/, 11 July 2020.
Voignier-Marshall, J., "Looking for Pauline Clairmont in N.S.W.," *The Byron Society in Australia Newsletter*, 7 (1983), pp. 25–31.
Vrišer, S., *Maribor* (Motovun: Niro Motovun, 1984).
Walker, R. B., *Old New England, A History of the Northern Tablelands of New South Wales, 1818–1900* (Sydney: Sydney University Press, 1966).
Walsh, G., *Pioneering Days: People and Innovations in Australia's Rural Past* (St. Leonards, NSW: Allen & Unwin, 1993).
Wardle, R., (ed.), *Godwin & Mary: Letters of William Godwin and Mary Wollstonecraft* (Lawrence: University of Kansas Press, 1966).
Williams, J., *Mary Shelley: A Literary Life* (New York: St. Martin's Press, 2000).
Wilson, G., *Murray of Yarralumla* (Melbourne and New York: Oxford University Press, 1968).
Witcher, H. B., "'With Me': The Sympathetic Collaboration of Mary Godwin and Percy Bysshe Shelley," *Forum for Modern Language Studies*, 52:2 (2016), pp. 144–159.
Wladika, M. "Egon Schiele, Mutter und Kind II, 1912," 2011. Leopold Museum. www.leopoldmuseum.org/media/file/166_dossier_schiele_mutterkindii.pdf, 12 July 2020.
Wollstonecraft, M., *The Works of Mary Wollstonecraft*, eds. J. Todd and M. Butler (London: Pickering and Chatto, 1989).
———, *Letters Written during a Short Residence in Sweden, Norway, and Denmark*, ed. I. Horrocks (Canada: Broadview Press, 2013).
Wollstonecraft, M., and W. Godwin, *A Short Residence in Sweden And Memoirs of the Author of 'The Rights of Woman'*, ed. R. Holmes (London: Penguin Books, 1987).
Woodland, J., *Money Pits British Mining Companies in the Californian and Australian Gold Rushes of the 1850s* (Farnham and Burlington, VT: Ashgate, 2014).
Wright, O., *Wongwibinda* (Armidale, NSW: University of New England, 1985).

Image 3 Photographic Portrait of Pauline Clairmont, c. 1875.

Source: Visual Materials from the Carl H. Pforzheimer Collection, c. 1875. Photograph.

Credit: The Carl H. Pforzheimer Collection of Shelley and His Circle, The New York Public Library, Astor, Lennox, and Tilden Foundations.

2

PAULINE CLAIRMONT'S AUSTRALIAN JOURNAL (1855–1857)

<u>Tagebuch</u>
v. m.
<u>Lebensbuch.</u>

Fortsetzung
VIII

Sontag den 6tn Mai 1855*

English translation by Ann Sherwin:

<u>Journal</u>
from my
<u>Life Book</u>

Continuation
VIII

Sunday, the 6th of May 1855

Sunday evening
May 6th 1855[1]

After a little trip of 8 days I returned this evening – Some moments were worth remembering – but few – We had very bad weather & I was much disappointted – First day Sunday to Wyagdon[2] 9 miles Monday Sofala[3] 11[4] staid all day with the Bowlers[5] E.B. – in the evening the Johnsons & Cloete[6] came to see us next day Pyramul[7] 20 F. disagreeable – Wednesday Luisa[8] 12 & on to Long Creek[9] 6 with A. Sp. & G. Spr.[10] Wretched filthy place – thursday lost our way back to Luisa M^rs T[11] very kind – Spring interesting[12] – Friday rained all day – Saturday ditto started for Pyramul Sunday pored Started for home dined at Sofala called at Wyagdon – got home late nearly bogged[13] – Found everything so nice & cheerful quite pleased to get home –

Der Mann F ist ein gemeiner Kerl ich bin froh dß ich ihn los hab – aber H. hat sentimentale große blaue Augen – er ist ein guter Junge u ich hab ihn recht gern – der Große war freundlich u heiter aber blaß –[14]

English translation of the German by Ann Sherwin:
   The husband F is a mean fellow. I am glad to be rid of him. But H.[15] has large, sentimental blue eyes. He is a good boy, and I like him very much. The big one was friendly and jocular but pale –

2[16]

ich will nicht mehr mit ihm koketiren

English translation of the German by Ann Sherwin:
I don't want to flirt with him any more.[17]

3ten Juni

Und ich hab auch nicht koketirt seit ich von Sof. zurück bin welches schon ziemlich lang ist die Worte kann ich mir verwahren aber die Blicke kaum – Es ist mir aber in neuerer Zeit eingefallen dß es doch nicht gar so lächerlich wäre wenn ich ihn heiratete – hier im Busch will man ja nicht blos ein maitresse in seiner Frau finden sondern auch eine verständige Freundin – u das kann ihr[?] A nie sein – denn sie ist dumm. Aber er ist noch lang nicht reich – u es war mehr Wahrheit in seinen Worten als er ahnte als er sagte Damp wood won't burn. Aber es wird eine schöne Frucht warden u ich kann die Schwachheit in seinem meinem Herzen für ihn nicht tilgen – aber ich bin in weiter Entfernung. Die Fs haben sich sehr schlecht gegen mich benommen u ich will nichts mehr mit ihnen zu thun haben –

English translation of the German by Ann Sherwin:

June 3

And I haven't flirted either, since I've been back from Sof[ala][18], which is already a rather long time. The words I can tuck away, but the looks – hardly. It occurred to me recently, however, that it wouldn't be all that absurd if I were to marry him.[19] Here in the bush men[20] don't want just a lover in a wife but an intelligent friend as well – and A[21] can never be that to him, because she is dimwitted. But he is far from rich – and there was more truth in his words than he guessed when he said, "Damp wood won't burn."[22] It will become a beautiful fruit, however, and I cannot overcome the weakness in my heart for him – but I am so far away. The Fs[23] treated me very badly, and I want nothing more to do with them.

June 5 Tuesday Wednesday

Heute waren die Bs hier Abschied nehmen, u mein junger Herr war wie gewöhnlich sehr koket – , aber daran liegt mir jetzt nichts mehr ich lieb ihn nicht mehr seit dem 29ten Oktober Septb 1854. Das ist aber keine Ursache warum ich ihn nicht zum Mann nehmen sollte – Ich hab über diesen Punkt neuerlich meine Ansichten geändert. Das Zureden mehrerer Leute hat mich auf die Idee gebracht z B. C B. mein Bruder u E. Was liegt daran dß er jünger ist als ich? Das ist ja für mich nur ein Vortheil – u am Ende will man zwar oft eine maitresse in einer Frau aber noch öfter eine Freundinn

English translation of the German by Ann Sherwin:

June 5 Tuesday Wednesday

Today the Bs[24] were here to say goodbye, and my young gentleman[25] was very flirtatious as usual – but I don't care any more. Since September 29, 1854, I no longer love him. But that is no reason why I shouldn't take him as a husband – I have recently changed my mind on this point. I arrived at this idea through the persuasion of several people, e.g. C.B., my brother, and E.[26] What difference does it make that he is younger than I? That can only work in my favor. After all, though a man often wants a lover in a wife, more often what he wants is a friend,

4

u eine Freundinn würde ich ihm immer sein, eine resource reichere gebildetere verständiger als A. – u ich glaube es ist nicht unmöglich ihn zu bekommen – Ich hab heute etwas starkes gesagt u sie waren alle wie versteinert die Pedanten, aber wenn man mit solchen ungebildeten Leuten lebt einmal man unwillkürlich ihre Manieren oder, besonders so eine Affennatur wie ich bin – die wahre Natur will manchmal heraus kommen, aber ich muß mehr politisch sein – Ich hätte nicht die geringste Reue über den Gedanken, ihm aber Worte gegeben zu haben ist mir leid

English translation of the German by Ann Sherwin:
and I would always be a friend to him, a richer, more cultured and intelligent resource than A.[27] – And I believe that it is not impossible to get him. I said something shocking today, and they were all petrified, the pedants, But when one lives with such subliterate people one forgets one's manners, or – especially for a mimic[28] like me – one's true nature will sometimes come out. But I must be more politic – I wouldn't feel the slightest remorse over the thought, but I regret having spoken the words to him,

weil es zu meinem Nachtheil war ach wär ich reich u unabhängig wie ganz anders würde ich handeln. Muß ich nicht hypokritisch sein?

―――――

W war sehr spröd – der dumme Junge glaubt er muß mir sein displeasure zeigen – in einer Beziehung liegt mir etwas dran – denn obwol er vor der Falle steht u vielleicht hinein gehen wird, ist er doch noch nicht drinnen, u es ist mein Bestreben dß er hinein gehe.

―――――

Ich wünsche er ginge Morgen mit uns damit ich Jemanden hätte zu sprechen – aber es ist fast beßer er bliebe hier denn die temptation ist zu groß zu kokoetiren ist zu groß u das darf ich nicht thun –

―――――

English translation of the German by Ann Sherwin:

> because it reflected poorly on me. Oh, if only I were rich and independent, how very differently I would act. Am I not compelled to be hypocritical?

―――――

W[29] was very aloof – the silly boy thinks he has to show me his displeasure. In one sense, that does matter to me, for although he stands in front of the trap and might enter, he is not in it yet, and it is my endeavor that he enter.

―――――

I wish he were going with us tomorrow, so I would have someone to talk to – but it is almost better that he stay here, for the temptation to flirt is too great, and I must not do that.

―――――

6

June 6 Per[30] June 8

Came from Sofala[31] – at W. last night Ja ich bin froh dß er nicht mit war denn wir hatten einen traulichen Abend beisamen – E saß neben mir – mein Fuß ruhte auf seinem aber seine Augen waren auf sein Buch geheftet – er sprach nicht – dreimal drängte sich die Kleine zu ihm, u jedes mal verließ er sie u kam zu mir endlich boudirte sie – erst sehr still aber ich sah in seinen Augen ein sanftes Feuer –

Gestern kam G. zurück u meine Kl hetzt ihm jetzt nach ich muß wirklich mit ihr sprechen den sie benimmt sich gar zu naiv – W hat wieder seinen gute Laune erlangt u drückt mir die Hand beim Schlafen gehen

English translation of the German by Ann Sherwin:

June 6 per June 8

Came from Sofala – at W. last night. Yes, I am glad that he wasn't along, for we had an intimate evening together. E[32] sat next to me – my foot rested on his, but his eyes were fixed on his book. He didn't speak. Three times the little one[33] sidled up to him, and he left her each time and came over to me. Finally she pouted – only very quietly, but I saw in his eyes a soft glow –

Yesterday G[34]. came back, and my little one is now chasing after him. I really must speak with her, for she is behaving much too naively. W[35] has his good mood back and squeezes my hand before retiring for the night.

7

aber der Zauber ist hin – Wie viel schöner u reizender u liebenswürdiger scheint mir G. Er ist schöner als je wäre er nur reich u wäre es nicht meiner Brüder willen ich heirathete ihn trotz seiner Armuth – Denn er hat was goldeswerth ist ein good temper u das fehlt Willi – nein ich mag seinen Charakter nicht – er ist zwar gescheidt u schön u reich – aber conceited grob heftig mit Männern u mit Frauen entweder koket oder verächtlich many a true word is spoken in jest – für mich ist eine Heirath nur eine Spekulation – ich achte G zu sehr, u hab zu warme Wünsche für seine Zukunft als dß ich ihn heiraten dürfte – ach es kostet mich einen tiefen Seufzer ihn ganz aufzugeben – jetzt da er wieder wie einst zu mir zurück gekehrt ist – u W's Gegenwart hat allen Zauber verloren jetzt da ich daran denke ihn zu heiraten –

English translation of the German by Ann Sherwin:

> but the allure is gone. How much more handsome and charming and amiable G seems to me. He is handsomer than ever. If only he were rich, and if only it were not my brothers'[36] will that I marry him despite his

38

poverty. For he has something precious as gold, a good temper, which Willi lacks. No, I don't like his character. Granted, he is smart and handsome and rich – but conceited, uncivil, heavy-handed with men and with women, either coquettish or disdainful. Many a true word is spoken in jest. A marriage for me is mere speculation – I respect G too much and my wishes for his future are too warm to allow me to marry him. But alas, the thought of giving him up entirely makes me heave a deep sigh now that he has come back to me again as before – and W's presence has lost all its allure now that I am thinking of marrying him –

8

wenn wir einmal verbunden sind soll er so viel Freiheit haben als sein Herz wünscht u ich auch – ich hoffe nur dß ich nicht mit Kindern geplagt sein werd wen immer ich heirate – ich bin neugierig wie sich die beiden jungen Leute benehmen werden wenn Fräulein A kommt –

English translation of the German by Ann Sherwin:

If we ever do tie the knot, he shall have as much freedom as his heart desires, and so shall I. I just hope I won't be plagued with children, whomever I marry.[37] I am curious to see how the two young people behave when Miss A[38] comes –

June 27 – thursday

Lottie's[39] birthday – 7 of her cousins here – very good & consequently very happy – cheerfulness is such a delightful thing – M⁽ʳˢ⁾ Beverley[40] is a dear kind creature – how fond she is of her children – & very sensible with all – for love & sense seldom go together –

Ja Fräulein A kommt morgen – was wird Wilhelm thun – wie wird er sich benehmen – ich weiß es kaum –

English translation of the German by Ann Sherwin:

> Yes, Miss A is coming tomorrow. What will Wilhelm[41] do – how will he behave? I hardly know –

9

es aber nur psychologisch interessant sonst nicht – G ging den 25ten fort auf lange lange Zeit – könnte ich nur in die Zukunft blicken – u wüßte ich ob ich je seine Frau sein sollte so wäre ich zufrieden – Wir sprachen neulich von AG u ob sie eine gute Frau machen würde – er sagte Ja, aber es ist ein groß Veränderung unlängst geschehen dann brach er ab – ich ahne was er meinte – ich würde ihn nehmen wenn er mich wollte, obwol er arm ist – u ich nicht sagen kann dß ich ihn liebe – u der Andere zu dem ich mich so magnetisch hingezogen fühle den wollte ich nicht. –

English translation of the German by Ann Sherwin:

> but it is merely of psychological interest, nothing more. G[42] left on the 25th for a long, long time – if only I could look into the future and know whether I will ever be his wife, I would be satisfied. We recently spoke of AG[43] and whether she would make a good wife. He said yes but that a big change had occurred not long ago. Then he broke off – I sense what he meant – I would take him if he wanted me, even though he is poor – and I can't say that I love him – and the other, to whom I feel myself drawn like a magnet, him I wouldn't want. –

10

June 30
1856[44]

You need not be so dejected my dear friend[45] – you are as bad as the young ones rushing from one extreme to the other, & if you can not succeed in the twinkling of an eye give it up in despair. No no why should not you be bent on victory as well as she?[46] We have equal chances – let us make a fair start – such a prize is well worth contending You have beauty I have the mind you have youth I have experience, it is true you do not see him so much as I do living in the same house – but then you are a novelty a change which is of great importance – besides you have

11

all your family to assist you while I have no one either to advise or help me. – After all if I do get him I shall consider that I have not made a firstrate bargain for I dislike the idea of marrying a man so much younger than myself – but nevermind about that – I like him very much I admire his beauty his wit his cleverness he is well to do in the world – he can help my brothers[47] and so! here goes –

Do I not remember this day 3 years ago? I was not much handsomer then & yet what was the result? What may have become of that poor boy – I have one of his letters still – what feeling what devotion what passion

12

& he was faithful though surrounded by temptation. Have I not said it a hundred times and is it not a fact that a man & particularly a clever man like Willy living a solitary bushlife like they do here wants to have a friend & companion in his wife as well as a mistress he wants elegant & clever[48] conversation music wit & mirth to spend the evenings pleasantly, books, arts sciences & many other things are to be discussed, so that when he comes home from his out of door occupation[49] where[50] he has perhaps had to do with vulgar low people heard bad language,[51] he returns to

13

elegant apartments finds himself with a lady & feels himself a gentleman – certainly people without refinement & education would just as soon sleep or smoke the whole evening or gossip away half an hour with his wife (uneducated like himself) or the maids or the stockman, but a man of such natural ability such a good education &[52] such a taste for books & learning as that young man has, could not possibly be happy with a girl who can barely read & write who would never from year's and to year's end open a book who does not understand the poetry in our nature

14

& whose conversation is utter commonplace – What signifies the difference of a few years in a country like this where the natives fade away so fast & only the Europeans keep their freshness of complexion

Two years ago I was repeatedly taken for 19 once by a lady too & my brother thought A. was 23 which is 5 years older than she really is – so much for looks – M^{rs} TS.[53] looks older than I now & she is several years younger – all the Europeans look younger in proportion than the natives, with very few exceptions – & then her features are of that kind that will very soon look

15

wizened – nose & chin meeting – & though on the whole she is very handsome, yet I do not think I have in my face a feature so out of proportion as her nose is – But then I being plain one bad feature would not strike one so much – I must set to work slowly & prudently –[54]

July 8, 1855

On the 30th of June I wrote in my little note book some words in deep dejection – how little did I think then how soon they would come true – "My heart is like a church-yard – there is one new grave the newest of all, perhaps the last"[55] – & since then another grave has been dug that contained her who loved me best in this world[56] the dearest & sincerest friend I had the only one whose home I ever called my home the only one who knew what I

16

had suffered on the second of February the only one who felt that day as I did – & she is gone the ocean is between me & her grave & his grave[57] & no one else understands the language of my heart – And here where with a bleeding heart I laid down on the altar of selfsacrifice[58] that jewel that was offered me, here I am accused of reserve of flirting of want of dignity of envy of selfishness What have I done to deserve all this? oh Clari if you can do so make me better kinder, take that vanity that covetousness that jealousy out of my heart that must make me disliked – My consolation is that most likely she knew nothing of her illness nor how dangerous it was – & how much sooner would I suffer all this pain than that

17

she should do so – How infinitely more miserable would it make me to think she was suffering all this – or perhaps had she lost her husband[59] or had he been laid on the bed of sickness unable to work what would then the state of my mind have been to think that she wanted my assistance & I not be there & not able to do anything for her – There is some consolation in this certainty – but then again the when I remember the many happy hours I spent with her – that sweet little cottage at H.C.[60] where she used to sit by the fireside of an evening a pink shade thrown over the lamp – & she would now & then walk to the window look in the black night & wonder when [illeg.] & Plin[61] would come

18

from town, or in the morning when we sat in the breakfast room looking out on the Park[62] & her little white hand was so busy at her work & K[63] was smoking a cigar, & I would look at that picture of happiness & my heart would overflow with gratitude towards the Disposer of all things that that sweet delicate flower was safe & protected from the storms of the world that she whose whole soul was love should have found a husband worthy of her, who made her happy who was all the world to her, to whom she unfolded all the treasures of her rich heart, who valued her like a jewel[64] – She was called away – & he is left desolate lonely & solitary – I dare say the wide world is all alike to him – it must be all a waste, for where could he find such love – & what happiness is equal to that of love?

Dohl[65] if you could have thought of the void your death would have you would have cried tears as burning as mine, to think that your poor sister should be so unhappy – to think that her courage should be so broken down, hope energy & mirth gone, to think ~~that~~ she was so sad, that she only wished to be in the cold grave & at rest. Oh I hope dohl you never knew anything of this & this & much more would I bear if you could be saved even a moment's pain Poor little Emy[66] says at the end of her letter "give me a little of the love you once give to her" –

20

What a hard hearted unfeeling rude rough brute I have often been not to be sensible of the meek affectionate heart of that good girl – what though she is not brilliant witty or clever what if she has not read so much as others have what if she has little imperfections of temper – who is responsible for their talents what good is it educating the intellect at the cost of the heart, & who is there that has not many faults & weaknesses & I in particular who am always wanting in charity – my dear Emy it is for me to beg your pardon for my heartless conduct [~~illeg.~~] pride & envy – but it is all done away with – my heart is

21

open to you my child & you shall always have a warm & faithful friend in me ready to help & sympathize <u>on every</u> occasion.[67]

<u>July 13</u> Friday

What a spirit of contradiction is in man woman & child! I could not have believed it, & I begin to think that I have not quite so much of it as other people or perhaps it takes another form. A little occurrence yesterday & to day which was certainly very satisfactory for my vanity though altogether incomprehensible to my feelings –

Ich versteh den jungen Mann durchaus nicht – denn dß er mit sich selbst über diesen Punkt raisonniert bin ich überzeugt – wie es aber kommt dß er meiner Gleichgültigkeit zu lieb thut was er für die Auszeichnung die ich ihm einst zeigte nicht thun wollte ist mir unbegreiflich – denn ich würde mich mehr hingezogen fühlen durch Liebe

English translation of the German by Ann Sherwin:

> I don't understand the young man at all – for he is arguing with himself over this point, of that I am convinced. But I find it incomprehensible that now, in face of my indifference, he does what he didn't want to do back when I was singling him out for attention – for I would feel more enamored by love

22

u Eifersucht als durch Gleichgültigkeit. Er aber nicht – als ich ihm damals meiner Natur gemäß meine Neigung u die dadurch entstehende Eifersucht zeigte wurde er stützig u that gerade was ich nicht wollte – darüber würde ich bös u sagte es ihm, wir stritten ein wenig, er ging fort u ich nahm mir vor ihn ganz aufzugeben – denn seine Tyrannei u Grobheit war zu arg – er wollte nicht nur allen Mädchen die Cour machen sondern pretendirte dß ich mit Niemanden ein Wort spräche – Während seiner Abwesenheit hielt ich mir lange Predigten wie unvernünftig unwürdig zwecklos demüthigend u peinlich alles dieses wäre wie unähnlich mir selbst mich von so einem übermüthigen Jungen schmähen zu laßen, u ich nahm mir fest vor, obwol ich viele Thränen darüber weinte, u oft mit Schmerz seine blauen Augen u seinem schönen Kopf ansah ich nahm mir vor mich an Demokritus die irländische Philosophie zu wenden, zu lachen mich ohne ihm des Lebens zu freuen ihn dann in Gottes Nahmen seinen eignen Weg gehen zu lassen. "Wenn der" sagte ich zu mir selbst "so großes Vergnügen in Fräulein As gesellschaft finden so kann er unmöglich meine Vorzüge würdigen."

English translation of the German by Ann Sherwin:

> and jealousy than by indifference. But not he. Back when I showed him my fondness and, in keeping with my nature, the jealousy it engendered, he balked and did precisely what I didn't want. That annoyed me, and I told him so. We quarreled a little, he went away, and I decided to give

him up entirely, for his tyranny and incivility were excessive – not only did he want to court every girl, but he also insisted that I never speak a word with anyone. During his absence, I preached long sermons to myself about how unreasonable, ignoble, pointless, mortifying, and embarrassing all this was, how unlike me it was to let myself be so abused by such a cocky boy, and I firmly resolved – even though I shed many tears over it and often beheld his blue eyes and handsome head with pain – I firmly resolved to turn to Democritus,[68] the Irish[69] philosophy, to laugh, to enjoy life without him, then in God's name let him go his own way. "If he finds so much pleasure in Miss A's company," I said to myself, "then he cannot possibly appreciate my merits."

23

Als er zurück kam war ich zwar Freundlich aber sehr kühl gesprächig aber alles offner Scherz – keine verstohlenen Blicke doppelsinnigen Worte, keine Annäherung Händedruck etc – ich schrieb ihm einen kleinen Zettel welches sagte – "Wenn ich auch nicht spreche ich habe immer treue schwesterliche Freundschaft für Sie" – Ich scherzte ebensoviel mit dem schönen G. ich ritt mit ihm – kurz ich war lustig u schien ihn u die schöne Vergangenheit ganz vergeß[en] zu haben – denn nicht die leiseste Anspielung auf Liebe oder etwas Vorhergegangenes erlaubte ich mir – Ich muß gestehen dß ich diesen neuen Plan mit etwas Furcht began, denn der Gedanke ihn ganz zu verlieren machte mich traurig – u wenn mir so eine Behandlung wiederfahren wäre, hätt ich mich gekränkt zuerst. Dann aber gerechtfertigt gefühlt meine Gefühle u Aufmerksamkeit auf einen andern Gegenstand überzutragen – Mein junger Herr aber ganz im Gegentheil – Zuerst war er ein wenig trotzig u wollte es nicht glauben, boudierte mir u sagte bißige Worte, koketirte mit Fräulein A, als er aber sah dß es Ernst war bei mir – ward auch er ernst zeigte

English translation of the German by Ann Sherwin:

When he came back, I was friendly but very cool; conversational but it was all open banter – no stolen glances or double entendres, no approaching, hand squeezes etc. I wrote him a note that said "Even if I don't speak, I always have true sisterly affection for you." – I bantered just as much with the handsome G.[70] I went riding with him. In short, I was jolly and pretended to have totally forgotten him and the lovely past – for I didn't allow myself to show even the slightest innuendo of love or any prior history. I must confess that I began this new plan with some anxiety, for the thought of losing him entirely saddened me – and if I had been subjected to such treatment, I would have felt resentful at first but then justified in transferring my feelings and attention elsewhere. But my young gentleman was just the opposite. At first he was rather defiant and didn't want to believe it; he pouted at me, uttered caustic words, and flirted with Miss A;[71] but when he saw that I was serious, he grew serious too, showed

24

mir ein Gedicht von Shelley "The Serpent that is shut out from paradise" sehr melancholisch verließ einst Frl As Seite um mit mir zu reiten (was er sonst noch nie gethan hatte) war einen ganzen Abend hier ohne fast ein Wort mit ihr zu reden – u heute wo sie ihn u Mr A engagirte mit ihr zu gehen zu seiner Tante u wo ich fest überzeugt war er würde ihrem Reiz u dem Zureden seiner Tante u seines Freundes den Abend dort zuzubringen nicht wiederstehen können, siehe da als wir beim Thee waren ging die Theure auf u er kam herein – meine Verwunderung war groß u meine Eitelkeit jupelte ich ließ aber nichts merken blicket nicht auf – er war zwar den ganzen Abend etwas disgrazios ich aber benahm mich gerade wie den Abend vorher – diesen Wiederspruchsgeist begreife ich nicht mir würde es ignoble im höchsten Grade demüthigend erscheinen mich durch kalte Vernachläßigung leiten zu laßen u tausendmal lieber unterwürf ich mich der Liebe. –

English translation of the German by Ann Sherwin:

> me a poem by Shelley, "The Serpent that Is Shut Out from Paradise," very melancholy[72]. He left Miss A's side to ride with me (which he had never done before), was here for an entire evening, and hardly spoke a word with her. And today, when she asked him and Mr. A to go with her to visit his aunt and I was sure he would be unable to resist her charm and his aunt's and friend's coaxing him to spend the evening there – Lo! as we were having tea, the door opened and in he walked, much to my astonishment! I exulted in my vanity but I didn't let on, didn't look up. He was somewhat graceless the whole evening, but I acted just as I had the evening before – I don't understand this contrariness. It would seem ignoble and extremely humiliating for me to let myself be swayed by willful neglect. I would a thousand times rather submit to love.

July 19th 1855

July 18.1855 Miss Hawkin's[73] wedding

It is two years to day that I came to Brucedale & that a new life began Strange are the vicissitudes the ever varying shades & lights storms & sunshine, pain & harmony that have passed through my mind Two years have I lived with this kind family – how winning was dear little Herby[74] – he seemed so pleased to see me again after an absence of two days – how unvaryingly kind has Mrs Suttor[75] been – & how much attention & respect was shown me yesterday at Miss H's wedding by all & everyone – My duties have been light & successful though I am always too sanguine – Carry[76] has improved in mind knowledge manner & appearance, I hope she may not forget her governess as most girls do – & what shall I say of him[77] who has been a source of so much pain & pleasure to me?

26

I do not understand him – I think of him often & often, I wish to see him happy, I would give anything – yes I would give my own happiness to make him happy – He would not go with us for a ride to day, & there again I do not understand him – why would he not come, does he not care for A[78], or does he not trust himself? She is pretty & good & might make him a good wife! – But why do you thus hate & avoid me? When at one time you thought I loved you, you left me for her, & now that I offer you sisterly affection, you do not seem pleased either – Can nothing that I do please you? What have I done to you to be thus despised? Put up my pride – up self esteem up independence up & find all the rich sources of enjoyment

27

of compensation & hope that are within your own mind without looking for satisfaction elsewhere – But let me live my life – and my sincerest wish is for your happiness –

Long is the time to look back upon how many pleasant incidents could I call back up to the 27th of October[79] 1854, how happy was I when our love had no cloud on its sky – but all that was premature, or else the exclusiveness of love is not in your heart – And how bigotted I am, because one man's mind & body are differently constituted from mine, do I say he does not understand this thing? Why not take him as he is? –

I cannot tell why a certain old gentleman is so often recurring to my mind this evening – is he still in existence I wonder –[80]

Abercrombie[81] says: keep a stern control over your imagination I will & above all things be <u>always ready</u> & prepared for the worst –

July 27

Went to Bathurst from thence to Sydney[82] – Enjoyed many things there as my little note book will show – some wisdom is daily revealed has not the light of knowledge dawned upon me since that winter? – Yes & I am always learning new things – Oh balcony of that house oh balcony like the other balcony that looked out over the old ruined fortress ages have rolled over it & I am now[83] partly happy partly unhappy – I liked my Sydney[illeg.] idleness & would not return to my 17 or 18 with the prospect of going through all I have for the whole world

Septb 13

Came back to Brucedale – one of the pleasantest moments in all this interval was a certain concurrence of events on the 11th Dear Mrs Suttor received me most kindly & really seemed pleased at my return – & I must say if ever the idea of home could be

29

pleasing to me it was this time

You do not know what a lasting & great benefit you are bestowing upon your children by giving them a good education – for in the bush[84] where you are out of the way of comparison or competition you are scarcely aware of your own powers, but in a place like this where so much intellect is concentrated you soon find the immense virtue of not only capability of appreciation which is the first step but also of entering into & taking part in the most brilliant witty instructive & amusing conversation in fact it gives you a position in society – [illeg. illeg.] which wealth cannot always I know it from my own experience & had I children of my own & the choice of giving them a refined mind & leaving them beggars or giving them wealth

30

of incalculable amount without education I should say – Let them have those treasures of the mind which can either secure worldly riches or make happy without them. I see here more than ever (of course there are exceptions) that mind is far superior to beauty – you must not think that this conviction arises from some private philosophical argument I have been having with myself to console myself for the want of beauty – no my individuality is out of the question – I write like one not belonging to the world a looker on at a distance stating facts & drawing conclusions therefrom. I sit in a little corner of a drawingroom & make my remarks on people their looks, actions & words; & what do I see? Beauty always admired but the attraction is

31

of short duration, talent always admired & the attraction is ever new increasing instead of declining – & would I poor unknown insignificant music teacher[85] be received as I am – treated as a friend by most of the ladies as an equal by all the men if I had not education & good manners? No certainly not even[86] if I had supreme beauty did not you say yourself that I would receive attentions where a hundred Adelaides would remain unnoticed? think then dear Mrs Suttor what your daughter will be – having besides a better education than nearly any girl in the colony the advantages of beauty wealth & connexions[87] –

32

these are two or three curious facts I have noticed in that book (Navy Surgeon).[88]

I How is it that although the fingertips so exquisitely distinguish the soft hard rough surface of things yet would not feel a fly or a creeping insect as much as any other part of the body?

II what is the difference ~~produced by~~ of the vibration produced by <u>sound</u> & <u>wind</u>?

III How is it that mercury divided into imperceptibility in powder or pill will mix effectually with the blood, while mercury swallowed crud in 50 times the quantity passes through the system without effect.

Atkinson's argument in favor of cures effected by Amulets or more properly speaking sympathy is the following:

33

We see diseases produced by the most imperceptible outward influences as temperature contagion we see daily the influence of the mind & the nerves upon the body – we <u>do not</u> know how far electricity is connected with the mind & particularly the imagination, why should we not believe that amulets when worn with faith should effect cures – does not faith in (note: faith in written above) religion effect moral cures why should not the faith in the amulet give you hope courage & strength – thus far it can act morally – besides which it might act upon the body either by smell, by absorption or penetration if a vegetable amulet or upon the nerves of a mineral one – Lord Verulam[89] says we should not reject everything of this kind, because it is not known how far those things are of superstition or depending on natural causes.

Septb 18

Es ist allerdings schmeichelhaft aber sehr unbequem dß alle diese Frauen so eifersüchtig sind – Über C. bin ich noch nicht im Reinen ob sie ihre Freundlichkeit wirklich meint oder ob sie sich nur ihrer Eifersucht schämt – S. ist sehr liberal gesinnt aber man darf doch nicht zu weit gehen wenn ich meine position erhalten will – u den reichen Sohn erlangen will – als wir heute ausritten u ich alle die schönen Güter das schöne Haus Wiesen u Felder dacht ich bei mir selbst das wäre doch schön, wenn das alles einst mir gehören sollte. Wäre S. ein Witwer oder ledig – ich möcht ihn denn er kann ganz angenehm sein wenn er will – Nur müßte er den schönen Sohn nicht haben denn das wäre eine gar zu große Temptation u ich seh es ihm an wenn es thünlich wäre würde er sich mir nähern aber C ist so eifersüchtig u nicht aus Liebe (wenn das überhaupt

English translation of the German by Ann Sherwin:

Sept. 18

It is certainly flattering but very uncomfortable for all these women to be so jealous. As for C.,[90] I have not yet figured out whether her friendliness is really sincere or whether she is merely ashamed of her jealousy.[91] S. is very liberal-minded, and yet I must not go too far, if I want to hold my position – and win the rich son.[92] When we rode out today and I saw all the lovely manors, the lovely house, meadows and fields, I thought to myself, it would indeed be lovely if all this should some day belong to me. If S were a widower or single – I would like him, for he can be very pleasant when he wants to be. – Only it would be better if he didn't have the handsome son, for that would be too great a temptation, and I see it in him: if it were feasible, he would approach me. But C is so jealous and not out of love (if that is even

möglich ist) denn sie hat ihn nie mögen das hat sie mir selbst gesagt sondern aus Eitelkeit, ich muß sie aber darin nicht indulge nicht weil es gegen mein Princip wäre, sondern weil ich meinen Zweck nicht erreichen würde – u da ich den Vater mit dem Reichthum nicht haben kann – muß ich den Sohn mit den expectations nehmen. Mein Herz ist oft Traurig denn ich sehne mich nach Liebe so wie ichs in meinem Innersten meine u in der Ehe kann u darf keine Romanz sein – u ohne Romantik wäre ich nicht ich selbst – Ich seh in die Mondhelle Nacht hinaus u erriner mir jenen Moment in Wall wo ich mich so unaussprechlich nach W sehnte aber da sagte ich zu mir selbst – none of your nonsense une femme qui aime perd tout son pouvoir also nach W darf ich mich nicht sehnen – das ist auch nicht schwer – den alten S darf ich auch nicht haben obwol er mich anlockt – ich weiß eigentlich nicht was mich an ihn anzieht den moralisch passen wir gar nicht zu ein ander

English translation of the German by Ann Sherwin:

> possible, for she never liked him – she told me that herself) but out of vanity. But I must not indulge her in that, not because it goes against my principles but because I would not achieve my purpose. And since I cannot have the father with the wealth, I must take the son with the expectations. I am often downhearted, for I do so long for love, as I imagine it to be, deep in my heart, and there can and must be no romance in marriage – and without romance I would not be myself. I look out into the moonlit night and remember that moment in Wall[93] when I yearned for W so unspeakably but said to myself: None of your nonsense! Une femme qui aime perd tout son pouvoir [English translation "A woman who loves loses all her power"]. That is also not hard. Besides, I can't have the elder S,[94] even though I am drawn to him – I really don't know what draws me to him, for we are not at all suited to each other regarding morals.

36

es ist aber ein Gemüthsfülle Wärme u Kraft; u manchmal eine Sanftmuth in aller seiner Derbheit die mich ganz touchirt – u ich mag große starke Männer – War er heute nichtgerade wie sein Sohn als er mein Pferd selbst sattelte u herausführte u mich hinaufsetzte – Was haben wir den für eine Macht Männer wie Pferde zu zügeln – Wenn ich den jungen wirklich become so wird ich ihm alle Freiheit laßen die er sich nur wünschen mag. Er mag dann so oft er will nach W gehen (denn auch darin wird er wie sein Vater sein) er mag eine Nacht nach der andere von mir wegbleiben – wenn ich ein hübsches Haus ein schönes Klavier u prächtige Pferde hab, so hab ich alles das ich wünsche Kinder brauch ich keine u das übrige wird sich schon finden. Um die Wahrheit zu gestehen mag ich so ganz junge Männer nicht – sie sind nicht reich, ihr Blut ist kalt u ihr Geist ohne Erfahrung, sie kennen die Welt nicht, sie können nicht denken

English translation of the German by Ann Sherwin:

> But there is a wealth of feeling, warmth, and strength; and sometimes a gentleness in all his gruffness that I find very touching – and I like big strong men. – Wasn't he[95] just like his son today, when he saddled my horse himself and led it out and set me on it? What kind of power is this that we can harness men like horses? – If I actually get the boy, I would grant him all the freedom he could wish for. Then he may go to W[96] whenever he wants (for he is no doubt like his father in that respect as well), even if he stays away from me night after night. If I have a pretty house, a lovely piano, and splendid horses, I'll have all I could wish for. I don't need children, and the rest will take care of itself. I must confess, I don't like such very young men – they're not rich, their blood is cold, and their minds are inexperienced. They don't know the world, they cannot think

u auch daher nicht die Vorurtheile abschütteln die dem geselligen Verkehr so drückend sind. Wie verschieden sind Männer die S.DW. von WUG[?] u = meinem Bruder – die älteren haben manches mitgemacht das ihnen über Recht u Unrecht aufschluß gibt, die Jüngeren wißen nur was sie der Schulmeister gelehrt hat – die Älteren haben warmes Blut u Lebenslust in den Adern, die Jüngern sind scheu u schmachtend weil die Stimme der Leidenschaft noch nicht erwacht ist – kurz der Morgen des Lebens ist zwar wie der des Tagens poetisch schön u rein – Der Mittag aber ist warm u fruchtbar – ich sehe die Blüthe gern aber die Frucht ist mir noch lieber – u das weiß ich dß W für sein lebenlang an mir eine interessantere Frau haben würde als an A., u wenn er nach ein oder zwei Jahren an ihre gehaltlose Schönheit gewöhnt würde würde er meine[n] Geist u meine Bildung gar sehr vermißen

English translation of the German by Ann Sherwin:

> and therefore also cannot dismiss the prejudices that are so oppressive to social intercourse. How different men are the S.DW. from WUG[97] and = my brother[98] – the older ones have learned about right and wrong from experience, whereas the younger ones know only what the schoolmaster taught them. Older men have warm blood and a zest for living in their veins, while younger ones hang back and pine, for the voice of passion is not yet awake – in short, the morning of life is like that of the dawn, poetically beautiful and pure, but the noontide is warm and fertile. I like seeing the blossoms, but I like the fruit even better. And this much I know: that W would have a more interesting wife in me for his entire life than he would in A; and when, after a year or two, he becomes inured to her vacuous beauty, he will sorely miss my intellect and breeding.

Octb 2d

Who would have thought it? – not I certainly – I have but one course to take not dictated by feeling but by reason & – I cannot here analise[99] how certain ideas or rather principles originated & got such firm hold of my mind that I can now no more wish to uproot them than actually do so – but there they are & though I never act against them I often remain passive – I leave undone many things that I might do – (I alone know what this refers to) One principle however is uppermost in my mind that is justice bringing with it charity passive & active therefore it seems to[100] unjustifiable to give myself or another pleasure at the cost of a third individual – the argument that the thing I am here alluding to would give me not pain cannot hold good here, for pain like pleasure & many other things is merely relative – therefore I am not

justified in doing to others what would give them pain though if done to me would pass unnoticed. I really think there is more truth in that saying about the <u>coming events</u> than most people look for – Did I not that day say to myself as I was leaning against the chiffonier in M^rs S's[101] room – there must come a reaction – & so it has come at least I fancy so – or do I only fancy it? – I wish it were so, or at least that that change if change there is came from another Source than I suppose it to come from – Would that it were only general weakness physical prostration that causes that coolness that constraint that forced smile that effort at cheerful commonplace conversation which I never noticed before – I will wait & see before I say anything the least said the soonest mended – may she one day read in my heart that I would not for the world do anything to hurst the kind little soul, may she be convinced some day that selfishness is not in my composition & though many unforeseen things have crossed my path, & not unpleasantly surprised me, yet would I not buy any amount of happiness with the consciousness that were it known to her she would be vexed – & that without stopping to consider whether she was right or wrong, just or unjust, sensible or foolish in her perception of the thing – the idea that she might be hurt would make me pull up.

<u>Octb 8</u>

I hope I think I am radically cured this time, but I won't crow before I am out of the wood – that vile jealousy is a mean contemptible want of pride on one side, & a painful suspicion on the other – always absurd ridiculous & unsatisfactory to others & yourself for if you [illeg.]

40

are sufficiently intimate with a person to know be jealous, you must either know you can doubt them, or then there is no occasion for it, or you must know that it is no use at all – so that vile passion always comes off worst. I have felt the pangs of jealousy myself I have seen what my jealousy has produced in others I have seen how foolish & more than that how unjust cross & unkind others were made by it – how uncomfortable & unhappy it makes all around particularly those who love you best –

There is no such feeling as jealousy from love as I once thought – because there is no selfishness in love, & jealousy is all self [illeg.] love & variety – Vanity that is all – mortification as the seeming neglect or want of admiration, therefore blameable & condemnable as rank, poisonous, barren & thorny – Jealousy is a passion as some author observes that has no birth nor growth but starts from man's mind like Minerva from Jupiter,[102] fullgrown & armed ready for battle & it is unlike other passions because at no time of its existence does it afford its owner any satisfaction or pleasure however morbid – Revenge, Avarice – Intemperance in fact all the passions of the human mind have at one time or another a bright moment a pleasure an irresistible attraction that makes one forget the reaction which we call a bad conscience & which is some people of longer duration than the pleasure afforded by sin – But Jealousy stands alone of its kind – positively speaking it has not the idiosyncrasies of our other passions good or bad – it has not a small beginning

41

a rise & a fall – but it comes & it is there in all hidiosity[103] wickedness & absurdity without one feeling of happiness, entrâinement[104] temptation or hope, or even recklessness which is a powerful passion in itself –

I have searched my heart closely in the last twelvemonth & I find that vanity is at the bottom of every kind of jealousy [vanity] at the seeming neglect of those we do <u>not</u> love but to whose attentions we think ourselves entitled, vanity raises her bright-eyed head vanity distills the poison of jealousy when she is hurt & she is very easily touched vanity darts her sting of suspicion when she is half blinded by her own venom, & instills the subtle poison of distrust which flies through the body with the swiftness of circulation, & brings with it tremors of envy, sores of hatred, shrinking malice, corrupt foul emanations in look word & deed. Vanity therefore is the root of the evil there lies the core of the disease, not in circumstances & above all, not in divine <u>love</u> as some have degradingly said – And now I will show how impossible it is that jealously should exist coeval with love or friendship, it is said in few words.

Love & friendship are pure beams of the Deity in fact I know no difference between the two, there is not a grain of selfish ness in either – their desire is to devote all their energy to contribute to the happiness of the object of their affection – Love says Whatever makes you happy will please me – Friendship says I trust you even far away – Love only studies how to please, Friendship forbears, love might

42

weep in sorrow & solitude but will suffer in silence, friendship will gently seek explanation on what is doubtful –

And where is there room even for a shadow of jealousy? – there is none of that rank need in the garden of [illeg.] love therefore will I punish my vanity right earnestly & severely whenever it again appears in the shape of Jealousy.

Which is the most attractive <u>beautiful sin</u> or <u>beautiful virtue</u>? – Most people would say the latter – Partly from habit partly from faith, & partly from fear. But I say: Imagine to yourself something between the two – less black than sin less tame than virtue, – if I say sin I do not mean the principle which is intensely hideous, but a sinner in whom there is yet some good left – Read these lines = <u>Lucifer with beaming forehead</u>[105] goes through the gates of morn. What a splendid picture of genius independant strong will, selfreliance[106] & boldness starts to your imagination I see him in all the strength of manhood with all the experience of riper years, lead by the light of genius trusting his own powers more than the beaten paths of custom.

43

Walking apart from other mortals, for that in the general acceptation of the word is called <u>sin</u>. Oh what are human beings that I should conform to their laws! – For me, for my soul there shall be none but the law of God, & the wishes of those I love –

I have a great notion of letting fruit get ripe before I gather it – I acted up to this principle by intuition & only the other day it stood clearly before me – tell them it was not principle but feeling –

Shall I write anything more tonight? – No, not much for my thoughts are dreary & oppressive, – My heart wishes for <u>something</u> & that something it shall never have – must never have, can never have – I have imposed on myself a heavy task & have not the heart to go through with it – I sometimes turn away & say with a sigh – <u>no I cannot</u> do it – & yet I ought & must. There is no one, no not one to advise me help me assist me, thus I drift about – Could I get but one thing [illeg.] but I have always been always been in a false position & nothing will set me right

Octb 30.

Went to Wyagdon[107] in evening Emily[108] Caroline William[109] & I – How I do love riding Phreeny[110] was nearly too fresh – Mʳ W. has given up flirting with Miss B.[111] which is a pity since he always seems so vexed with himself whenever he has missed an occasion – like this time – I (correct as is) coming home he spoke part of the time to Emily but to C. and me he would not condescend to say even a word – Are not those changes of temper curious? He never will come near me riding except when there is no one else to talk to – & I had a good mind to tell him so the other night we were coming home from Carioymion[112] – I thought so & felt much inclined to address my part of the conversation to Carry[113] only – I tried however to preserve decent equanimity & said as many commonplaces to him as I could. Would it not be aggravating to think that you were only talked to faute de mieux, only a pis aller[114] that if whosoever else was there to side with to talk to, Mʳ W.[115] would not take the slightest notice of you – I am sure it would to anyone who had the least sensibility.

Dec 1

Spent a pleasant Day – M^{rs} S went to the parsonage – Mr Oldfield[116] & the two young gentlemen were here We rode to the Frenchmens place Mr Johnson[117] went with us – he does not seem so much frightened of me as he used to be – G[118] is gentle & soft but sulky – he was however a little more amiable to night – he stood close to my chair while I was playing[119] his hand was on the back of it & he was leaning against it – his eyes are so beautiful – oh he is so gentle & good –[120]

I have long settled in my mind that the terror of Death lies in the body in the nerves not in the mind – No enlightened person is afraid of death except feeling a regret at the loss of the pleasures of this earth – No the terror of Death lies neither in thought imagination nor feeling but in the constitution. the rupture of electricity is painful to us & more so to the suffering individual. Or else why would we pause & give a moment to reflection at the death of a person totally unknown to us a perfect stranger? Would any of us enter a room where a person was dying or dead, or see a dead body streched[121] across

the road without our attention being arrested our feet stopped & our eyes turned towards the corps? No I think not, & what can be the cause of it? A dead body of a stranger[122] can positively have no interest for our mind nor feelings as we can do nothing for it what is it therefore that attracts & painfully moves our sympathies & our feelings? I can find no other reason than that wrenching off our link of the chain of electricity that binds & holds us all, it is that that pains us though we attribute the pain we feel to another cause. For if it was not a physical cause what good mental cause could we set forward – could we Christianity fear for the future of a good soul? Could Atheists who do not believe in the immortality have anything to fear? Or are we so thoroughly selfish to regret their absence because they can no more give us what they gave us in their life time?

that might be with those we love, but what can be said in that argument for the Death of strangers, & yet as I said above every death affects us more or less – & a violent unnatural death more than a quiet natural one. It is true that some people feel this sort of sympathy very little, & many get quite used to it as physicians & nurses but they too feel it at first.

This latter argument upon further reflection rather upsets or shakes my previous theory[23] – in so much as the breaking of electricity I first alleged as cause of the pain of Death [illeg.] must be the same at every death more or less – how then could people though they witnessed it often come to get used to it? It must in this case have something to do with imagination – but the[124] how

49

the connexion[125] is invisible to me.[126]

Everything but thoughts on the past is pleasant – I feel esteemed liked & even nearly appreciated by these kind good people the dear little children love me, I have so much to be thankful for that I am so –

Sister[127] if you are still aware of [the]my[128] feelings & actions influence me as you did when you were in this world to be kind prudent & just.

I feel more & more how much the affection I have for Somebody is growing upon me – I see so much to love[129] in him so much to admire & yet he is not clever & yet his eyes are so seducing. I sometimes think I will fling all necessary considerations on one side & tell him how he has conquered my heart & entreat him to let me follow him. What a sweet peaceful happy life would I have in prospect – but I know I must not indulge

50

indulge[130] in those daydreams they are dangerous, & his heart is too noble too pure to be trifled with, oh I would not that he should suffer one minute's pain caused by me. – I <u>must</u> marry for money not for love unless the two can be combined. T[131]: – told me to day that I was <u>a schemer</u> & that I encouraged a certain engagement & subsequent marriage – but I really had nothing to do[y] with it – knew nothing of it till the day before they were engaged – & then when I found that the young Lady loved him so much that she would have him in spite of his poverty [I illeg.] & her mother being quite agreable[132], I thought it was quite unnecessary my making myself disagreeable

51

by interfering –

He is a fine young man good manners & a straightforward honorable character but alas a lack of tin[133] – But I declare most solemnly if I was not actuated by <u>two motives</u> I would rather marry with love & little money than without love & be ever so rich But the two motives are powerful one rather good the other rather the contrary – not bad in itself exactly only I will have to make up my mind to bear the consequences what ever they may be – & they <u>may</u> be something very awful –

61

3ᵈ

Had a long talk with him in the afternoon – my heart faints with sorrow – & his [eyes] soul[134] closes like the nightshade – He said "Supposing there were two!" –
But oh let the grave be closed upon it all & the tombstone of silence seal it with eternal oblivion. And am I right in thus crushing the sincerest

52

& purest emotions of my heart? Am I right in forming a resolution which goes against my feelings I will say what my reasons are they may be wrong but to the best of my belief they are not. First I think he is not in a position to incur more expenses than necessary as it would only keep him back instead of getting him on in the world thus it would in one way certainly be a disadvantage in the second place I feel that I am bound to assist my family which in marrying a poor man I could not do – I say nothing of myself for would I not endure anything for him, do anything be deprived of anything if I could be with him at his side & contribute my small powers to make him happy – & to see him cheerful sheds a sun of happiness into my soul – to see him smile – to hear his cheerful yet soft voice, to see

53

his eyes glow with love as they did yesterday as they did all the evening wherever I went his eyes followed me – but he disguises his feelings he will not let me read his heart because he says I handled him so roughly once – But[135] what oh wan[136]t can I do? At night I thought I was safe – & my heart thumped against my ribs like a hammer when I heard the door open & steps approach my bed – I curled up in a corner & said all I could think to dissuade him, threats gentleness, & anger but all to no purpose, he did however not succeed though I must say I was rather loath to refuse, for and finding how intent he was I jumped down at the foot of the bed & ran out of my room – he was then obliged to decamp. It was right – I know – it would have been more than my situation was worth – I can not not see the harm – but this time it does not suit my purpose so we must go without it – but I did not tell him so.

54

Dec 26th 1855

We are on good terms, which pleases me – She is ashamed of it herself & I have prudence though I do not sympathize with her – How must a woman's body be organized to be jealous after twenty two years marriage I do not know[137] – And it seems to me that I shall never be jealous again – if I married a certain person I should turn socialist at once as Henry H[138] used to say of me. Would that not be a good plan if only the others were not so stiff. Some exceptions could however be found I. & the T. & who knows how many others. But those I would like to proselytize would be ~~pout~~ of the pale of conversion I am afraid. Was I not always eccentric has my path not always run apart from others, & have I not done in innocence & justice what pride & prejudice would never dare – So will I this time do what seems to conduce to my future ~~happiness~~ satisfaction[139] without caring what the world may say.

55

& happy for me if it was but the opinion of the world that I shall have to trample upon – happy if with the attainment of that one object [illeg.] my heart could also be satisfied – But at my time of life though the heart may still retain its tresure[140]s of love to give & the desire of love to receive yet vanity & ambition [illeg.] which at eighteen or twenty lay dormant have now grown into powerful adversaries so powerful that they over rule the soft longing of the heart, the gentle submissive affectionate heart. I confess that were it not for the empire that vanity & ambition hold over my soul, I would go & be <u>his Slave</u> <u>his</u> servant <u>his</u> submissive loving faithful wife, I would serve him truly all the days of my life, & be as happy as the day was long – for <u>he</u> is the man that with one word one look could make me happy – But it will not be so – Vanity & ambition are urging me forward, holding out [illeg.]all the advantages that riches & position can give

56

all the pleasures of vanity ~~gratified~~ gratified, all the satisfaction of doing good to my family & to others all the personal comforts that will be mine, & that indeed one must have, where the heart has nothing to hope for. I know one thing however that G does not like me half so much as I love him, if he cares at all – for he is more distant than ever more reserved than[illeg.] ever, & more attentive to everybody else than ever – & it is best that it should be so – I must keep out of the way of temptation, for I feel as if one moment's weakness could pull down the whole fortification of resolutions.

63

Jan 14.1856.

Had a great row this morning with Georgey[141] – cannot get on – got excited was in the humps all day long – Mr Barton & Miss Drane[142] came in the evening – Mr B is a most amusing person kept us laughing all the time – has nice eyes & beautiful teeth, when he laughs you see two white crescents of oval opaque looking teeth pure & spotless to the very wisdom teeth – he is a gentleman how pleasant it is to converse with people that have been trained in their youth – to associate with people who do not always set themselves up for idols in their mole eyed selfishness.

It is in the middleage of human life that the character is fully developed & comes into full vigour & action

58

there is a great charm about the freshness of youth, but it is only like a dream like scent imaginary no real enjoyment either of mind or person – B looked at me rather significantly – if I had moral courage – but after all I am better as I am – Ernest B.[143] was here too the poor boy looks very ill indeed – he said once – You might kill a poor fellow at once instead of —

– but I am sure he does not bestow one thought upon me unless he actually is before me – he is so very quiet take care of yourself Ernest –

Jan 18

Mrs Bowler Adelaide & Ernest came they seem one & all to appreciate the comforts of Brucedale – why are they all so honey sweet except A she is cold as ice & sulky as a snail. She blushes when W is mentioned but I know she does not love him for all that – affairs do not seem very promising for M^rs S is the only one that would perhaps take my part – & she perhaps has no influence – could I but see into the future – the gentleman in question is coming back soon but I have bad prospects for next winter as we shall most likely be in Sydney & he up here as the house must be left in somebody's charge –

Rode to Wyagdon & spent a very pleasant evening – they are kind agreable people – wie wol thuend ist es mit Leuten umzugehen denen gute Manieren natürlich sind – die von Jugend auf civilisirt waren die die Welt gesehen haben – die Bs sind

English translation of the German by Ann Sherwin:

> how gratifying it is to associate with people who are naturally well-mannered, who were civilized from their youth, who have seen the world. The B's[144] are

von dieser Art – sie sind unglaublich höflich u freundlich mit mir. Was ist das mit Ernst pretendirt er nur? ich trau u glaub ihm nicht recht – denn er naht sich mir gar so ungenirt u nimmt gar keine Notiz von C. dß es mir fast vorkommen wollte als ob es nur pretendirt wäre. However das ist nur ein kleiner Zeitvertreib, u kein so schlechter den er ist ein gutter Junge u hat adle Züge. – Schmeichelhaft ist es mir auch dß dr junge F. sich zu mir neigt er steht neben mir er spricht mit mir trotz der Gegenwart dieser allgemein bewunderten Schönheit – Vielleicht ist sein Bruder wie er – nur älter u stolzer – es mag kommen was da wolle ich bin in meinem Thurm gegen alle Wetter verschanzt – Mrs S sagte einst lang vor sie eine Idee hatte nächsten Winter nach Sydney zu gehen Wenn ihr Sohn verheiratet wäre

English translation of the German by Ann Sherwin:

> this kind of people. They are incredibly polite and friendly to me. What is it with Ernst? Is he just pretending? I don't quite trust or believe him – for he approaches me so artlessly and takes no notice of C,[145] such that I almost get the feeling that it is all pretense. However, this is just a little diversion and not a bad one at that. For he is a good boy and has noble qualities.

I also find it flattering that young F[146] is well disposed toward me. He stands next to me and speaks with me, despite the presence of this universally admired beauty. Perhaps his brother is like him only older and prouder. But come what may, I am secured against any weather in my tower. Mrs. S. once said to me, long before she had any notion of going to Sydney next winter, that if her son were married, she would

61

wolle sie von ihm [illeg.] laßen u down the country gehen mit der ganzen Familie – das wär mir schon recht ich ließ ihr dann alle Tag nach W gehen – Wird die Zeit einmal kommen wo er wünschen wird ich wäre etwas mehr eifersüchtig u ich dß er ofter nach W. ginge? Neulich sagte ich ich wäre zu alt zu heiraten sie aber antwortete never mind you must not say that there is a brave heart in store for you yet – was meinte sie damit vielleicht gar nichts vermuthlich so – dr Ring aber den sie mir neulich gab hat der nichts zu bedeuten? Ach nichts vielleicht als eine freundliche Aufmerksamkeit. Wenn auch daraus Alles nichts wird kann ich in S. beßeres finden.
– Oh G wie bist du mir unvergeßlich mit deinem stillen treuen Herzen – sieh aber dß ich auch etwas Ehre habe – ich bin viel zu gering u schlecht für dich –.

English translation of the German by Ann Sherwin:

> leave from him [illeg.] and go "down the country" with the whole family. That would be fine with me. Then I would let her go to W every day. Will the time ever come when he will wish that I were more jealous and I, that he would go to W more often? Recently I told her that I was too old to marry, but she replied, "Never mind. You mustn't say that. There is a brave heart in store for you yet." What did she mean by that? Maybe nothing. Probably so. But the ring she recently gave me, did it mean nothing? Alas, maybe a mere friendly remembrance. Even if everything comes to naught, I can find better in S. – Oh, G, how unforgettable you are to me with your silent, loyal heart. But look! I have some honor too. I am of far too little regard and bad for you.

62

I am a wretched little man – I have sore throat toothache heartache am bilious which comprises everything else – Cross to a degree – vexed with the present disgusted with the future & sorry for the past – B.[147] says I am a divine woman – I think I will return to him now. I am sure he loves me still & though he is white haired we might be happy still. G. certainly is fascinating to almost an irresistible degree – but what part have I in him such a heart I do not deserve – Caroline made me "fess" as she calls it that I had a flirtation with George at the Turon[148] – she said it laughingly – but oh would I had never known him

Jan 26.

M^r & Mrs Bowler & Adelaide & Major Ch.[149] rode to Alloway[150] rather quickly Caroline was as ill tempered & cranky as an old crow – pale with rage – bless the man that gets her for a wife – – the more I think of it the more I am impressed with the impossibility of the thing – Fate may decide I'll take it easy.

– and yet I can not come to any other satisfactory conclusion & resolution – I want a home & my vanity & pride make me long for this very one that I know is coveted by some one else – it is the rivalry that leads me on – that alone will carry me through it – for what else could? I want thus much – my present Salary settled for life as p[illeg.]in money & Brucedale for our residence & the other part of the family to take a place somewhere near Sydney so that we might go down & spend one or two of the cold wintermonths down there. I also want this Piano left here Several good horses & 2 servants

31st

Went to Sornbank[151] & spent a very pleasant day came home rather fast Mary & Ch[152] went with us –

Feb 1.

Drove Mrs S. to Alloway Bk.[153] It was one of the lovliest evenings I ever beheld – a sort of evening that would disperse what W. calls a fit of the blues – I was disappointed to day very much so & unexpectedly I am low – not what Major C. calls P.D.[154] – but things may may rise again, & I may yet come off with flying colors. – We are all canvassing[155] – Mrs S. too & I was perhaps foolish to refuse her assistance – but after all I think I did right –

Got a very kind letter from Knox[156] yesterday – life has no real interest no heartfelt attachment for me now –

It is high time that I were married – not that I feel more inclined to it – – no the very word conveys to my mind a consumation[157] of disgust barbarism selfsacrifice & endless annoyances far too great to make up for the positive facts which are pleasant the grievance to me is double – first the necessity that obliges me to it & secondly the thing itself – but I have come to the conclusion that [illeg.] it is perfectly useless unless one is a genius & comes at the right time when that genius is wanted to swim against the stream of custom, established law & prejudice – Certainly a revolution is made by many but it is headed by one, an army fights a battle but is lead[158] by one & thus it is that the individual is lost in the multitude unless it leads that multitude by the power of genius.

And I though I might be clever & remarkable am not a genius & must therefore run with that multitude perhaps against my will or must stand apart & walk my own way – this I could certainly do, did I not want the assistance of that same despised multitude

Were I of independent fortune I might & would stand apart – "I heard with narrow foreheads"?[159] – No never not mentally – I am obliged to live among them, do as they do, seem as they seem or are imitate their ways & manners sanction what they sanction condemn what they condemn in order to get money without which element I die & in so far I am dependent on them –

they allow little or no margin for difference of constitution if you walk on the side of the road & set but your foot halfway over the boundary they will push you hustle you hurl you thrust you down the precipice of degradation whence no woman returns – And yet strange to say I like Brougham's[160] Devilsdusk love the outskirts – I walk on the edge of propriety, I frequent shady places & I even love to lie on the very edge of my bed. Depth is always a disagreable extreme – even in thought we can only bear it because our intellect is so very limited & that depth small as it is to what we do not know – is painful & exhausting –

Now I wish someone would come forward & say they did not understand what I meant for I <u>could</u> make it much clearer

68

thus I wander away from that baneful word marriage – never was there any moral human institution so contrary to my nature through & through – View it from whatever side I will it seems to me the same barbarous remnant of uncivilized ages – One step it is true <u>we have</u> made since the creation of the world – there was a time when men were the only human beings in the world – that is each man had so much land so many cattle so many wives – now a man has so much land so many cattle & he has <u>one</u> wife who is allowed to consider herself mistress of <u>some</u> part of the property & shares his pleasures & sorrows – but when will the time come when woman will have so much land so many cattle & need

69

not have any husband at all if she does not want one! –

Feb 6.
Ashwednesday[161]

Had service at Kelso[162] then went to Bathurst shopping – Saw such a handsome man – Ravenblack hair & deepblue eyes – He looked intensely at me, I dropped my eyes & looked up again there was that gaze still – Ah who could look at ripe fruit & not wish for it – who indeed! – the second time he was lying down & a green branch was over his forehead & under the leaves I still saw those gleaming eyes – Socialism in idea I never will give up – Socialism in reality I am doubtful about – I would have gone into that butcher's shop & stood before that man – just near enough to touch him – & looked into his heavenlike eyes & spoken to him – to read his soul – my nerves were suddenly unstrung & in going home I felt agony sweet & piercing

delightful yet fearful – twice it came over me & I felt my eyes grow dim till my horse suddenly shyed & stopped cantering then the spell was broken – what a pity that I should be thus excluded from the most entrancing part of the society of men – For all the intercourse I have with men I might as well talk commponplace out of a dialogue book – Mrs S. was cut out for a parson's wife & no mistake she holds me tight no one must come near me[163] – And what shall I gain in the end by submitting to all this? – Here of all places in the world I enjoy less of men's society than I ever did before – & those there are, are of the most uninteresting description – Half & half neither Patricians nor Plebeians[164] Just enough [illeg.] to raise themselves above the lowest class of men, enough education to make them look down upon those who cannot read & write enough polish of manner to abstain

from beating their wifes[165] – but properly speaking without [illeg.] refinement Yes refinement is what is wanting everywhere – in mind in feeling in body in manners in social intercourse in their houses in their garden in their occupations – in everything in short & as I said before with only as much civilization[166] as will make them despise that refinement – those are the men that I associate with with the exception of one or two – Among such men women of course stand little higher than the horse & the cow – indeed perhaps not quite so high seeing that physical strength is the only thing valued – It stands to reason that in a country like this where manual labour is the only thing at present wanted – intellect must be at a discount.

But where have I got to – from my admiration of the handsome men –? I think the pleasures of love are not so great as those of imagination.

Sat 9th

Fred[167] came this day last week & Willy & D. Bowler[168] came today Fred has a nice moustache W. brought a charming likeness of himself – il est comme toujours – je ne puis pas – non je ne puis pas – mais que faire – Il n'y a rien à dire sur ce suject – que n'est-il 10 ans de plus ou au moins 5 – mais cette union serait deplorable – je laisse tout au course du tems[169] – mais il est décidement ce qu'on appelle soft en anglais amoureux de chaque fille – il deteste son beau cousin plus que jamais je suis bien punie de ma cupideté – J'abandonne un beau aimable jeune homme que j'aime de toute mon âme pour ce garçon rien que pour

English translation of the French by Sharon Joffe:

> W. brought a charming likeness of himself – he is like he always is – I cannot – no I cannot – but what to do – There is nothing to say on that subject – why is he not 10 years more or at least 5 – but this union would be deplorable – I leave all to the passage of time – but he is decidedly what one calls soft in English in love with every girl – he hates his handsome young cousin more than ever I am well punished for my greed – I am abandoning a handsome decent young man whom I love with all my soul for this boy only for his Fortune.[170]

Sa Fortune[171] – Feb 19

Diese Frau ist ein unausstehlicher Affe muß sie eine Mutter von 10 Kindern auf das sie sich so viel einbildet sich benehmen wie ich eine independente junge Person? Ich kann keine Mode erfinden sie imitirt sie, keine Meinung aus sprechen sie wiederholt sie Mir keine kl. Eccentricität erlauben aber sie muß alles nachmachen – so eine Affennatur hab ich noch nie in einem menschlichen Wesen gesehen. Es wär viel passender wenn ich mit ihrer Tochter gleich wäre aber das erlaubt ihre grenzenlose Eitelkeit nicht – 7/8 von ihr ist humbug u das achte achtel ist leer – ein Strohhalm ein Korbstoppel ein Draht – unverläßlich, seicht.

English translation of the German by Ann Sherwin:

> This woman is an insufferable ape! Must she, a mother of 10 children in whom she takes such pride, behave like an independent young girl? I can create no fashion without her copying it, express no opinion without her repeating it, allow myself no little eccentricity without her mimicking it – never have I seen such apery in a human being before. It would be much more fitting if I were like her daughter, but her infinite vanity doesn't permit that. She is seven-eighths humbug, and the eighth eighth is hollow – a straw, a piece of stubble, a wire – unreliable, shallow.[172]

March 3ᵈ

Living so much alone, or being restricted to the incourse of very few people is next to solitary confinement very injurious to the mind – as much so as if a horse's shoe was never taken off his hoof all his life – nothing in nature stands still, & every thing that is to keep in harmony must follow that forward – impetus – he who does not advance goes backwards, for there is no such thing as standing still. Our mind through the fiction of thought through the medium of books or conversation is constantly undergoing changes modifying, adding here throwing off there, generally gaining strength & light till the climax is reached & then decreasing with the strength of the body

If however these mediums of improvement as reading & conversation are wanting (the latter particularly) then the mind that is a healthy strong one, becomes fretful morbid captious unjust abschized[173] & at at[174] last settles in some mental or bodily disease. – I feel very much that way sometimes – now that I have lived so long in this seclusion – deprived of intellecttual intercourse deprived even of the comuning of my own thoughts by incessant stifling duties claims upon my time & my thoughts & my actions – To a mind accustomed to intellectual intercourse of a high order, to books of importance, & to solid useful occupation when left to itself commonplace conversation on subjects whatever are is

most distressing – compared to it the prattle of children the busy life in the streets, the noise of a factory is not half so wearying as commonplace repetitions on subjects otherwise perhaps interesting. And that is exactly my case – there is not a creature here that understands me my derivation my education my early impressions my principles – I have nothing in common with them further than that we are all human beings – I am obliged always to listen with a smiling face to the trivial nonsense of one, & the colonial amour propre[175] of the other – [illeg.] without either contradicting or expressing any personal opinions but those generally received in the country.

In consequence I have become as I said above morbid to which I was already predisposed. Trifles put me out of temper I impute wrong motives to the most innocent things I waste hours in ridiculous nonsense, or idle away my time in fancyful imaginations which make me wish for an impossible reality & dissatisfied with the present Sometimes I say to myself Why dont you take up the study of some science or undertake to write a book both of which you have often contemplated, give some serious deep occupation to your mind instead of letting it run rampant in the domain of imagination upon worthless unprofitable[176] sickly subjects – why not

78

rather fix your desires & appetite on something attainable healthful & satisfactory?. then I answer How can I perform any mental work when all my time except when asleep is taken up by something or ~~other~~ somebody – not being a genius though I may have very good talents & more perhaps than many others – but only just enough to make me[177] feel to ~~myself~~ isolated – & my mind being deprived of its native atmosphere & soil frets & makes me so cranky sometimes –

 Mrs S.[178] said something contrary to what she wrote once before – but it did not affect me much – the time is past when my heart was that way inclined – But always represent things in a pleasant light –

79

You <u>are</u> a little Humbug! –[179]

March 29.

Mʳ Suttor's nomination day[180]

He started in the dog cart driving Tandem & followed by 40 or 50 horsemen – I sometimes think I like the boy – but I am afraid B.P.[181] have something to do with it – it would really be a pity to loose[182] that chance – Could I, oh could I but look into the future – then I should be suddenly satisfied – je me rejouirais du succès ou je me ferais raison de la défaite – A vrai[e] dire tout pour le moment ressemble à une deroute complète – le seul éspoir qui me reste et qui est bien faible est son ancient penchant pour moi – mais hélas que peut un amour de garçon contre un amour d'homme la beauté de cette demoiselle et tous les encouragement des deux familles? Je crois qu'une retraite honorable est ma seule ressource

English translation of the French by Sharon Joffe:

> I would rejoice from success or I would make sense from the defeat – to tell the truth all for the moment resembles a complete derailment – the only hope that remains to me and which is quite weak is his former feeling for me – but alas what can a boy's love do against a man's love the beautify of this young woman and all the encouragement of the two families. I think an honorable retreat is my only resource

80

have forgiven long long ago but I can never forget – Miss B[183] came here to day April 2ᵈ[184] but never went near the schoolroom – We did not go to the races at which she was probably offended for she did not come back at all that night – I wonder what tomorrow will bring I expect W&E. A[185] will go but we not – & what will Friday be – W. said to me: Suppose we take a ride in on Friday?" – Now I feel sure he would not propose our going if A had not been there –[186]

April 4.

The third day is come & gone – & he bore his disappointment very well though certainly he <u>might</u> have got a horse, though not his own mare) but he did not seem overanxious about it – & this is the first time in my life since that morning we went to O. that he <u>in my presence</u> neither flirted with Addy[187] – nor wrapt himself in sulky silence nor looked sentimental[188] so it was a pleasant day – in fact I never saw him behave so well –

81

Saturday

It is a mystery to me, a perfect labyrinth – out of which I can never find my way except by climbing & jumping over all the intricacies contradictions &[189] paradoxes [illeg.] inexplicable unravellable combination of ups & downs pro & cons, faith error courage struggle firmness & weakness that obstruct the straight path of reason logic & experience in that particular subject – Is there a preference why deny it, is there a struggle why keep it up – is there no preference why that pallor that hiding behind the newspaper that sudden shake of the nerves if there is no struggle why that theory quite uncalled for that absurd argument – – which through its very existence & presence proves the necessity of a strong preventive?

82

I could certainly answer all these questions & doubts by something that I have in my mind, – I could say that he is extremely impressionable in that quarter & that her extreme beauty her gentle & ladylike manner make a kind of electric physical impression & the imaginations fancies behind the pleasing exterior something still more beautiful which there is however not in this case there is no mind & perhaps no feeling – & he knows that, if [illeg.]he thought that she loved him he would perhaps not be able to resist – but as it is – she has no mental attractive powers there is no moral communion between them – (& fortunately so else my cause would be a lost one) He is very intellectual & like his mother & my brother values mind even in a woman therefore I have power over him.[190]

83

All this I would say to myself & rest content – but I distrust my own judgement in this case – & here to this silent book I may confess that there is a mysterious attraction that draws me towards that young man something that makes me feel as if it clouded my reason though it sometimes brightens my heart. An attraction that till now I have not been quite able to up root although I have succeeded in keeping its growth down – the thing is that he always encourages me & draws me further by all the means that love has to make it self known but that can also be imitated. Why does he press my hand why does he come & sit near me & do those many little things that so sweetly deceive one if in reality he prefers her? – Or does he love her without knowing it & is he all the time deceiving himself & me? & will at the time when I expect a crisis all the truth break forth like a pent-up stream? – then I

84

must forget & when I must I will – In the mean time I will take care too much is not said of me. – that loss would though great in itself yet comparatively small to the 2d of Feb & the 5th of March[191] – Have I not lived am I not still alive though

78

so much changed under that eternal sorrow? – Can anything affect me more than the loss of that father & sister that where the whole world to me – no nothing in the whole world – for though there is a closer & stronger communication between W. & me than me & anyone else, & often takes the shape & form & color & voice of love – yet I have never indulged in that feeling, it is but the seed that would grow into a powerful tree was it not enclosed in the iron bands of selfcommand. To loose[192] you would cost me a pang but only a momentary one, & the waves of pride &

85

imagination would soon sweep away all trace of such idle thoughts – the sunshine of cheerfulness the calmness of philosophy & the perfume of hope would soon again bring back joy & veil the void that your absence would cause –

April 8 –

M. S. est défait et j'en tire mauvaise augure –[193]
I take it as a bad omen –
Vous m'êtes trop cher Guillaume pour que je vous sacrifie a mon interêt – Soyez heureux et je me consolerai de ma perte – but keep a stern control & command over yourself –

English translation of the French by Sharon Joffe:

> You are too dear to me William for me to sacrifice you to my interests –
> be happy and I will console myself with my loss

17[194]

I have enemies here & there but I may say I have friends nearly every where by my foes dwell to the northward I heard a tale to day from a person that I would trust as soon & sooner than my own ears – what Mr D[195] has been trying to insinuate – the young pappy thinks he can manage a double edged sword – but as

86

yet he has only learned to use his jackknife – I always mistrusted that set – one & all those [illeg.] quiet people are always deceitful

– but no I must pay them even that compliment – I am convinced it is nothing but that lurking spiteful selfish spirit of contradiction that once made him flirt with her – for to say that he flirts now or looks sentimental which I dislike above all things would be positively untrue – he does not talk to her more than he would with any other pretty <u>artful</u> girl that made such <u>avances</u>[196] as she does – it would be more than man's nature could do –

Nuit et jour je pense à lui (parce que vous n'avez rien d'autre à faire) je ne puis me persuader qu'il viendra un tems[197] ou il sera le mari d'une autre – (parcequ'il a une belle fortune) et vous series[198]

English translation of the French by Sharon Joffe:

> Night and day I think of him (because you have nothing other to do) I can not persuade myself that he will come back one time where he will be the husband of an other – (because he has a big fortune) and you would be

87

fachée de la perdre) – mon orgueil est vaincu je voudrais être son ésclave plutôt que sa maîtresse (c'est l'esprit de contradiction parce que vous n'êtes pas tout à fait sûre de lui – une fois sa femme et vous deviendrez indifférante comme du brouillard) Je souffrirais tout de lui sa froideur ses insultes son manque d'attention ses liaisons mêmes si je croyais qu'il m'aimât – (oui par cette même indifférence – une fois que vous auriez remporté ~~une~~ la victoire[199] sur votre rivale satisfait votre ~~vanite,~~[200] amour propre que vous auriez acquis un mari beau jeune admiré riche et spirituel et ainsi satisfait votre vanité devant le monde, et je préviens votre mari qu'il trouverait fort difficile de vous impatienter ou de vous rendre jalouse –

English translation of the French by Sharon Joffe:

> angry to lose it) – my pride is conquered I would like to be his slave more than his mistress (it is the spirit of contradiction because you are not entirely sure of him – once his wife and you would become indifferent

like the fog) I would suffer all from him his coldness his insults his lack of attention his attachments even if I believed that he loved me – (yes by this same indifference – once you have won a victory over your rival satisfied your (vanity) self love that would have acquired a handsome young admired rich and spiritual husband and thus satisfied your vanity in front of the world, and I warn your husband that he would find it very difficult to get impatient or to make you jealous

88

What once was a painful disguise is now become a pleasing reality – the wide wide world once again[201] takes its preeminence – Science occupies reason Arts satisfy the feelings, & travelling excites the imagination & thus I can be happy through myself. I told W. to day that I thought it a fine thing to be independent in [illeg.]getting a living & that as soon as I had finished his sisters education I intended visiting America – & that I quite wondered at myself at having remained so long in one place – this morning M^r S said something about some people that he knew – W. brushed his hair and off his forehead & walked out of the room – whether M^r S said it intentionally or not I can scarcely guess – but he is perfectly right

89

the very idea of it has always gone against my feelings. –

No! not even if I married him would I allow my heart to love him – He would trample me in the dust if he thought I loved him – he is one of those sort of people that must be kept at a respectful distance, & held with a tight rein & a firm hand – or else his presumption knows no bounds – that <u>one</u> fact I never will understand it is so contrary to all that I have ever thought or felt on similar occasions – never mind it is of very little consequence that I should understand his feelings & consequent proceedings –

April 30.

M Bowman[202] came here to day lovely day had a little holiday for L. & H.[203] went to Bathurst M Suttor dreamt a dream that she would not tell me – it was about me. – the same night W. dreamt that he was crying bitterly – him I did not ask what it was about

May 2d

Wyagdon baby christened to day Florence Adelaide[204]; I fully expected there would be a little Adelaide Suttor in anticipation of the big one to come – but it was not so & Ad would not have anything to do with the baby so she said – I think it was a disappointment to Mrs T.S.[205]

Yesterday I showed W. a poem which I found in Dr Smith's book & which ran thus:

>Go youth beloved in distant glades
>New friends new hopes new joys to find
>Yet sometimes deign midst fairer maids
>To think on her thou leavst behind
>My love thy fate dear youth to share
>Must never be my happy lot
>But thou mayst grant this humble pray'r
>Forget me not forget me not

>Yet should the thought of my distress
>To[206] painful to thy feelings be –
>Had not the wish I now express
>Nor even feign to think of me –

>But of if grief thy steps attend
>If want if sickened be thy lot
>And thou require a soothing friend
>Forget me not; forget me not[207]

And this evening he said giving me a newspaper "Here is something in answer to what you showed me – last night – it ran thus:

>Trace to thy loud misgivings
>These fruitless tears give o'er
>No absence can decide us love
>No parting part us more
>Mountain & seas may rise between
>To mock our baffled will
>But heart in heart & soul in soul
>We bide together still.

Where'er I go, or far or near
I cannot be alone
Thy voice is ever in mine ear
Thy hand is in mine own
Thy head upon my pillow rests
Thy words my bosom thrill
And heart in heart & soul in soul
We bi[illeg.]de together still.[208]

92

Vanity would whisper soft delusive words but I dashed the gay deceiver to the ground, She wounded & deceived me once – & I will never again believe her – & now I am quiet & happy at least content.

May 4.

It is no use disguising the truth. To my own heart I may confess that consuming anguish that willing submission, that silent sorrow, that faithful spirit that pentup stream that powerful love – & he does not love me – He thinks he tries to think to make himself believe that he does love me, that he is faithful "with quiet eyes unfaithful to the truth but he deceives himself & me & his mother unwillingly unconsciously – but the time is coming when that

pent up stream will break all bonds pass all bounds, when it will burst forth from dark caverns clouds & deep places in all its power & radiance like the sun from a heavy stormy sky – He will then come to me with his honest face & say – Forgive me I knew[209] not myself, I thought you were indifferent & this passion born from a passing impression & imagination has grown overwhelming in its power I love her with all the strength of manhood – you had the blossom of spring the dew of dawn – – Thus will he speak to me – & I shall say "Anything brother that pleases you shall make me happy – & truly so it shall be – for long since have I banished all thoughts of self –

May 17.

In Septb 54 was the day that wrought the change that night I said "it must be" – but it was not till June following that my heart would believe – a year has passed since then & I am now so far indifferent that I could marry him for his fortune only – thus goes the world – Had I a fortune of my own or the means of making one I would not have recourse to such means for sustenance Had G. the fortune then indeed I should be happy but as it is I <u>must</u> make the best of it. We, or rather they were talking of [illeg]. this evening – oh how sad it makes me to think of that place

<u>Visions</u>

My hand is strong my heart is bold
My purpose stern I said
Nor shall I rest till I have wreathed
Fame's garland round my head
No! men shall point to me & say
See what the bold can do
"<u>You dream</u>" a chilling whisper said
And quick the vision flew.

Yes I will gain I musing thought
Power, pomp & potency
Whate'er the proudest may have been
That straightaway will I be
I'll write my name on human hearts
So deep 'twill ne'er decay
"<u>You dream</u>" & as the whisper spoke
My vision fled away.

"I'm poor" said I, but I will toil
And gather store of gold
And in the purse the fate of kings
And nations I will hold.
I'll follow fortune till my path
With wealth untold she strew
"<u>Again you dream</u>" the whisper said
And straight my vision flew.

96

Of I can gain nor name nor power
Nor gold by high emprise
Bread to the hungry I will give
And dry the mourners eyes
Through me the sun of joy shall find
It's[210] way to sorrow's door
"The wildest dream of all" then said
The whisper, "you are poor.

I'm poor unheeded but I'll be
An honest man, I said
Truth I shall worship, yea & feel
For all that God hath made
Though poor the honest man can stand
With an unflinching brow.
Before earth's highest". Such I'll be
The whisper spake not now.[211]

This poem was given to me last night to read – & why does Fate bring such tempation[212] in my way? Why must I refuse that which would make me happy for that which will be an endless source of misery from which like a labyrinth or a horned dilemma there is no escape – I am doomed to unhappiness to sorrow & pain

97

My nerves are like David's[213] my heart roareth for very unquietness – & no peace shall I find till death – Oh George gentle & nobleminded let me speak to you in my thoughts as I dare not do so any other way My love for thee is like the milk of the cow, like the scent of the magnolia, & dark like approaching night & sorrowful separation. How beautiful admirable was your conduct to day – Every action every look every word proves the aristocracy of the soul – Would that he whom I would wed for his fortune were like you – No wonder poor little Carry's[214] heart melts like wax in his presence when my weatherbeaten castle trembles beneath his glance. He is too good for any of the girls that I know – Some too stupid some too flighty some too matteroffact some

98

too wordly[215] no I can not see a woman worthy of thee & I am the unworthiest of all. I am not so vain as to think that he ever gave me two thoughts except perhaps of anger or scorn & blame – for I am hard rough rude unamiable unloveable My few good qualities are stern & bitter & yet I am a woman in folly vanity & [illeg.] Could I ever expect to make a man happy to make a good wife? No never – the fact is that I have an utter horror of matrimony in its best shape & color. Love that fanciful airy imaginative hue of the soul seen & felt only as a vision in the rosy sky fluttering like a butterfly passing as a perfume in the evening breeze, coming & going & coming again like the tints of sunrise & the setting

99

"sinking behind Delphian cliffs"[216] the sun rises again after that purple evening & the silent resting night but it is another day another epoch in our lives.

Thus is ~~life~~ love, & could ~~that~~ the[217] rainbow ripen the wheat for our bread, could the silver light of the moon milk our cows, could the hues of the sunset build us houses? No & no more can love be chained by the fetters of matrimony Oh man who hast first shaken with they gentle voice & thy large grey eyes that prejudice of my youth; thanks to thee!

Oh in what errors are we all brought up, & how we cling to those first youthful impressions – For prejudice has a double fang with which it holds upon our mind That of feeling & that of reason – How foolishly we hold to what we like though

100

reason can demand it – And strange to say feeling has the strongest hold – Reason is open to arguments but what weapons can we bring to field of feelings? Reason no for ~~they are~~ it is of a nature that it cannot act upon the other. no more than wine can dissolve gold or milk iron. the principle of Duality & Trinity[218] is often times repeated in the visible & invisible world –

June 1.1856

M[r] W. showed me two of the lovliest sonnets by Shakespear[219] that ever were written so full of gentle sorrow & faith – But I will not be humbugged any more – I must not love if I want to keep my power & M[r] Cupid[220] shall be at a discount with me – Yes that is decided for ever – that love

101

must never again move my heart – Abercrombie has not spoken in vain –

George looked so handsome he was sad & silent what was it that drove the smile from those lips – George I love you too well too disinterestedly too truly too sincerely too honestly ever to allow you to know it. I feel I shall make a wretched bad wife for my love is like a gust of passionate wind – I feel I should make you unhappy for I hate the very idea of marriage, & if ever I enter that chamber of moral horrors it shall be with a golden key But I say you without unveil not what is hidden for you would discover what would make you shudder & you would curse the day on which you pledged your faith with mine –

102

So would every man, did he enter my blue chamber – but it would be veiled to a man I did not love – Oh Boy I loved you with all the strength of my ardent soul – but you did not know or understand it – The fault was neither yours nor mine, I spoke while you were yet in dreamland, I spoke a language that you will perhaps never understand. I spoke of the sun shine before the rising I spoke of the spring in the winter & you heard me not. And I turned to George gentle & true – but would never marry him – as for you, when I loved you I banished all thoughts of marriage – now that the charm is broken I contemplate the idea of marriage with a calculating eye, & might make if not a good wife an attractive mistress – but mark – since you dashed my flowers of love to the ground I am a socialist

103

Yes the sun has risen again after that tempestuous setting which tore the red & grey clould[221] of heaven, & raised the billows of the ocean, & dashed my little bark into the depth of Death, it dawned again after that stormy night & "calm is the forehead of the outer sea"[222] & with sad love that would lay down & die do I now pray for George's happiness; he & I must never wed – for near the man that I love do I feel my own unworthiness for love makes us humble – but near the man I do not love, I feel my power for coldness of heart makes us strong.

June 6.

The blue Ss. went to Orange[223] G. to Wyagdon –
 "Nothing that you would come to know[224] – at least so I suppose –
 Oh mystery of the heart –
 He is the only man that I would be faithful to – His faith would

make me faithful – but the other one is like his father, & therefore socialist, therefore suited to me therefore I dont like him Oh George be unkind to me rude indifferent cold; treat me with contempt seem not to notice me, be spiteful flirt with others make a show of your love to them, show them attention frown on me, make yourself disagreeable to me in every possible way, – but that you cannot do – & so I must love you –

June 6th

This Day I received poor M's[225] letter Her youngest & perhaps dearest daughter is gone[226] – she is no more with her, her voice is no more heard her quiet soft hazel eyes [illeg.] no more look up in charity & intelligence her small thin hand no more is busy for the comfort of others & that heart is full of love & sorrow has ceased to beat. – Silent is her place at table empty her chair at the Piano

she whom I taught to string those notes in harmony – Ah could I but know of hereafter – how it is & if she & Clari[227] & our father feel each other's presence & look down upon my existence I hope that it is so –

June 11.

What I wrote on the 6th about G. he had done or rather been made to do – I think him faultless in my eyes he is so. Why can I not be so artful as others – even young Carry beats me in that – but would it do me any good? No I am like G there I would not stoop to any artifice let alone meaningless to gain my point. What she thinks or whether she is aware of what she does goodness only knows but it is certainly strange conduct. She wont speak a word to anyone else but him, she leaves every body to go to him, & when even he goes away from her she runs after him. I do not wonder at his feeling flattered – though when a certain gentleman is present poor G. goes for nothing at all – Oh [illeg.] some of them appreciate him. He came to me several times & Miss C[228] looked round with a red nose & a

cross mouth & would not answer her Aunt at last she stopped till we came up & left M^{rs} K[229] to ride all by herself. I then rode up to M^{rs} K & she little artful thing managed to get longside of G. then she was satisfied – After a while G. came up to me again at which she cantered on by herself a few yards & finding that G did not follow her she stopped close before us so that if we walked one step further she must get between us – thus she went on, & as I did not wish to seem to show any particular desire of having G at my side she at last in going home succeeded in getting him on a head all the way back – My heart was so sad as I looked on the beautiful evening red & the pink rays of the setting sun the tears came in my eyes, & my whole soul leaned towards George as I beheld his splendid profile against the grey sky & bitter were the tears that filled my eyes till I could see nothing before me, that I must not encourage him, that I must not allow myself the faintest ray of hope – for his I shall never be – no never – How could I with

my family depending on me marry a poor man!

June 29.

Yes it was a pleasant day of dreamy pleasures & pleasant realities – But let me say it all – In the morning I had a good ride to church Mr Fox[230] preached the first time – Rode hard to keep up with the dogcart – If Miss B had been here other arrangements would have been made – but however – I expressed myself neither one way nor the other, but allowed Mr T. to lift me from my horse in his peculiar manner. At dinner Mr G. sat near me, & whether it was that he wished to show C that he did not care if T. sat near her or not, or what else it was that inspired him he talked very much & seemed in a state of excitement but oh how gentle & handsome he is – In the evening we went for a walk – I did not ask W because he seemed so deeply immersed in Moore's poems[231] that I made sure he would not come – But I sent Carry in & behold – forth started at the [illeg.] my young gentleman much to my surprise & we had a very pleasant walk – Coming home Johnson[232] walked at my side – he said he was very lonely

in his little cottage at Sofala,[233] & what a treasure a good wife was & went on like that I thought but did not say so: Why the dash don't you get a wife – I can see he longs for it – I was tired in the evening & leaned back on the sofa – T. came & sat near me – half leaning too & when I went to bed he for the first time in his life pressed my hand & held it longer in his than usual, at which I was rather surprised for I thought all along that both he & George are very much taken with C's beauty & innocence. – Templar[234] that exquisitely handsome dangerous man was near me nearly all the evening spoke poetry to me fixed his beautiful black eyes upon me till my heart thrilled – his profile is splendid purely grecian & there he stood in his fiendlike beauty like an Appollo[235] – he must be irresistible in his soft gentle moods if such ever happens – – & Mr Willy – what shall I say of him – he is getting tame he too pressed my hand as I said good night – & looked at me with his true blue eyes[236] –

July 4

Sie sind alle fort – Fast alle die mich einst geliebt alle unter dem Rasen hügel u mir bleibt nicht eine einzige Schwester – Dohl schrieb in einem alten Brief – Du allein hast den Schlüßel zu unserer Jugend – u so ist es – niemand versteht die Sprache u Niemand sieht die Farben. Ich stehe einsam u allein in dem Garten so voll Duft u Blumen aus der Vergangenheit – Mein Herz liebt euer Andenken Ihr Theuren wie euch selbst – Wol dß ich den Schmerz der Trennung hab u nicht ihr – nicht du – du meine Dohl für die ich jeden Schmerz der Welt ertragen möchte. Ihr seid alle außer dem Bereich ds Bewußtseins wenn überhaupt die Seele nicht ins All zurückgeht – Was hab ich o Schicksal gethan dß du mir solchen Schmerz sendest – Wohin ich blicke ist nur Trauer – die ich liebe verlaßen mich alle – so auch Wilhelm

English translation of the German by Ann Sherwin:

> They're all gone – practically everyone who ever loved me, all lie under the sod, and I don't have a single sister left.[237] Dohl[238] once wrote in an old letter: "You alone hold the key to our youth." And so it is. No one understands the language, and no one sees the colors. I stand deserted and alone in the garden, so full of the fragrances and flowers of the past. My heart loves your memories, dear ones, as much as it loves you. I'm glad that it's I who suffer the pain of separation and not you – not you, my Dohl, for whom I would endure every pain in the world. Even if the soul doesn't return to the universe, all of you are outside the realm of consciousness. What have I done, o fate, that you send me such pain? Wherever I look, I see only sorrow. All those I love desert me. Even Wilhelm,[239]

denn ich bin nicht der Liebe würdig. Worin liegt es denn dß mich die verlaßen müßen die ich liebe Ist denn nicht alles das ich in meinem Herzen gegen Wilhelm sage nicht selbstbetrug schale Sophisterei womit ich mir G[l]eichgültigkeit u Leichtsinn aufdringen will – u kommt es mir nicht hundertmal so klar so deutlich vor die Seele dß ich nur ihn liebe u dß er mich nicht einmal mit gemeiner Höflichkeit behandelt – Liebt sie ihn? Nein keine Spur – die Leute wißen nichts davon. Mein Glaube allein dß mein Streben danach durchaus nichts nützt halt mich von zu vielen Grämen ab. – Denn dß sie den Triumph haben wird ist kein Zweifel, dß sie siegreich ihn nach Hause führen wird u mich mit Verachtung zurück laßen ist auch kein Zweifel – Sie sparen keine Mühe – Schmeichelei wird mit vollen Händen aufgetischt – u sowol er als seine

English translation of the German by Ann Sherwin:

> for I am not worthy of love. Why is it that those I love have to leave me? Is not everything I say in my heart against Wilhelm self-deception, shallow sophistry, attempts to project indifference and frivolousness – and is it not plain and clear to my soul a hundred times over that I love only him and that he doesn't even treat me with common courtesy? Does she love him? No, not one bit – those people know nothing of love. The belief that my striving after it is utterly futile is all that keeps me from excessive grief. – For there is no doubt that she will triumph, nor is there any doubt that she will lead him down the aisle in victory and leave me behind in contempt. They go to great pains – flattery is served up in lavish degree – and both he and his

111

Mutter können eine unglaubliche Quantität davon vertragen. Wie wäre es denn möglich dß ich gegen solche Schönheit so viele eifrige Feinde im Rückgrund ich die ich allein ohne Jugend ohne Schönheit die mächtigste Waffe gegen Männer dastehe, etwas erlangen könnte – Nein ich sehe die Schlacht als vorloren [sic] an, u dr schein bare Vorzug den ich bisher habe wird von dem so lang gehemmten Strom fort geschwemmt werden – Mein Bruder sah es auch u sagte es mir denn er wußte nicht welchen Schmerz er mir dadurch machte – Sie thut alles das in ihrer Macht steht oder vielmehr die Alten stehen hinter ihr u soufliren alles das sie sagen u thun muß – denn von sich selbst ist sie ein Strumpf an Dummheit. Sie lernt jetzt Musik damit auch durch die Künste sein Herz bezaubern können – u Kunst u Schönheit verbunden müßen unwiederstehlich sein – Was bleibt denn mir noch für ein Vorzug? Als meine treue Liebe die wird aber selten belohnt Warum druckt er mir die Hand alle Abend? – Aber wozu zähl ich alle die für u wider? –

English translation of the German by Ann Sherwin:

> mother can tolerate an incredible quantity of it. How could I possibly win anything in face of such beauty, with so many zealous foes in the background, I who stand there alone, lacking both youth and beauty, the most powerful weapons against men? – No, I regard the battle as lost, and the apparent advantage that I've had up to now will be swept away in the long dammed-up stream. My brother saw it too and told me, for he didn't know what pain it would cause me. She does everything within her power – or rather the elders stand behind her and whisper everything she must say – for on her own, she is the epitome of stupidity. She is learning music now, so she can captivate his heart through the arts – and art and beauty are bound to be irresistible. What advantage am I left with other than my true love? But that is rarely rewarded. Why does he squeeze my hand every evening? – But why am I counting all the pros and cons? –

112

Sonntag den 27 ten Juli 1856

Heute vor einem Jahr ging ich mit Willy nach Sydney gegangen wo ich außer meinen eignen Gedanken nur Erfreuliches erlebte – Es war eine süße Mußestunde – Heute aber bin ich fast ebenso elend Emi u Sidi diese reinen Kinder sind mir frisch im Herzen, den wir liebten einander getrennt mehr als früher – sie sind fort wer weiß wohin? Wer weiß ob die Dohl noch ist wer weiß ob ihre Seele voll Liebe Reinheit u Güte nicht zerfloßen ist – Wenn sie ihr Bewußtsein noch hat so liebt sie mich noch davon bin ich überzeugt, aber dß sie mir davon kein Zeichen geben wollte ist mir unbegreiflich – Wie immer wenn sie noch lebt so ist sie glücklicher als auf dr Welt weil ja alles nach Beßerung strebt –

English translation of the German by Ann Sherwin:

Sunday, July 27, 1856

A year ago today I went with Willy[240] to Sydney, where, except for my own thoughts, I experienced only pleasures – it was a sweet hour of leisure. But today I am nearly as miserable. Emi and Sidi, these uncorrupted children, are fresh in my heart, for we loved each other apart even more than before. But they are gone to who knows where. Who knows whether Dohl still exists?[241] Who know whether her soul, so full of love, purity, and goodness, has dissolved. If she still has a consciousness, then she still loves me, of that I am certain. But that she didn't want to give me any sign of it – that I find inconceivable. As always, if she still lives, she is happier than she was on earth, because everything aspires to become better –

113

The want of charity however good they may be is most unharmonious to say the least of it – I could at once enter into particulars – but I will first generalise as Dr Warren[242] says it is such a prominent feature of my character & writing – there are two kinds of uncharitableness one objective in not making allowance for others the other subjective in valuing one's own opinion too highly. The first says to a man who has stolen a loaf of bread to give it to his starving child – you are a thief & must be punished, or to a young Lady who talks to a gentleman – you are a desparate flirt which is very wrong & blameable making in the first case no allowance for a father's feelings & in the second for difference of character, between a dull person who has nothing to say for herself & a lively one with a pleasant flow of spirits – This is the first kind of uncharitableness – the other says – you dont think like me, consequently.

114

you must be wrong, in error & blameable –

This uncharitableness of both kinds is the only fault that I see Mrs Suttor – for I do not count weakness or frailty a fault else I should be as uncharitable myself – Only most unfortunately in Mrs S.[243] there is always a little spice of envy – I do not wonder now at W's accusing me of bitterness & conceit seeing that he has so much of it himself But I must go on with my subject, & now that I have generalized I will particularize[244]

116

He who humbleth himself shall be exalted –[245]

We must bear the cross of humiliation before we can receive the crown of glory –[246]

My eyes are unsealed –

Sunday Aug 4th
1856.

I was beginning to read Angels' love by Moore[247] & Mr W. said: The first am I – consequently I read attentively & the following was the result:

> Pure & ~~innocent~~ unmoved she stood as lilies in the light – so innocent the maid whom it was my destiny to love – Had you but seen her look when from my lips the first avowal burst Not anger'd no – So fixed & frozen my heart failed me the spell was broken, how could I leave a world which, or lost or won,

117

made all to me – that minute from my soul the lights of heaven & love both passed away & I forgot my home my birth, till I became what I am now –[248]

Poor boy I understand he thinks he has no chance of winning her because his own timidity still spell=binds him[249] – did he but know what I know & see what I see – then would life rise on the wings of hope –

Yes I feel morally certain that he would not give me his arm if she was there, that he would not[250] speak to me if he could speak to her, that he would not ride near me if she was with us – and that knowledge ought not only to <u>cover</u> my feelings with impenetrable indifference but also govern my feelings – only the one is much easier done than the other – that I have a

118

preference for him it would be impossible to deny – but can one not have a preference for a dear brother, a friend who though the husband of another may have for you & you for him the purest sincerest affection? I love my brothers[251] better than any other men in the world & Willie Suttor shall rank equal with them – & then I can say that I have screwd myself up to harmonious concert pitch.

Saturday Aug 9. Nina's[252] birthday

Went to Wyagdon[253] rather ruffled in this morning – got on pretty well always prepared for the worst much the best place – W. for the first time in his life <u>did not</u> flirt, nor seemed inclined to flirt nor was rude to me, nor was cross – my own sweet Willie boy would I not give my own happiness to secure yours – I have now the truest sisterly affection for you – and could Ad.[254] but make you so happy as I long to see you made

I will tell Mrs Wise though that one thing beginning with LP. & Mr B & ending with Mr P. & I will also tell L.P about Maria's[255] laugh – For I know they dont spare me – W. was riding on ahead of us all as he often does, & Ad left us all rode up to him & never left him till we got to Mrs Kerr's[256] place & then <u>he</u> left <u>her</u> – I feel sure she has been told by her mother not to be so backward – upon Mrs Ch S's[257] principle of: Did beauty but know its power etc – that sounds well & true but when you come to think of it, it wont quite bear analyzing – for beauty like Adelaide's lies in its statuesque calmness & [illeg.] like silence not in ervarying feeling clouds & sunshine, & emotions of all kind expressed in the face & the attitudes – If A's face underwent all the changes that mine for instance does she would only loose[258] by it

Sunday Aug 10.

W. has really forgotten how to flirt – he was so good all day – but oh pent up stream oh fate of Kate!²⁵⁹

But however there was not that constrained sentimental manner that I so much dislike to see – He drew her portrait he read poetry to her he sits near her & talks, but always in that quiet manner that he had never shown before

Indeed he might say a great many more things lively & piquant with out my being in the least displeased, but it all depends on the manner.

<u>A little later</u>[260]

(Dream of Poison)[261]
I crowed too soon – But never mind. I am out of it – But I think they are both a little deceitful – for when I am there she never speaks a word nor raises her eyes, & he too scarcely seems to notice her – but when I am away – I hear them talk & laugh merrily & have plenty of fun – But so long as I can gain <u>my end</u> that is of [illeg.]

121

little or no consequence – How could the son of such a father the nephew of such an uncle be anything else?
To excuse himself he shows me Moore's Poem Cupid & Psyche[262] & sa[illeg.]ys its his principle always to make himself worse than he is – I call that would – be cunning but very shallow withall[263] I wish to goodness I had M<u>rs</u> Bowerman's[264] ready smile & commonplace quick & deep dissimulation is highly necessary for a person of deep feeling like myself & above all I wish I could be with a brazen face –
Pardi s'il etait mon mari je m'en ficherais – mais je ne puis pardonner a l'amant[265]
What we call love is nothing but electricity the communication of the electric fluid between two bodies – if only between two it may be very powerful if di –

122

vided – Division always lessens the strength – If a man & a woman have electric communication, between them it acts upon the moral as well as the physical system thereforein love is different from friendship & a combination of circumstances is necessary to make <u>first love</u> of such importance in the moral part of our constitution – If I take the electricity I have given combined with moral approbation or even without[266] to one person, from <u>that</u> person he or she will suffer bodily & mental pain because that fluid is vitally connected with our life. the person that deprived of electricity will express himself according – Sometimes in bad temper, sulkiness extraordinary merriness [illeg.] excitement, depression of spirits headache & flushes – all this

123

is called Jealousy – Hence it is so easily explained why people when they are jealous go & spitefully flirt & affect feelings that are not really in them – Jealousy or the withdrawing of electricity is causes an irritation in the deprived party, whose electricity being roused in an unsatisfactory manner tries to find vent in some kind of retaliation. Then [succee] jealousy subsides & the two previously inclined united bodies become neuter. Thus I could not spontaneously have pressed W.s hand tonight because he had spent his electricity & I mine on another object – Our bodies have an instinct of this & it is surprising wh how easily shortly[267] disunited bodies attach themselves or attract others even that have never felt an approach before – – like a match that has just been blown out catches fire much sooner than a fresh one –

124

Monday Aug 11.1856.

Carry's[268] birthday – Adelaide here had a very pleasant evening played at cards, laughing took my headache away very good thing – A. was a little more lively – W. all the more sulky – he was so all day long for what reason goodness knows – perhaps a mouse ran over his liver

———

I feel lucid to night there is a kind of phosphoric light in my brain, I feel a moral livelyness that I have not felt for long – the first time I have laughed heartily for a long time – I dare say the poor conceited boy thinks I am jealous – I was going to write him a note only I have it still in my pocket but I [illeg.] will feign indifference & gaiety till I really feel it.

125

– At this moment a note is s[p]lipped under my door – I open it, it is from him – he says I am changeable, & have no right to expect more than friendship from him & that I shall be disappointed if I think he loves me still –

———

I feel morally certain that I shall be unutterably miserable if or when[269] a certain thing happens – for there is no reason to think that it will be any better than it is now – on the contrary –

———

Aug 15

Was it not strange this evening ~~this evening~~ his manner towards me? <u>Something</u> that I do not know of her either preceeded or is to come – & I rather think she knows of it for she was not crosser not colder than usual with me – He brings out his poetry books to read with her it is a pity she does not understand that language – I wish to goodness I had some worthier occupation than all this nonsense & rubbish – got a letter from Mr Wood[270] to day

126

That girl young as she is has fifty times more artfulness & dissimulation than I ever dream of – it is but too true "Fair & false".[271]

    Miss A came home this evening in high ill humour & her <u>good night to me</u>[272] was arctic – What can be the cause for it?
    He does not flirt that is true – but I dont see why that should give you such immeasurable satisfaction It rather proves that his admiration for her is too great to express itself so flippantly – But of one thing I am heartily glad viz that he has put aside that most ridiculous aggravating sentimentality –
    Wont I! ___ ! ____ that's all!![273]

you have no chance! –[274]

127

Every body notices his penchant – even Carry – Well it is done – she has him but why on earth must he be so rude so bitter towards me – why can he not treat me with the same indifference as I show him –

Sunday Aug 24.1856.

To night for the first time I felt angry – really angry with W. & I said in my heart – Go, do not speak to me. I dont care for you He seems to study to do all he can to vex, annoy, hurt, provoke & aggravate me – But I say to myself I <u>will</u> dissimulate & appear totally indifferent – by constantly feigning a thing it becomes natural – When he spoke those rude harsh untrue words to me I turned my back & went on talking & laughing to Carry[275] just as if he had not spoken at all – upon which he sat down & never spoke a word till half past eight when he said Good night I am sleepy & went to bed

128

I have reasoned myself into reason & am quite prepared to hear that he has proposed to her, & to begin my roaming life again – It was an illusion, a short dream of a happiness that <u>might</u> be but it was only a dream, that happiness was never to be realized Perhaps I should never have been happy with him – I will believe so – We were not made for each other we never did understand each other never was there any <u>moral sympathy</u> between us, whatever other attracttion there may have been – but that goes for very little when Psyche[276] does not wake up at the same time. Be it so – we will have less to regret.

Aug 25.

It is evening I return to my own room I close the door & stand before the fire – "My lost William" It is so, I cannot disguise the truth any longer, nor deny facts – He is lost to me, & the dreaded moment of parting has come, the parting of hearts, when I must think of <u>my Willie</u> as dead, & look on William Suttor Jun[r] as a stranger.

129

I dare not look up to his true blue eye[277] lest he should read in mine – I dare not speak to him lest my voice should betray, I dare not stand near him lest my heart should tremble – & forget that I have no part in him – the stream of passions is swelling & will soon sweep away all restraint – they think me far away – they think of me I dare say what I seem – but memory still lingers over that once loved scene only the silence of the grave, or the gay laugh & cold indifference cover the burning tears of sorrow.

– And why do I thus hide my sorrow from him – why do I feel that impulse that struggle to go far from him – & yet always come back again – why does every thing disappear when I stand near him – why do I not hear or notice any but him? Why indeed? I cannot answer any of these questions, nor can I argue away the reality of these facts – there they are & will be – my only & last ~~dissimulation~~ resource is – dissimulation.

130

that there <u>has been</u> a communication I can see even now – & strange coincidences sometimes take place – this morning I was standing at the fireplace reading – W. came in & as a sort of atonement perhaps for last night's rudeness he said good-morning rather more kindly than usual – I felt a sudden thrill – "But no" I said to myself, <u>if</u> there is any communication yet between us, it is as slight as an almost invisible thread – & that will soon break I added & returned my thoughts to my book – & this evening he expressed the very same idea, either out of a book or his own head –

What D[278] said is very true, true in perfection because it is a fact a condition a sine qua non[279] Let [~~illeg.~~] him come to you –

131

Go, my good fellow to your much admired AB[280] & see what you can get out of her, except children[281] & see what you can find in her except her beauty – I was very glad E.A.[282] gave me his arm to night & not M[r] W. – I never know what to talk to him – I should like to hear some of his conversation with AB, it must be essence of wit, intellect & poesy

———

Rain makes the plants grow but what does tears produce? are they the evaporation of sorrow? or are they productive of wholesome afterthoughts

---

Why do I not like to take wine with him? why do I not like to ride or walk with him, why do I not talk to him? – why? – Because when Ad. is here he treats me not only with marked indifference but positive rudeness – that is why –

132

I have asked myself the question why I am so altered towards him. there are more reasons than enough First that letter in which he says that if I think he still loves me I shall be disappointed, then his manner towards me, his rudeness his bitterness his willful & wrongful accusations all which I only overlook with indifference because he knows no better, & thirdly his evident inclination for Ad – which more people than myself noticed for perhaps I should not in that case have trusted my own perceptions – Are not these reasons allpowerful & all plenty, & could I with any self respect seem to be as I used to, & as I still would be.

But even were all these reasons not – I should feel justified in this species of dissimulation for it would be cruelty to bind such a young man to such an old woman –

133

If I. or G.[283] offered – I feel that I could marry either of them, though I. . . . . . loves an other, & make a good wife though I loved another –

Whether the time will ever come when I shall forget W. & that sweet time although so short when I loved him more than life, & when I could read the same affection in his eyes, is doubtful indeed I think it will always be like a beautiful dream – like all my loves are, except music & even that seems like a distant harmonious chords brought be[284] the breeze & passes[285] (the es is added in pencil) out of sight again –

One of the kind things W. said was that line of Tennyson's about the jingle of the guinea[286]

134

Septb 9th Tuesday

Went to Bathurst to get all the black things for the mourning for poor M[r] Francis[287] Death – it was such a soft bright day – one of those days that make me feel I shall regret leaving Australia

---

If you think my young gentleman that you can go on that way with me you are mistaken – When Ad is here you treat me with the utmost rudeness & coarsness[288]. & as for riding with me or speaking kindly to me that is out of the question or to showing me the least attention you would despise and now that she is gone you come to me you want to ride with me you pay me compliments you want to enter upon arguments or laugh

135

& joke but I can tell you its no go. the tables <u>are</u> turned now – <u>she</u> runs after you <u>I</u> run away from you – & I wish you may be as happy as <u>you</u> can with her –

It is an ordeal that I must go through, whether or no – if there is any[289] power I cannot know it too soon if there is little let that little evaporate –

Wie dr Felsen uraltes Erz Ewig derselbe bleibet mein Schmerz

Meine Augen füllen sich mit Thränen wie einstmal, als meine Seele in Sehnsucht gebeugt nach Liebe u Gegenliebe seufzte – u jetzt! –

English translation of the German by Ann Sherwin:

Like the age-old ore in the rock,
my pain remains ever the same.[290]

My eyes fill with tears as in former times, when my soul groaned, weighed down with longing to love and be loved[291] – and now! –

Septb 15

Wohl unser Goldlosi ist zu dir gegangen ihr 3 seid beisammen – oh Dohl schau auf mich herab aber wein nicht sei nicht traurig – viel lieber leid ich als dß ihr littet – aber wenn es dir möglich

English translation of the German by Ann Sherwin:

Sept. 15

Indeed, our Goldlosi[292] has gone to be with you. The three of you are together. Oh, Dohl,[293] look down on me, but don't cry, don't be sad. – I'd much rather suffer myself than have you suffer – but if possible

ist schick mir nur einen Strahl von Hoffnung u Freude – denn du weißt nicht wie mein Herz von neuem blutet, wie es um dich geblutet hat – sei aber dem W. den du auf dr Welt nie gesehen hast nicht gram wenn er mich auch mißhandelt er meints nicht so bös – dß er nicht so fein u edel ist wie du ist nicht seine Schuld – Wenn ich nur wißen könnte ob ihr alle glücklich seid ich hoff es denn den Glauben an eine ewige Gerechtigkeit hab ich nicht verloren, ihr die ihr so gut auf erden wart müßt jetzt glücklicher sein, denn es strebt ja alles nach Vervollkommnung –

English translation of the German by Ann Sherwin:

send me a ray of hope and joy – for you don't know how my heart bleeds anew, the way it bled for you – but don't harbor any ill will against W[294], whom you never saw on earth, even if he mistreats me; he doesn't mean any harm – it's not his fault that he isn't as fine and noble as you. If only I could know whether you are all happy. I hope so, for I have not lost faith in an eternal justice. You who were so good on earth must be happier now, for everything strives toward perfection –

I suppose I must not send my love to anyone else –
   oh never mind if it is locked up he will give it to me when he comes back –
– I will take it as a bad omen if you dont –
Interpretation of dreams –
   Far from being vexed I am pleased at it – Nothing could have been more cold & distant than her "good morning" to me, & her fixed & stony stare as I sat down with my crochet near the window – nothing more expressive of dislike & ill will than her "good-bye" to me – she scarcely touched my fingers & turned sullenly away as she did so –

T.P.[295] says there was a little flirtation between her (Ad) & W. an inclination on both sides – but I have a notion that it was not a very satisfactory one or else Miss A.

138

would not[296] have been so cross with me. Pedremo[297] – fate cannot be helped – If I get it I shall crow double if I dont – alors je m'enferai raison.[298] The crisis is approaching – circumstances are beginning to condense around me, – did he not say "Evidence was strong against me" – & may he not say so again – & do people not outlive a great many flirtations & marry the most improbable parties after all –

Did she not at one time think G. all perfection – & did she not quarrel with Carry about Mͬ T. & now I dare say she thinks W. all perfection, at least she has been told by her mother that he would be a desirable husband for her – & so she makes up to him –

Sunday Septb 21.

Heard to day something about a gold nugget![299] Things are beginning to look suspicious, it is getting dark round me. In vain would hope whisper, her little voice is drowned by the thunder of reality & hushed by the sternness of facts – Had I never come here it would have been better for me – Certainly I have never indulged much in those sweet fancies – No it must not be Reason sets herself against hope & what can bright winged Hope do but fly away – far over the blue mountains, & perhaps like Hiawatha[300] be drowned lost vaporised in the golden distance of the setting sun over the ocean Would that I had never seen those blue eyes changing like an April shower, would that I had never felt the pressure of that hand now relaxing like the cord after the arrow is flown, never heard that voice now cold & distant never kissed those lips that

140

now speak but bitterness & contempt. What have I done that you are thus changed – Did you ask me that question one world would answer you & justify me – <u>Selfdefence</u> is the word – To shield myself my heart my happiness from your cutting words your sarcasm even your indifference, have I thus retired from you – But why am I ~~thus~~ wasting my thoughts upon you, why do I weep over a heap of ashes, why do I speak to the dead whose memory even I dare not love And have I not cause to be indignant to reproach you, did not the storm of anger give way before the mild rays of that love which ever will shine through sadly in my heart

141

Hope like a heavenly genius powerful beyond earthly sorry & obstacle is for ever falling & rising like the evening star sometimes hidden by the clouds & the blue mountains sometimes coming down so close to me that I can feel the soft flitting of his rosy wings on my cheek – he does not speak but only cheers me by his presence, he does not even look – still like faith which wants no proof <u>I feel his presence</u> And then I sink into soft dreams of the past & the future I sit & think & think & one by one he brings sweet thoughts of his own & lays them at my feet and my heart, & crowns my forehead with roses – Can he be the gay deceiver that some think him to be? Does he deceive himself & me? Oh let us not think of the tearing of that veil – It was one night coming from W. that he wrote

142

me a letter in which he says: "I gave all that I had a heart I gave what was worth worlds for worlds cannot restore those pure feelings for ever gone – but I must strive to behold you with quiet eyes unfaithful to the truth.

That letter made me very sad & I said is his love for ever gone; must I leave him & forget him? And I spoke little <u>my</u> eyes too were unfaithful to the truth –

But eight months afterwards he showed me the following lines
    Oh never say that I was false of heart
Though absence seem'd my flame to qualify
As easy night I from myself depart
As from my soul which in thy breast doth lie
that is my home of love; if I have ranged
like him that travels, I return again
Just to the time, not with time exchanged
So that myself bring water for my stain[301]

And do you really return to me after having ranged so far & so long? said I to myself & is your soul still in mine like once

in olden times? But yet I spoke nothing but was gay & laughing then Ad came & I still laughed He thought it was disguised jealousy & wrote to me "What right have you to be jealous if you think that after all you have said & done ~~you~~ I can still love you, you will be disappointed" – & he said I dreamt that Ad was feeding me with figs & you were looking as though you would poison me" – All these unkind words hurt me & I was more silent & distant than ever as I said before in selfdefence to shield my self from his arrows –

And what will come now will he say again, I might as soon depart from myself & from my soul which lies within thy breast – Oh would that he returned again how sweet would his words sound in my heart, oh how willingly

would I give him all that I have to give – her love can not compare with mine, if she has any at all – at all events it would not stand <u>his test</u> which is silence – she like T.P. says she would like to send her love to some one else but the female part of the congregation – & sends him messages by Carry & asks him for books & scent & often talks in laughing of him & he does the same, confesses at the dinnertable that he is in love with her, says he had desperate flirtations with her & so on – how does all that agree with what he said to me very seriously about George? He said: I am sure G. loves you – What makes you think so? said I – Why because he never so much as mentions your name, & I take that to be a strong sign of it. – (I think so too)

Vous croyez que c'est moi qui l'empêche de se jeter à vos pieds – vous vous trompez car je ne fais rien du tout – je suis là et je lui laisse son entièrè libertè – mais peut être – sans moi – ne se fait il jamais approché de vous –

Vous (Pauline) êtes trop sévère trop dure trop rigide – Je sais bien que de la chaleur de votre constition même vient cette tension de nerfs qui ne peut s'adoucir sans être satisfaite – mais il faut un peu dissimuler cette crude verité – vous avez changé de positions ce qui me semble être à votre avantage Une femme doit être douce comme la brise du printems[302] pliable comme le roseau attrayante pas de faiblesse et non sa force, elle doit

146

commander en ayant l'air d'obeir Je dois descendre de mon haut cheval quand il reviendra –

English translation of the French by Sharon Joffe:

I think that oiling the heart strings was a little bit of a dodge. Monsieur did not take his dashing new whip nor his fine gloves nor his stunning neck tie – perhaps he thought he would conquer without those auxiliaries –

> You believe that it is me who prevents him from throwing himself at your feet – you are mistaken because I do not do anything at all – I am there and I leave to him his entire freedom – but perhaps – without me – would he never come near you – You (Pauline) are too severe, too hard, too rigid – I know well that even the heat of your constitution comes from this tension of nevers that cannot soften without being satisfied – but it is necessary a little to dissimulate this crude truth – you have changed positions which seems to me to be to your advantage. A woman should be soft like the spring breeze, pliable like the reed attractive no weakness and not her strength, she must command while having the appearance of obeying. I must descend from my high horse when he comes back –

Octb 2ᵈ

Anne Piper[303] & Adelaide came – & I should really like to be a clever person one for instance that could see into a stone wall further than another – to explain this curious fact this phenomenon of some kind or other – Whenever Ad is here W. seems to feel an almost undisguisable dislike to me – whether he flirts with her or not in her presence he treats me if not with downright rudeness yet with coldness & contempt. Now I can examine these facts calmly & cooly whatever may have gone before

Just like his father[304].

& having a good deal of causality & being of an enquiring mind I ask this question. "What causes this change" as quite apart from present[305] feeling or future plans – Is it physical or psychological I am half inclined to the former or both[306] view being rather of that class of philosophers who like to reduce everything to physical causes – I sometimes think I would like to ask him how he feels all the time & to explain some of those symptoms – but it would be of little use, – he is too like his mother of quick perception but superficial without depth of reasoning powers.

Is it voluntary or involuntary? If the latter it would agree with the first reason above mentioned but if it is voluntary it must be the result of some argument he has had with himself the nature of [illeg.] which I cannot imagine – & which that vile principle of theirs "the least said the soonest mended" has always prevented him from telling me. It may also be half one reason & half the other – it may be because consti –

tutional, & it is a curious circumstance that his dislike seemed greatest at the same time that he pretended to like me most & is proportionately decreasing as the loving communication between us seems diminishing

Octb 8.

Quoth the Raven, "Nevermore"[307] – Il a fait des avances ce soir – faute de mieux[308] je suppose – but it is over – I can suppose only two motives either his above noticed indifferent familiarity or he is preparing for our next ride to Wyagdon which is to be to morrow or the day after – Can he not leave me in peace – he has had his turn & is now seeking pleasure else where – Pass on young heart & leave me – I ask nothing else for you have nothing else to give.

———

My dear Carry – after all the rudeness unkindness & sorrow that I have experienced through your brother you must not be surprised or hurt at the indifference with which I treat him.

that I once loved him you perhaps know – that there is still a preference for him in my heart I even now cannot deny nor perhaps sufficiently disguise but my only answer to myself has been it cannot be & that struggle has sometimes placed me in a false position.

I understand the French saying now "L'amour est une affaire sérieuse a trente ans"[309] – One has passed the thoughtlessness of childhood & youth – & in the same proportion as we do not feel sorrow in youth we neither feel pleasure – for the body is not ripe for it – that again confirms me in my theory of physical causes. A child does not feel the pain of a friend's death or any other mental grief or pleasure as its soul[310] awakens or is matured by some moral influence it becomes aware of things that were invisible before – but still sensations of all kind are

transitory easily excited & easily effaced – the death of a friend parent[311] which to the little child passed unheeded is felt more by the daughter of 15 but yet far more deeply by the daughter of 30. In the same way would a young girl who was in love & separated from the person soon forget – but love at 30 becomes a serious thing indeed.

———

How changed is Mʳ W. but that too is only a fit – But whatever comes I am content I have made up my mind & will abide by it – this last resolution has spread a calm over me which quite lights up my dark existence – I shall go back to my mother & to many friends who I trust have remained faithful[312]

& I shall part from this country which has afforded me much pleasure with affectionate feelings. –

Calm like a lake had my mind been all day – I forbore to rejoice at several things, because Prudence was at my side & Firmness – & I feel I am strong enough to hear the song of the Syren[313] because Mentor is holding my hand – Oh never never leave me again thou faithful friend[314]

Du wankelmüthiges Geschöpf warum läßt du mich den gar nicht in Frieden – Nicht ein Wort werd ich sprechen, wir werden uns trennen wie wir uns gefunden – Du magst jetzt zuschlagen du kannst mir nicht mehr weh thun.

English translation of the German by Ann Sherwin:

> You fickle creature, why don't you leave me in peace? – Not a word will I speak. We shall part just as we found each other. You can lash away now, but you can't hurt me any more.

152

Sunday Octb 12.

It was a peaceful day no acidity no ruffling no smothering no inward scowling & outward grieving no friction, no illusions or insinuations & the like disagreable things –

We went to church – & I still maintain that I feel convinced if AB. had been there W. would – but I know the rest & act thereon. I am still firm in my conduct showing as much indifference as possible without pique in my manne – Nothing short of something –

there is an alliteration which combines two of our initials expressing the only quality that we have in common which is S. & C[315] & stands for Spirit of Contradiction

———

& I really think if it was not for AB I should have forgotten it long ago –

153

Alte Sünden steigen wie Geister auf u verlangen Rache – 0 du Schicksal du hast mich so lang in Fesseln gehalten – wie bitter bereue ich jenen abscheulichen Moment wo ich die freudenlose häßliche Sünde berührte – u jetzt muß ich vielleicht so viel so theures dafür aufgeben – Was hat mich so lange Jahre abgehalten jenen Fleck reinzuwaschen u ohnedem! Nein niemals dazu bin ich zu gewißenhaft es bleibt nur ein Ausweg meine Abreise so lang als möglich zu verschieben u nach Sydney zu gehen u sehen ob ich dort Heil finden kann – Doch das Schicksal ist unerbittlich –

English translation of the German by Ann Sherwin:

> Old sins arise like ghosts and demand revenge. O fate, you have held me in chains for so long. How bitterly I regret that hideous moment when I touched joyless, ugly sin – and now I may have to pay so dearly for it. What kept me from washing that spot clean[316] all these years anyway? No, never. I am too scrupulous for that. There is only one way out: postpone my departure as long as possible and go to Sydney and see whether I can find salvation there. Yet fate is unrelenting –

You sweet little bird do not repeat that name so often before my window.[317]

154

Thursday Octb 16.1856.

Dear Mrs Suttor & all the party came back to day – We went to meet them as far as Mrs Campbell's[318] fence – it was a long & lovely ride – although! they are all looking so well & they are so happy – only over me[319] is a shadow cast – I know well what makes me so sad – but it serves me right & is just punishment for my double impudence – Now it is useless to say I will never do it again – I went out on the moonlight verandah & heard again that song – oh it was so cold & inside all were so happy – oh would that I had never come here –

It is inexpressibly sad to me it so completely overshadows my heart & my mind that I feel my face growing deadly pale – my mind wander far away to moments of happiness

155

in the past & the blank desert of the future, so that I can scarcely hear or understand what is said to me – What will become of me! 2 months more of this silent sorrow & then separation to the grave – When he is married I will come back not till then – May my strength last long enough – may he never know it all, & yet how I long sometimes to pour out my whole heart to him – how handsome he looked on the verandah to day – but no he has not one thought of sympathy for me – he lies on the sofa the whole evening without ever speaking a word – he goes to bed in silence without raising his eyes – It is true I scarcely ever raise mine – mine are now quiet eyes unfaithful to the truth – had I but known all this sooner – how much pain I should have been saved.

156

I have quite made up my mind that I will not do the least thing towards an approach – yet I do not see the necessity of keeping at such pitch – fork distance.

I knowing my own strictness sternness severity & hardness – I may relent a little – would I not wish to spend the short time that is left to me in in peace with a dear brother – let us part in friendship Willy you will ever be dear to me as a brother & dearer – too dear for a husband – Much wrong have I done myself by my pride, my unbending iron muscled pride I have fought a hard battle which is not yet ended –[320]

157

The pain of parting is deep & bitter & can it seem strange that I should wish to go – Yet reason is so preponderating so evidently on my side – that although it cannot lessen the pain – yet it gives me strength to dissimulate & I talk laugh & play when I would rather sit down in silent sorrow & let the tears stream down my cheeks – Yes Willie you do not know it nor does anyone else how deeply I love you – & yet I will part from you for ever without a word – It is the punishment due to my sins – And when I am gone you will laugh & say she was not worth having – & I am quite satisfied that you should not regret me for else you would be as unhappy as I am & may that never be may you rather condemn & forget me than be be as unhappy as I am. –

158

It was our fate that we should not understand each other

> My heart is sair, I dare na tell
> My heart is sair for somebody
> I could walk a winter night
> For the sake of Somebody
> Oh – hon for Somebody
> Oh – hey for Somebody
> I could range the world round
> For the sake of Somebody.
>
> Ye powers that smile on virtuous love
> O sweetly smile on Somebody
> Fra ilka danger keep him free
> And send me safe my Somebody
> Oh – hon for Somebody
> Oh – hey for Somebody
> I wad do – what would I not
> For the sake of Somebody.[321]

———

159

Wandering Willie.

> Here awa, there awa wandering Willie
> Here awa there awa, haud awa home
> Come to my bosom my ain only dearie
> Tell me then bringst my Willie the same.
>
> Winter winds blew loud & cauld at our parting
> Fears for my Willie brought tears to my ee
> Welcome now Simmer, & welcome my Willie
> The simmer to nature, my Willie to me.
>
> Rest ye wild storms in the cave of your slumbers
> How your dread howling a lover alarms
> Wauken ye breezes roll gently ye ~~waves~~ billows
> And waft my dear laddie once mair to my arms
>
> But oh! if he's faithless & minds ne his Naunie
> Flow still between us thou wide roaming main
> May I never see it, may I never trow it
> But dying believe that my Willie's my ain.[322]

119

160

Nov. 15

Il faut se faire raison[323] – & I hope Mr Gouldesbury's[324] words may prove true – & that it will be but the parting that is painful – What & should there not be one[325] among the handsome clever talented civilized men of Europe one who could make me forget this roughshod Australian lad! I shall find many to love me more – & that may attract my attention too – After all what can I find to love like admire or regret in him? He is clever & tolerably well educated but still more conceited & presumptuous he is handsome but rude & overbearing – he is tender <u>sometimes</u> but generally cold & inconsiderate – it aime par élan comme moi[326] – only with

161

the difference that when my fit is over I am quiet while he goes from attraction to repulsion – Could I ever have been happy with a man who though of high principles & honest conduct is so different in manner – with an unshaven unpolished unhewn narrow-minded colonist whose idiosyncracy is all over the world is prejudice ignorance & conceit – Could one possibly put a roughsplit log of timber & a finely polished piece of wood together into the same piece of furniture without creating great want of harmony? No – therefore W & I would never have been happy together – I should always have been obliged to conceal my superiority & he from envy & pride would have made my life miserable. I who value polite calm gentle kind people so much –

162

no give him the silly uneducated unfeeling girl, whom he can look down on to whom he can be as rude as he pleases because they both know no better –

What kind of a plant is Love? Is it a hardy or a delicate one is it luxurious spreading sweet – scented fruitful bright to behold hidden under leaves betraying itself by its perfume – or is it a weed thorny & prickly growing among rocks, thriving is battering storms, or bending to the tempest raising its head its sunshine – or is it a tough pine dark & solitary – or a stern oak hiding its virtue in its innermost heart, or wavering & light as the silvery birch or is it a rosebud scorched in the

163

heat of the day, or a primrose crushed for ever by one rude footstep? – Whenever I think of love I come to the conclusion that I know nothing about it – Sometimes I fancy I love then again I am thoroughly convinced that it is all but a dream – who can tell me whether he & I love each other? Could we thus leave each other to all appearance for ever if we loved – & yet my heart so often calls in pain & pleasure I love him Love has been so much talked spoken & written & thought of that it ought to be a great thing or is my feeling of duty equally great that or even greater that it can master love? – All the other passions rise in rebellion against love they always side with reason & love this time is almost conquered – chained fettered imprisoned but not dead – no it will never die –

164

I understand W. a little better than formerly – but never could he by actions manner or look convince me that he loved me – on the contrary[327] he manner always went to prove the opposite – but <u>now</u> I make allowance for that want of steadiness & selfpossession he has his father's love of the sex & his mother's flightiness how could he see what he does & looks. He has the most excitable nervous system I ever saw the least thing makes his eyes flash his cheek grow pale, raises his anger or makes him weary ashy – grey – what wonder then that he should be affected by the presence of such a large & handsome body as AB. I really do not think now that he loves her[328] with all his mind & all his soul & all his body – it is only that sort of attraction that one body feels for another & would feel if they were blindfolded – that I have felt a hundred times towards

165

other strangers where love was out of the question – <u>remember the man at Penrith</u>[329] that was most decidedly only a physical attraction an awfully powerful one certainly – that is the way love is pleasant but marriage in our acceptation of the word[330] is truly abominable it may be necessary but it is beastly – How many can I remember that have created that sweet passion of the moment in me which when combined with mental admiration is the divinest feeling I know, but like the rainbow it can last but a few moments. – I: – do you remember that night! we were both entranced & saw not nor knew what we were doing the same trance I felt at at[331] S. & at O.[332] only that the last had a most unpleasant aftertaste or reaction – but that pleasure must be bought by long fasting & abnegation of mind & body for thinking or talking too much of love spoils the appetite like poking about the kitchen spoils your desire for dinner

166

Nov. 18

Something was the matter with W. to day We had a strange conversation at breakfast in which 2 things were manifest – the cause of his dislike of M[rs] Barton[333] very prominent & M[rs] Suttors opinion of me as to my taste for bushlife[334] – she may be right though I scarcely know it for a fact myself – after all I should positively be thrown away if I had to wash up dishes make bread & mend old rags in a bark hut – What would be the use of my ever having learnt to read or to play on the Piano[335] if my end & aim in life is to be such work as the commonest Servant can do? & endure so many other unpleasantries besides – No – let birds of a feather flock together. I feel certain that AB will make him an excellent wife five hundred times better I could have done.

167

Would that I were gone – although I wish to stay for M[rs] Suttor's sake, He shows me such perfect indifference & such unbounded admiration for her which he himself neither can nor tries to deny – that my love for him sinks deeper & deeper into my heart – not even to his mother can I speak of it much less to any one else – No indifference does not express it – Aversion dislike, coldness – he says I rewarded his love with cruel suspicion – but we never understood & consequently never loved each other –

Nov 26.

Caught in an awful thunderstorm coming from Alloway Bank[336] – M^{rs} S can not believe that I am going –

What beautiful eyes that boy has – oh never shall I forget my Australian lad – his eyes have an expression of deep & unuttered – something –

Like in all great but particularly sad events in my life it takes me a long time to realize & bring to my mind as fulfilled those passed & dreaded facts –

How many times have I thought of things that I would write or send to friends long out of this world – & then suddenly the reality flashes across my mind – So it is again now – the necessity of leaving him & if possible forgetting him often vanishes out of consciousness & the old so sternly repressed love rises up in my heart expanding its powerful wings in the sunshine of hope – But how soon does the bitter cold gale of unpleasant reality sweep over the snowy rosy wings & love furls & folds then hiding its downy beauty stooping in silence seeking to understand what is commonly called contentment.

It so often strikes me as impossible – & yet the contrary seems just as improbable –

170

Dec 6.

It is a balmy evening after a thunderstorm – I never saw such a splendid sunset By some impulse my thoughts turned towards the mountains toward W. – But I am so thoroughly convinced of finding no sympathy there, that they come back to me echoless – It is like an amputation that I am putting off from day to day – yet knowing that it must come, wishing it was over.

I made a paramouche[337] for George & am going to write him a few lines with it – but am puzzled what to say or rather how to say it[338] –

171

My dear M.ʳ George – No that will never do – & yet I dont see why I should not – well My dear M.ʳ George – Your mother told me you wanted a Paramouche & I begged leave of her to make you one – that you might remember me as doing a kind office for you – & I chose the blue color the Australian blue because this sunny land with all its recollections will ever be dear to me, when I am far away in Solitude – it would be the country of my choice did Fate not again drive me out on the wild ocean of life – I am going – but I trust you will all remember me – I was sorry to hear your

172

brother F was ill, & hope he is quite well now – Pray give him my kindest – I will not say love for that he would not care for – but kindest remembrance & the same to M.ʳˢ Acrec[339] & I shall always be glad to hear through M.ʳˢ W H. Suttor how you are all getting on –

Oh what blockheads are these wise persons who imagine a child should understand everything it reads.

It would not take Malthus[340] big volume to prove that no existing circumstance could at this time be what it is unless all preceeding circumstances had been from the beginning of time precisely what they were[341]

Dec 13. Saturday

Went to Bathurst – W. est malelevé au possible[342] – I however took no notice of it – we asked him to come to Carwinyan[343] – he gave no answer probably because of our difference last Sunday & my silence at the woolshed – In the evening I walked in the garden – I had talked to Maro[344] & his sweet Italian voice & accent reminded me of days gone by of Gianetto & Pietro[345] I gave him a book – & the Sun with last rosy blush lit up the sky – the wind blows seaward & I must go – I was walking in the perfume of the honeysuckle & oh that music wrung my heart with fear anticipation & regret – I shall walk in the glittering ballroom in glittering dress in the crowded operahouse[346] surrounded by

music perfume elegance wit mirth & flattery all my senses charmed with magic art – & like a dream like a vision on the distant ocean shall I see Australia with her sad gumtrees her starlight her rocky solitudes her silent calm moonlight nights & I shall see Willie & remember the time when we loved each other.

A youngster like that may do very well to flirt with or peradventure to marry if he should have the qualities necessary for a husband – but to love!! give me the ripe man who creates & feels pleasure! –

Sunday Dec the 14.

Heard M.̲ʳ Schwin[347] preach a sermon on "Who is this that cometh out of the wilderness like pillars of smoke, perfumed with myrrh & frankincense"[348] – I thought it good & impressive & in some places poetical though the delivery was sometimes affected –

AB. came in the afternoon, & W. without exactly flirting always kept near her & let neither EA.[349] nor Ten approach which trouble he might have saved himself for she turns her back to all of them except the one whose "<u>prospects are not exactly dark</u>".

When she was gone W. gammoned to be very affectionate with me & all sorts of nonsense & brought me flowers & offered me his arm but it did not make much impression except that it reminded me of former days. Whatever can it be if it is not love that influences him to whenever she comes – & ~~to~~ raises his spirits so high that a reaction must come –

<u>Monday</u>

And come it did – to day he is in deep gloom & thought he speaks to no one, he is away all day long dines by himself & in the evening having him on the sofa in the diningroom till about 10 o'clock he at last makes an effort & comes into the drawingroom[350] & asks to hear the song we used to sing at Boree[351] – I am glad that I acted yesterday as I did – showed as much indifference as I possibly could without beeing rude – & really according to my old theory what one pretends a long time at last becomes actual & upon my word I know what I thought when I went to bed about W. & Ac.

177

I am impatient to be gone.

It tantalizes me for I cannot deny it there is still a silent hidden preference for that boy in my heart[352] that I shall never be able to conquer – the least moment of indulgence of inattention, or slackening of rein, the least little breeze of sentiment would blow up a blazing flame & the steeds of my soul would bolt at once into a mad career & plunge Pallas[353] into unknown depths of misery – I like to write about him & to think a little of him although it is forbidden fruit.

The other night at Carwinyan[354] that beautiful music went streaming through my heart till the fountain of tears sparkled in the moonlight – & I said in my innermost heart – oh Willie leave me not be my stronghold & my support for I am weak.

Dec 16.

I think W. feels that he was a little inconsistent the other day – this evening he said good night to me with that steadfast look that seems to say "<u>Trust me</u>" & with that lingering gentle shake of hands that seems to say "<u>leave me not yet</u>" – but it may also mean nothing at all – et je resterai impassible – en tous cas il faut se faire raison.[355]

Dec 20.

Had a very long ride & it was very hot – I noticed a peculiar coolness on Mʳ W's part on one occasion – which seemed strange I walk about as one in a dream it is in vain I talk myself into the belief of <u>something</u> – & why I cannot be more indifferent is too me a perfect mystery – Why can we not live near each other in peace – why why why? a thousand things? –

179

Guillaume est jaloux de son frère c'est inexplicable – mais Sa fierté est indomptable – Ma foi je voudrais me venger de ce jeune homme quand même toute ma vie fut sacrifiée[356] mais je n'ai point de génie c'est qu'il faudrait tout feindre et si adroitement, ah si j'avais quelqu'ami qui m'aidat – Mais pourquoi ne pas chercher l'assistance de sa mère? Je voudrais l'épouser et ceremonie faite lui lancer la fouder aux pieds et l'envoyer chez Mademoiselle – car il ne mérite pas mieux que je suis bête et miserable de me tourmenter pour un jeune vaux-rien un coureur un

180

malhonnête, tour a tour gallant et brutal auprès des femmes rempli d'amour propre de vanité de fierté d'ignorance de morgue et d'inconsistence

– Et pourquoi est ce donc que je l'aime pourquoi ai-je refusé George & Edouard? D'abords il est jeune et beau et riche et puis – il me maltraite – et pourtant à présent dans ce moment[357] je l'épouserais pour me venger – Ah plus à Dieu que j'éusse assez de volonté pour accomplir cela.

– Mon aimable petit Frank[358] comme tu es gentil avec tes beaux yeux et ta bouche ravissante et ta douceur et ton silence rêveur tu comprends que mton frère me deteste et pourtant sa vanité le

181

fait être jaloux – tu le suis car en sa presence tu n'oses t'approcher de moi, à peine si tu lêves les yeux sur moi –

English translation of the French by Sharon Joffe:

> William is jealous of his brother it is inexplicable – but his pride is indomitable – My faith I would like to take revenge for myself on this young man even as my life is sacrificed but I have no genius it is that it is necessary to pretend all and so skillfully, ah if I had a friend to help me – But why not look for help from his mother? I would like to marry him and ceremony done kick him and send him to Miss – because he does not deserve more that I am stupid and miserable to torument myself for a young nothing a rover a dishonest, by turns gallant and brutal towards

women full of self love of vanity of pride of ignorance of hautiness and of inconsistence

– And why is it thus that I love him why did I refuse George and Edward?

Firstly he is young and handsome and rich and then – he mistreats me – and however at present in this moment I would marry him to get revenge – Oh more to God that I had enough will to accomplish that.

– My lovely little Frank[359] how you are kind with your beautiful eyes and your delightful mouth and your kindness and your dreamy silence you understand that your brother hates me and however his vanity makes him be jealous – you know it because in his presence you dare not approach me, if you hardly raise your eyes on me –

Dec. 25. Christmas day

It was a long hot fatiguing day – & yet had W. not been as he was I should have been happy – But he cannot see my heart how full of love it is & my eyes of tears – or else he does not care – & a flash of revenge shoots across my heart – But no he is not so indifferent or else he would show it in his manner

---

Would that I were dead rather than endure this misery –
I am impatient to be gone.

Had music in the evening but it came not from the heart – I was quite out of sorts & would rather have sat down & cried – than laugh

& talk with those gentlemen – When AB flirts he yawns & stretches himself – but when I flirt he shuts himself up & wont talk to me – can it be possible that he is jealous of –––––[360] ? No – Impossible – He has a curious way of trying to prevent me from occupying my thoughts with other people So he did with George with M̄ʳ Bode & M̄ʳ Acres. & Ernest[361] – But it is no use speculating – I must chance it & noft fret.

Monday[362]

There are always so many people staying at Brucedale that one cannot enjoy one's life at all – I wish they were all gone, & we could have a quiet evening to ourselves – But wishing it as idle as sorrow – I almost wish to see W. smile & happy although it would show he did not care – It seems to me sometimes that I cannot go that I shall not go & my imagination clings with tenacity to that thought but it is all deception – the separation is fulfilled in truth "Love lies bleeding"[363] those words that I heard & heeded not sound now like a dirge – Oh Willie farwel[364] you love me not – or you could not be so silent. The wind is howling loud & the clouds are sweeping over the cold sky – on such a night I stood on the Verandah at Wallawa[365] & deeply did I long for you to love me & protect me through life. But you came not –

184

New Year's day. Thursday Jan 1.1857.

this day is always of sad recollection to me this day 10 years ago the Countess K.[366] came into my room before breakfast & fatal & yet happy was the result – Yes happy because I came here where I met the only man I have ever truly loved the only one I will ever love On this day far back in the recess of my childhood we used all to assemble round my fathers[367] table – there were the mysterious presents for all, the children to the parents what their small means afforded & the parents to the children what was pleasing & useful – there we need to find long & secret wishes realized through the divining power of love there tears of gratitude & pleasure would fill our youthful eyes, & Father & mother[368]

185

stood by in silent pleasure watching the happiness of their children – Then came the family breakfast the only one throughout the whole year & the harmony & peace were exquisite – And now – where are they all gone? Round the small table shall sit but three where once were 9.[369] their hearts are filled with sorrow – & mine is doubly so – & my eyes are full of tears when I think of Willie whom I am going to leave never to see again.

What is it my boy that weighs on your mind that drives the smile from your lips, that makes your brow so pale? Is the pent up stream gushing eddying foaming & rising within your heart? I know you would lay down & die for her she occupies your thoughts day & night & her beauty is ever present before your eyes – her sweet

186

voice is ever ringing in your ears & her soft look is still thrilling your heart – her touch is magic her presence a charm – What oh[370] what keeps you back? – Do you not know that every thing is favorable to your wishes <u>except one</u> & that might be overcome for the love of you. Cheer up my boy hope shows you the bright to morrow My love for you unworthy of your notice as it may be is too deep for leaden selfishness to sink into it.

187

The moral like the physical world has two sides to it, a dark & a light one. Hope is the light that shows us the creation brightly & despair darkens what otherwise would be seen if not bright yet[371] clear in the [illeg.] calm twilight of contentment. To be led away by either of these is want of faith anciently called compensation.

Compensation & Hope are sisters but how often does the night of despair seem to annihilate them – I am in the middle of night now – when every thing wears a different aspect from what it does in the light of Hope – Trees sun ghosts rocks mountains rivers like oceans there is a mysterious murmuring in the forest & flowers, clouds

Jan 11

A fortnight more & then I must go – Farewell you all Mother & son[372] Farewell.

Sunday Jan 18.

Last Thursday Friday & Saturday I was very ill – & not much better to day – in the bitterness of my own blame I must say it serves me right – but it was my fate & I suppose I could not help it – it is a lesson for the future but what is the good of that –

It is inexpressibly touching to me how Willy looks at me or comes & stands near me when any other person says anything about his heart or his love – Somebody once said at dinner "Where can your heart be"? – He blushed & looked up at me expressing as plain as looks could say it – you know all about it – & today again when Mrs Wise[373] said "he does not know where his heart is" – dear W. came near me & looked at me with his dear honest face –

You are the West – Wind & I am the willow tree –[374]

Sunday Jan 25th

Mrs Suttor told me to day I had better go – when Mrs G. S. goes – –[375] & so I must – away with this weakness that makes me linger & put off my journey – He has no spirit to move him – it is all evaporated – & that is love – but what is love – how foolish it is to allow those romantic notions to take root in a young persons head – now I am disappointed – when B[376] & I broke our engagement I did not care half so much

I was not disappointed then for Love of life was still in me – –[377] & even now I will not be disappointed I will not be bowed down – "my faith in time is large"[378] – I forget all the charms of old Europe the delight of travelling the romance of history the beauty of a civilized & cultivated country the charms of refined society the magic of music of moral independence the perfume of liberty the pleasure of seeing my old friends & last but not least of all the satisfaction of doing what I consider to be my duty –

– And why should I regret so much to leave that one being ~~who~~ with whom I have no sympathy or rather who is perfectly indifferent – Am I such a fool & so weak – & is my

reason & my good sense so entirely obscured that I can not perceive plain facts which have stared me in the face these two years & more & which I distinctly remember to have seen even more clearly than I do now – But no – I have faith in myself in my[379] strength in[380] my lightness – & I trust that the sunshine of cheerfulness the calmness of philosophy & the perfume of hope will veil the void his absence will cause – Love never was a serious thing with me & now I shall know no more about it – with this last event shall close all that I shall ever have to do with it – & so ends my sojourn in Australia.

Had you loved me as I loved you nothing would have separated us but where there is no [illeg.] there is no strength –

192

Sunday feb 1.1857.

Too many people here to be happy – rode to Alloway B.[381] in the evening was almost sorry poor little C.[382] was there how many things I would have said to W. – Oh how that boy can touch the inmost chords of my heart – how he came & sat near me on that sofa that his elbow touched mine – oh that I should leave you my own sweet Willie

Feb 2ᵈ 1857 Monday left Brucedale[383]

Baulkham Hills[384]
Jan 6. Friday[385] –

Old Germany beckons to me in the distance like an old neglected friend who now is ready to welcome the traveller back with treasures of pardon in his heart – Yes I will go back & sit by my own mother's side & hear the wind roaring outside & have a frosty Christmas once more – & see the snow drifted against the window You Southrons[386] do not know the soft calm snowlight –

193

However painful I feel I have done my duty in resisting – for we both can do better – he is too like his father & I know what that means. Every door is shut except that leading to Romance only I would never let him think that I did not love him that would not have been true may he remember me as the first blush of the rising sun on a glorious day.[387] May I marry my soldier's son & he his soldier's daughter – she is just the sort of person he could love or ill-use ~~what~~ without her feeling in the least disturbed by either.

Boy's love is a beautiful plant though so delicate that the least storm destroys it – sometimes it ripens into manhood but rarely –

But Love real strong love outraged set at defiance outlives all bides his time & takes his revenge.

Love might say of himself Im Sturme wachsen mir die Flügel[388]

194

There is a deep meaning in that legend of the Spartan boy[389] who suffered the stolen fox to gnaw his very vitals the while he covered him with his tunic, & preserved on his brave face a calm smile of unconcern. Most of us have a stolen fox somewhere, but the weak nature writhes & moans & is delivered from its torment while the bold unflinching spirit preserves a gallant bearing before the world & scorns to be relieved from the fangs that are draining its very life away.

Greycliffe[390] Saturday
Feb 21.

Brother mariness[391] we will wander no more – say the Latos eaters[392] & I must leave this lovely country these true & kind people – I must go back to that land that will bring back to my mind so many bitter thoughts of past & present

195

How much I have suffered there, how much more will I suffer now that those whom I knew & who knew me are gone My mother my only friend there to you will I return you are the only attraction –[393]

How beautiful to the mind & the eye is this[394] Harbour[395] where I had hoped to be at rest at last. How deep blue the sea how bright the sun, how pure the breeze – how tired I was last night & my tired eyelids fell upon my tired eyes & I went to sleep with the sighing of the seawaves – My eyes have grown dim with gazing upon the polarstar – I gaze forward neither up nor down – for there is so much before me & round me –

196

I hope it may be my fate to see Tennyson[396] – In mind I imagine him like M[r] Maitland[397] in appearance like old Beethoven[398] – What a vision that young M. was – not a handsome one either but not to be forgotten. With his intelligent little dark eyes & his large nose & his long legs – as we sat on the grass under the rose-bush eating watermelon – & C[pt] B. with his fine profile against the evening sky slowly smoking his cigar – that was on the 4th of March 1855. a Sunday I think it was. Him I shall never see again how strange that all those I feel attrackted to I must never see again –

March 1 Sunday

J.B.[399] is really one of the most fascinating men I have ever known – & I am pleased to see he is on such good terms with his wife – He drove me to Coodgee Bay[400] & there we sat on the rocks watching the roaring waves what words he spoke to me then but in the evening how cold how cutting how Satanic he was & yet – how soft & gentle he can be

March [illeg.] 6.

Old Man worries me to death what shall I do? I wish he would give me my money pay my bill & be off – though he really ought to give me a whip it was too shabby presenting me with that stick –

My hat looked very well almost too stylish – foolish old man did not see it wants me to – – but I said no no –

198

What a sweet pleasant evening I spent. I came in early & there he sat never looking at me & still I felt his presence – he walked home with me & he gently pressed my arm – it made me quite thoughtful – but his heart is locked & the[401] old love alone has the key of it. I like his laugh & what clean white teeth he has – but he is a very nervous irritable temperament Sometimes his eyes glare sometimes they are softly half closed – he did not give me his arm till he were heard the door close, for[402] the old Lady looked after us –

I wish he would come with me tomorrow – but he wont –

199

Son I went nearly stark staring mad when I heard you talk to George –

Father I'll go crazy if you don't.

He is determined it must come to a conclusion – but I have made up my mind – & must see what can be got out of him. –

March 8. Sunday

Spent a pleasant enough day at Wooloomooloo[403] – In the evening went to see M[rs] Francis[404] – & such a hullabaloo there was & poor me got into & when I offered to come & help I was told to please myself – & when I went home how distant how cold he was – he never offered me his arm & how he said goodnight! – But what am I thinking of why should I wish him to be otherwise – it has always been my fate where I feel attractted there seems a corresponding repulsion

200

Farewell F.N.[405] you shun me, good night – I will retire into my solitude

9.[406]

Spent the evening at home it poured heavily – & Cornelius W.U.[407] was there it was as good as a comedy. I wished there was a Piano. At all events it made us laugh – I went to the[408] window & looked in the direction where F.N.[409] lives but he does not think of me –

<u>Wednesday</u>

Had another pleasant evening ~~at home~~ in Cumberland St[410] We looked at Burns[411] works & he read many of his poems how sweet & easy to him is the scotch tongue to him – M^r F said what a strech[412] on caledonian liberality to bring home that Pineapple[413] – but he has none of that closeness about him only necessary economy – I could not afford to spend so much did

I not get it so easily – but however there we sat, looking at prints reading Poetry & talking though not one word of love – could he be submissive I think he could – In the evening I made them some toddy & they got quite excited over it – but oh if my father was alive I would ask for no other home but to be with him. Sometimes I feel quite biologised – that evening I could not have raised my eyes to him – though I sat near him & he came closer & closer his arm almost touched mine I asked him some question about the engravings before us & he leaned over till his glossy black hair touched my cheek it sent a thrill through me I drew back slowly I was in a trance –

202

12[414]

Rain all day long went out driving with M<u>r</u> Barton – Expect old man is vexed – he gave me Vanity fair[415] & asked me who my jeweller was. In the evening I went to M<u>rs</u> Francis[416] – F. N.[417] showed me a beautiful book – but then he went away & never came back the whole evening – but no – I will not be disappointed – like George I suppose he thinks it necessary to screw up sometimes.

Friday the 20th

Went to Parramatta[418] in the steamer with Mr Barton had a tête à tête dinner champaigne & cold chicken it was all very nice – Is it not strange coincidence that George & I should come out the very same day – who knows but no – he is too proud to come

near one a second time it is a pity I might have made him a very good wife. He is very good looking neither too clever nor too stupid very good tempered & tolerably well off – now that I am free I need not mind marrying a poor man – He sat very near me this morning but I should never have courage to tell him what[419] I think he said something this morning about "Long long ago" what did he mean – Will he come out on Friday – I fear not –

Willy is a dear good boy he is not quite reconciled but I trust it will turn out well –

came back by rail – in the evening Tochet[420] was there – he is a nice looking timid young man of 23. a Creole from the Mauritins[421] passionately fond

of music – he has the softness of the southern climate – & his face[422] is generally pale & calm – yet sometimes soft rays of expression glide gently over it or a momentary thought brightens his large gray eye – he played at Whist with me – heart is his favorite color like Ws. I [illeg.] [illeg.] to play Diamond[423] for the sake of AB.

– And where is the Napier[424] romance? Where? I dont know? he was too much of an Anchorite[425] for me –

March 23rd

Dined at the Wauts[426] I should not like to see either of those girls married to ~~the~~ W. if they were ever so rich – Alice sings well – were too late for train had to wait sat at the station talking of the future – oh why did George write those initials of the table –

24

Picnic on Manly Beach[427] – got wet through it was all very calm & pleasant Mr Barton is a little bit of a flirt – but I will let him be – he is a good fellow for all that.

Thursday March 26
1857.

Got up early to see the eclipse It was getting cold & dark I stood alone against the Flagstaff when a well known form appeared among the people – it was F.N[428] – I know his walk & figure from a thousand & his smile & his thoughtful intelligent look but he did not come near me T.[429] came & asked me in his gentle voice if I was afraid – I was afraid but not[430] of [illeg.] earthly things.

206

At last that grand Picnic is over – some of the men were not bad but rather conceited – I can tell Mr C. that I will take his impudence down a little before I have anything to do with him. Diverty[431] is also going they are fine looking men – Mr Cardiffe[432] was also there but such a doleful looking face I have not seen this long time – a smile seems out of possibility

In the evening I played at cards with Tochet – his eyes were sunk – he looked languid & when I said goodnight to him, he did not raise his eyes – he is very like Willie only more gentle & wellbred

Friday 28.

My own good Willy left to day & a pouring wet day it was we were a party of 9 horse – George rode only with M[rs] Doyle[433] & An.[434] with me – he came out a little more – I like all the Suttors – Would that I had courage to tell George what I think but the words will not come over my lips – perhaps it is better not – how soft they all are – I never saw the like – What shall I do will the spirit move me & put irresistible words into my mouth –? –

M[r] Barton gave me a beautiful bracelet – & I want several things more S.[435] succeeded beyond expectation

---

Would that my wish could be realized – I wish it with all my heart – but see no chance –

208

29.

I have resolved to write to him he shall at all events not mistake my motives for they were as pure as crystal –

31.

I have written to him – he was eager to get the letter – but when he had it he hid himself & did not appear for ever so long – However we talked much about it though in an unsatisfactory manner – he said "will you not be my friend because I cannot say I love you with all my heart" – I said I dont want half of your heart – But he is a good boy though so gentle & as we ran to the steamer that cloudy morning – he said It is not fair you punish me too hard to say you will never bestow a single thought upon me – He said in his sweet voice come out on Friday night that is the

best plan – & that voice haunted me all day long – May I soon forget him –

How cold it is – came down in the steamer all by myself it poured torrents of rain. Good old Barton was there waiting for me – he is a kind old fellow – How bitter Mrs Simpson[436] was about people who get [illeg.] more than others out of others – Perhaps because neither she nor her daughter are so successful –

April 1. Wednesday

Did a lot of business – dear old Barton very kind did not insist on dragging me out – & spent such a pleasant evening at home – How handsome Martin, how interesting Tochet & how well Massé[437] sings but of all I prefer T. – One man soon makes me forget another – Yesterday I fancied I heard George's voice all day

210

& to day Tochets dark blue eyes haunt – me – he is so like Willie – those same eyes that are grey by day ~~light~~, & light up phosphorescent blue in the evening – we played at cards & won everything – how he blushed when I said I was thinking of him – & how fond of music he is – there he sits in the corner of the sofa near the Piano his head leaning on his hand, Byron[438] attitude his eyes bent down – emotion rises to his forehead when I have done playing he gets deadly pale

Massé seemed lost in thought when I played that Nocturne[439] I am very fortunate in finding such good company in a boarding house –[440]

211

Rain rain rain & nothing but rain all day long – today however I was not sorry as it gave me a pretext for remaining at home I think T. was a little jealous yesterday seeing B. always about me – he walked sulkily out of the room – B. is hard to shake off sometimes – but however I got him into good humour again – & by chance we always come to be partners at cards & curious to say when it was his lead I said in my own mind – Tochet do play hearts – & by chance he <u>did</u> play hearts – that happened twice – is there a communication between him & me? –

April 3ᵈ

Ride the mare Peggy every day fine delightful horse – had a party at Mʳˢ Bzellats[441] last night – that odious Clarkson was there – I like Deverty[442] fifty times better – I biologized Cardiffe at supper – he looked up with his large blue eyes & after a while when I was drinking champagne returned the compliment several times I stood him near in the quadrille[443] & while we were doing the grande ronde he held my hand so gently & looked down into my eyes for he is very tall so slowly & quietly – but still I think him stupid –

not to be compared to my little Tochet in gentleness nor in beauty to Martin nor in cleverness to Marcel Massé – We had such a pleasant soirée musicale at home – Massé sings very well & Roquelle[444] plays beautifully Tochet listened to me – I saw the color rising to his fair forehead – I sat on the chair & he on the sofa & he leaned his arm towards me still far away – but oh how sweet is his presence – What was the impulse that led him out of the room when I sat near B? Ah me – how intemperate I am – fortunately I get sober so quickly –[445]

April 5.

this is my last Sunday in Sydney so I suppose –

Quelle chose que l'amour – n'arriverais-je donc jamais à savoir ce que c'est – je ne puis pas dire combine de peine T. me fait – il me fuit il m'attire et qu'ai je donc fait pour qu'il me traite avec tous de dedain – du premier moment il m'a fait impression je ne l'oublirai jamais – tu ne sais pas le plaisir que j'éprouve en me trouvant vis à vis de toi à la table de jeu où de te voir près du piano quand je joue de voir ton attention à la musique comme tu comprends bien mes morceaux favoris – ah j'aime tout jouer ceux que tu aimes entendre – Dis moi donce – pourquoi tu[446] m'évites – pourquoi êtes vous si silencieux? Sont ce les visites de M. B qui vous contrarient? qu'en pensez vous – il est d'ageun[447] age à être mon père, il est marié sa femme ainsi que sa fille sont

mes amis – il voit que mon frère est parti et que je ne puis pas à moi seule faire tous les préparatifs du voyage il m'offre sa voiture il m'aide et me conseille comme il le ferait pour sa fille – N'ai je mes assez de chagrin dans ce monde pour que vous ne m'en fassiez pas aussi –

Vous ne me parlerez plus j'en suis sûre je ne verrai plus vos yeux si pleins de douce mélancolie "Vous n'avez pas besoin de moi" avez vous dit – vous vous trompez

———

Vous jouez comme une femme doit jouer – et une femme doit avoir du sentiment.[448]

English translation of the French by Sharon Joffe:

> What a thing is love – would I never thus come to know what it is – I am not able to say how much sorrow T. gives me – he runs away from me he attracts me and what have I thus done that he treats me with all disdain – from the first moment he made an impression on me I will never forget it – you do not know the pleasure that I feel on finding myself opposite you at the game table or to see you near the piano when I play to see your attention to the music as you understand my favorite pieces well – oh I love to play all those that you like to hear – Tell me therefore – why do you avoid me – why are you so silent? Are these the visits from M. B.[449] that make you contrary? what do you think of it – he is of an age to be my father, he is married his wife as well as his daughter are my friends – he sees that my brother has left and that I cannot make the preparations for the trip all alone he offers me his car he helps me and advises me like he would do for his daughter – do I not have enough sadness in this world that you cause me worry too –

You will not speak to me more I am sure of it I will not see any longer your eyes so full of sweet melancholy "You don't need me" – you are mistaken

You play like a woman must play – and a woman must have feeling

One thing is certain that I must not let Mr B. come here any more

---

I find myself getting very like W.

It is a pleasure to sit down & write about T – as I cannot see him not speak to him – I saw them all in the gardens though they did not see me – I know his voice & figure out of hundreds Allons faire la ronde par ici[450] – he said – but never looked up perhaps he did not want to see me – I shall ask him tomorrow if I can muster courage it is absurd how awkward one sometimes feels although he is too much a stranger to be intimate & still too much of an acquaintance to be shy –

But so it is – to Massé I could talk & say anything & when T. comes I feel like in the warm spring air after a cold winter – And he of all men avoids me & treats me with the completest indifference – I must mind what I am about as well with B. as with T.

How stupid this book is getting – no more bursts of enthusiasm on any subject

---

On Easter Sunday I saw P.T[451] for the last time as I stood at the window

Vous me quittez – je vous regrette mais vous ne le saurez jamais[452]

Friday April 17.1857.

It was a lovely day & I was out for the first time after my illness Massé has full play now that his friends are gone & he enjoys it He is here as often as he can & spends his evenings with me & sings & talks so pleasantly

J'ecoute vos paroles puisque c'est la dernière soirée que je dois passer avec vous[453] – how aimiable[454] French people are he is one of the few little men that I like – that sweet french language in the mouth of a Parisian – I bought a superb shawl from him to day – but still he is a gentleman – how unbearable the same class in

England would be – snobbish & conceited – he asked me to write to him – But I must not forget a most kind & pleasant visit I had from Do/arvall[455] to day – he was so gentle & kind so forgiving so courteous – I really think he likes me – for what other object could he have in saying those golden fascinating words Did ever a man understand flattery so well as he? – His eyes were softened into tenderness & he sat there & looked at me as if he would give his life for a kind word from me – He said – Never have I been so unkindly used as by you, others throw roses

on my path – but you – you strew thorns – oh why did I come here – why had I not strength never to see you again – but when I saw your writing & read your words – my heart melted – & here I am like a fool –

& I liked him all the better for his folly –

I drained for poor old B. he is almost on the dry but still he could not refuse me 20 which is 10 less than what I wanted & in my horror I write to D scarcely expecting an answer & that kind heart gives me his hand once more & I can now get that beautiful shawl –

220

April 19. Saturday

Embarked! with a whole cargo of strangers – was sick for nearly a week & then had another accident – most disgusting – I wish I was on shore[456] –

M[r] & M[rs] Redall[457] are in the honeymoon – the Captain is a most gentlemanly & well-informed person – among the gentlemen passengers there are only two that attract my notice – M[r] James Osborne[458] & M[r] Clarkson – the first goodlooking very like Prince Albert[459] tall young honest bushman – the other just at that age where the passions are warmest without being too hot with all the strength of manhood

221

without the massiveness of later years – I dare say something past 30. very curly hair & fine teeth & well made but not handsome – He is an original in many ways – & pretends to be rude & rough & sarcastic – mais au fond je crois qu'il a des trésors de tendresse dans son coeur qu'il cache sous cet éxterieur froid & indifferent.[460]

———

He told me to day of the love of his life & how unkind she was to him & what he bore for her sake – & it made him quite pensive for the rest of the evening – he owned that he was very jealous – I feel that he never would take the least notice of me except here on board ship where he has no one else to talk to – [illeg.] so I will not give him another thought –

222

The captain read me a little lesson last night about M[r] Clarkson – but I have a very good conscience – & to day C. speaks not a word to me – is he vexed with me? for he got part of the homily My heart is of most curious construction How like a buoy it floats on the top of sorrow & misfortune, it must be a light heart else it could not bear all the jolts & downfalls & thunderbolts & roaring of torrents & howling of wind that have met it ever since I was born. With grief I left Brucedale I secluded myself saw no one spoke to no one, the fact is[461] I was moulting casting off my skin, & at last crept out of my larva a[462] fresh & new being I awoke to new joys, my nerves braced up to new exertion, though still a little delicate. the first thing that presented itself to my gaze was Paul T.[463] he is[464] in the first blush of rising feeling a second Laszlo[465] a second Willy[466] – it was a short & sweet hour I spent with him & he vanished. then there was silence around me – words were[467] spoken & forgotten, sounds heard & forgotten facts happened & were forgotten & I unwillingly embarked for an other long voyage – C[468]. said what

223

I have often said to myself before = I am the wandering Jew. –

And here is a life of general misery – except some few moments of compensation – that is a piano[469] good dinners & now & again a slight communication[470] between

C. & me. I like O[471] too tho'[472] that is a calm every day concern. But C. makes me phosphorescent – forgetful of what is going on around me & what I am doing – What an ear he has for music – & a fine voice – sometimes he sings when he is not asked but when he is asked he shuts himself up – so I just let him do what he likes & seem to take little or no notice this morning I was sitting at work in my cabin humming little tunes to myself so low that I am sure no one outside the cabin could possibly have heard me – & presently there was a low whistle beginning the same song I was singing Katty Darling[473] the same key – & was that chance or did he hear me & answer me? He comes near me sometimes & slightly touches me, rien q'un

224

frôlement[474] – & it makes every nerve tremble – I was leaning against the post last night with my face so that he could not see me & then he came nearer & nearer & first looked round the post bending his head down[475] close to mine saying "Are you playing hide & seek with me?[476]

I breathed a little & was talking to Mrs Drysdale[477] – when he leaned also against the post slowly & quickly – it quite frightened me – I dont know how it is when such things happen – it quite takes my consciousness of every thing else away – & I feel as if everything was vanishing except the one. – – but I gathered myself up & went to my little roost as he calls it. Does he or does he not feel attracted? he used to come near me – but now it is all over – he will never say "Allow me the pleasure" again he will never sit near me again

Well perhaps it is better so – I might possibly have got into another fausse-position[478] & refuse

225

a good offer for the sake of a caprice of the heart which can never do any good – but is it not hard for all that to be [illeg.] kept on such short allowance of happiness or rather fun in this short life & on this dull ship – where one really has nothing else to do but talk & laugh –

I think you had a motive C^pt Young[479] or do you fancy I am vexed & therefore try to be more attentive? – C.[480] has not spoken to me all day long – nor I to him – when will that end –

It is my belief that you are jealous.

– Thus passed 24 hours in silence.

Of all the men I know none has such sensitive irritable nervs[481] as Mr C. I should like have a bed large enough to stretch myself all lengths upon it –

226

There is a deep melancholy in the heart of every man, bound up in the very bundle of his life, which like the breath of myrrh is ever ready to spread itself by a secret influence over all his being; & in spirits of the deepest tone there is most of this for this is the greatness of the soul reaching after its true proportion – & this may at any time make the life of any man restless & sad unless he learns indeed to lean his soul upon God –

Samuel Wilberforce
Bishop of Oxford.[482]

And is that the cause of all my sorrow my sensitiveness my acute feeling of the smallest things – is that the reason of my present utter depression of spirits? Yes it is that want of harmony

227

so essential to finely organized beings – I read another sermon to day that was composed of three elements superstition, cant & philosophy – the first always a silly imagination the second as usual shallow & the third bottomless – – Now I think the Mahomedan[483] religion more sensible as it is more practical more useful – it says "Do this & do not do the other – & never have I found in the Koran such contradictions such shallow arguments & reasoning as in the Christian doctrines. For instance – We can do nothing of ourselves – we must pray for the Grace of God without which all prayer is vain – & more such rubbish – human workmanship peeps out at every corner – – – –

C. said this evening – if you are in a stew for pity's sake walk through the pain but dont let your neighbours know – he is coming round perhaps he will come to me again, but what would be the good the old fellow would only be at me again.

228

Day after day passes in monotonous solitude, without warmth light or pleasure without interest without a smile without a laugh a word to cheer no not even sorrow to remind one[484] of a possible reaction. the sound of my own voice frightens me & so still is my face day after day & night after night that if by chance I look into a laughing book & take some of the contagion my [illeg.] muscles unused to that novel use they are put to long to return to their grave proportions fatigued by the short exertion.

– And merryness & cheerfulness is to me like the breath of life, as necessary to my happiness as the warm sun & the blue sky – I am weary of this existence, I don't digest my dinner I am pale tired cold languid & stupid – & all this for that ridiculous old man's interfering – I never speak to any of the gentlemen here & they not to me particularly Mr C. who studiously avoids me – but it is not that which grieves me car je puis bien m'en passer[485] but the wretched dullness of all circumstances combined.

I cannot look old Rumpus[486] in the face as formerly – he has spoiled all the pleasure I could possibly have had on this passage & that is little enough – – And I go solitary sad & slow to my small – roost C. has the nerves of a woman – & he a soldier – what strange colored eyes he has – almost impossible to tell the color there of – He is quite an original & a comic one too.

I fancy I detect some symptoms of imitation – quiet & almost imperceptible there is something of a woman in his face & manner – but where it lies I cannot tell – & yet he is a tall strong well made man – he said this evening how much he disliked being by himself in his cabin particularly – how often have I thought of him when I lay shivering & lonely in my little berth – but of those things I dare not think – Good night C Shall we for ever remain so distant as we are now? – Anger is like to rise in my heart when I think of that old fox – he may be assured that I will not speak to him so long as he

230

wont let me talk to Mr Clarkson. Perhaps C thinks as I do that if our mutual wish to speak to each other was <u>very</u> great we would not mind the old meddler. – Perhaps he is right

Comment ai-je remarque un mouvement d'humeur de la part de M. Cl. ce soir? lorsque je me suis mise a l'autre table de jeu – Je s'approche mais soit coquetrie soit timidité il n'ose point m'offrir le bras à la promenade à peine s'il me parle – Mais ce soir lorsque nous jouions il était d'abord très gai et les fesait éclater de rire – puis tout d'un coup, il devient sombre ne désserre plus les dents et le jeu fini il se lève brusquement, prend son chapeau et quitte la chamber – lui qui restait toujours à causer jusqu'a l'heure de coucher –

English translation of the French by Sharon Joffe:

> How did I notice a movement of mood on the part of Mr. Cl. this evening? When I placed myself at the other game table – I approach him but be it coquetry or be it timidity he does not dare offer me his arm for a walk and he hardly talks to me – But this evening when we were playing he was at first very gay and made them burst into laughter – then all of a sudden, he becomes somber no longer opens his mouth and the game finished he gets up briskly, takes his hat and leaves the room – he who always stayed to chat until bedtime –

At times he is very comical & strange – he said to day – I wish to goodness I had a wife that I might abuse her & say – here look what I've got for my money why not a pen'orth[487] – he must get a small wife – another time he said – Would I had a wife only for six hours – & then stopped & added laughing – to sow my shirt buttons on – He looked at me & said – "You ought to have been mine – only you shant – but that was before my old bug bear had interfered – Now it is different – we scarcely ever notice each other except when music is going on. I think I must do a little bit of the

231

civil to the old fellow that he may have no just cause to complain – he would not send me any more pudding to day – so it wont pay to quarrel with him – I think I have shown him my displeasure long enough.

there was a blush like a peach on young Harry Osborne's[488] cheek when I played with him to night & he said I was a partner to his mind & somehow I forgot to look over to the other table where C was playing

No blush to night I saw –

C.s irritability of nerves deceives one into an idea that his heart is also impressionable Sometimes one then another – Sometimes then Myra then M^{rs} D[489] & so by turns – this evening it was first one & then Mrs D. I saw the start of it – He put his arm round the post & said: this is the beloved wife of my bosom – it made me shake – would that I could sleep one night with him – he looks so strong & warm – he would growl & be fierce like a tiger – no one night would not be enough – We sympathize in one thing we both prefer the forbidden fruit to matrimony – But I will give up all thoughts of him – & stick to O[490] – he says he must get a wife by hook or by crook he is handsome good tempered & stupid[491] such a husband I should like – & would make him a good wife – too sensitive people hurt me & I hurt them we would do not amalgamize – & still I have that indomitable itch to flirt with Clarkson – But is not the charm [illeg.] in sunder – by that rough awkward sailorhand –

232

You say you are restless – Oh come to me I can cure I have a remedy that will give you peace – a calm contemplative heart by day, gratitude to Fate, love to all man – kind, hope & strength in danger & adversity, pleasure in virtue, deep slumbers by night from which you will ride satisfied & strong in the morning – I care not if you thank me afterwards I care not if you forget me when health has returned – for then we shall be ripe for separation – but now your pain is my pain, your sigh is my sigh & your sorrow is mine – I mean that when I see you so restless unhappy your eyes half closed looking into the vague your limbs half extended a half frown upon your brow & sweet anguish upon your lips then sorrow strikes into my heart like lightening & I would give of my happiness to make you happy my joys to make your life beautiful – but – to whom say I all this – who is there that hears me in the loud roar of waves – who cares for me in their world so full of treasures

Another rush to night! He was cross all the evening – he can be so cold – then he starts up from the table after his – "shmoke" – & never comes down till we have all gone to bed.[492]

Vous reverrai-je jamais Toché? Pensez vous à moi quelque fois – Mais vous êtes loin de moi en Meurice peut-être vous m'avez oubliée et jamais je ne vous verrai –

English translation of the French by Sharon Joffe:

> Will I ever see you again Toche? Do you think of me sometimes – But you are far from me in Mauritius perhaps you have forgotten me and I will never see you –

Seeing that I am of an enquiring mind I cannot help reducing every thing to phisical[493] causes – all our mental[494] feelings are produced by bodily sensations –
Do not leave me altogether C. why do you not come near me. Sometimes when the old fellow is away? Why do you not give me one look worth having – but I know you like Myra the best – therefore you do not come to me.

Never did I experience such succession & combination of adverse circumstances. the cold is atrocious the damp detestable the cabin the most uncomfortable the sky cheerless the decks wet, the floors just washed & neither warmth nor air to dry them, the vessel going very slowly These are some – then the disagreable[495] feeling the restraint created by the captain's untimely interference which acts like a wet or at least a damp blanket upon my spirits & those of another person at which result the old lady is highly pleased – I dare not speak to any one of the gentlemen except perhaps good morning & how do you do – but when I give half a laugh at dinner or breakfast I see his cunning eye peeping down just only for a quarter of a second – and Cl is just as much awed as I am – he dare not come near me – did you observe the little hesitation & indecision before setting down to read? He did not make love to Myra what was the cause of that?.

234

My sins have been great & are not yet forgiven – for ages pictures of speoch[496] have been handed down to us till we take them for facts – that was the language of the Hebrews & the Asiatics altogether – the Bible is full of those similies – thus a bad conscience is another expression for suffering for our imprudence – as my sins are not forgiven means, I have not yet found that remedy which will relieve the suffering of my body – & many such –
the more I think of it the more I find that [Fatali] the belief & the doctrine of Fatalism[497] is an essentially Christian article –
We believe that the God that we adore to possess all knowledge he knows <u>every thing</u> & can do <u>every thing</u> then if he knows every thing he must know our future

fate, if he knows it must be all predestined consequently rob of the possibility of stepping off that path of fate –

Cl does say queer things sometimes – he was rather in a state of excitement this evening & as he said "as hot as a furnace & turned down his collars & looked for all the world like Henry VIII[498] – He talked & laughed incessantly & made us positively roar at the Piano I wonder what put him into such a state of excitement – it must have been flirting with Myra – Had it not been for that his excitement might have been contagious but as it was I remained neutral & as cool as a cucumber all the evening – he said he used to be as savage as a young tiger just what I thought of him – I would

235

not be game to offend for something But he takes so utterly no notice of me that I am gradually partaking the same feeling

The Captain looked more [illeg.] than ever.

It is a curious fact & one peculiar I believe only to beings of the human species that the approach of the two bodies without mental connection looses[499] half of its virtue – that I experienced to a certainty last night – C. & I had been rather ~~cold~~ distant all day – & in the evening he came & sat near me apparently with the greatest sang-froid[500] talking indifferent things & to other people all the time Once he leaned so close to me that I was almost squashed against the post & it made all the blood rush to my heart – & I felt that he was somewhat attracted because at every minute his arm touched me & like AB.[501] he had the fidgets under the table in his legs – <u>but still</u> – <u>strange to say</u> there was not that thrill that has run through my very body & soul when he has only touched my skirt Now how ever does that come! it is more than I can say

Nous sommes tous les deux arrivés a cette époque de la passion ou on souffre tellement qu'on saisit n'importe que[~~illeg.~~] moyen pour se soulager[502]

Is it not strange that he should ask me for a remedy for his sleeplessness after what I wrote in my book the other day on page 232 Oh would I could show him that page –

It is curious fact how like W.HS.[503] he is –

What frightful weather we have – bitter cold bleak sharp wind & a wintry sky – the ship rolling tremendously every body is wake nearly all night gets tossed out of their beds every in the cabins upset inkbottles spilt over their faces, water cans all over the floor – all the gentlemen are upon deck half the night C. gave me his arm this morning for a walk but he seemed thoughtful – only he said – Again I could not sleep – he makes the best bow I ever saw – he is most graceful – but rather supercilious –

236

I would not mind making a small bet that to morrow there will be a grand flirting with Miss Brown —[504]

the whole day I felt oppressed with a weight upon my heart – I could not laugh or speak & my cheeks glowed like fire – I felt that C. was looking at me but he said nothing & was all the evening more reserved than usual. It pains me to be on such distant terms with him but what can I do? All yesterday he would not speak to me for why I cannot guess – & to night it seemed as if he was sorry – there he was slowly putting on his coat opposite me, & for the life of me I could not help looking up once or twice – the same when he was sitting silently against that post – then he went to bed & I saw he turned his head at the door towards me but I dared not turn mine as the Captain was looking at me –

But what of tomorrow's bet? – this evening I had the most extraordinary run of cards – twice running 6 trumps with H honors in my hand –

Sunday night

No he did not flirt – he was quiet & silent all day long – Mrs Brown called him – he would not be drawn into conversation – at the children's tea he did not come forth nor to the music – After tea I went & talked to Mrs Drysdale he was near her – & conversation began – how sweetly did the evening pass altho he spoke so much of Mrs Wrench[505] – he seemed to brighten up like the evening sky after a thunderstorm – & so did I –

237

Two or three times he left the room – but oh how soon did he return! He was pale with excitement the whole evening – oh would that I dared give him the sleeping draught – he so longs for –

mais tout cela n'aboutir à rien —[506]

But I must not play that trick too often – & remember that howwell[507] it succeeded with W.H.S. J^{nr}[508] at first [illeg.] still [illeg.] I played it once too many –

It is blowing & snowing fearfully the sails are all reefed my bed was covered with snow during the day time I never stir out of my cabin but lie rolled up in blankets & only come out in the evening – C. was cold & pale & silent

I played with James O.[509] at whist[510] – he too got excited – does that man pay any attention to me – if so I shall be pleased – but some words that C said made him start & me blush alltho' I pretended not to hear – it was when the Stewart found my bed covered with snow – had O thought for a moment he would have been silent but he was excited with the game –

I don't know how it is that I always feel a secret satisfaction a sort of consciousness of having done right when I have neglected C. not be rude to him or snub him or be pert but when I have quietly & coldly shown others as much if not more attention than him – it is a little revenge for the Picnic – & he shall have more of it before we are done – the message I sent to Deverty[511] I know vexed him – & now like George he says "Mind you never speak against D he is my most particular friend

238

that man is terribly fascinating – one can not resist – M[r] Drummond[512] looked at me with reproachful looks – but I heeded him not – C was near me – & glowing warmth went down my side – his eyes were half closed & so soft – he turned round towards me he was uneasy the whole evening – he breathed hard & his knee touched mine – oh I felt the burning red come over my face – I know – & why should that disturb me – that this approach is only physical nervous – what else do I want? – But I will tame that young tiger before I have done with him –

the 28th of May we got to the point of the horn[513] such bitter cold such sunless days such a dreary life – better were not to live at all. the Captain has made the voyage 4 times before & bears it all without complaint – had he not interfered so disagreably[514] I would think him very interesting.

Per 7. June

7 weeks have we been on board & are now in 45 lat.[515] we have been so far as 58 which in point of cold is equal to 68 in the northern hemisphere – It is gradually getting a little warmer but I still have chilblains – the sky is leaden the ocean a little darker & not a ray of sun –

Trinity Sunday June 7.[516]

On this day I saw the first funeral at sea – it is a melancholy sight the soldier had died of consumption

& there he lay shrouded in the brittish[517] flag the union Jack – M^r Cl.[518] read the service over him & all the soldiers & sailors stood round in silence –

I had a sort of strange sensation as I looked down upon the crowd to discover the head of the person one likes but among so many – there he is – I thought in my heart – but what part have I in him? – None – he neglects me more than ever – for every one he has a joke or a kind word only me he passes in silence – he is just like W.H S.[519] in that – & why is it that I must always like people that dont like me? it is as sure as fate.

I am thriving on Fatalism & getting quite fat – that is good

Joshua Chap X. v. 12. the moon in Ajalon[520]

Saturday the 13th of June I saw the first ray of sun in the morning before I got up –

14th the ocean looked blue for the final time to day & a feeling of Spring came over me as young Leslie[521] walked out of the door into the morning air – & I felt distinctly that the purest pleasure lies in the imagination –

It would be a curious & interesting search to make to find out all the relations the connecting branches of

Of[522] ancient & modern things – but particularly in religion, religious matters superstitions & mysterious rites & ceremonies. Often has it struck me with surprise in reading some old historical book to find there the origin though somewhat modified of our modern customs. Most clearly is that to be seen in languages.

Things are going on as they ought tho' not the most pleasing – that prediction about the <u>Bs</u> is coming true again – & I think I might add AB. but that is neither here nor there. Bauman Bentzel Bowler Böhm Brown[523] I have wholesome tenor of names beginning with a b.

I know what I ought to do & what I wish to do – but alas it will be a hard task if ever it comes so far, which perhaps it may not.

What glorious hours <u>I could</u> spend with C. if he chose to be a little less disagreeable but as you seem so fond of secondhand articles you may go & enjoy that high nose – where he wanted to flatter me he said a woman ought to have a straight nose now like the other W.H. he seems to prefer the high Roman – Soyez le bien venu mon cher – allez vous amuser le plus que vous pourrez en attendant il faudra que vous vous passiez de quelque plaisir et quand Madame sera accouchée alors! –

English translation of the French by Sharon Joffe:

> Welcome my dear – go amuse yourself the most that you are able to while waiting it will be necessary that you spend some pleasure and when Madame will be lying in thus –

241

I long to write to dear Mrs Suttor & tell her all about it – she will call me a flirt but I will end by telling her that no person however fascinating should ever make me forget my Australian lad.[524] – neither they will – altho' imagination there again did more than reality –

Why does he act so strangely?

———

One thing I feel a little flattered in mentioning – that was last night's conversation on desk in the twilight

What man strongly feels – he naturally seeks to express –

Wednesday June 17.ᵗʰ 1857.

J'ai été fêtée aujourdhui[525] – It so happened that they all three said & did undeniable things to day My heart is glad that C has returned to me – with his own dear hands he carved a paper knife for me, out of honduras mahogany[526] – he did not flirt with Mʳˢ B.[527] but he sat at my feet as he used to when I played the Accordion – oh the sun shines not brighter in my heart than his smile is there or is there not sweet gentle love under that rough outside – he not the gentleman a great deal more so than D's[528] nasty familiarity.

242

the dear old Captain[529] ever came to me & held kind discourse – I see it – he gently took my hand & this evening I saw for the first our old European friend the great bear – he is truly kind & refined the most gentlemanly person on board –

June 18.

Waterloo day to day – I had a cleaning in my cabin & [illeg.] it looks so pretty it is the nicest fitted & the most cosy looking – I went then & sat on deck with my work – & a pleasant sweet dream came over me – C. lay out at my feet half sleeping talking laughing & whistling his whistling goes straight to my heart – In the evening I expected he would go & pay his usual devotions to Mrs B. but he did not & came & sat near me – J.O. also came & Leslie & John[530] whom I call Juan & we had great fun – But I am a great fool for writing all this –

243

By evil inspiration I said something last night to C. about Mrs B.[531] & he evidently was annoyed – I regretted much – but he came round again in the evening though at first with the appearance of [illeg.] on – I feel convinced that he will flirt with her to day to spite me, for it is plain he can not divest himself of the idea that I am jealous if ever so little – & he –? – what does he mean? does he want to make a fool of me – or does he think me impervious –? And still I would not give up his attentions for anything –

How doth everything disappear
When . . . . is near!

The finest bird ever I heard whistle was a man, & that man is he – Like a lark like the swallows at home singing their long notes through the evening sun & the blue sky – like the voice of my little Charlie.[532] But how can I indulge in these thoughts when I know that he not only does not care for me but loves some one else & had just as soon talk to Widow B. or – as to me there is no person so unfortunate in these things as myself – these two W.H. are a match

---

I cannot disguise to myself a certain fact – a slight dash of jealousy – but I will not be hard he <u>might</u> like me – for all that – do not I study not to make any difference between him &. O – & has he not a hundred times imitated me?

244

My nerves are in supreme irritation between those two men & M~rs~ B. In my own [illeg.] mind there is no doubt about the preference – that electric communication was in full force to night – oh how fascinating he can be – so eh much that I dare not go near him dare not look at him & my pride rises at the thought of his total indifference – Almost rather had I he never spoke again to me than see him flirt –

Osborne's heart is full I see he tries to suppress his jealousy but he cannot bear my singing with C. – Do not torment me so leave me in peace to rest on James' faithful heart – When he (J)[533] comes into the room he sits walks straight up to me & sits down & whispers – he is guileless – honest rough yet kind – with him I would lead a quiet sober life – –

~~Saturday~~ Sunday

I will not stand this nonsense any longer. –
How sweetly he sang last night –!
It reminded me of Schönstein's[534] singing only that that I was too stupid then to appreciate – there was a strong communication between us –

Sunday

One thing I could not help seeing with pleasure this morning when we all came on deck to Church – he had had a restless night & was as much excited as I had been the night before – there he walked up & down in figure he is one of the handsomest men I ever saw – such grace & strength combined – only he is already getting too stout at 25 he must have been perfection –

But I will now look upon him as one who is attached to another & only occasionally flirts with Mrs B. because he thinks her harmless.

Monday 22ᵈ

Yes I know the exact course I ought to run – & am in the right track now but to keep it is the difficulty –

Always perfectly good humoured but always indifferent take no notice of his rudeness no spiteful repartees no bitter allusions no retaliation in flirting with J.O. no sulky retiring when he is making himself agreable to Mʳˢ B. – But[535] – <u>not allow the slightest flirtation with yourself</u> give up that silly satisfaction of vanity, it is the way to win O's heart & punish Mʳ C. & in fact retain the esteem of all the company on board –

Mʳˢ B. evidently does not like his advances poor thing I wronged her – she is right I. should consider it an insult in her position

246

those two men are really very queer – there they want me to play for them goodness knows how long while they dance & romp with these children & when some one else plays they have not the politeness to ask me – & that other conceited fool goes buzmaking & sentimentalizing after Mʳˢ B. altho' she treats him with as much indifference as is possible without actual rudeness & then he wants me to be always ready to play for him to listen to him & all the rest of his nonsense. –

He is really in love with her – the utmost stretch of vanity will not allow me to think he does it to spite me – for he is always about when I am not there & so – but I know all the rest – it is all as it ought to be –

J. O is getting on swimmingly & C. divides his attention between Mʳˢ B. & me – mine is not divided but never mind about that – Today the 26ᵗʰ we spoke a vessel an American & there was so much noise & commotion & excitement that it shook my nerves & I had to go to my own cabin & sat down on the floor & had a cry – C must have noticed for he left Mʳˢ B's side for a little while & came to me – he also in the evening alluded to Cpt Y[536] paying attention to me – Perhaps he thinks in his own mind that I flirt quite as much as I think he does –

247

& maybe he is right for we can never see ourselves – James[537] sat near me in the evening – & once the blood did ruch[538] to my face & made me feel all overish – I should not wonder if he was to try that trick again –

Saturday night

A deep blush to night I saw so deep it communicated itself to me – as we played at Backgammon – & emotion softened his usually sparkling eyes – how gentle men get & how submissive when touched by woman.

And what was the matter with our chivalrous Captain – he is really what Bentzel would call [illeg.] he spoke not to me the whole afternoon & evening – & late when he came down there was something in his countenance that told me he had suffered –

C. is coming round again – he delights in tormenting for me – he would like to take them all away – but he found that JO. did not enjoy the widow's society so much as he did & came back to me – & to my surprise he (C) also returned & this evening I was surrounded by multitudes much to the disgust of others C. came nearer & nearer, he said that he had oceans of feeling in his heart he was restless & reserved – he said a man loves only once, & that is over with me – no it is not over – what am I to conclude but that his love he left in Sydney – I can not dissimulate & pretend to like those I do not – that accounts for your rudeness to me I said –

Saturday is an eventful if not an unfortunate day for me on board this vessel – On a Saturday I got that lecture from the captain – the Saturday before last C flirted assiduously with M^{rs} B all day long – but in the evening he came to me he sang so sweetly that night that all my nerves trembled he sat near me at cards, he was gentle again – & the next morning I could see that the swaying of the waters had not yet subsided – & last night a Saturday again occurred that event with my shawl that made one person start up from his chair & walk away a few steps & then come back – but still I do not think he loves me – & is the Captain jealous? did he long to give me a lecture last night? Both he & Mrs Drummond are very prim today – Fortunately they were not in the room when J. O came near me – he was very rude certainly – I dare say only his rough way of expressing his feelings – still I must keep him at a distance if I want to make anything of him which I certainly do – he is the man I want altho' C. has the Apple Blossom my life with him would be a succession of squalls gales hurricanes water spouts & spouts of all kinds, a fair breeze now & then, sometimes tho' rarely a calm & sunshine mountainous waves rough seas sweeping over poop & quarter deck right into my own private cabin, dark & stormy nights glaring hot days – & where would be the soft twilight hours that I once thought of? Last night for the first time he sat near me at the twilight hour & how I am rated for it – What will he do to night – he will not come partly from

perverseness & partly from shyness: –

He seems to have brass sometimes but he is as easily influenced as a woman. He is undoubtedly the strangest mixture of ferocity & tenderness overflowing spirits & melancholy frankness & reserve ~~of~~ strength & softness, determination & mutability spirit of contradiction & submission that ever was found united in human form. –

Entre autre[539] he said one remarkable thing last night – about watching the proceedings of others – I would never go after a person to see what they were about – if I could not trust a woman to keep quiet in my absence all my watching would do no good – I recognized my theory of Fatalism in those words – for what is trust but Fatalism with the hope that things will turn out well without our interfering.

As for the other chap I knew him by heart the first day I spoke to him – he is the dull good boy who[540] does his work on week days goes to church on Sunday smokes his pipe & gives one a pinch by way of expressing his affections.

I shall be very dull when I get on shore for these 3 men so different in character are all of the valuable –

My nerves [~~illeg.~~] were sent into such swing last night even to day I have not found my balance yet –

[~~illeg.~~]

<u>Sunday night</u> June 28.

It certainly is a satisfaction to my vanity to see how attentive all the men are & how jealous the women – M^{rs} D – & Mrs B. & Mrs R.[541] all poked their heads together & whispered – And I had the C^{pt} & Mr C. near & the Osbornes all except James whose voice was not heard all day poor boy he looked very down hearted all day I will cheer him up to morrow – The C^{pt} was more attentive than usual & with him[542] conversation never flags – C. also came out – Salmon on Monday – very fine, allow me to observe – he is going to begin a new system of flirtation to morrow – he did not flirt with Mrs B. altho' she tried hard to get him by herself on the other side of the poop but it was no go – he came & sat down near us –

June 30.

Action not words – Practice not Theory Facts not intentions & resolutions – shall prove my mind – Certainly Theories & resolutions must precede facts – but only in your own mind – I shall only be despised if I put forth intentions & speak vain words if ~~my~~ they do not coincide with my actions – And I will not play second fiddle, nor will I go in double harness – & he says he can make a pair go as well as a single – She the Bee is as jealous as she can be, more so than she dare show – the idea of making her my rival – I have not the presumption to stand against such powers – & will therefore retreat.

251

Forgot the 30th of June – thus things pass away – but since my treacherous heart has forgotten to regret W.[543] I wonder at nothing

July 1st crossed the line[544] –

July 2d Per.[545]

C.s impudence has no bounds – but there is such a thing as going too far, altho he thinks himself alpowerful – I trust it may be my fate to conduct myself well this time – I will be a small Ceasar[546] in my way & have all or nothing –

Was that the meaning of "Je triomphai j'[illeg.] dans l'air?[547]

[~~that illeg.~~]

July 4
Saturday again a

disagreeable day – Unwell – squally & gusty in every sense of the word – C. devotes all his time to M^{rs} B & in the evening when she is not there he wants to come & sit near me & I am to laugh at his jokes & do all that he wants – & <u>I wont</u> – so none of your humbugging for me – & Mr Osborne is just as bad – – You treat me very cavalierly but <u>you</u> may go to [illeg.] without that I send only one thought after you –

C sang "When time hath bereft thee"[548] & laid great stress upon the 2^d verse – but I kept as quiet as I could altho' my nerves quivered every minute – I had to get up but it is not he that does that – but music

Associating with <u>such</u> people as I have done for the last 4 or five years is enough to make the most humble minded thickly conceited – Is there a single tho[t] rough bred lady or gentleman among them? – – I think & think & find none & still I have seen beauty talent & even education among them – but that hideous disgusting sickening vanity spoils darkens sullies distorts every imaginable good quality

Is there one among them that can speak more or be silent & quiet with ease & grace – without fancying that every look word or gesture is watched & criticized with jealous uncharitableness or with unbounded admiration by all around. – No – they all seem to say – Now, how do I look – or what do you think of me now – or am I not a wonderful creature? – often these questions are not satisfactorily answered & still oftener they would give worlds to feel that they were not watched or at least to feel as if they did not mind it – but that is impossible for if they do try & work themselves within the boundaries of "Dont care" – they rush madly into the contrary extreme of desparate[549] recklessness – & come to be hung. – that frivolous vanity that morbid shyness has been the bane of my life – tell me that I am morbid? it may be so, but I may add my morbidness is more out of the way of general sanity than yours – for yours one can detect a long way off & coming within your precincts it is visible in highways & by ways in every corner on every path on the mountain tops & in the valleys among the flowers & thorns in palaces seated in sickly array in velvet couches, paralizing the noblest talent rusting angelic beauty destroying innocent pleasure artless conversation, & guileless feeling – even down to the cottage door, the poor-house, that corroding corrupting petrifying & mortifying disease is to be found.

Many people could I name that would be truly fascinating without it – Mrs Barton is I think one of the least afflicted that I have known for a long time & Mr Suttor is another – but they are few & far between – When will nature assert her rights – & what is the cause of it – is it the bile of the mind? is it the dampness of the climate that gives Brittish[550] nerves & muscles the rheumatism & puts green & yellow glasses before the eyes of imagination – Is it a disease of the mind or the body or are the two inseparable – is the cause mental or physical?

You have taken your choice – I hope you are pleased with your bargain –

I have often admired the richness of conversation that is going on in the morning light the twilight & the moonlight – you northerners have a strange way of making love – I am the fool for not understanding you

Sunday the 5th

Spoke an American vessel the Marcelens from Boston the Captain Mr Baxter came on board & gave us provisions in exchange for a chronometer – It was a source of excitement to all except me – J.O. & Mr Leslie went on board – he is a good boy – But all the ladies sadly illtreat me because they are jealous – I might really say with Miss Lydia Languish[551] I wish I had not such beautiful eyes.

Again I am knocked on the head & cannot recover myself – I am a most unfortunate chap – always getting into scrapes – but certainly I never was so much snubbed scolded found fault with scowled & frowned [illeg.] at, calumniated put down & kept under abused crowed over, tantalized neutralized & perhaps envied – as on board this ship. no – not envied – for that sweet scented plant was only had time to shoot out a tiny little leaf when it was chocked by jealousy spite malice hatred & all uncharitableness. For my part they may have all the gentlemen to ourselves – I have enough resources in me not to be dull when I am alone.

I really do not understand that blessed English character yet – or else it is only this class of people that I cannot make out – I am sinking lower & lower in my associates What have I come to? Curses on my low habits – But no – low people I would not mind for a change – but these half bred underbred people I cannot digest – As I said before there are only 2 gentlemen on board & of those one is natures nobleman that is he is not educated I am truly a fool for good nature – my elegant refined manners my politeness are so many pearls thrown before pigs[552] – & still I would not for the world become like one of these – this may seem Pharisaism[553] – but

I ask would any one willingly[554] descend from a painter of landscapes to painting doors & chairs & tables – or from the officer to the common soldier or from or from[555] the lordly table to the servant's hall?

& could educated as I am with my inherent love for arts & sciences have any communication with such people – the only wonder is that I still wonder at their want of manners. At Brucedale at least I had my schoolroom with sensible occupation & Carry to appreciate it – I had the pleasure of unfolding that fine young mind as the rosebud spreads before the sun – & I had my Piano – & the liberty of the bush to think & meditate when those people overpowered me with their folly & vulgarity – but here! –

And what do I get for my good nature? Rudeness from the men & scowls from the women. It will be best for me to make myself scarce – & I can tell you Mr O. it is precious little music or kind looks you will get out of me after [illeg.] the total want of attention you show me – & C. the same – tho' to do him justice he is never rude – but teases me another way – but that is past – we[556] have nothing more to say to each other –

I really think O is conceited as C. & that is not a little Oh W.H s & big roman noses how have ye persecuted me.[557]

– Now tell me without forethought afterthought or thoughts of any kind following only the voice of nature which chamber would you enter?

When they are both quiet? there is no doubt – when C leaves me I turn slowly to O. when O leaves me I turn with my whole heart to C. & he seems more attractive than ever – but alas he is another's property – & really if he intends becoming Myra's father he flirts a little too much with his future daughter in law – but who knows perhaps he intends to wait for her – but I quite forget what I was going to write – something about Brucedale – yet I fear it was all my fault – he could not bear such strong food – how true were his words – had you been experienced it would have been better – or in other words – had you been younger & your blood less warm – the fruit of love would have slowly ripened instead of being scorched –

255

that which becomes the aristocrat the elegant man ill suits you – you clumsy country pumpkin you raw Irish praty[558] – What C does with grace you imitate with bearishness what is amusing & comical in him is vulgar coarse & stupid in you – that is the worst of those big men – they are so coarse – & if you think you are going to win me by that off-hand manner you are mistaken – be yourself as you were first & you may do – but if you [illeg.] the monkey you wont –

July 10.

What a sleep I had last night after all my anguish on that dear old grey shawl –

C remarked to day that I spoke to him for the first time since 4 days – he counts the time then – but he has not fasted enough yet – to day he has given up the widow – but never mind – whether he goes back to her or not – it will make no difference to me –

Sunday

As I have nothing else to do this blessed Sunday I may as well report a little progress. C. is still sulky with the widow[559] & me – he speaks to neither she speaks to him with the widow & me she speaks to him but I don't – these are curious goings on – I speak very little to any one – but him I neglect altogether for very good reasons it is the only way to tame him – he is now finding out the length of his tether – & wonders perhaps where the end is. perhaps he thinks like Paddy[560] that the other end is cut off – I am almost beginning to think he did it to spite me – but no – this morning after church[561] he wandered about her like a spirit & only some firm resolution seemed to keep him from her – & did not Mrs Drysdale tell me that they had quarrelled – I can only say nevermind – James is very handsome & good-natured something in the Rawdon Crawley[562] style – just the right sort of husband for a clever woman – a Lord Byron, a Darvall[563], would have made me miserable but a Rawdon Crawley a J.O. might make me happy –

Another species of calamity – that cantankerous old harridan is so jealous at having no one to flirt with that she wont let anyone talk to me – & there am I with no one to talk to, the gentlemen all fighting shy of me – the ladies all scowling for Mrs B. & M^{rs} R are just as bad – all day passes & I speak scarcely a word at least only to those I dont care for – such as L. or the odious drunkard D.[564] a shaking tottering blear-eyed doughey fellow – & L a flush intrusive rattling little fellow always after girls – Hamstead very much the same style such is my company – & J.O. & C. & the C^{pt} my old beldam not only keeps from me but tries to get for herself – how often would I like to speak to C. he is so clever & elegant – but he is; indeed we are both rather shy whatever aplomb we may seem to have. In 21 days we shall be near Gravesend[565] I shall be sorry not to see any of then again –

256

– Yes what is it? Unconscious imitation that sort of similarity that vague sympathy that often appears before me like a thought a feeling of mine coming from him – there is no doubt that he is not as he used to be – a sort of soberness tacit reflective charmless & dry – does he read my thoughts – I wonder when I think how few things I have learnt from books or teaching – & how much from myself & the world. Yes flitting thoughts & vague dreams & fancies my purest happiness of the past that is the commencement of the end of my flirtation with C. often make me pensive – but no I dare not indulge – reason & knowledge forbid it – & if C. perhaps knows my secret he has it not from me – & J.O. knows it not & where ignorance is bliss it is folly to be wise.

Eversince I have not spoken to C. he has not gone near Mrs B. nor even looked at the children – to day I asked him after a long time to sing a song which he did & turned quite pale & excited – but no sooner had we had tea than he rushed up & lay down on the sky light opposite to her, upon which she instantly got up & went down stairs – In the evening he said "Lover's quarrels are love renewed"[566] & in a thousand sweet little ways tried to attract my attention – I however am determined to talk no more to him than I can help so as not to deserve Os remarks about bad tempered people. Perhaps C. thinks we shall be all as before but that is a mistake – may it be my fate to bee[567] Os wife – I could not wish better. I wish I was not so jealous – it is physical I know & must take some remedy soon.

Saturday again July.

Two days has he been trying to conciliate me – on Friday James was very rude to me C. & Henry felt it & how did they act C. began to talk & laugh to amuse me & make me laugh & forget J's ill conduct – Henry on the contrary was silent & the next day he came & talked in a very offhand manner calling me a sneak trying as it were to justify his cousin's conduct by his own – the next day C. never went near M̄ʳˢ B. & in the evening James & I & C & Henry played at whist & there was constant

257

crossfiring & I perceive that James is not quite so indifferent as he seems – to be. By[568] the bye what impulse induced him the other night when we quarrelled to say so quickly that he would go off to Ireland & get a pretty little wife of sixteen – or no I'll go back to that nice little girl I left behind me? What? – Vedremo.[569]

this Sunday morning Mʳ C. is making up to Mʳˢ B. & she receives him very graciously there are not many widows now a days who would be burnt alive or buried in their husband's tomb. Foolishly I mentioned last night to Mʳ C. "How is your driving getting on?

"Oh very well" said he with a slight laugh – only one of them kicks most tremendously.

– Now I have an easy part to play comparatively for without changing any thing in my conduct I can avoid him, need not speak to him nor take any notice of him whatever – <u>if I choose</u> but the fact is, amusing people are too scarce here for one to be so particular – I shall report some more progress this evening.

I have spent a most pleasant morning in my own cabin – I am always happy in this little dominion of mine where I am Lord of all I survey – Having had a very good breakfast & prayers on deck where Mʳ C. turned his face to Mʳˢ B. & his back to me – I went down into my own pretty room – the fresh seabreeze blowing through the curtains & I lay down to dream & read <u>the Lament of Tasso</u>[570] & notes of Wilson's[571] which might just as well describe C's character & Francesca di Rimini & many notes & Don Juan[572] & was happy – In the evenings I smoke before going to bed & long have I not enjoyed anything so securely & thoroughly – with visions that come without a sleep – What a dream was that of going to H.C.[573] with Lord William & taking his arm as we walked through the picture gallery & being caught in the storm & somehow I never came to a conclusion.

258

On the other page I said I would report progress – the events are various & still merge into one. Instead of C. giving all his attention to Mʳˢ B. he divided it & gives half to her & the other to Mʳˢ D. who also seems pleased whatever her husband may think of it. He goes away & leaves us there – I saw C's emotion as he stood so near Mʳˢ D. & that went on the whole evening – J.O. was rather silent he wont speak to me – & that is settled – I often wonder I dont care more at being so little thought of among these people Willie would say those foolish words

"When a woman discovers unappreciated treasures in her bosom etc – that everlasting "Don't care" has been my misfortune thro' life. Remember the words that Prussian officer said years & years ago – they have come true – – the moment C heard the bees were going up on deck – he shut up his writing & dashes up – & JO. goes into his cabin & sings you may go to Hong Kong[574] for me – How is it these men look at me with deep glowing eyes & still dare not come near me? I believe that either they or I am overcharged with electricity – there is a remedy for that which I shall employ as soon as I can get that wholesome ointment.

Per 23ᵈ

Raw wet muggy half rainy half sunshiny day English summer is making itself felt. C. studies equality – & it is good – J. is coming round a little but he seems to distrust himself & me – he is very jealous that is a bore. C's whistling is truly fascinating – sweeping up & down like a duet of swallow & nightingales the variations he whistled last night extempore to that march of the violet was superlative

259

I never met a man with whom I seemed to have so much similarity – he is also something like George Osborne in Vanity Fair.[575] I saw James writing a long letter yesterday perhaps it will be like the Prince of Orange[576] of tender memory. I will ask him illeg. about it. It was [illeg.]

Before I go to bed I must note one small event – We were playing at cards this evening Mʳˢ Drysdale & James & C. & I – I laid down the ace of hearts & said – Who will have that – James got quite pale & confused & at last he said with a sigh It is not my fate to have it I see. – Do you really care for me James? I know you are bashful – & so perhaps it is not to be – C kept calling me Mʳˢ Clarkson all the evening & such fun we had he does not mean anything I know full well.

Saturday night

It is very flattering to me that I should attract all those young men – certainly there is not much other attraction but still M[rs] Redall with her grand airs does not seem so successful – I saw the love light in James eye this evening he seemed to me handsomer than ever – It must have been evident to others for they all left us except M[rs] Drysdale – all C. Henry & M[r] Fulton[577] & the captain all disappeared that sort of influence always gives me le vertige[578] morally speaking – & I found myself with my patience cards & James at my side – M[r] C. sang "when time hath bereft thee[579] beautifully & then When a girl gets bothered among too many lovers. He sang things sometimes that go straight to my heart – but still I feel morally convinced

260

that tho' he might flirt quite seriously with me & even like me he would never marry me – & I must think of that now – I am past thirty, want a home & will not be called an old maid – In music he said we get on very well, but whether we would in other things is a question – his whistling gladdens my head & makes it ache – he would have had the preference had he not so perseveringly flirted with M[rs] D. But I gave him a warning & he took his choice – & J –? – I feel that it is better so.

Had Clari[580] still been in London than I could not have imagined a happier life than to be C's wife – but as it is the old world is but a grave yard to me & I must make a home & a bower in the new one.

this evening I remarked something curious. I was playing Piano J. O sitting on the floor near me rather close – O. never took his eyes off me that I felt & once or twice said some little endearing word "Oh" said Clarkson who was standing on the other side of James – declarations going on here" – & in a minute I noticed that C. was silent & turned away to the back of the Piano – What ho! my Lord are you jealous?

27. Monday.

this <u>has</u> been a disgusting day! although it began very well – I played on the Piano in the morning & C. & James came & Henry poor Hutton[581] is very unwell I sent him several messages during the day – C. I sang "Gin a body meat a body"[582] & in the second verse James looked at me I felt it – perhaps he wanted me to look up at him – but I did not – I let things take their course – But even the wind [illeg.] round – C. flirts as hard as he can with the daughter when he can't get the mother – all the morning they

kept singing to me "Too many lovers puzzle a maid"[583] – but they soon all flew away & flocked round Mrs B. C. did not seem quite sure of his game for several times left her – but at last he settled down in a very sentimental position – & James & Henry are such donkeys in regular sheep fashion if one jumps they all jump & when one lays down the others all squat & so they all follow the bell-wether Clarkson. James however seemed sorry & when Mrs B. went down & C followed he came to me but <u>then</u> I went away – For C. I dont so much care for he seems booked to the widow but that Osborne should leave me gives me pain. In the evening I had to sit near C. playing at cards for I wished to avoid playing with him he said "In Sydney I used to play till 2 oclock sometimes & loose[584] too – now if I had had a wife I should have gone to the small roost & forgot all about cards – & his foot trembled violently under the table – but I avoided touching him – – Ah soon we shall be out of this ship & then I shall forget all this nonsense – it is unworthy of me. –

What will tomorrow bring?
My birthday & it was a dull cold day – Mrs S.[585] surely thinks of me – this day the first time James did not follow M^r C's lead but walked up & down & then came to me – & at last went & sat down all by himself – I think he is jealous of poor Leslie.

Yes that <u>is</u> the fact I cannot make up my mind – & many a true word is spoken in jest – too many lovers bother a maid – I know it, I feel it – I could have either of them – but to which give the preference that is the question –? What shall I do would that some one was here to advise me – I think I incline to Osborne as being more likely to make me a steady quiet sensible husband in the country where my brother is & my mother[586] is going to – he is kind good natured honest & hard working – not very brilliant or highly educated, but his strong arm & cheerful temper would uphold me in days of sadness – he is not a flirt & would not irritate my nerves. But the other again is refined sensitive witty elegant beautiful figure (but James is much handsomer) has exquisite taste for music draws very well sings shines in the drawing room, has the most dandified little foot imaginable & splendid teeth. but he is a flirt & after all only Lieutenant past 30 & not rich! – He will pay me off to morrow I know – but all that will soon come to an end – What was the matter with him these two evenings I know not but he certainly was not himself something has gone wrong with him – ~~he~~ I am treating him like Cordelia[587] used to the people she did not like but was obliged to be civil to.

263

I think I was perfectly justified in not playing this evening I was sorry to disappoint the others, but as they were none of them particularly civil to me – I don't see that I need be at their beck & call. they have adopted M^r C's fashion which he does only out of spite of all standing round M^rs B when she designs to show herself on deck & when she goes down they all come round me – now I wont stand that – I told C. I was not used to play 2d fiddle – & so while they were on deck I played when M^rs B retired they all came round the Piano & wanted me to sing & play for them upon which I cooly[588] left the Piano & took up a book – they were all rather taken aback & I[589] only wish they may guess my motive.

You are going-going-gone – Well I wont
say you may go to Hong Kong[590] because I dont feel spiteful enough for that – but let me say – Goodbye –

It always pleases me to trace that principle of Dualism through all the works of nature. this morning before getting up I spent a delightful hour reading de l'Orme[591] – & found one passage not exactly new to me but very well expressed – there is a constant struggle ~~he~~ says the cardinal[592] between feeling & reason in the human ~~mind~~ breast. In youth feeling has the ascendancy ruling like a monarch with imagination for her minister – in after years reason succeeds to the throne to finish what feeling left undone. Consequently you & I (Richelieu[593] & de l'Orme) would read Ovid[594] ~~very~~ as[595] differently as the wax

264

is from the honey the bee gathers from the same flower. What touches you is the sweet poetry the wit the luxurious pictures presented to your imagination – while I through a thousand splendid allegories the great & sublime truths robed in the garment of light.

———

Last night I spent a very delightful evening we had a little talk about Mrs Drummond & her bad behaviour towards me – it seems I am quite a martyr which pleases me not a little I told James O. I was hurt at his calling me badtempered – as the only reason of my altered manner was the remarks made by some of the ladies – & ~~we~~ I[596] had a tacit reconciliation with him & C. O said in the evening do you believe in making up quarrels – yes I said I do – so do I said he & I never forget the look he gave me – & all the funny dear little things C said to amuse us – he spells my name Pawline which 3 first initials stand for <u>Pauline & William</u> – Thursday – To day he did not flirt with M[rs] B – what a wonder – & tho' she went down quickly after him[597] he soon reapeared[598] on deck "that tack don't answer" said M[rs] Drysdale. After tea I was sitting at the Piano, & James with his good honest face came & sat on the floor at my feet – that great big bear listening to my singing when C came & sat down the other side of me that was too much for J. he got up walked away & lay down on the locker & never spoke another word the whole evening – he is the most jealous man I ever saw. but is jealousy the smoke the[599] precedes & surrounds love? then he would love me if his love was proportionate to his anger when any one speaks to me – for that is the reason of his coolness to John & Leslie – C says if he marries he will have a small wife that she may stand in awe of him – to day he was looking at me putting my bonnet on – I must get a new one soon – It is quite good enough my dear – & he dashed up the steps – Good night both of [illeg.] –

265

I dont know – but I think it is no go –

———

Howard Hutton[600] is the gentlest most reserved person ever I knew – so silent so quiet so sad so thoughtful so observing & so warmhearted withal – in all these little squabbles he has faithfully & quietly taken my part there is a kind gentle expression in his eyes – & his manner is the same – he has very good features which look quite classical when he is well – I often look at his fine grecian profil[601] as he sits leaning sideways against that post – but a shade of melancholy is spread over that landscape that softens all the light & shadow – he is consumptive – he is teaching me the Maori[602] language he comes & stands near me to translate & sometimes when there is no one in the room his arm gently touches my shoulder – but not with a start – he glides away & comes again often up & down on deck it seems as if a soft slight attraction brought him to me & took him away again – like the evening breeze brings the scent of rocks & waves it away.

———

Henry is a sort of thermometer –

Aug 1.[603]

Les[604] he is a good boy – he has plenty of spirit & flashiness, & true Irish fire – a heart full of feeling & a tongue that can talk, & pluck ready to rise at a moment's notice – & still to me he is as submissive as a dog – I dont say that he loves me at all – no he does not – nor pretends to, & what gives me that power over him I know not – but my every word look or half expressed wish seems to him a command – if I went to the M[605] I should like him to come too – tho' perhaps O. would not approve of it – for he is as jealous of him as Y.[606] is of C.

Last night was Saturday again & what a pleasant evening we had music & talk & laugh. Jim[607] sat on the table behind me – every time I looked around his eyes went deep into mine & once I heard him say to himself "I will" – I never saw him so excited . . . "Alles ds Neigen von Herzen zu Herzen ach wie so eigen machet es Schmerzen"

English translation of the German by Ann Sherwin:

> "All the leaning of heart toward heart, Oh, how personal the pain it causes[608]."

Cl. kept at a little distance for he saw O was too near but still he was in good humour –

this evening he said you are like the boy & the tarts, he had so many he did not know which to eat first[609] – the sweetest said Drummond[610] who was as drunk as a fiddler – but which is the sweetest that is the thing said Hutton – they evidently see that I cant or wont make up my mind & that is about the size of it – & I should not wonder if they were both to make a fool of ~~them~~ me – if they think I am fooling them.

Aug 3^d

Saw land for the first time – the Lizzard lighthouse[611]

Every body in a state of excitement except me & perhaps Cl. In the morning it was nice & warm & I sat on deck working while C was making his little ship I put out my hand for the [illeg.] & he bent his face so low down as almost to touch my fingers with his lips – Osborne was sulky all day – those blessed Reddalls are manoeuvring against me The little Misses wont let James play with me He always wants that nasty song the gay Cavalier[612] sung – he shall have it & go to Hong Kong after it – if that is all he has to say – he never said a word to me – & now he talks of being disappointed & humbugged & all that – does he expect me to run after him – I need not be as that too able for there are always plenty people about me – there is that old Captain always bugsnacking

Henry was in a certain mood all day long pale with swimming eyes, languid attitudes, a soft silent gaze & then drooping eyelids – he looked so fascinating – he is a dear boy sometimes

But altogether it was a stupid evening – for we did not play – Cl was out of tune & voice his nerves too were on the stretch – he looked at me once with half closed eyes – away with all these thoughts – this is Monday – on Wednesday next we shall all disperse never to meet again –

Plenty of Pilot boats about – the end of a thing is always disagreable unless it is the beginning of something else which is agreeable – now I wish I was on shore – It serves me right – but I cannot decide now – not to save my life – my years bring me folly instead of wisdom – there are so many pros & cons on either side that I have not decision in my mind to say or know what I will do – Reason or rather inclination says sometimes one sometimes another – When O comes out very independant & sings the gay Cavalier[613] I think well of C beauty & all his fascination & how happy I could be with him that I could – but when he flirts with Mrs Brown it seems again that only a bushlife would suit me & J.O. make the best of husbands so quiet & goodnatured, & thus I go on till they will both leave me & serve me right.

there is one dark spot in my life that I shall never forgive myself – & that is my conduct towards Willie[614] – may I live to tell him to & to have his forgiveness –

Aug 5.

Calm & foul wind all day long off Beachy Head[615] We shall soon be starved short of sherry claret[616] brandy arrow root & all sorts of things last pig killed all the fowls gone – C got very vexed at being so stinted – & so it is most provoking not even to have a glass of grog – we had all expected this would be our last evening on board – C sat near me – & 'pon my word I could not resist – I am glad to think I have no choice – for it would be hard – for that I know I could have either of them –

Aug 7. thursday

Arrived again in old England – the coast looked beautiful & the landswell was delightful – all day long I was mournful from the morning – James & C. avoided me all day long & in the afternoon went on the steamer that was to take us in tow at which my [illeg.] were not much raised but I reflected that they might as well be away as they could not talk to me –

At tea C was silent almost sad – he took up a paper & read & James left the room & there they sat & we all looked on to the manoeuvres of the Pilot – M[r] Waters[617] a very fine man. At dusky nightfall I went down & played & soon James appeared – M[rs] Drysdale was there – & we talked about meeting in London – at last I mustered courage & said to Os. I will give you my address in London & hope you will come to see my Aunt[618] & me – I have taught them both not to be jealous C. for some reason or other would not play cards this last night? Query – Why? but we had plenty of music & my vanity was fully satisfied – I began to play that little Organ tune Waltz – but C took

268

my hand off the Piano & said "Not that not that dont speak to me like that you dont mean it – it is waste of breath – before we went to bed he kissed my hand – had I but been alone with him! – I am now convinced that I could have either of them which I have been slow to believe – C – you Lord William I dare say I shall never see again – he was in a great state of excitement all the evening – oh had my Clari[619] been in London – then I should have been happy – but as it is I may as well go & bury myself alive in the bush, & ride & cook & forget all refinement – Oh when I come to think of it – I dont know now that I shall be able to do it –[620]

Paul Toché[621]
Marcel Massé Georges
    Martin
Mr Roeckel Pianist
Mr Harden
Mr Beeber Traveller
The officers of the 11th/Clarkson, Peebles, Deverty Vigors/
M^r & Mrs Breillat
Eliza & George –
C^{pt} Young of the Waterloo
Mr Knight & Mr Leslie
M^r & Mrs Drysdale
M^r & Mrs Reddall
Family Osborne
Mrs Drummond
Mr F. Drummond
Mrs Brown a widow
Mr Howard Hatton

People known in Australia

Sir William Dennyson the Governor[622]

C[pt] Macleane	Bill Oakes
C[pt] Napper	M[r] & M[rs] Campbell
The Hon[ble] B. Morton	(Sornbank)[623]
William Maclay Sen[r]	M[r] & M[rs] G Campbell
William McClay jun[r]	M[r] & M[rs] T. Campbell
M[r] Gardiner	2 Misses Campbell
M[rs] & Miss Milford	M[r] & M[rs] David Campbell
E Baulanger	Francis Elphinstone Gouldesbury[624]
M[r] & M[rs] Rawack Pianist[625]	F.R. Bode[626]
	Miss Drane (Meggie)[627]
	Miss Arabin
C[pt] & Mrs Hovelle	M[r] Elwin
M[r] & M[rs] Wrench[628]	M[r] Teukins (Artist)
C[pt] Bloomfield 11th	M[r] Colquhoun
M[rs] Mayne & & family[629]	
M[rs] Sandy Campbell[630]	M[r] Napier of the Herald[631]
M[r] & M[rs] George Waut[632]	Andrew Suttor[633]
M[r] Hutton (Painter)	M[r] Cob.
Patch Nathan	M[r] Burn
M[rs] Vinner	Frederic {
The Rev[d] & M[rs] Reay widow	Langloh {Parker[634].
M[rs] Severn (Henry) Widow[635]	M[r] de Ayala
M[r] Haege	Sp. Consul
M[rs] Walton	Thomas Mort.[636]
M[r] & M[rs] Keele	Francis Napier of Glasgow[637]
M[r] Flemming	M[r] & M[rs] Woolner
M[r] W Lee S[r638]	Miss Onge
M[r] and M[rs] T. West	M[rs] Andrew McDougall
M[r] & the Misses Foster	M[rs] Doyle Widow
William Stephen	Wallace & Kenneth M[c]D.
M[rs] Roland Oakes	Elizabeth McD.
	M[r] Hawkins {D[r]
	Miss Ch. Darcy {Horn[639]

198

My prospects are not the most clouded —[640]

Damp wood wont burn

Wait till it gets dry —
Happy is the bride the sun shines on —
Happy are the dead the rain rains on[641]
Oneida[642] You love me not[643]
Simla[644] Uncles & brothers have I none
European[645] that man's father was my father's son —[646]
Columbian[647]

Credit: Unpublished. Text: M.S., Pf. Coll., CL'ANA 0176 (unpublished manuscript, Pforzheimer Collection of Shelley and His Circle, New York Public Library, Astor, Lenox, and Tilden Foundations)

Notes

* The title of Pauline's Australian journal, "Journal from my Life Book Continuation VIII" (translation and transcription of the German words provided by Ann Sherwin), provides insight into her rich creative output. It is one of a possible few she wrote while a governess for the Suttor family at their estate, Brucedale, in Bathurst, New South Wales, Australia. Pauline composed this journal (number VIII) between 1855 and 1857, beginning some two years after she arrived in Australia in 1853. She was a prolific journal writer who wrote at least sixteen known journal volumes, fifteen of which have been lost. Only this Australian journal remains extant at press time. The fact that she included the words "Continuation VIII" implies that she recorded those first two years in Australia in Volume VII and possibly in part of Volume VI. The introduction to this volume provides additional information about the search for Pauline's lost journals after the Second World War. When Marion Kingston Stocking visited Walter Clairmont (the recipient of Pauline's journals after the death of his sister, Alma Crüwell-Clairmont) in Munich in February – March 1949, she noted that volumes one through seven of Pauline's journal "had apparently already been lost" ("Miss Tina and Miss Plin," p. 374). Stocking examined the remaining journals which she describes in "Miss Tina and Miss Plin" and which enabled her to construct the narrative of Pauline's life. She describes them as "about the same size, roughly 5 ¾ x 8 ", hardbound notebooks" (p. 375). The extant journal meets Stocking's description. It is wrapped in a brown linen cover and contains 274 pages, each one numbered sequentially by Pauline. A small label on the front cover says "VIII 1853–57" with the words "to keep" written at the top in blue ink. Mary Claire Bally-Clairmont may have written these words when she collected the Clairmont family artefacts. The back inner cover has a small yellow seal which states: "144 Blatter K.K.a.p. Double-Raster von M. Trentsensky Wien. Domherrenhof Nr. 871 C. M." The numbers 144 (next to "Blätter"), 517, and 4S have been written in black ink. The seal provides the number of leaves (144 Blätter), the fact that the pages are "double grid" pages (Double-Raster) and the name and address of Matthäus Trentsensky, publishers (Domherrenhof Number 871). K. K. means "kaiserlich und königlich" (Imperial and Royal, referencing the Austro-Hungarian dual monarchy for which Trentsensky was an approved purveyor). C. M.

refers to the currency at the time. I quote here from *The Clairmont Family Letters*: "In *Picture of Vienna*, under the section entitled 'Value of money,' the author described the two different types of currency used in Vienna: '*Schein* or paper money; the other *Conventions-Münze* or good money' (p. 39). The anonymous author of *Picture of Vienna* recorded that only C. M. (Conventions-Münze) was used for large transactions, while Schein was offered for smaller purchases. Another term for 'Schein' was 'Wiener-Währung' (abbreviated as W.W. and translated as Viennese Currency) while 'Silber' (Silver) was the term used for C. M. According to the author, one florin in C. M. was equal to two and a half Schein. C. M. money was not frequently used and was often not in circulation. In *Beyond Nationalism*, István Deák explains that the Austrian currency was the gulden and that it was written as 'f' (florins). Each gulden contained 60 kreuzer (kr.). Fl. CM was worth 2 fl. 50 kr. WW. In 1858, the Österreichische Währung replaced the former currencies. The gulden was then divided into 100 kreuzer (New York: Oxford University Press, 1990), p. 115" (*CFL* I: 11). In black ink, we find the number f45. Additional information about the genre of journal writing and life writing can be found in Chapter 5 of this edition.

As I noted in my "Editorial Standards and Practices," for Pauline's journal, numbers included within each printed page in this volume (written at either the right or left hand margins) indicate where Pauline started a new page in her journal. As she handwrote her entries, the pages do not correspond to longer printed pages. I have chosen to create page breaks at the beginning of each journal entry which I identify by a change in date rather than to divide the pages according to the way Pauline structured her journal.

1 By this point in her narrative, Pauline had been in Australia since 1853. As recorded in her letters to her aunt Claire Clairmont, she had arrived intent on securing a position as a governess. Pauline and Wilhelm had migrated to seek their fortunes to support themselves and their mother and siblings and to avoid illness, which was rampant in Europe at the time. Their brother-in-law Alexander Knox, husband of their sister Clara Clairmont (who herself would die in 1855), provided some financial support for the outward journey. They had departed from the Downs, England, on 17 January 1853 on the *Zeepaard*, a Dutch vessel with 32 people on board (28 crew and 4 passengers) and captained by T. Giltjis. On 6 May 1853 the ship docked at Port Jackson, in New South Wales. Page 2 of the *Sydney Morning Herald* of Saturday, 7 May 1853, documents the ship's arrival (National Library of Australia, http://nla.gov.au/nla.news-page1507368, p. 2) and records that Mr. and Miss Clairmont were passengers onboard the ship: "May 6. – Zeepaard, Dutch barque, 787 tons, Captain T. Gilltjis, from the Downs 17th January. Passengers – Mr. and Mrs. Culvert, Mr. and Miss Clairmont. Gilchrist, Alexander, and Co., agents". They stayed a period in Sydney, which Pauline described in a letter to Claire as "a very bad place" (*CFL* I:154), Pauline took a position as a governess for George and Charlotte Suttor. Their estate, Brucedale, was located about 12 kilometers (7.5 miles) northeast of Bathurst. She wrote with satisfaction to Claire: "You will be pleased to hear dear Aunt that I have preferred settling in the country with a family to the uncertainty of lessons in such a low place as Sydney" (*CFL* I:154).

The Suttor family continues to live at Brucedale today. On the property's website David Suttor (b. 1961) notes: "Dating back to 1800 ours is the oldest family business in Australia. Seven generations of the Suttor family have lived and worked on this property. Located in the Peel district, 15 minutes drive north of Bathurst on the Sofala Road, our 2800 acre property straddles Clear Creek and the Winburndale Rivulet. With its gently undulating landscape Brucedale is a very picturesque property. Ideal for country walks, picnics, fishing or just relaxing and soaking up the beauty of the area. Historic tours of the farm are available on request. And if you're in Bathurst in

March you might like to consider coming along to the annual Brucedale Twilight Concert in the garden! Bathurst is the oldest inland city in Australia (population 37,000) and there are many scenic drives to nearby villages such as O'Connell, Sofala, Hill End, Millthorpe, and Carcoar" (www.brucedale.com.au/property.php Accessed 24 February 2020).

2 Members of the extended Suttor family lived at Wyagdon (also spelled Wiagdon), which is situated a few miles from Brucedale. Bathurst, which is about 200 kilometers west-north-west of Sydney, New South Wales, is the closest town. A chronicle of the family, *Dear William: The Suttors of Brucedale*, explains that George Suttor found the Brucedale land grant too small for his projected plans and requested a grant at Wyagdon. By 9 December 1835, Suttor recorded a purchase of some 864 acres at Wyagdon. He left the estate to John Bligh Suttor in his 1856 will (Judith Norton, *Dear William: The Suttors of Brucedale* [Sydney: Sydney Pub. Committee, 1993], p. 291). Norton explains that the estate was almost 10,000 acres when it was sold in 1890 (pp. 70–71). In his letter to Wilhelm Clairmont, possibly dating from 1888, Willie Suttor recorded that his brother Herbert Suttor married one of the "Wyagdon Suttors" (See *CFL* II: 253).

3 In May 1851, gold was discovered in Sofala, a town some 45 kilometers from Bathurst, a month after the gold rush began in Australia with its discovery in Ophir (42 kilometers from Bathurst). Pauline may have visited both locations.

4 11 miles.

5 The initials E.B. refer to Ernest Ulysses Bowler (1830–1896). He would express affection for Pauline as her journal will show. His younger sister, Adelaide Agnes Henrietta Bowler (1837–1920), married Pauline's one-time lover, Willie Suttor, in 1862. The parents of Ernest and Adelaide (and their brother Adolphus Bowler) were John Bowler and Francis Mary Jane Raitt. Together, Adelaide and Willie had seven children (one son and six daughters). While Stocking records the name of Willie and Adelaide's first daughter as Pauline (see *CC* II: 568), the family chronicle *Dear William* identifies their daughters' names as Dora Henrietta, Isabel Adelaide, Grace Agnes, Lilliane Charlotte, Kathleen Francis and Una Leonora (*Dear William*, pp. 322–323). Adelaide's sister, Julia, married Willie Suttor's uncle, John Bligh Suttor. See www.wikitree.com/wiki/Bowler-657 and www.wikitree.com/wiki/Bowler-666 for additional information (Accessed 19 May 2020). As this journal will show, Pauline was unimpressed by Adelaide whom she considered an inappropriate choice for Willie. See Ruth Teale's article in the *Australian Dictionary of Biography* for more information about Willie Suttor (Ruth Teale, 'Suttor, William Henry (1834–1905)', *Australian Dictionary of Biography*, National Centre of Biography, Australian National University, http://adb.anu.edu.au/biography/suttor-william-henry-4936/text7733, published first in hardcopy 1976 Accessed 20 May 2020).

6 Unidentified.

7 Pyramul is located in New South Wales, about 55 kilometers from Bathurst.

8 Unidentified.

9 Long Creek, New South Wales, is about 70 kilometers from Bathurst.

10 Unidentified.

11 Mary Suttor (1808–1889), the wife of Thomas Charles Suttor (1804–1889). Thomas Suttor was William Henry Suttor's older brother and the uncle of Willie Suttor. Mary Suttor was the sister of Charlotte Suttor, Willie Suttor's mother. Thomas and Mary Suttor had seven children. They lived on an estate called Mount Grosvenor in the town of Peel which combined a 300-acre land grant Thomas Suttor had received from Governor Brisbane in 1824 known as Grosvenor Farm as well as an additional 769 acres of land on Clear Creek that he purchased in 1837 (*100 Years of Peel and District*, pp. 3, 170; *CFL* II: 254).

12 Pauline's spelling for "interesting".
13 Pauline means that they were almost stuck in mud.
14 See Chapter 5 for more information about the use of foreign languages in nineteenth-century journals. Pauline frequently writes in French or German when she records intimate details about people or events. Her ability to code-switch shows her remarkable facility with each of these three languages. This may reflect a desire to obscure intimate details from a possible reader such as her employers, although there is no evidence that she had any suspicion they might review it intentionally.
15 Pauline frequently used abbreviations to indicate people she did not want to identify. As Chapter 5 notes, journal writers often resorted to this tactic in order to prevent identification of personal events or situations.
16 As noted in the "Editorial Standards and Practices" section of this edition and in the endnote for the title page of Pauline's journal, numbers included within each printed page in this edition (written at either the right or left hand margins) indicate where Pauline started a new page in her journal. As she handwrote her entries, the pages do not correspond to longer printed pages. I have therefore elected to break the pages at the beginning of each of Pauline's journal entries rather than to divide the pages according to the way in which she wrote her journal.
17 By her own description, Pauline engaged in numerous relationships with men through the years (she provides evidence of her many relationships in this journal), one of which culminated in the birth of her daughter, Johanna Maria Georgina Hanghegyi, in 1864. The identity of her daughter's father remains hidden to this day, but speculation abounds as to his identity. In "Miss Tina and Miss Plin," Stocking records that Pauline had identified Georgina as a "child of mine & free America" (Stocking 1978: 378), suggesting perhaps that the father was an American. Herbert Huscher believes that the name Hanghegyi is "an attempt at a translation of the name Clairmont into Hungarian" (Huscher 1955: 47). Stocking further notes that Pauline used many names for Georgina in the now-missing journals: "from 'Dot,' to Jane, Anna, Iana, and Georgie" (p. 384). Pauline spent time with Wilhelm in 1863 on his farm in the Banat during the pregnancy, then left the baby with Countess Károlyi in Rakičan, Hungary. Pauline had previously served as a governess in Rakičan, a city now part of Slovenia. She continued living with Wilhelm until 1865 when she returned to Vienna. In 1871, Georgina joined Pauline and Claire in Florence. Claire thoroughly enjoyed raising Georgina and had hoped to leave her money after Pauline's death. She also expressed a desire to sell the Shelley letters, aiming to give the proceeds to Pauline with the expectation that Georgina would receive an inheritance from the sale (*CC* II: 661). However, Georgina died in 1885 in Florence.

A letter to Claire from 8 July 1853 indicates that while in Sydney and prior to assuming the position of governess to the Suttor family, Pauline received a marriage proposal from a man who "after a fortnight seemed desperately smitten & popped the question!" (*CFL* I: 153). She told Claire that Wilhelm and her friends had "advised me so strongly against it that at last I was persuaded to say no . . . I was never so much courted as here" [meaning in Australia] (*CFL* I: 154).
18 See Pauline's journal entry of 6 May 1855.
19 The context makes it apparent that Pauline references Willie Suttor. She would have lost her position if the Suttors had known of the affair, which likely explains her choice of German, to keep her lover's identity a secret. See chapter 5 of this volume for more information about code-switching.
20 The Australian "bush" refers to the outback. In a letter to Claire Clairmont written on 3 September 1856, Wilhelm Clairmont refers to the "miseries of bushlife" (*CFL* I: 211). In her letter to Claire dated both 23 and 27 March 1854, Pauline expressed negative thoughts about Australian men. She referred to them as "squatters" and

"scrubbers," noting that Wilhelm had advised her not to "marry a squatter for it would be neither more or less than hiring yourself out for life time as maid of all work" (*CFL* I: 166). She further stated that "men are worse tyrants here than in Europe – Regular turks (except the plurality of wives)" (*CFL* I: 166). "Scrubber" was a known slur for people living in the Australian bush; "squatter" was as well, and it referred specifically to men who farmed illegally on vacant land. Gerald Walsh notes, of such men farming beyond the borders of the original Nineteen Counties, that their lives in the 1830s and 1840s "might well have been 'a sordid, filthy, existence'" (*Pioneering Days: People and Innovations in Australia's Rural Past* [St. Leonards, NSW: Allen & Unwin, 1993] p. 229). Pauline seems to echo these negative stereotypes.

21 Adelaide Agnes Henrietta Bowler (1837–1920), Willie Suttor's future wife. See Pauline's journal entry of 6 May 1855.
22 Perhaps an oblique and somewhat inaccurate reference to Proverbs 26:20: "Where no wood, is, there the fire goeth out" (*King James Bible*).
23 Unidentified.
24 The Bowler family.
25 From the context of this entry, it is apparent that Pauline refers to Willie Suttor. She states that her "young gentleman" is "younger" and that she would be a more "intelligent resource than A" (Adelaide).
26 "My brother" refers to Wilhelm Clairmont, in whom Pauline must have confided her affection for Willie Suttor. "E" is possibly Ernest Ulysses Bowler, Adelaide's brother. I am not able to identify "C.B."
27 In her journal, Pauline constantly compares herself to the younger Adelaide whom she found to be unintellectual and not attractive enough for a man like Willie. In her journal entry for 30 June, she describes Adelaide as follows: "then her features are of that kind that will very soon look wizened – nose & chin meeting – & though on the whole she is very handsome, yet I do not think I have in my face a feature so out of proportion as her nose is – But then I being plain one bad feature would not strike one so much".
28 According to Ann Sherwin, translator, the German word is "Affennatur" which has a number of meanings, including one who mimics. She notes that it is difficult to find an appropriate translation without knowing the exact context: "Mimic doesn't sound right to me, especially considering that she applies the same word *Affennatur* very negatively to someone else a few pages later". Sherwin suggests perhaps "madcap" or "eccentric" for the translation (Translator's notes, 4 September 2018).
29 Willie Suttor. Pauline's use of single letters to identify him indicates again her reluctance to have him identified should her journal have been discovered.
30 Latin for "through".
31 See 6 May 1855.
32 Probably Ernest Ulysses Bowler.
33 Adelaide Bowler.
34 Probably George, to whom Pauline will refer as the journal progresses.
35 Willie Suttor.
36 Wilhelm Clairmont.
37 In spite of her reluctance to have children, Pauline would give birth to her daughter, Georgina Hanghegyi, in 1864.
38 Adelaide Bowler.
39 Lottie refers to Charlotte Augusta Anna Suttor (1848–1926), the seventh child of William and Charlotte Suttor's thirteen children. She married William Colburn Mayne (1838–1901) in 1870 and they had five children.
40 Judith Norton's genealogical tables in *Dear William: The Suttors of Brucedale* indicate that Sarah Cordelia Suttor (1806–1894) was Willie Suttor's aunt and mother of

his five cousins. She was the younger sister of Willie's father, William Henry Suttor. She married William Beverly Suttor in 1829 (the son of Henry Suttor [1773–1848] and Miss Beverley) with whom she had five children. Henry Suttor and George Sutter (1774–1859, William Henry Suttor's father) were brothers.

41 The German spelling for "William," representing another reference to Willie Suttor.
42 George.
43 The abbreviation is unclear. If it is AB, then Pauline refers to Adelaide Bowler, which makes sense in the context.
44 The number 6 has been crossed out and replaced with a 5.
45 Pauline poignantly addresses Willie and refers to Adelaide in this journal entry.
46 There is short dash underneath the word "as" in order to separate the two parts of this page.
47 Wilhelm and Charles Gaulis Clairmont (Charley).
48 Pauline writes the words "& clever" above the word "elegant".
49 See entry for 3 June 1855, for information about the Australian bush.
50 Pauline writes the word "where" above the word "occupation," thereby indicating that she actively involves herself in editing her journal.
51 In a letter to Claire Clairmont dated 8 July 1853, Pauline notes the behaviors of the Australian men. Of her stay in Sydney, she comments: "I think I never saw so many public houses & drunken people about as here all day long but the nights are comparatively quiet . . . There are very few places of public amusement, & those that there are are low places more calculated to attract diggers & their class. I have not once been to the theatre Willy says it is too horrid for ladies to go to" (*CFL* I: 154; Pauline repeats the word "are").
52 We find further evidence for Pauline's journal editing as she adds the symbol "&" above "education".
53 Mrs. Thomas Suttor refers to Mary Anne Grosvenor Francis Suttor, the wife of Thomas Charles Suttor (1804–1889). Thomas Suttor was the older brother of William Henry Suttor, and therefore Willie's uncle.
54 In this poignant section, Pauline muses on her feelings for Willie and her antipathy towards Adelaide Bowler, his eventual wife. As the text suggests, Adelaide was less educated and younger than Pauline. She references Wilhelm Clairmont ("my brother") and Mrs. T.S., the wife of Willie's uncle Thomas Suttor. In her next entry, Pauline will comment on the "deep dejection" she experienced while writing her entry for June 30. This sadness would be nothing compared to the pain she would feel after the death of her sister, Clara Knox, who died in 1855. See 8 July 1855.

Pauline's sense of being "the plain one" would worsen with time; in 1878, she would reference what she perceived as her waning looks in a letter to Wilhelm from Florence, Italy where she resided with Claire. She exclaims as follows in her letter of 9 June, possibly 1878: "You will see by my photo how stout I am getting . . . if you have turned grey – in the course of years (which is better than being bald) I have lost my teeth which is much uglier than grey hair" (*CFL* II: 234).

55 Perhaps a reference to Thomas Gray's "Elegy Written in a Country Churchyard," written in 1751. Gray was an important eighteenth-century poet (1716–1771).
56 Pauline alludes here to the death of her younger sister, Clara Knox (née Maria Johanna Klara Gaulis Clairmont, 1826–1855). Marion Kingston Stocking states that Clara died of "pulmonary consumption", a fact she credits to Betty Bennett who gave her a copy of Clara's death certificate (See *CC* II: 548). While the Clairmont family employed a variety of names to reference their daughter, for example Clärchen or Cläri, Pauline referred to her as "Dohl" in her letters and journal. As this word is not the German name for "doll," we can assume that the family made up that word to refer to their sister. In 1849, Clara departed Vienna for England to stay with her aunt,

Claire Clairmont. Wilhelm was already residing in England with Claire. Mary Shelley invited all three to visit her at Field Place in Sussex. As Wilhelm was ill, Claire decided to stay with him in Kent and she sent Clara alone to visit Mary Shelley. While at Field Place, Clara met Alexander Knox (1818–1891), a friend from Trinity College of Mary Shelley's son, Sir Percy Florence Shelley (1818–1889). Clara and Knox immediately fell in love and eloped, much to Claire's chagrin. They married on 16 June 1849. Claire blamed Mary Shelley for the elopement and an irreparable quarrel ensued between the two stepsisters which remained unresolved when Mary Shelley died on 1 February 1851. After the loss, a bereft Claire wrote to Sir Percy Florence to express her discontent over not having been informed of Mary Shelley's final illness: "I have heard to-day that your Mother is dead. I have no wish to add any thing to your affliction, but indeed it was most unkind in you never to let me know she was ill. Most unkind. Now I can never see her more!" (*CC* II: 536). The stepsisters had been relatively close throughout their lives. Lady Jane Shelley (1820–1899), who had married Sir Percy Florence in 1848, was also involved in the courtship. Stocking quotes in *The Clairmont Correspondence* that Lady Jane Shelley said the following nearly fifty years later to Maud Rolleston about Knox's plan to marry Clara ". . . I fully agreed with him that the plan would not be a bad one, if he felt they could make each other fairly happy. When I told Mary [Shelley] she was much troubled, and said, 'Don't allow it, dear, don't allow it; they don't love each other, and the Clairmont blood always brings misery'" (*CC* II: 508). In a letter written to his parents dated 16–17 August 1849, Wilhelm observed that the dispute with Claire had impacted her health: "She was very well at Malling, but these insolences of the Shel.s and Knoxee's have so upset that she never has had a days health since Clara's marriage" (*CFL* 1: 39, Wilhelm's spelling). He also explained Claire's feelings towards the Shelleys in that same letter: "Mama asks in her letter whether my aunt told to me and Clara of her opinion of the Shell. A.C. answers that she told us every thing because she never would think of having secrets with her own relations, so Clara knew perfectly well what she put her foot into, but she was so infatuated that she would not believe one word my aunt said to her. and Mr K. of course is furious against my aunt for speaking so openly all she knew about him; now A.C. says she is determined to make the Shel. pay the piper for it. A.C. says you ask why she never complained of the S. before; and she said that she never mentioned particulars about them, but always complained bitterly of them to you at Paris; and told you there that Mr Trelawny had told her many years before that Mrs S. was the bitterest enemy she ever had" (*CFL* I: 39). Mr. Trelawny refers to Edward John Trelawny (1792–1881), Percy and Mary Shelley's friend. Together with the Shelleys and Lord Byron, Trelawny was part of the Pisan Circle of 1821. He published his *Recollections of the Last Days of Shelley and Byron* in 1858. His grave is next to that of Percy Shelley in the Cimitero Acattolico in Rome. A. C. in this quoted passage refers to Aunt Claire; the abbreviated forms of S and Shel refer to the Shelleys; K. refers to Alexander Knox.

Additionally, on 16 May 1852, Wilhelm wrote to Claire as follows about Claire's disagreement with Mary Shelley and her family as a result of the marriage, and Knox's financial promises: "You request me to write to Percey and remonstrate with him on the pain he ~~caused~~ allowed his wife to inflict upon you and us all – it is a difficult task ~~for~~ to remonstrate on a thing the truth of which it is so difficult to prove, though we may be convinced of it – ; for he would simply say that neither he nor his wife had anything whatever to do with Clara's marriage; ~~but~~ or the more likely thing is that he would not take the slightest notice of my letter; and so our purpose swould not be gained. – The chief difficulty however is that K. promised to send Mama £ 20 every year as long as Charl.'s education lasts and I am afraid he would seize upon this as an opportunity of shaking off his obligations towards us. I am afraid I can not in the present critical moment risk to deprive Mama of any pecuniary support, without the certainty of some great end being gained" (*CFL* I: 129). "Charl" refers to Charley Clairmont (Charles Gaulis Clairmont).

In this same entry, Pauline references "the second of February". Here, she refers to the date her father, Charles Gaulis Clairmont, died in Vienna. Charles had been English tutor to the Imperial family, specifically to the future Emperor Ferdinand Maximilian of Mexico (1832–1867) and his younger brother, Karl Ludwig (1833–1896). Their older brother, Franz Joseph (1830–1916), was crowned Emperor of Austria and Apostolic King of Hungary in December 1848. The Dual Monarchy of Austria and Hungary terminated in 1918. In response to Charles's death, Archduchess Sophie (the mother of the three imperial sons) recorded the following in her journal on 3 February 1850, which Hubert Huscher quotes in "Charles und Claire Clairmont": "Nous allâmes chez L'Empereur et y trouvâmes Seeburg[er](?) qui venait d'apprendre la mort subite du pauvre Clairmont, le maître anglais de Maxi-Charles-Schoenborn, et des Mensdorff etc. . . . Je la chachais à Maxi lorsqu'il vint vers 6 h. ¹/₂ chez moi accompagner son père à la première 'Faust'. J'allais un moment chez Charles qui fut très painé aussi de la mort de Clairmont . . . Je dis a Maxi la mort du bon Clairmont qui l'affligea beaucoup" ("Charles und Claire Clairmont," p. 65). Translation: "We went to the Emperor's place and found Seeburg(er) who had just learned of the sudden death of poor Clairmont, the English teacher of Maxi, Charles, Schoenborn, and some of the Mensdorffs, etc. . . . I hid it from Maxi when he came to me around 6:30 to accompany his father to the premiere of 'Faust.' I went for a moment to Charles's place who was also very pained to hear of Clairmont's death . . . I told Maxi of the death of good Clairmont which distressed him a lot" (English translation provided by Sharon Joffe).

Charles's demise caused both financial and emotional difficulties for his spouse and children. Antonia discovered that Charles had been unfaithful to her when his affair with Mrs. Kollonitz was revealed, and the family also suffered financial hardships. These financial difficulties would be mitigated by Claire whose support of her brother's family would continue throughout her life. Claire not only provided financially for Antonia and her children, but in her later years she would help raise Pauline's daughter, Georgina Hanghegyi. Claire also provided the support which enabled Wilhelm to purchase an estate in Marburg (today's Maribor in Slovenia). See Appendices B and C for more information about Wilhelm's years in the Banat.

57 See the photograph in this collection of the Clairmont family tomb. Charles was initially buried in Währing in the eighteenth district of Vienna, and Pauline refers to this location here in the journal. The cemetery today is Schubert Park. Composers Ludwig von Beethoven and Franz Schubert were originally buried in Währing, but their graves were moved to the Zentralfriedhhof (Central Cemetery) in 1888.
58 Pauline writes "In the alter of selfsacrifice" above and after the word "down".
59 A reference to Clara's husband, Alexander Knox. Knox outlived his wife by some thirty-six years, during which time he maintained connections with his wife's family. Knox also provided financial support for Pauline and Wilhelm when they traveled to Australia. A letter he wrote to Charles Clairmont in 1849 gives his background. He told Charles (who communicated this information to Claire) that he was the son of George (a merchant who worked in Jamaica) and Letitia Knox (who died in childbirth; see *CC* II: 513–514). A lawyer and a writer, Knox met Percy Florence Shelley when they were students at Trinity College, Cambridge. He accompanied Percy Florence and Mary Shelley when they traveled to the continent. From those travels, Mary Shelley wrote *Rambles in Germany and Italy*, her 1844 book of travel literature. Knox was the author of *Giotto and Francesca and Other Poems* (1842).
60 Unidentified.

61 Pauline was known as Plin to her loved ones, a contraction of her first name. According to Stocking in "Miss Tina and Miss Plin," she was variously called Paula, Paola, Paolina, Plin, and – according to a letter from Professor Huscher [Herbert Huscher, see the bibliography for this edition's Introduction] – in the family she was usually referred to as 'die Ampel' (i.e. a hanging lamp), a further contraction of 'Aunt Plin.'" (p. 383).

62 After his marriage to Clara, Knox wrote to Wilhelm from 77 Warwick Square, Pimlico, and the letter was dated 18 June 1849. Pimlico is located in London, beside Belgravia. A letter from Clara to Claire on 9 July 1849 has no accompanying envelope to identify an address, but she wrote to Wilhelm fifteen days later from 77 Warwick Square. On 21 November 1849, Wilhelm told his parents that Clara and Knox were moving into a new house in Kensington (about three kilometers southeast of London's center). On 4 January 1854, Antonia told Claire that Clara and Knox were living in East Sheen, Surrey (*CFL* I: 164). East Sheen is located in Mortlake parish in Surrey County.

63 Alexander Knox.

64 Before her move to England, Clara was employed as a tutor by the Prince and Princess of Liechtenstein. Charles told Claire in July 1849 that Clara would have "lost all character" with people such as the "princess L – " had he and Antonia not protected her reputation (*CC* II: 504).) Notwithstanding the Clairmont family's initial disappointment over the hasty marriage, it appears that Knox and Clara were happy together. Letters reveal that after their initial shock Charles and Antonia took a sanguine view towards the young couple. Indeed, Knox proved to be a good husband to Clara, a notion Pauline's journal entry confirms. However, Claire's anger and disappointment lasted a long time.

65 Pauline used this name for Clara in a letter written on 8 July 1855 to her sister, Emily Clairmont, after Clara's death: "whenever I tried to write my eyes came full of tears & I began to think of all that our dear Dohl had ever said & done, & I could not write" (*CFL* 1:178). Later, in that same letter, she states in German: "Meine liebe gute Emi jetzt da wir unsere schöne Dohl verloren haben" (English translation provided by Ann Sherwin: "my dear, good Emi, now that we have lost our beautiful Dohl").

66 Emy refers to Pauline's younger sister, Emily Clairmont (1833–1856). The parish register of the Church of St. Michael in Vienna (Michaelerkirche) recorded her name at the time of her birth in 1833. Emily was a governess as well, a fact Antonia noted in her letter to Claire of 21 November 1853: "Emmy continues with the family in town and comes now and then to see us" (*CFL* I: 160). On 4 January 1854, Antonia mentioned Emily's employer: "Emmy continues still with Mrs Löhner" *(CFL* I: 164). Emily later became engaged to Frederic Drathshmid in 1855. Of the engagement, Pauline wrote to Emily in German on 8 July 1855: "Über deine Verlobung liebe Emi hab ich mich sehr gefreut denn ich hör viel Gutes über dem jungen Mann u wünsche nur dß er dich glücklich mache – u merk dir liebe Emi good temper ist eine Hauptbedingung zu einer glücklichen Ehe – Schreib mir etwas mehr Ausführliches über das 'Wann u wo" – ich hoffe dß wenn die Zeit heran kommt werd ich dir einen Beitrag zur Aussteuer schicken können aber es muß nicht zu bald sein denn die letzten 50 f hab ich der Mama geschickt u die nächsten 100 hab ich versprochen dem Willi zu leihen wenn er nach Neuseeland geht" (*CFL* I: 178–9). English translation of the German by Ann Sherwin: "I was very pleased about your engagement, dear Emi, for I am hearing so many good things about the young man and only hope that he makes you happy – and take note, dear Emi: 'good temper' is a primary requirement for a happy marriage. Write me more details about the 'when and where' – I hope that when the time approaches I can send a contribution for your trousseau, but it must not be too soon, for I sent Mama the last 50 gulden, and the next 100 I've promised to lend Willi when he goes to New Zealand".

Emily died in 1856, the same year as her sister Sidonia (1836–1856) and her brother Charley. The 6 March 1856 edition of the *Oesterreichisch kaiserliche Wiener Zeitung* [number 55] lists her as "Emma Clairmont" who died on 2 March 1856 (Austrian Newspapers Online, Österreichische Nationalbibliothek [Austrian National Library], p. 11): "Tochter der Frau Antonia Clairmont, k.k. Professors-Witwe, alt 22 J., Landstrasse Nr. 671." It identifies her as the daughter of Mrs. Antonia Clairmont, a "professor's widow," and states her age as "22 J" (22 years). Antonia tragically lost three of her seven children within the timeframe of a year. Mary Claire Bally-Clairmont wrote as follows on the rear of a photograph about the Clairmont family tomb: "at the churchyard of Matzleinsdorf in Vienna: tomb (in german gruft) Nr. 3 bought by the Clairmont family in 1850; first burial for Charles Gaulis Clairmont; then his daughters Sidonia and Emily; no idea where his wife Antonie is buried. Next William Gaulis = Willhelm, a.s.q." (no CL'ANA number, Unpublished document, Pforzheimer Collection). See the photograph in this edition of the family tomb.

On 12 May 1856, Claire mentioned Emily's fiancé, "poor young Mr. Drathsmid," who Stocking mistakenly could not identify (*CC* II: 549). On 26 December 1856, Antonia informed Claire: ". . . poor general Drathshmid has been very ill of the typhus fever – I don't know whether I told you that they lost their eldest son suddenly – it is just a year, he was shot by accident – it was a dreadful blow, and then the loss of poor Emmy whom they both loved as a daughter, and which affected them doubly, for herself and for Frederic's sake for he loved her so dearly, it will take years ere he recovers her loss, and so the poor parents had to mourn the death of one son and the happiness of the other" (*CFL* I: 232).

67 In her letter to Emily written after Clara's death and dated 8 July 1855, Pauline admitted her ill-treatment of Emily and asked for her sister's forgiveness. Pauline expressed in German: "Meine liebe gute Emi jetzt da wir unsere schöne Dohl verloren haben, schmerzt es mich noch mehr dß ich oft gegen dich so unfreundlich war sie hat oft gesagt die arme kleine Emi thu ihr nichts – Ja liebe Emi die Trennung u Entfernung haben mich in vieler Beziehung verändert, ich glaub ein bischen weicher u besser gemacht aber ich werde doch immer ein derbes hartes gefühlloses Ding bleiben, aber die wenigen die von unserer familie zurückbleiben werd ich doch immer lieb haben – so sehr es so einem wilden bißigen Hund wie ich bin möglich ist – es ist an mir dich zu bitten die Vergangenheit zu vergessen u wir wollen einander treue Schwestern sein – Ich wollte nur es stünde in meiner Macht Euch allen zu beweisen wie lieb ich Euch hab" (*CFL* I: 178). English translation by Ann Sherwin: "my dear, good Emi, now that we have lost our beautiful Dohl, it pains me even more that I was often so unkind to you. Poor little Emi, she would often say, don't hurt her. – Yes, dear Emi, separation and distance have changed me in many respects, made me a little more gentle and better, I think. Even though I remain a rude, harsh, unfeeling thing, nevertheless I will always love few members of our family that remain – insofar as possible for a savage, vicious dog like me. It is up to me to ask you to forget the past; let us be true sisters to each other. If only it were within my power to demonstrate to all of you how much I love you" [*CFL* I: 179]).

68 Greek philosopher (c. 460 BCE – c. 370 CE), best known for his theories concerning atoms. According to Democritus, the universe is made up of atoms.
69 The connection with Democritus and "Irish philosophy" seems unclear.
70 George.
71 Adelaide Bowler.
72 Percy Bysshe Shelley's poem, "To Edward Williams." The first stanza of the poem reads as follows: "The serpent is shut out from Paradise. / The wounded deer must seek the herb no more / In which its heart-cure lies: / The widowed dove must cease to haunt a bower / Like that from which its mate with feigned sighs / Fled in the April hour. / I too must seldom seek again / Near happy friends a mitigated pain"

(www.online-literature.com/shelley_percy/complete-works-of-shelley/154/ Accessed 25 February 2020*)*. Edward Ellerker Williams (1793–1822) resided near the Shelleys in Lerici, Italy, with his partner, Jane Johnson (styled as his wife, Jane Williams) and their two children. He drowned with Percy Shelley in the Gulf of Spezia on 8 July 1822 when their boat, the *Don Juan*, capsized in a storm.

73 Unidentified.
74 Herbert Cochrane Suttor (1850–1939). The genealogical table in the family chronicle, *Dear William*, records that Herbert married Emilie Henrietta Suttor, the daughter of John Bligh Suttor who was Herbert's uncle.
75 Charlotte Augusta Anne Francis Suttor (1817–1879), mother of the Willie Suttor and wife of William Henry Suttor, Senior (1805–1877). Charlotte and William likely named their daughter after their governess. Sarah Pauline Suttor was born in 1853.
76 Caroline Elizabeth Suttor (1841–1921). The daughter of William and Charlotte Suttor, Caroline would marry John Edye Manning (1831–1909) in 1859.
77 Clearly a reference to Willie Suttor, whose behavior towards Pauline was a constant source of chagrin.
78 Adelaide Bowler.
79 Pauline deletes the word "October" via pencil and inserts the word "September" above. These incidents were probably parsed in an earlier part of Pauline's now no-longer extant journal.
80 Pauline had no shortage of suitors. In a letter dated 8 July 1846, Antonia told Claire that Pauline had "an offer of an elderly lover but has decided against it" (*CFL* I: 8). Wilhelm referenced Pauline's social activities too. In a letter he wrote to Claire on 28 February 1860, he documented Pauline's "little 'solo' excursions to Venice" which she kept from him and which provided her with a "happy manner" in "seeking recreation from the fatigues of her duties" (*CFL* I: 349). In a letter, dated 17 March and probably 1863, Pauline wrote to Claire from Wilhelm's farm in Bobda, Romania. She was pregnant at the time: "I am a sinful & wicked creature in the eyes of the Lord – & he has seen fit to punish me" (*CFL* II: 32). This last comment seems unexpected as neither Claire nor Pauline generally held negative perceptions of relationships. Societal perception could have had an impact on Pauline's ideas too. Stocking identified Pauline's Viennese lover as "Adolphe L" (*CC* II: 621). The identity of her daughter Georgina's father remains a mystery.
81 A reference to John Abercrombie (1780–1844), a Scottish physician who wrote *Inquiries Concerning the Intellectual Powers and the Investigation of Truth* (1830) and *The Philosophy of the Moral Feelings* (1833).
82 Pauline spent some time in Sydney when she first arrived in Australia in 1853 and disliked it; she called it a "bad place" in a letter to Claire (*CFL* I: 154). On 31 July 1853, she informed Claire of Mrs. Armstrong's "lodging house" where she resided while in Sydney (*CFL* I: 155); it is possible that she stayed there again in 1855. This may have been a boarding house advertised in the supplement to the *Sydney Morning Herald* of 27 July 1853. Buyers interested in purchasing a five-ton wood boat were encouraged to visit "Armstrong's Boarding House, next door to the Patent Slip Inn, King-street West" (National Library of Australia, http://nla.gov.au/nla.news-page1507810, p. 2S). In 1867, the Sydney *Almanac and General Calendar* identified a boarding house belonging to "Mrs. A. Armstrong" of 188 Princes Street (Sydney: John Sands, 1867, p. 224. Web. 4 July 2015. http://cdn.cityofsydney.nsw.gov.au/learn/history/archives/sands/1858-1869/1867-part3.pdf). In her letter to Claire of 8 July 1853, Pauline referenced a romantic relationship she had while in Sydney: "so Mr Blair a very handsome young man, says who lives in this lodging house where I am but alas he is poor & proud – So we settled that it was no use thinking of marriage but we would contribute to our mutual amusement as long as we were both in Sydney – So there I see his

beautiful bright eyes & his dark curls of hair daily – he reads Tennyson's poems to me, & when we come to hear about love in a cottage we shut up the book & sigh! – Is not that a pleasant little passe tems!" (*CFL* I: 154; Pauline misspells "passe-temps," a French term meaning "hobby, diversion or pastime." She refers to Alfred, Lord Tennyson's poem "The Lord of Burleigh" which includes the line "Love will make our cottage pleasant").

83   Pauline adds the word "now" above the word "am".
84   See 3 June 1855 in this edition for more information about the Australian bush.
85   Pauline was a highly accomplished piano player, at least, according to a letter Charles Clairmont wrote to Mary Shelley dated 1–23 November 1845. He noted that Pauline was "quite a proficient on the Piano" and "considered one of the best female dilettanti" in Vienna. She was, her father exclaimed, "Beethoven mad" and could "no doubt, that in case of necessity . . . earn her lievelihood by it" (*CC* II: 462). Charles was by no means an impartial observer, but his letters to his stepsister do not reflect frequent boasting about his children. Jacqueline Voignier-Marshall records that John H. Suttor, the great-grandnephew of Willie Suttor mentioned to her in 1982 that there had been a piano at Brucedale ("Pauline Clairmont in New South Wales," p. 30). This piano is likely the instrument Pauline mentions in her letters home and on which she may have provided instruction as part of her governess duties.
86   Pauline writes the word "even" above the word "not".
87   Pauline's spelling.
88   John Atkins (1685–1757). Atkins was a surgeon who published *The Navy Surgeon: Or, Practical System Of Surgery. With A Dissertation On Cold and Hot Mineral Springs; And Physical Observations On The Coast of Guiney* in 1742.
89   Sir Frances Bacon (1561–1626) was made Baron Verulam in 1618. He was Lord Chancellor of England, a philosopher, and a writer.
90   The identities of the people mentioned here are difficult to establish. However, context suggests that "C" refers to Charlotte Suttor, while "S" refers to her husband, William Henry Suttor.
91   See 26 December 1855 for more information about William and Charlotte Suttor's marriage.
92   If as I propose "C" and "S" are "Charlotte" and "[William Henry] Suttor," "The rich son" is likely a reference to Willie Suttor.
93   Unidentified.
94   A clear reference to William Henry Suttor, Senior.
95   William Henry Suttor, senior.
96   Possibly Wyagdon, where members of the Suttor family lived.
97   Pauline exhibits strong evasiveness here to identify these subjects. WUG (the German is difficult to decipher) is placed next to an equal sign which indicates that "WUG" possibly stands for Wilhelm and (possibly) their other brother, Charley Gaulis Clairmont. The "S" refers possibly to the Suttors, while "DW" could be the German for "the Williams" (which would reference both Suttor men to whom she was attracted).
98   Probably a reference to Wilhelm Clairmont.
99   Pauline's spelling.
100 Pauline's spelling.
101 Charlotte Suttor.
102 Pauline alludes to Roman mythology. Minerva was the Roman goddess of War, the counterpart to the Greek Athena. Minerva was said to have sprung, fully-grown and dressed in battle armor, from the forehead of her father, Jupiter (Zeus, to the Greeks). Her mother was Metis, a Titaness.
103 Pauline's spelling.
104 French for "instruction".

105 British poet Mark Aikenside (1721–1770) wrote his three-volume poem, *The Pleasures of Imagination*, in 1744. This line is from Volume 1. The stanza reads: "Know then, whate'er of nature's pregnant stores, / Whate'er of mimic art's reflected forms / With love and admiration thus inflame / The powers of fancy, her delighted sons / To three illustrious orders have referr'd; / Three sister-graces, whom the painter's hand, / The poet's tongue confesses; the sublime, / The wonderful, the fair. I see them dawn! / I see the radiant visions, where they rise, / More lovely than when Lucifer displays / His beaming forehead through the gates of morn, / To lead the train of Phœbus and the spring" (ll. 139–150. See www.poemhunter.com/poems/imagination/page-1/22680716/ Accessed 4 June 2020). Here, Lucifer is the morning star who brings in the dawn with his torch. He is also known as the pre-fall Satan.
106 Pauline's spelling.
107 See 6 May 1855.
108 Siblings Caroline and Willie Suttor.
109 Emily refers to Emilie Henrietta Suttor, the daughter of John Bligh Suttor, and Willie and Caroline Suttor's cousin.
110 Possibly the name of her horse.
111 Willie Suttor. Miss B. refers to Miss Bowler (Adelaide).
112 Unidentified.
113 Caroline Suttor.
114 "Faute de mieux": French meaning "for want of something better". "Pis Aller": French for "last resort" or "poor substitute".
115 Willie Suttor.
116 Mrs. S. is Charlotte Suttor. Mr. Oldfield is unidentified, as is the French man mentioned in the next sentence.
117 Unidentified.
118 Here, "G" refers to Pauline's suitor whom she liked but could not have considered marrying due to his lack of financial stability.
119 A reference to Pauline playing the piano.
120 Pauline writes this entire journal entry in pencil and then copies over the pencil in black ink.
121 Pauline's spelling for "stretched".
122 Pauline wrote the words "of a stranger" above the word "body".
123 Pauline writes the word "previous" above the words "my theory".
124 Pauline may have meant to write "then" instead of "the".
125 Pauline's spelling.
126 Pauline separates this section from the next with a line.
127 Probably a reference to Clara Knox.
128 Pauline writes the word "my" above the elided word "the".
129 Pauline adds the word "love" above "to".
130 Pauline repeats the word "indulge".
131 Unidentified.
132 Pauline's spelling.
133 Slang for "money".
134 The elided word "eyes" and "soul" are written above.
135 Pauline underlines the word "but" five times.
136 Pauline mistakenly writes "want" for "what".
137 Pauline's comment indicates that she and William Henry Suttor (Senior) engaged in some type of flirtation and that the relationship angered Charlotte Suttor. William and Charlotte Suttor were married on 24 December 1833, twenty-two years before Pauline penned her journal.
138 Unidentified.

139 Pauline writes the word "satisfaction" about the elided word "happiness".
140 Pauline's spelling for "treasure".
141 Possibly George Roxburgh Suttor, William and Charlotte Suttor's younger son. He was born in 1844 and died in 1928. He married Eveleen Dargin with whom he had four children.
142 Mr. Barton is unidentified. In her list entitled "People known in Australia" which she includes at the end of her journal, Pauline lists "Miss Drane (Meggie)".
143 Ernest Bowler.
143 The Bowler family.
144 Caroline Suttor.
146 Francis Bathurst Suttor (1839–1915), the son of Charlotte and William Suttor, and Willie Suttor's younger brother. Francis would marry Emily Jane Hawkins in 1853.
147 Possibly a suitor.
148 The town of Sofala lies next to the Turon River. See Pauline's 6 May 1855 journal entry.
149 Major Ch. is unidentified.
150 Captain John Piper first owned Alloway Bank before the Suttor family purchased it in 1845. In his will of 31 August 1876, William Henry Suttor bequeathed Alloway Bank's two thousand acres to his wife and, after her death, to his sons Horace Melbourne Suttor and Norman Lachlan Suttor (*Dear William*, p. 301). Pauline told Wilhelm in a letter dated 20 January 1874 that she had received a letter from Mrs. Suttor. The Alloway Bank house, she noted, had been replaced with a new home: "Do you remember Allowaybank house the residence of old Mr Suttor – that is pulled & a new fine house built & it is called Cangoura a native name, & Willie & his beautiful wife Adelaide are coming to live there" (*CFL* II: 218). Willie Suttor inherited Cangoura from his father. Norton cites Suttor's will: "I give and devise to my said son William Henry Suttor the younger All those five hundred acres (more or less) of land adjoining Alloway Bank which I purchased from the late John Savery Rodd and was conveyed to me by Indenture dated the first day of October One thousand eight hundred and fifty two and now known as Cangoura and upon which my said son William Henry Suttor the younger has lately built a house" (*Dear William*, pp. 301–302).
151 *The National Advocate* (a Bathurst newspaper) of 24 March 1908, page 2, includes a notice of a public sale of cattle, sheep, and household items belonging to Mr. C. Armstrong of Sornbank, Brewongle, whose lease had expired. Brewongle is about 6.4 kilometers (4 miles) south and east of Bathurst. See https://trove.nla.gov.au/newspaper/article/157196542 Accessed 20 May 2020. See also the list of people Pauline met while in Australia where she lists Mr. and Mrs. Campbell of Sornbank.
152 See Pauline's 9 August 1856 entry. She references here Mary Anne Grosvenor Francis Suttor and Thomas Charles Suttor, Willie Suttor's aunt and uncle.
153 See 26 January 1856.
154 Unidentified.
155 William Henry Suttor, Senior, had political aspirations. Although he had been active politically for eleven years and had been a council member during that time, he lost the Roxburgh seat to William Lee in 1856, an event that Judith Norton characterizes as leaving him "bitterly disappointed" (*Dear William*, p. 151). Suttor later won the seat for Bathurst in June 1856.
156 Alexander Knox.
157 Pauline's spelling.
158 Pauline's spelling for "led".
159 Unidentified.
160 An enclosed horse-drawn four wheeled carriage with a driver who sits upfront but who is not enclosed in the carriage. Named for Lord Brougham (1778–1868).

161 Christian holy day, marking the first day of Lent. It heralds the six weeks of penitence before Easter.
162 The word "Kelso" is written above. There are 8 kilometers between Bathurst and Kelso. Holy Trinity Church was erected in 1835 and still holds Anglican services today. The "Statement of Significance" about the church on the government of New South Wales's web page about it notes: "Holy Trinity Kelso is of State significance as the first church built west of the Great Dividing Range, in the Bathurst district near Sydney, in 1835. It has historical associations with the opening up of inland Australia for European occupation by convict labour, in particular, the crossing of the Blue Mountains and the establishment of a Christian settlement in Bathurst in the early 1800s. It has been in continuous use as a place of worship and burial from 1826 until the present day. Its pioneer graveyard is the earliest European cemetery west of the mountains. Its rectory is an intact although modest example of the domestic design of the renowned ecclesiastic architect Edmund Blacket. The group is likely to be of State and local significance for its associations with Anglican ministers including the Reverends Samuel Marsden, Rowland Hassall, Thomas Hassall and William Grant Broughton, and architects including Blacket as well as the Bathurst pioneer and original grantee James Blackman. Although the design of the original church building is naive and its author unknown, the church has a landmark position sited impressively at the top of a hill. Extensive alterations and additions have been carried within the group by prominent architects, adding considerably to the aesthetic significance of the church and demonstrating a high degree of religious commitment and technical achievement for a pioneer settlement where materials and skilled trades were in short supply. The fine stained glass east window of the church was manufactured c1902 in England to a design by Pre-Raphaelite artist Edward Coley Burne-Jones. The church organ (c.1882) is one of few Hunter organs to have been imported into Australia from England, and is intact. The Holy Trinity Church Group is of State social significance to the Anglican Church in NSW as a pioneering parish still using the site for worship. The archaeological potential of the Holy Trinity Group is of State significance because of the site's early settlement, continued use and limited disturbance. It is representative at a State level for retaining many of the original elements of a functioning nineteenth century Church of England property – including the rectory and the burial ground, as well as the church. It is of State significance for its rarity as an intact group of ecclesiastic structures in continuous religious usage since the early years of inland occupation of Australia" (www.environment.nsw.gov.au/heritageapp/ViewHeritageItemDetails.aspx?ID=5052122 Accessed 26 February 2020).
163 In her letter to Claire dated 22 and 27 March 1854, Pauline expressed her discontent. She wrote, "I am literally imprisoned night & day in a house & garden a hundred yards square & as for going to any place beyond a mile it is such an unheard of piece of independance in the eyes of these narrowminded colonists, that the first & only time I attempted a little stroll by myself – terror seized all the inmates of the house when they became aware of my absence horses were saddled, bellmen were sent out the native cooy was sounded & at last they discovered me sitting under a tree at about 5 minutes walk from the house. Then there were questions asked, signs of terror & surprise given, what could have induced me to wander away in the bush, had I lost my way (I had only been absent half an hour) did I hear the bellman & the cooy why did I not answer the latter? Till I at last said – be quiet with all your nonsense, I only took a little walk to refresh my wearied spirit in the cool bath of solitude & commune with myself on the different duties I had undertaken" (*CFL* I: 166–167); The word "cooy" is a misspelling of "cooee" which *Collins English Dictionary* defines as "a call used to attract attention, esp (originally) a long loud high-pitched call on two notes used in the Australian bush" ("cooee." *Collins English Dictionary – Complete & Unabridged*

164 Two classes of Roman citizens in ancient Rome. Patricians were the nobles of Rome and members of the class were originally leaders in the Roman Senate. The plebeian class was the less noble class. The term refers to the ordinary citizens of Rome.
165 Pauline's spelling for "wives".
166 Pauline writes "civiation" and adds the letters "liz" in pencil.
167 Perhaps Frederic Parker, one of the people Pauline records in her list of people whom she met in Australia.
168 The original is unclear. The letter could either be a "B" or a "D." A "D" would refer to Adolphus Chorley Robert Bowler (1834–1912), brother of Ernest and Adelaide, who was known as Dop. See www.wikitree.com/wiki/Bowler-374 Accessed 20 May 2020.
169 Pauline means to write "temps".
170 Pauline writes the words "sa Fortune" on the next page of her journal. I have translated it here.
171 French for "his fortune" or "her fortune".
172 Charlotte Suttor had ten children in 1856. The use of German here likely reflects the desire to shield these sentiments from the Suttor family should they read her journal.
173 Pauline means to write the word "abscised," meaning "to cut off".
174 Pauline writes word "at" twice.
175 French for "self-esteem".
176 Pauline cites from Shakespeare's *Hamlet*: "O, that this too too solid flesh would melt / Thaw and resolve itself into a dew! / Or that the Everlasting had not fix'd / His canon 'gainst self-slaughter! O God! God! / How weary, stale, flat and unprofitable, / Seem to me all the uses of this world!" (I.ii.129–34). http://shakespeare.mit.edu/index.html Accessed 26 February 2020.
177 Pauline writes the words "make me" above the word "to".
178 Pauline writes this final section in pencil.
179 This sentence is also written in pencil.
180 William Henry Suttor, Senior, hoped to win a seat on the Roxburgh council during elections held in March 1856. He was not elected (see Norton, p. 151).
181 Unidentified.
182 Pauline's spelling.
183 Possibly Adelaide Bowler.
184 Pauline writes "day April 2^d" above the word "to".
185 Pauline refers to Willie Suttor and his cousin, Emilie Henrietta Suttor. A. is a reference to Adelaide Bowler.
186 Pauline writes the first part of this journal entry (before the 4 April demarcation) in pencil and then copies over it in black ink.
187 Adelaide Bowler.
188 Pauline adds the words "nor looked sentimental" in pencil.
189 Pauline adds the symbol "&" above "paradoxes".
190 She references Wilhelm Clairmont in this passage.
191 Pauline alludes to the deaths of her father on 2 February 1850 and her sister, Clara Knox, on 5 March 1855. Stocking notes that Clara died of "pulmonary consumption" according to her death certificate (*CC* II: 548).
192 Pauline's spelling.
193 French for "M. S. is defeated and I take it as a bad omen." M. S. identifies Mr. Suttor (William Suttor, Senior) who lost his election.
194 This number does not correspond with Pauline's pagination and therefore is assumed to be a date change.
195 Unidentified.

196 Pauline's spelling.
197 Pauline's spelling for "temps".
198 Pauline's spelling for "serez".
199 Pauline adds the word "la" above "Victoire".
200 Pauline writes the words "amour propre" over the elided "vanité" (which she misspells).
201 Pauline adds the word "again" above.
202 Norton identifies William Bowman, esquire, as a member of the Legislative Assembly for New South Wales (see p. 157). In August 1856, William Suttor, Senior, was also sworn in as a member of the Legislative Assembly.
203 Siblings Lottie and Herbert Suttor. Lottie refers to Charlotte Augusta Anna Suttor (1848–1926), the seventh child of William and Charlotte Suttor. Herbert is their son, Herbert Cochrane Suttor (1850–1939).
204 Florence Adelaide Suttor (1856–1933) was the daughter of John Bligh Suttor (1808–1886) and Julia Francis Nina Bowler (1829–1901). John Bligh Suttor and William Henry Suttor were brothers. Julia Bowler was Adelaide Bowler Suttor's sister. See Pauline's journal entry of 6 May 1855 for more information about the Wyagdon Suttors.
205 Mrs. T. S. refers to Mary Anne Grosvenor Francis Suttor, the wife of Thomas Charles Suttor. Mrs. Thomas Suttor was the sister-in-law of John Bligh Suttor and Florence Adelaide's aunt.
206 Pauline's spelling for "too".
207 Amelia Alderson Opie's poem, "Song," written in 1802. Opie (1769–1853) was a friend of Mary Wollstonecraft. Opie's husband, John Opie, painted Wollstonecraft's portrait which hung in the Godwin home. The portrait is in the National Portrait Gallery in London today.
208 Unidentified.
209 Pauline writes the word "knew" above "not".
210 Pauline's spelling.
211 The poem is unidentified.
212 Pauline's spelling.
213 Biblical King David.
214 Caroline Suttor.
215 Pauline's spelling for "worldly".
216 From Lord Byron's poem, "The Corsair," published in 1814. In Canto 3, he describes the sunset, noting that the sun, "Behind his Delphian cliff he sinks to sleep" (line 18). In "The Curse of Minerva," Byron's poem of 1811 which addressed the issue of the Elgin Marbles taken by the British from Athens to England and which was unpublished during his life, Byron repeats lines 1–54 (including this line) from Canto 3 of "The Corsair". "The Curse of Minerva" was eventually published in 1828. Byron died in 1824. See Peter Cochran's analysis of "The Curse of Minerva" (https://petercochran.files.wordpress.com/2009/03/the_curse_of_minerva1.pdf Accessed 6 March 2020).
217 Pauline writes the word "the" above "that".
218 The notion of religious dualism affirms that there exists two opposing principals or parts to existence such as good versus evil. The Christian doctrine of the Trinity asserts that there are three parts to the Godhead, namely the Father, the Son, and the Holy Spirit.
219 Pauline's spelling.
220 The Roman god of love. Cupid was the son of Venus (goddess of love) and Mars (god of war) and is known as Eros in Greek mythology.
221 Pauline's spelling.
222 A reference to Lord Byron's play, *Manfred*, first published in 1817. In Act II, scene 2, Manfred states: "Beautiful Spirit! in thy calm clear brow" (line 27). See www.bartleby.com/18/6/22.html Accessed 6 March 2020.

223 Orange, New South Wales, is roughly 29 kilometers (18 miles) from Ophir.
224 Pauline thinks perhaps of two possible quotations: "For I determined not to know any thing among you, save Jesus Christ, and him crucified." 1 Corinthians 2:2, *King James Bible*. Alternatively, Socrates (Greek philosopher, 469 BCE – 399 BCE): "As for me, all I know is that I know nothing".
225 "M" stands for "Mutter" (German for "mother) or the English word, "mother". Antonia Clairmont's letter to Pauline informing her that Sidonia Clairmont had died had evidently reached Australia.
226 Born in Vienna in 1837, Sidonia Clairmont died on 29 January 1856 at the age of nineteen years. She would be one of three of Antonia and Charles Clairmont's children to die in 1856. Antonia wrote to Claire on 7 February 1856 of the loss: "our dear Sidi was taken ill and in short 12 hours, her angel soul passed on to that better world, when we shall once join her, but are now left to struggle and suffer" (*CFL* I: 184). It may be that an earlier ailment had made Sidonia vulnerable, as Charles Clairmont informed Mary Shelley in a November 1845 letter that Sidonia had suffered "a scrophulous complaint . . . She appears to have overcome the scrophula as far as exterior symptoms go; but the spine, just at the root of the neck has taken a wrong direction . . . she is however lively and healthy, has an excellent appetite and walks far and well" (*CC* II: 164). Writing to Mary Shelley on 1 August 1845, Claire Clairmont described Sidonia as "sickly and the Doctor says quite frankly that he cannot think she will grow up to live, for her lungs are much affected. She is only eight years old and her breathing is so short she cannot mount a staircase – there is a mal conformation of the heart or of the spine" (*CC* II: 454). On 23 August 1856, Claire wrote an inscription for Charles, Sidonia, and Emily's tombstone which was erected in the Währing cemetery (see *CC* II: 580–581).
227 "Clari" refers to Clara Knox. The family frequently called her Clari.
228 Caroline Suttor.
229 Possibly Elizabeth Suttor (1815–1862), the sister of William Henry Suttor, senior, who married William John Kerr in 1835. See journal entry for 9 August 1856.
230 Unidentified.
231 Poetry by Thomas Moore (1779–1852), English poet and friend of Lord Byron.
232 Robert Johnson, Esquire, was a member of Parliament for New South Wales in 1856 (Norton, p. 157).
233 See journal entry of 6 May 1855.
234 Unidentified.
235 Apollo, the Greek god of the sun. This is Pauline's spelling for Apollo.
236 In 1888, Willie Suttor wrote to Wilhelm Clairmont, noting how he had changed over the years: "The slim lad you knew in myself has grown into a stout, portly elderly gentleman of great girth & weight some 15 stone 7 lb. with grey beard & alas I fear, a little bald patch on the top of his crown is beginning to show itself" (*CFL* II: 253).
237 Emily Clairmont, Pauline's younger sister, died on 18 March 1856 at the age of twenty-two. See journal entry for 8 July 1855 for more information about Emily Clairmont. On 5 April 1856, Antonia told Claire: "when the cold set in poor Charley became worse, Emmy at the same time, she got the typhus, but Charley soon ralied [spelling original], was out of bed, grew quite strong again, and promised very fair, but two such lapses to fear, without bad consequences was not to be hoped; since Emmy's death, he is getting weaker and weaker every day" (*CFL* I: 187).
238 One of many direct addresses to her sister, Clara Knox.
239 Wilhelm was working on his farm, Kangaroo Hills, by 1856. In 1855, he purchased Kangaroo Hills near Armidale, New South Wales, together with his partner, Julius Duboc. That enterprise failed by 1857. He then went to work on various runs for the Twofold Bay Pastoral Association until his departure for Europe in 1861.
240 Pauline's brother, Wihelm Clairmont.

241 Clara Knox died in 1855 while Emily and Sidonia Clairmont both died in 1856. Charles Gaulis Clairmont would die in 1856 too. See the journal entry for 8 July 1855.
242 Possibly Alexander Warren, Esquire, a member of Parliament for New South Wales in 1856 (see Norton, p. 157).
243 Charlotte Suttor.
244 Pauline leaves a page between this final paragraph and the entry that starts on page 116.
245 Luke 14:11: "For whosoever exalteth himself shall be abased; and he that humbleth himself shall be exalted" (*King James Bible*).
246 "The Crown of Glory" is a biblical term. We see references to the term in 1 Peter 5: 4 "And when the chief Shepherd shall appear, ye shall receive a crown of glory that fadeth not away" (*King James Bible*) and Proverbs 16:31 ("The hoary head is a crown of glory, if it be found in the way of righteousness"; *King James Bible*).
247 Pauline refers to Thomas Moore's "The Love of the Angels". Moore was an Irish poet (1779–1852) who published his poem in 1832. Moore was a friend of Lord Byron and wrote *The Life of Lord Byron* which was published by John Murray in 1832.
248 Pauline quotes partially from the poem here. She quotes from the First Angel's story. Moore's lines read as follows in the poem: "pure and unmoved / She stood as lilies in the light" which is later followed by: "So innocent the maid, so free / From mortal taint in soul and frame, / Whom 'twas my crime – my destiny – / To love, ay, burn for, with a flame / To which earth's wildest fires are tame. / Had you but seen her look when first / From my mad lips the avowal burst; / Not angered – no! – the feeling came / From depths beyond mere anger's flame – / It was a sorrow calm as deep, / A mournfulness that could not weep, / So filled her heart was to the brink, / So fixt and frozen with grief to think / That angel natures – that even I / Whose love she clung to, as the tie / Between her spirit and the sky – / Should fall thus headlong from the height / Of all that heaven hath pure and bright!"

Subsequent lines include: "How could I leave a world which she, / Or lost or won, made all to me?" and "That minute from my soul the light / Of heaven and love both past away; / And I forgot my home, my birth, / Profaned my spirit, sunk my brow, / And revelled in gross joys of earth / Till I became – what I am now!" (https://allpoetry.com/The-Loves-of-the-Angels Accessed 23 January 2020).
249 "Spell=binds" is separated with an equal sign.
250 Pauline placed the word "not" above and between "would" and "speak".
251 Wilhelm and Charley Clairmont.
252 Julia Nina Sofala Suttor (1851–1917) was the daughter of John Bligh Suttor (1808–1886) and Julia Francis Nina Bowler (1829–1901). The family lived at Wyagdon. Norton records that Julia Nina Sofala Suttor was born on 9 August 1851 and died on 29 October 1917. In 1873, she married Henry Douglas Mackenzie, with whom she had six children (*Dear William*, p. 334).
253 See 6 May 1855.
254 W. is Willie Suttor; Ad. refers to Adelaide Bowler.
255 Mrs. Wise is unidentified. Mr. B. could refer to Mr. Bowler, possibly Ernest. Maria Suttor was the daughter of Sarah Cordelia Suttor and William Beverley Suttor. Sarah Suttor was the sister of William Henry Suttor, senior, and therefore Willie Suttor's aunt. Maria and Willie were cousins. Norton does not give a birth date for Maria Suttor. However, her older sibling was born in 1833 and her younger sibling was born in 1835. She would therefore have been born sometime in 1834.

It is difficult to discern if the initials are L.P or T.P. L.P would refer to Langloh Parker, one of the people Pauline met while in Australia and listed together with Frederic Parker at the back of her journal. Langloh Parker would have been Willie Suttor's friend. He was born in Tasmania in 1840 and died in 1903. His wife was the author

Catherine Eliza Stow, whose pseudonym was K. Langloh Parker, and his uncle was Augustus Morris (c. 1820–1895), a co-worker of Wilhelm Clairmont's. Langloh and his brothers, Frederick ("Frederic" in Pauline's journal) and James, were pastoralists who worked at Paika, a farm managed by Augustus Morris. Morris was a pastoralist who managed and then owned sheep stations. He worked as a manager on the Tala, Yangar, Nap Nap, and Paika stations. Later, in 1853, and together with T. S. Mort, Thomas Holt, and T. W. Smart, Morris purchased stations from William Wentworth in the Murrumbidgee area (see 'Parker, Langloh (1840–1903)', Obituaries Australia, National Centre of Biography, Australian National University, http://oa.anu.edu.au/obituary/parker-langloh-14738/text25894 Accessed 22 May 2020, and Barnard, Alan. "Morris, Augustus (1820–1895)", *Australian Dictionary of Biography*. National Centre of Biography, Australian National University. 1974. Web. http://adb.anu.edu.au/biography/morris-augustus-4250/text6867 Accessed 22 May 2020).

"T.P" might refer to Thomas Piper (1838–1919). Piper was born in New South Wales and he died in Bathurst (https://australianroyalty.net.au Accessed 22 May 2020).

256 Elizabeth Suttor (1815–1862), the sister of William Henry Suttor, Senior, married William John Kerr in 1835. They had no children. They lived at Peel House in Peel Village. The house still stands today. In October 1856, the *Bathurst Free Press* wrote about "a suitable mansion . . . erected by W. J. Kerr, Esq on a picturesque little hill overlooking the swamp" (*One Hundred Years of Peel and District*, p. 37). I quote here from footnotes to *CFL* (I: 158): "Elizabeth Suttor Kerr began a Church of England Sunday School (*One Hundred Years of Peel and District*, p. 154, 171) and the *Bathurst Free Press* recorded the opening of the school in November 1859 with forty children and four teachers at the Kerr's house (p. 59). Peel Church has a stained-glass window dedicated to the memory of Dr. and Mrs. Kerr. Smith notes that Elizabeth Suttor Kerr donated £10 in 1857 to the Church of St. John the Evangelist building fund (p. 126)".

From *CFL* (I: 157): "In June 1851, an indigenous Australian worker found gold on the run of William John Kerr, brother-in-law of William H. Suttor and husband of William's sister, Elizabeth Mary Suttor. *The Bathurst Free Press and Mining Journal* of 19 July 1851 titled its discovery article, 'A Hundred Weight of Gold' and boldly declared, 'Bathurst is mad again. The delirium of golden fever has returned with increased intensity' (National Library of Australia, http://nla.gov.au/nla.news-page6172011, p. 2). The press reported that the gold weighed roughly 106 pounds, 'all disembowelled from the earth at one time,' and that the discovery 'set the town and district in a whirl of excitement.' The *Maitland Mercury and Hunter River General Advertiser* of 23 July 1851 compared the Californian gold rush to the Australian gold rush and, as a result of the discovery of gold near the Meroo Creek area where Kerr's run was located, the newspaper published the following: 'whether the Californian gold fields exceed ours in general richness or not, no such quantity of gold as this has yet been found there in one mass. This finding of a hundred weight of gold, as it has been aptly termed, has produced considerable excitement in the colony . . . Increased immigration from neighbouring countries may be looked for as an immediate consequence, and the news will reach home just in time to swell the stream of immigration hither which the first intelligence of our gold discovery will have induced' (National Library of Australia, http://nla.gov.au/nla.news-page127012, p. 2). On 14 July 1851, Charlotte Suttor termed the Kerr find 'the wonderful heap' and recorded that it was kept in the dining room cupboard until it could be placed in the bank (*Dear William*, p. 131)".

257 Mrs. Charles Suttor. Here, Pauline refers to Willie Suttor's aunt, Mary Anne Grosvenor Francis Suttor, the wife of his uncle, Thomas Charles Suttor.

258 Pauline's spelling.

259 Unidentified.
260 Pauline sections this entry separately from the previous one.
261 The words "Dream of Poison" are written in pencil. The line is from Percy Bysshe Shelley's 1816 poem, "Mutability". The first line of the third stanza states: "We rest – a dream has power to poison sleep" (www.poetryfoundation.org/poems/54563/mutability-we-are-as-clouds-that-veil-the-midnight-moon Accessed 21 May 2020).
262 "Cupid and Psyche" by Thomas Moore (1779–1852). In Moore's poem, the final stanza reads as follows:
"Farewell – what a dream thy suspicion hath broken! / Thus ever. Affection's fond vision is crost; / Dissolved are her spells when a doubt is but spoken, / And love, once distrusted, for ever is lost!" (www.poetrynook.com/poem/cupid-and-psyche Accessed 26 January 2020).
263 A short line divides the two parts of this page.
264 Perhaps William Bowman's wife. See 30 April 1856.
265 The following French lines are written in pencil and then copied over in black ink. The lines read as follows: "Pardi s'il etait mon mari je m'en ficherais – mais je ne puis pardonner a l'amant". Translation: "Good lord yes, if he was my husband, I would not care – but I cannot forgive the lover" (French translation by Sharon Joffe).
266 The words "or even without" are added in between "approbation" and "to one person".
267 The words "easily shortly" are written above the word "how".
268 Caroline Suttor, Willie's sister.
269 Pauline wrote the words "or when" above "if".
270 Unidentified.
271 These words are written in pencil and copied over in black ink. They allude, perhaps, to Shakespeare's *Macbeth*'s "Fair is foul, and foul is fair" (I:i), the concluding couplet of the three witches' initial appearance on stage.
272 The words "to me" are written above "night".
273 Pauline writes these words in pencil. They are traced over in ink and are written in a larger script than the rest of the entry.
274 Pauline writes these final words in a smaller script.
275 Caroline Suttor.
276 Probably a reference to Moore's poem, "Cupid and Psyche". See journal entry "A little later" (no date provided).
277 The word is written in the singular.
278 Unidentified.
279 Latin for "Without which, not".
280 "AB" refers to Adelaide Bowler. "E. A." is unidentified. "Mr. W." refers to Willie Suttor. The later reference "Ad." is again to Adelaide Bowler.
281 "Except children" is written in pencil and above the word "her".
282 Unidentified.
283 "Or G" is written above. I. is unidentified. "G" stands for George.
284 Pauline meant to write "by" instead of "be".
285 The letters "es" have been added in pencil, possibly by a later reader.
286 Pauline enjoyed the poetry of Alfred, Lord Tennyson. Christoph Clairmont and Mary Claire Bally-Clairmont speculated that a handwritten manuscript of poetry now in the Carl H. Pforzheimer Collection belonged to her. The anonymous author of the manuscript copied Tennyson's "Charge of the Light Brigade" (written in 1854). Pauline also referenced Tennyson's work numerous times in her journal and letters. See, for example, *CFL* (I: 154) when she describes her romantic interest, Mr. Blair, who reads Tennyson's poetry to her. The "jingle of the guinea" is a line from "Locksley Hall" which was published in 1842: "But the jingling of the guinea helps the hurt that Honour feels, / And the nations do but murmur, snarling at each other's heels" (lines 105–106).

287 Henry Francis died in 1856. Charlotte Suttor was the daughter of Henry Francis and Ruth Grosvenor (1778–1860). Henry Francis was born in 1774 in London. He married Ruth Grosvenor in 1801 in London and the family emigrated to Australia. Charlotte was the ninth of their ten children (www.asletts.com/node/6 Accessed 2 February 2020).
288 Pauline's spelling.
289 The word "any" is written above "is".
290 Per Ann Sherwin, Translator: "The German version appears in many places online, part of a poem or song – often quoted without attribution. This is my non-rhyming translation" (translator's note, 6 September 2018).
291 Ann Sherwin, translator, suggests that these words could also be a quotation, but she was unable to identify the quotation (translator's note, 6 September 2018).
292 The Clairmont family suffered a third loss in 1856 when Charles Gaulis Clairmont died on 7 May 1856. On 8 May 1856, Antonia wrote to Claire of her son's death: "Yesterday 7th May at ½ past two in the afternoon my dear poor Charley departed this life for a better world where there are no cares no sorrows, he is an angel as pure and free from sin as dear little Sidi" (*CFL* I: 192). Word had not reached Wilhelm by 28 November 1856, as evidenced in a letter he wrote to Claire, which referenced his sisters' deaths, but expressed uncertainty about his brother: "I can never dispell from my mind the gloomy thought that poor dear Charley too is perhaps consigned to his eternal resting place while I am writing these lines" (*CFL* I: 227). Thus the letter informing Pauline of Charley's death likely would not yet have reached Australia and this journal entry references Emily's death in March 1856. "Goldlosi" may refer to Emily and is perhaps a form of "Goldilocks". Charles Clairmont told Mary Shelley in a letter dated 1 November 1845–23 November 1845 that Emily "is the prettiest of the three younger ones, and will doubtless grow up something of a beauty". Her 1854 pencil and watercolor portrait shows she had light brown-colored hair (see Clairmont Family Papers, Pforzheimer Collection), which may support the name "Goldlosi".
293 Clara Knox.
294 Willie Suttor.
295 As with apparently the same initials appearing (without only one period) in the 9 August 1856 entry, it is difficult to discern if Pauline wrote an "L" or a "T". The "L" could refer to Langloh Parker, while T. P. could possibly be Thomas Piper. See 9 August 1856 for more information about these two men.
296 Pauline wrote the word "not" above "would".
297 Portuguese for "stone".
298 French for "so, I will be right".
299 See 9 August 1856 for information about the gold rush in Australia.
300 Hiawatha was the chief of the Onondaga people in the fifteenth century. He was instrumental in forming the Iriquois Confederacy, a league of five nations (six, after 1722) committed to working together during the French and British conflict over the conquest of North America. See www.britannica.com/topic/Iroquois-Confederacy (Accessed 2 February 2020). Henry Wadsworth Longfellow wrote "The Song of Hiawatha" exploring the legend in 1855, a poem with which Pauline might have been familiar. The final lines of the poem referenced Hiawatha's death: "And the people from the margin / Watched him floating, rising, sinking, / Till the birch canoe seemed lifted / High into that sea of splendor, / Till it sank into the vapors / Like the new moon slowly, slowly / Sinking in the purple distance. / . . . / Thus departed Hiawatha, / Hiawatha the Beloved, / In the glory of the sunset, / In the purple mists of evening, / To the regions of the home-wind, / Of the Northwest-Wind, Keewaydin, / To the Islands of the Blessed, / To the Kingdom of Ponemah, / To the Land of the Hereafter!" (www.hwlongfellow.org/poems_poem.php?pid=296

Accessed 2 February 2020). It appears that these lines inform Pauline's comment about Hiawatha's death.
301 William Shakespeare. Sonnet 109: "O! never say that I was false of heart, / Though absence seemed my flame to qualify. / As easy might I from myself depart / As from my soul, which in thy breast doth lie: / That is my home of love; if I have ranged, / Like him that travels, I return again, / Just to the time, not with the time exchanged, / So that myself bring water for my stain. / Never believe, though in my nature reigned / All frailties that besiege all kinds of blood, / That it could so preposterously be stained, / To leave for nothing all thy sum of good; / For nothing this wide universe I call, / Save thou, my rose; in it thou art my all." (www.poetryfoundation.org/poems/50301/sonnet-109-o-never-say-that-i-was-false-of-heart Accessed 2 February 2020).
302 Pauline misspells "printemps".
303 Possibly Sarah Ann Piper (1836–1918), sister of Thomas Piper. See jounal entry for 9 August 1856. (https://australianroyalty.net.au/individual.php?pid=I67900 Accessed 2 February 2020).
304 These final words are written vertically on the right side of the page.
305 Pauline adds the word "present" above "from".
306 Pauline adds the words "or both" in pencil above the word "former".
307 From Edgar Allan Poe's poem, "The Raven" published in 1845.
308 "Il a fait des avances ce soir – faute de mieux je suppose." French for "He made advances this evening – for lack of anything better, I suppose".
309 "L'amour est une affaire sérieuse a [Pauline's spelling for "à"] trente ans". French for "love is a serious affair when one is thirty years of age".
310 The word "soul" is written above "awakens".
311 The word "parent" is written above "friend".
312 Here Pauline anticipates her return to Europe. She talks of returning to her mother, Antonia Clairmont, who lived in Austria.
313 Pauline's spelling for "siren". The sirens were Greek mythological characters who enticed sailors with song, leading to the sailors' deaths.
314 The German words that follow are all written in pencil and copied over in dark ink, with the exception of the final five words.
315 Suttor and Clairmont.
316 Shakespeare, *Macbeth*, Act V, scene i: "Out damned spot! Out I say". Ironically, like Lady Macbeth, Pauline strives to cleanse herself of her sins.
317 Pauline writes this final line in English.
318 Pauline has written "Mr C's" and then added "ampbell's" in pencil underneath. In her list of people whom she met in Australia, Pauline identifies "Mr. and Mrs. Campbell" of Sornbank. See also the journal entry for 31 January 1856.
319 The word "me" is added above "over".
320 Pauline writes "which is not yet ended" in pencil.
321 Poem written by Robert Burns in 1794, "For the Sake O'Somebody". Burns was a Scottish poet who flourished during the Romantic era.
322 Robert Burns, "Wandering Willie," written in 1793.
323 "Il faut se faire raison". French for "You have to be right".
324 Pauline records "Francis Elphinstone Gouldesbury" in her "People Known in Australia" list.
325 "One" is written above.
326 "Il aime par élan comme moi". French for "he loves like me by impulse".
327 Pauline's spelling. Additionally, she writes the word "he".
328 The word "her" is added above "loves".
329 Penrith is located some 50 kilometers west of Sydney. The city was named in honor of Penrith, England. British settlement began in 1815.

330 "in our acceptation of the word" is written above "marriage".
331 Pauline repeats the word "at".
332 S. and O. possible refer to Sofala and Ophir, two cities referenced in Pauline's journal entry of 6 May 1855.
333 Unidentified.
334 In a letter to her aunt, Claire Clairmont, written from Brucedale between March 22 and 27, 1854, Pauline observed as follows about men in the Australian outback: "Willy wrote to me a short time ago – Take care my dear sister you don't marry a squatter for it would be neither more or less than hiring yourself out for life time as maid of all work. I told him there was no fear of that, as I did not intend marrying at all – let not that vex you dear Aunt, – but men are worse tyrants here than in Europe – Regular turks (except the plurality of wifves)" (*CFL* I: 166). She also discussed life in the Australian bush in her journal on 3 June 1855.
335 See Jacqueline Voignier-Marshall's article, "Looking for Pauline Clairmont in N.S.W" for the information about the piano at Brucedale (*The Byron Society of Australia Newsletter*, [7] 1983, pp. 25–31), and various references in *The Clairmont Family Letters* where Pauline describes playing the piano at Brucedale. See journal entry for 13 September 1855.
336 See journal entry for 26 January 1856.
337 Pauline probably refers to a handkerchief (in French, "un mouchoir"). A "pocket handkerchief" is "un mouchoir de poche".
338 These lines were written in pencil and traced over in black ink.
339 Unidentified.
340 Thomas Robert Malthus (1766–1834) was a British economist who wrote *An Essay on the Principle of Population as It Affects the Future Improvement of Society, with Remarks on the Speculations of Mr. Godwin, M. Condorcet, and Other Writers* in 1798.
341 This final paragraph is written in pencil and traced over in black ink.
342 "W. est malelevé au possible". French for "W[illie] is completely badly brought up".
343 Unidentified.
344 Unidentified.
345 Pietro is the Italian for Peter. Gianetto is an Italian version of John, typically styled as Giovanni.
346 Pauline's spelling.
347 Possibly the local preacher.
348 Song of Solomon, 3:6: "Who *is* this that cometh out of the wilderness like pillars of smoke, perfumed with myrrh and frankincense, with all powders of the merchant?" *King James Bible*.
349 EA and Ten are not identifiable.
350 Pauline's spelling for "dining room" and "drawing room".
351 Borree Creek, located some 80 kilometers (50 miles) from Wagga Wagga in New South Wales.
352 The words "in my heart" are added in above after "boy".
353 Pallas was a Titan in Greek myth. He was married to Styx, with whom he fathered children, and was the Titan of warcraft.
354 Unidentified.
355 "et je resterai impassible – en tous cas il faut se faire raison" is French for "and I will remain impassible – in all cases, it is necessary to be reasonable".
356 The final "e" is added in pencil.
357 Pauline writes the word "ce" (English for "this") above the word "moment".
358 Pauline writes "rank" (without the letter "F") in blue ink.
359 Francis Bathurst Suttor (1839–1915), was the third child of William Henry and Charlotte Suttor. He married Emily Jane Hawkins, with whom he had nine children.

William and Charlotte's second child, Edwin John Piper Suttor, was born in 1837 and died in 1838.
360 Pauline writes five dashes here.
361 "& Ernest" is added in in pencil above "Acres." *The Australian Dictionary of Biography* identified F. R. Bode as the father of Annie Isabel Jane Bode who had married Alfred John Cotton (1861–1941), a pastoralist, in 1891. Cotton and his wife farmed on Bode's farm, Bromby Park, at Bowen (see Michael J. Richards, 'Cotton, Alfred John (1861–1941)', *Australian Dictionary of Biography*, National Centre of Biography, Australian National University, http://adb.anu.edu.au/biography/cotton-alfred-john-5786/text9813, published first in hardcopy 1981 Accessed 23 May 2020). Bowen is in Queensland, Australia. Enid Kerr wrote a pamphlet on Frederick Robert Bode entitled "Frederick Robert Bode of Bromy Park: he rode with Dalrymple: from a paper prepared for Bowen Historical Society" (mid-twentieth century).
362 Pauline gives no date, but this is evidently a different day.
363 Opening line of William Wordsworth's 1845 poem, "Love Lies Bleeding": "You call it, " Love lies bleeding," – so you may, / Though the red Flower, not prostrate, only droops, / As we have seen it here from day to day,/ From month to month, life passing not away". Wordsworth (1770–1850) was a British Romantic poet.
364 Pauline's spelling for "farewell".
365 Possibly Walla Walla, a town in New South Wales, Australia.
366 Unidentified.
367 Charles Clairmont.
368 Antonia Clairmont.
369 Pauline, Wilhelm, and their mother, Antonia, were all who remained from the original family of nine.
370 The letter "h" of the word "oh" is added in pencil.
371 The words "if not bright yet" are inserted above "seen".
372 Willie and his mother, Charlotte Suttor.
373 Unidentified.
374 A reference to Percy B. Shelley's 1819 poem, "Ode to the West Wind." In the poem, Shelley asks the West Wind to "Make me they lyre, even as the forest is: / . . . / Be thou me, impetuous one!/ Drive my death thoughts over the universe / Like wither'd leaves to quicken a new birth! / And, by the incantation of this verse, / Scatter, as from an unextinguish'd hearth / Ashes and sparks, my words among mankind!" (www.poetryfoundation.org/poems/45134/ode-to-the-west-wind Accessed 29 June 2020).
375 Pauline adds two dashes. Mrs. G. S. refers to Mrs. George Banks Suttor, the wife of the brother of William Henry Suttor, Senior. George Banks Suttor (1799–1879) married Jane Johnston (unknown date – 1882) in 1826. The couple had seven children (*Dear William*, p. 320).
376 Possibly Mr. Blair, the young man Pauline met while in Sydney. See journal entry of 27 July 1855.
377 Pauline adds two dashes, perhaps to reflect her emotional state.
378 Unidentified.
379 the word "in" is added in pencil above "my".
380 Pauline first wrote the symbol "&" in pen. Then she wrote the word "in" in pencil over the ampersand.
381 Alloway Bank. See journal entry of 26 January 1856.
382 Caroline Suttor.
383 This sentence is written in pencil.
384 Baulkham Hills is about 29 kilometers north-west of downtown Sydney, Australia.
385 Pauline miswrites the date. February 6 would have been Friday's date, but Pauline mistakenly records it as January.

386 Typically, a term used by the Scots to describe people living in England (i.e. south of Scotland). Pauline uses the term to describe people living in the Southern hemisphere.

387 Jacqueline Voignier-Marshall quotes Willie Suttor, who stated in his *Memoirs* that Pauline was "the first woman of marked intellect and high attainments whom it had been my fortune to meet". He then added: "And now couldn't help – thrown together so much as we were – feeling a stronger feeling than mere friendship for her" ("Pauline Clairmont in N. S. W", p. 29). Suttor also recorded that Pauline exuded a "certain spice of devilry in her," thereby captivating a "raw country lad with all his passions just ripening into manhood strength" (quoted in Voignier-Marshall, p. 29). Although Pauline was jilted, Suttor later attributed the end of their relationship to Pauline's supposed deferred interest in his cousin (p. 30). In his 1887 book, *Australian Tales Retold: and, Sketches of Country Life*, Suttor probably referenced Pauline when he wrote his story, "A Cattle Muster on the Plains." He described the character possibly based on her as "a late arrival from England, but has lived much on the Continent, and being somewhat self-willed, would defy conventionalities and make one of the party" (*Australian Tales Retold: and, Sketches of Country Life* [Bathurst, N.S.W: G. Whalan, 1887)], p. 82).

388 German for "In the storm my wings grow".

389 Plutarch told the story of a Spartan boy who stole a fox, intending to eat it. However, to avoid detection, he hid the fox under his tunic and stoically suffered as the fox scratched him.

390 Greycliffe is located in Sydney, Australia. Today, Greycliffe Gardens form part of the Sydney Harbour National Park. The website to Greycliffe Gardens states: "The gardens rub shoulders with the lovingly restored Greycliffe House. This historic sandstone mansion built in 1852, is one of the best-preserved examples of neo-gothic Victorian architecture in Sydney" (www.nationalparks.nsw.gov.au/venues/greycliffe-gardens Accessed 4 February 2020). Greycliffe House is listed as a historic home: "Of the numerous Gothic villas which dot the Harbour side, no doubt no other has survived in such an idyllic situation. The house, its setting, and its historic connections make it a building of outstanding importance. The house is believed to have been built on the original Vaucluse Estate by W C Wentworth in the late 1840s ostensibly as a present for his daughter. Subsequent owners included W S Willis (1850–70); Wentworth family 1872–76; Lady Martin 1876; Mr Miller 1899" (www.environment.gov.au/cgi-bin/ahdb/search.pl?mode=place_detail;place_id=2498 Accessed 4 February 2020). Vaucluse is located about eight kilometers east of Sydney's main business area.

391 Pauline's spelling.

392 Although she misspells Lotus, Pauline references Alfred, Lord Tennyson's poem, "The Lotus-eaters" (first published in 1832). The final line of the poem reads "O, rest ye, brother mariners, we will not wander more" (www.poetryfoundation.org/poems/45364/the-lotos-eaters Accessed 4 February 2020).

393 Wilhelm Clairmont remained in Australia until 1861, when he returned to Europe to farm. Pauline's return to Vienna meant a reunion only with her mother, as all of her other siblings had passed away since her departure for Australia.

394 The words "is this" are added in pencil.

395 Sydney Harbour.

396 Alfred, Lord Tennyson, British poet (1809–1892).

397 Mr. Maitland and Captain B. are unidentified.

398 Ludwig van Beethoven (1770–1827), German-born composer and pianist.

399 Pauline departed for Europe aboard the *Waterloo* on 19 April 1857. The ship was commanded by Captain Young. *The Shipping Gazette and Sydney General Trade List* of Monday, 9 March 1857, records as follows in its section on "Arrivals and Departures"

from the port of Sydney: "Per Waterloo, Captain Young to sail 27th instant: Mr. and Mrs. Reddall, Lieutenant Clarkson in charge of detachment of invalids, the Miss Osbornes (4). Cargo: about 1300 bales wool with oil and sundries" (page 67 https://trove.nla.gov.au/newspaper/article/161171727 Accessed 22 February 2020). *The Sydney Morning Herald* of 9 April 1857 lists the following upcoming departure: "Waterloo, ship 960 tons, Young, for London, to sail 16th instant. Passengers – Mr. and Mrs. Osborn and two children, Mr. J. and H. Osborn, Miss Claramont, Mrs. Drummond, Mr. F. Drummond, Mrs. Brown and four children, Mr. and Mrs. Drysdale and two children, Lieutenant Clarkson, in charge of detachment of 52 rank and file 11th Regiment, 7 women and 4 children, invalids" (page 4, https://trove.nla.gov.au/newspaper/article/12993949 Accessed 22 February 2020; Pauline's name was incorrectly spelled). In its "Departures for England" section, *The Sydney Morning Herald* of 15 May 1857 documents the departure: "April 19 – Waterloo, ship, 893 tons, Captain Young, for London. Passengers – Mrs. Reddal, Mr. and Mrs. Drysdale and two children, Mrs. Brown and four children, Mrs. Drummond, Miss Claramont, Messrs. Osborne (2), Masters Osborn (2), Mr.Hulton, Lieutenant Clarkson, and 21 invalid soldiers. Cargo: 869 bales wool, 45 casks tallow, 214 hides, 93 casks sperm oil, 60 bundles old metal, 670 bags gum, 5 packages" (Page 12 https://trove.nla.gov.au/newspaper/article/12995619 Accessed 22 February 2020). An advertisement placed on 7 March 1857 in *The Empire*, a Sydney-based paper, notes as follows: "For London, under engagement to sail on the 27 March the Waterloo, A1, 898 tons, John Young, commander; is now fast filling up, and has superior cabin accommodation. Apply to Captain Young on board, Circular Quay; or, Smith, Campbell, and Co., Macquerie-place. February, 28th." (https://trove.nla.gov.au/newspaper/article/60275823 Accessed 22 February 2020).

In her passenger list, Pauline has written the letter "D" in pencil above the "B". The passenger list records the presence of Mr. and Mrs. Drysdale. It is entirely possible that Pauline referred to the Drysdales as she mentions this individual's wife in her journal entry.

400 Coogee Beach is one of Sydney's beaches.
401 Pauline added the word "the" above the line of text.
402 Pauline added the word "for" above the comma.
403 Woolloomooloo (Pauline spells it incorrectly) is part of greater Sydney today and is about 1,5 kilometers from the city's downtown. This section of Sydney was settled in 1793 by John Palmer. See www.environment.nsw.gov.au/heritageapp/ViewHeritageItemDetails.aspx?ID=2421506 Accessed 26 May 2020.
404 Ruth Grosvenor Francis (1778–1860), the widow of Henry Francis and the mother of Charlotte Suttor. See 9 September 1856.
405 In her list generated at the back of her Australian journal, Pauline mentions "Francis Napier of Glasgow." She writes the words "of Glasgow" in pencil. She also records meeting "Mr Napier of the Herald," with the words "of the Herald" written in pencil. Francis Napier explored the north coast of Australia as a member of Captain Cadell's expedition. Napier's cousin, James R. Napier, published Napier's account of his 1867 expedition, *Notes of a voyage from New South Wales to the north coast of Australia, from the journal of the late Francis Napier*. The work was published in Glasgow, Scotland, in 1876 (a year after Francis Napier's death).
406 This is a separate entry, although undated. It appears Pauline intended for it to be a new entry.
407 Unidentified.
408 Pauline adds the word "the" above the word "window".
409 Francis Napier.
410 Pauline was possibly residing with Mrs. Mary Simpson at 218 Cumberland Street. Mrs. Simpson likely owned the property and Pauline paid her rent. *The Sands and*

Kenny's Commercial and General Sydney Directory, for 1858–9 identifies Alexander Simpson as a carpenter who lived at 191 Essex-street (which was part of Cumberland Street; http://cdn.cityofsydney.nsw.gov.au/learn/history/archives/sands/1858-1869/1858-1859-part1.pdf Accessed 10 June 2020). By 1867, the directory references Mrs. Simpson of 218 Cumberland Street (See http://cdn.cityofsydney.nsw.gov.au/learn/history/archives/sands/1858-1869/1867-part4.pdf Accessed 10 June 2020).

411 Robert Burns. See 15 October 1856.
412 Pauline's spelling.
413 Probably a reference to Robert Burns's poem, "Will Ye Go to the Indies, My Mary." The second stanza includes the reference to the pineapple, a fruit with which Burns was undoubtably unfamiliar as he mistakes it for an apple growing on a pine tree: "O sweet grows the lime and the orange, / And the apple on the pine; / But a' the charms o' the Indies / Can never equal thine" (www.bbc.co.uk/arts/robertburns/works/will_ye_go_to_the_indies_my_mary/ Accessed 26 May 2020).
414 A probable date change, hence the editorial decision to make this entry a new section.
415 William Makepeace Thackeray published *Vanity Fair* in serial form between 1847 and 1848. A satire of British society, the novel tells the story of Becky Sharp and Amelia Sedley.
416 See 9 September 1856.
417 See journal entry for 8 March 1857.
418 Parramatta is located about 24 kilometers west of Sydney's downtown area. It sits on the Parramatta River.
419 Pauline adds the word "what" above the text in bolder ink.
420 At the back of her journal, Pauline lists the names of all the passengers aboard the ship and includes Paul Toché.
421 Pauline probably meant to write "Mauritians". Inhabitants of the island nation of Mauritius, which is situated off the east coast of Africa, Mauritians trace their ancestors back to southeast Asia, France, and Africa.
422 Pauline adds the word "face" above the text and in bolder ink.
423 Pauline references card games in this sentence.
424 Francis Napier.
425 Someone who has retreated from the secular world to embrace a religious life.
426 In her list generated at the back of her journal, Pauline mentions "Mr & Mrs George Waut" as "people known in Australia".
427 Manly Beach is one of Sydney's northern beaches.
428 Francis Napier.
429 Paul Toché, a passenger listed aboard the *Waterloo*.
430 Pauline adds the word "not" above "but".
431 Pauline lists the name "Deverty" at the back of her journal and identifies him as a passenger aboard the *Waterloo* who was an officer of the 11th.
432 Unidentified.
433 Pauline's list of people she met in Australia and recorded at the back of her journal included "Mrs Doyle Widow".
434 Possibly an abbreviation for Andrew Suttor, mentioned in her list of people Pauline met while in Australia. Andrew Johnston Suttor (1835–1871) was the fifth child of George Banks and Jane Johnston Suttor. He was a cousin of Willie Suttor. He married Elizabeth Smith in 1870 and with whom he had a daughter in 1871. He died a year after his marriage (*Dear William*, p. 320).
435 Unidentified.
436 See journal entry, "Wednesday".
437 Georges Martin, Paul Toché, and Marcel Massé were passengers aboard the *Waterloo* and Pauline records their presence in her list at the back of her journal.

438 Lord Byron (George Gordon Byron), 1788–1824, British Romantic poet. Lord Byron and Claire Clairmont had an affair and their daughter, Clara Allegra, was born in 1817. Allegra died in 1822.
439 Nocturnes were written for the piano by a variety of composers. The compositions were inspired by the night.
440 When Pauline first arrived in Australia in 1853, she boarded with Mrs. Armstrong. See journal entry for 27 July 1855. By the time of her return to Europe, Pauline seems to have been staying with Mrs. Simpson on Cumberland Street. See the journal entry, "Wednesday".
441 Possibly Mrs. Breillat. Pauline lists "M^r & Mrs Breillat" as passengers onboard the *Waterloo*.
442 Deverty, an officer of the 11th along with Clarkson, Peebles, and Vigors, all of whom Pauline records as being aboard the *Waterloo*.
443 Pauline writes the number "2" and then "1" above these words.
444 Pauline records "Mr. Roeckel Pianist" as a passenger on the *Waterloo*.
445 Pauline was clearly a woman who did not abide by the social mores and norms of her time. By her own admission, she drank alcohol, smoked cigarettes, enjoyed numerous romantic relationships, and had a child out of wedlock, Georgina Hanghegyi, in 1864.
446 Pauline writes the word "pourquoi" above the word "tu".
447 Pauline strikes through the first "age" and replaces it with "un" which she adds above.
448 Pauline writes this final sentence in pencil and then traces over it in black ink.
449 M. B. is likely Mr. Breillat whom Pauline identifies in her passenger list. See 13 June 1857. Mr. Breillat was travelling with his wife.
450 French for "Let us go round here".
451 Paul Toché.
452 French for "You leave me – I will regret you but you will never know it".
453 French for "I listen to your words because it is the last evening that I have to spend with you". Pauline misspells "écoute".
454 Misspelling for "amiable".
455 Unidentified. Pauline's spelling is also not definitive.
456 The first sentence is written in pencil and traced over in black ink.
457 Pauline records their name as "Reddall" in her passenger list at the back of her journal.
458 Pauline notes the presence of the "Family Osbourne" on the *Waterloo*. See her list of passengers at the back of her journal.
459 Prince Albert of Saxe-Coburg-Gotha (1819–1861) married Queen Victoria (1819–1901) in 1840. The couple had nine children.
460 French for "But basically I believe that he has treasures of tenderness in his heart that he hides under this cold and indifferent exterior". Pauline misspells "indifférent".
461 Pauline writes in pencil over the word "the". She adds the word "is" in pencil below the word "fact".
462 Pauline writes the word "a" again in pencil.
463 Paul Toché.
464 Pauline writes the word "is" in pencil above the word "he".
465 Unidentified.
466 A reference to Willie Suttor.
467 Pauline writes the word "were" in pencil above the word "words".
468 Mr. Clarkson.
469 Once again, Pauline's interest in the piano shines through her writings.
470 Pauline writes the word "communication" over another word which is illegible.
471 O and C refer to passengers aboard the vessel. On the final page, Pauline notes the presence of Mr. Clarkson and the Osborne family. "O" probably refers to James Osborne, one of Pauline's love interests. See journal entry "Sunday night" on April 20.

472 Pauline writes the word "tho" in pencil over an illegible word.
473 "Katy Darling" was a popular American song, first published in 1851. The first stanza reads as follows:
   Oh they tell me thou art dead, Katy darling, / That thy smile I may nevermore behold! / Did they tell thee I was false, Katy darling, / Or my love for thee had e'er grown cold? / Oh, they know not the loving of the hearts of Erin's sons Then a love like to thine, Katy darling, / Is the goal to the race the he runs. / Oh hear me, sweet Katy, / For the wild flowers greet me, Katy darling, / And the lovebirds are singing on each tree; / Wilt thou nevermore hear me, Katy darling, / Behold, love, I'm waiting for thee (https://tunearch.org/wiki/Annotation:Katy_Darling Accessed 19 February 2020. Source for the material: O'Flannagan [*The Hibernia Collection*], Boston, 1860; p. 16).
474 "rien qu'un frôlement": French for "just a touch".
475 Pauline inserts the word "down" above the word "head".
476 Pauline writes the words "Are you playing hide & seek with me?" in bolder ink.
477 Mrs. Drysdale is also mentioned in Pauline's list of passengers aboard the ship.
478 "fausse-position". French for "wrong position".
479 Captain Young, the captain of the vessel.
480 As she was wont to do, Pauline abbreviates the names of her love interests through her journal.
481 Pauline's spelling.
482 Samuel Wilberforce (1805–1873) was the son of William Wilberforce (1759–1833), the great abolitionist. Samuel Wilberforce was an Anglican bishop, who served as Queen Victoria's almoner. He became Bishop of Oxford in 1845. Together with his brother, Robert Wilberforce, he wrote a five-volume book about his father, *The Life of William Wilberforce*, which was published in 1838 (www.britannica.com/biography/Samuel-Wilberforce Accessed 19 February 2020). Samuel Wilberforce's commentary "Stillness in God" about Psalm 37:7 includes these words (www.biblestudytools.com/commentaries/treasury-of-david/psalms-37-7.html Accessed 19 February 2020).
483 Another spelling for "Muhammedan," Pauline's reference to Islam.
484 Pauline adds the word "one" above the word "remind".
485 "car je puis bien m'en passer": French for "because I can do without it".
486 Pauline uses this word as a proper noun. The word refers to a great noise.
487 Obsolete term for "pennyworth," meaning a bargain.
488 Probably one of the members of the "family Osborne" who travelled with Pauline on the *Waterloo*.
489 Mrs. Drysdale.
490 Pauline lists the "Family Osborne" in her list of passengers aboard the vessel.
491 Pauline writes the words "& stupid" above "such".
492 The final paragraph is written in pencil and traced over in black ink.
493 Pauline's spelling.
494 Pauline adds the word "mental" above "feelings".
495 Pauline's spelling.
496 Pauline's spelling.
497 A doctrine that supports the view that fate or destiny predetermines everything.
498 King Henry VIII (1491–1547), King of England. He married six wives, was the second Tudor king, and caused the Reformation in England when he divorced Catherine of Aragon to marry Anne Boleyn. Elizabeth I was the issue from his marriage to Boleyn.
499 Pauline's spelling.
500 French for "cold blood".
501 Adelaide Bowler.

502 French for "Both of us, we arrived at this stage of passion where one suffers so much that one grabs any way in order to find relief".
503 William Henry Suttor.
504 Pauline lists "Mrs. Brown a widow" in her roster of passengers.
505 Unidentified.
506 French for "But all of that will not lead to anything".
507 Pauline's spelling.
508 William Henry Suttor, Junior.
509 James Osborne, of the "Family Osborne" members.
510 A card game.
511 See the *Waterloo* passenger list. Deverty was one of the officers of the 11th aboard the ship.
512 Pauline lists Mr. F. Drummond and Mrs. Drummond as passengers aboard the *Waterloo*.
513 Cape Horn, the most southern part of South America. It is located off the coast of South America, on the Chilean-owned Hornos Island. In the nineteenth century, ships would return to England via Cape Horn. Clippers would sail from Australia to catch the strong westerly winds, known as the Roaring Forties. When the Suez Canal opened in 1869, voyages to Europe were much quicker. See the State Library of New South Wales's website for more information about nineteenth-century sea voyages. The website explains: "During the 19th century, emigrant ships travelling to Australia sailed into the Bay of Biscay (off the coast of France) before heading south to the equator. Stopping for supplies either at Cape Town or Rio de Janeiro, sailing ships could often spend weeks in the doldrums waiting for wind. Great Circle sailing took ships south into the Roaring Forties, where travellers faced freezing conditions and the risk of icebergs, before heading back up towards the Australian coast. With the advent of steam-powered ships and the opening of the Suez Canal, the time to reach Australia decreased significantly" (www.sl.nsw.gov.au/stories/emigrating Accessed 20 February 2020).
514 Pauline's spelling.
515 45 degrees latitude. Pauline hereby confirms that the ship was sailing in what was known as the roaring forties, defined as "areas between latitudes 40° and 50° south in the Southern Hemisphere, where the prevailing winds blow persistently from the west. The roaring forties have strong, often gale-force, winds throughout the year. They were named by the sailors who first entered these latitudes" (*Encyclopedia Britannica* "Roaring forties" www.britannica.com/science/roaring-forties Accessed 20 February 2020).
516 Trinity Sunday is the first Sunday after the Christian holiday of Pentecost, which is celebrated forty days after Easter. Trinity Sunday celebrates the Holy Trinity of the Father, the Son, and the Holy Spirit.
517 Pauline's spelling.
518 Clarkson.
519 Willie Suttor (William Henry Suttor).
520 Joshua 10:12: "Then spake Joshua to the LORD in the day when the LORD delivered up the Amorites before the children of Israel, and he said in the sight of Israel, Sun, stand thou still upon Gibeon; and thou, Moon, in the valley of Ajalon" (*King James Bible*). Ayalon Valley was located near Ramla in Israel.
521 Pauline identifies Mr. Leslie on her passenger list.
522 Pauline repeats the word "of".
523 While all these names are unidentified, Bohm could reference Dr. Bohm, the physician whom Charles and Antonia Clairmont consulted when Pauline lived in Vienna. Bowler refers to Adelaide Bowler, as does AB. On board ship was also a Mr. Beeber (whom Pauline indicates is a "traveller") and Mr. and Mrs. Breillat. The reference to "Madame" may indicate that the man Pauline was interested in was Mr. Breillat.
524 Willie Suttor.

525 French for "I was celebrated today". Pauline misspells "aujourd'hui".
526 Honduran mahogany (Swietenia macrophylla) is also known as big-leaf mahogany.
527 Probably Mrs. Brown, the widow Pauline identifies in her passenger list.
528 Mr. Deverty.
529 Captain Young of the *Waterloo*.
530 James Osborne and Mr. Leslie. "John" is not identified on Pauline's passenger list as she only provides last names.
531 Mrs. Brown.
532 Here, Pauline recalls her brother, Charles Gaulis Clairmont (known as Charley).
533 Pauline adds "(J)" above "he". "J" refers to James Osborne.
534 Unidentified.
535 Pauline writes the word "but" in bolder ink and in a larger font.
536 Captain Young.
537 James Osborne.
538 Pauline's spelling for "rush".
539 "Entre autre": French for "among others".
540 Pauline writes the word "who" above "boy".
541 Mrs. Drysdale, Mrs. Brown (or Mrs. Breillat) and Mrs. Reddall. All are passengers recorded on Pauline's list. As Pauline references Clarkson's flirtatious behavior, we can assume that Mrs. B. refers to Mrs. Brown.
542 Pauline writes the word "him" above "with".
543 Willie Suttor.
544 "Crossed the line" means to cross the equator.
545 "Per.": Latin for "through".
546 Pauline's spelling for Caesar. She references Gaius Julius Caesar, Roman military leader.
547 French for "I triumphed I [illeg.] in the air" (incomplete sentence).
548 Volume 1 of *Hamilton's Universal Tune Book: A Collection of the Melodies of All Nations* of 1844 lists "When Time Hath Bereft Thee (air)" in its contents. See Irish Traditional Music Archive (www.itmacatalogues.ie/Default/en-GB/RecordView/Index/88196 Accessed 1 June 2020). The words from each of the two stanzas of the 1872 publication by W. Hamilton of the song read as follows:
"When time hath bereft thee of charms, how divine, / When youth shall have left thee, nor beauty be thine, / When the roses shall vanish, that circle thee now, / And the thorn thou would'st banish shall press on thy brow, / In the hour of thy sadness then think upon me, and that thought shall be madness, that thought shall be madness, / That thought shall be madness, deceiver, to thee, / That thought shall be madness, deceiver, – to thee. – "
"When he who could turn thee from virtue and fame, / Shall leave thee and spurn thee to sorrow and shame, / When by him thus requited thy brain shall be stung, / And thy hope shall be blighted, thy bosom be wrung, / In the depth of thy sadness then think upon me, and that thought shall be madness, that thought shall be madness, / That thought shall be madness, deceiver, to thee, / That thought shall be madness, deceiver, – to thee. – "
(Cooke, T. *When Time Hath Bereft Thee*. Andre & Co., G., Philadelphia, monographic, 1872. Notated Music. Retrieved from the Library of Congress, www.loc.gov/item/sm1872.02527/ Accessed 1 June 2020).
549 Pauline's spelling.
550 Pauline's spelling.
551 Character in Richard Brinsley Sheridan's play *The Rivals* (1775). Lydia wants to chart her own course and not marry the man selected by her aunt, Mrs. Malaprop.
552 Matthew 7:6: "Give not that which is holy unto the dogs, neither cast ye your pearls before swine, lest they trample them under their feet, and turn again and rend you" (*King James Bible*).

553 The Pharisees were a Jewish sect who were important interpreters of the oral Biblical law. They lived in ancient Palestine between 515 BCE and 70 CE.
554 Pauline writes the word "willingly" above "one".
555 Pauline repeats the words "or from".
556 Pauline underlines the word "we" in pencil.
557 Pauline writes this sentence in pencil and then traces over it in dark ink.
558 Pauline means "prátaí", the Irish for "potato".
559 Mrs. Brown, identified as "a widow" in Pauline's passenger list.
560 The word "Paddy" is a pejorative term for an Irishman.
561 Pauline adds the word "church" above "morning".
562 Rawdon Crawley is a character in William Makepeace Thackeray's novel, *Vanity Fair* (initially serialized between 1847 and 1848). He marries Becky Sharp, much to his rich aunt's chagrin, but dies later in the novel.
563 Lord Byron (George Gordon Byron), 1788–1824, British Romantic poet. Darvall refers to Sir John Bayley Darvall (1809–1883), an Australian politician.
564 L. and D. denote Mr. Leslie and Mr. Drysdale.
565 Town in northeast Kent.
566 From Roman playwright Terence's *Andria* l. 555: "amantium irae amoris integratiost" ("lovers' quarrels are a strengthening of love") www.oxfordreference.com/ Accessed 20 February 2020.
567 Pauline's spelling.
568 Pauline's spelling.
569 Italian for "we'll see".
570 Byron's poem, "The Lament of Tasso," written in 1817. The poem is a dramatic monologue written in the voice of Torquato Tasso, a sixteenth-century poet, who suffered from mental illness and was hospitalized in St. Anna's hospital in Ferrara, Italy. Byron's poem, which begins with the haunting lines "Long years!–It tries the thrilling frame to bear / And eagle-spirit of a child of Song – / Long years of outrage, calumny, and wrong; / Imputed madness, prison'd solitude, / And the mind's canker in its savage mood," tells of Tasso's institutionalization in St. Anna. Eugène Delacroix (French painter, 1798–1863) painted his famous *Torquato Tasso in the Hospital of St. Anna at Ferrara*. An early version of the painting from 1824 is in a private collection and the 1839 version is in the Oskar Reinhart Collection 'Am Römerholz' in Winterthur, Switzerland.
571 John Wilson wrote a review of Byron's poem in *Blackwood's Edinburgh Magazine* in November 1817. Wilson (1785–1854) was a Scottish critic and author.
572 Pauline read Byron's translation of Dante Alighieri's *Inferno* in which Francesca da Rimini is first mentioned. Dante encounters Da Rimini and her lover, Paolo, in Canto V of the poem. *Inferno* is the first part of the three section *The Divine Comedy*, written between 1308 and 1320. Pauline also read Byron's *Don Juan* (written between 1819–1824), Byron's satiric and unfinished epic about Don Juan's exploits and travels.
573 Unidentified.
574 Pauline alludes here to "The Gay Cavalier," a song printed on an 1851 broadside from the Poet's Box in Glasgow, Scotland. In this bawdy song about a cavalier and his lover, the second stanza references Hong Kong: "The note was not long, / It was dated Hong Kong; / Short and sweet as a letter should be; / There was sketched in the middle, / A youth with a fiddle, / And under them fiddle-de-dee, / He turned it about, / "Meant for me I've no doubt; / "Some contemptible rival that's plain, / "If I knew who it was, / "I would cudgel him – poz! / "He should not be so pleasant again" (See Vaughan Williams Memorial Library, www.vwml.org/ and www.vwml.org/record/RoudFS/S396697 Accessed 1 June 2020). See also journal entries "27 Monday" and "August 3d".

575 George Osborne marries Amelia Sedley but is entranced by Becky Sharp in Thackeray's *Vanity Fair*. Osborne is a gambler, self-centered, and selfish.
576 Possibly William II (1792–1849). William was Prince of Orange and later King William II of the Netherlands. He spent time in England and was married to Grand Duchess Anna Pavlovna of Russia (the daughter of Paul I of Russia) with whom he had five children. He was the victim of blackmail as a result of his affairs with both men and women.
577 Unidentified.
578 French for "dizziness".
579 See 4 July 1857.
580 Pauline refers to her sister, Clara Knox.
581 Mr. Howard Hatton, listed on Pauline's passenger list.
582 From Robert Burns's 1782 poem, "Comin Thro' the Rye." The lines from the second stanza read as follows: "Gin a body meet a body / comin thro' the rye, / Gin a body kiss a body – / Need a body cry" www.poetryfoundation.org/poems/43801/comin-thro-the-rye Accessed 29 June 2020).
583 *The Cyclopedia of Popular Songs 2* of 1835 references this song. In 1893, Miss B. Bidder transcribed Mary Langworthy's recollection of the song that her mother, Anne Quarm, had sung to her. The Vaughan Williams Memorial Library provided the information and the transcription. The song's words are as follows:
   Young Susan so many lovers had she / She knew not on which to decide O! / For all spoke sincerely & promised to be / Well worthy of such a sweet bride O! / In the morning she gossiped with William / And then the noon spent with young Harry. / The evening with John, so amongst all the men / She could not decide which to marry / Heigh ho! Heigh ho! Heigh ho – I'm afraid / Too many lovers will puzzle a maid.
   Young William grew jealous & hurried away / And Harry soon tired of wooing / And John having teased her to fix on the day / Received but a frown for so doing. / So amongst all these lovers she's left in the lurch / And pines every night on her pillow / Till making a prayer on her way to the Church / She swooned & died under a willow / Heigh ho! heigh ho! heigh ho – I'm afraid / Too many lovers will puzzle a maid (www.vwml.org/ Accessed 1 June 2020).
584 Pauline's spelling.
585 Mrs. Suttor.
586 Wilhelm and Antonia Clairmont. Wilhelm was still in Australia and Antonia lived in Austria.
587 Pauline references Shakespeare's *King Lear*.
588 Pauline's spelling.
589 Pauline adds the word "I" above the word "only".
590 See journal entries "Saturday again July" and "August 3d".
591 Philibert Delorme (1510/1515–1570), French architect. His architectural writings "also attest to the way in which Delorme successfully grafted the spirit of Renaissance new learning onto the classic French tradition" (www.britannica.com/biography/Philibert-Delorme Accessed 24 February 2020).
592 Pauline adds the word "cardinal" above the word "the".
593 Armand-Jean du Plessis (1585–1642). Styled as the Duke of Richelieu, he was a cardinal and first minister of France under Louis XIII: "As both statesman and churchman, Richelieu was the acknowledged architect of France's greatness in the 17th century and a contributor to the secularization of international politics during the Thirty Years' War" (www.britannica.com/biography/Armand-Jean-du-Plessis-cardinal-et-duc-de-Richelieu Accessed 24 February 2020).
594 Publius Ovidius Naso (43 BCE – 17 CE), Roman writer best known for his fifteen-book poem, *Metamorphoses*.

595 Pauline writes the word "as" above the word "very".
596 Pauline writes the word "I" above the word "we".
597 Pauline adds the word "him" above the word "after".
598 Pauline's spelling.
599 Pauline probably means to write "that" instead of "the".
600 Pauline lists "Howard Hatton" as being a passenger aboard the vessel.
601 Pauline's spelling.
602 Maori are the original inhabitants of New Zealand. They migrated from Tahiti to New Zealand in 1300.
603 Pauline writes the date in pencil.
604 Mr. Leslie, aboard the vessel.
605 Unidentified.
606 Captain Young.
607 James Osborne.
608 Unidentified.
609 Mr. F. Drummond, who was traveling with his wife, Mrs. Drummond (see Pauline's list of passengers on the vessel).
610 Probably from Goethe.
611 Lizard Lighthouse is located in Cornwall, on the southernmost tip of the mainland of Great Britain. The lighthouse has been operating for over 250 years (www.trinityhouse.co.uk/lighthouse-visitor-centres/lizard-lighthouse-visitor-centre Accessed 24 February 2020).
612 See journal entries "Saturday again July" and "27 Monday".
613 See "Saturday again July".
614 Willie Suttor.
615 Beachy Head is located in East Sussex. It is the highest chalk headland in England.
616 Pauline writes the word "claret" above "sherry".
617 Unidentified. Possibly the pilot.
618 Claire Clairmont.
619 Pauline's sister, Clara Knox, now deceased.
620 Pauline's journal ends here. The concluding blank pages are indicated as follows: There are some unnumbered pages; page 271 is numbered on the right side, but Pauline does not write on it; there is no pagination on what would be page 272; pages 273 and 274 have no numbers; page 275 is the back cover of the book.
621 Pauline writes this final list of passengers aboard the *Waterloo* upside down.
622 Sir William Thomas Denison (1804–1871) was the governor of New South Wales and also the governor-general of New South Wales, Van Diemen's Land, Victoria, South Australia, and Western Australia from 1855 until 1861. Thereafter, he was governor of Madras, known today as Chennai, in the Indian state of Tamil Nadu.
623 See also the journal entries for 31 January 1856 and 16 October 1856.
624 See 15 November 1856.
625 Pauline adds the word "pianist" above "Rawack." Leopold Ravac (Rawack) was a musician from Silesia who settled in Australia in 1852. He married Viennese musician, Amalie Mauthner Rawack, but they divorced in 1861 and she returned to Austria. He was also a shipping agent. Wilhelm Clairmont frequently told Claire Clairmont to write to him care of Leopold Rawack. See http://sydney.edu.au/paradisec/australharmony/rawack-leopold-amalia.php Accessed 10 June 2020.
626 See journal entry 25 December 1856.
627 See journal entry 14 January 1856.
628 See journal entry "Sunday night" 1857.
629 Pauline repeats the ampersand.
630 Pauline adds a bracket to the left of Captain Bloomfield and Mrs. Campbell.

631 Pauline writes the words "of the Herald" in pencil.
632 See 23 March 1857.
633 See 28 March 1857.
634 Pauline inserts a bracket that includes both Frederic and Langloh.
635 Pauline writes the word "widow" above "Severn".
636 Thomas Sutcliffe Mort (1816–1878) was one of the owners of the Twofold Bay Pastoral Association. Wilhelm managed farms for the Association.
637 Pauline writes the words "of Glasgow" in pencil. See also 8 March 1857.
638 William Lee, Esquire, defeated William Henry Suttor, Senior, in the election for the seat of Roxburgh in 1856 (see 1 February 1856). He was a member of the Legislative Assembly of New South Wales.
639 Pauline adds one large bracket around the names "Mr Hawkins" and "Miss. Ch. Darcy".
640 Pauline writes her last page (unnumbered, page 275) on the inside back cover of her journal. She uses pencil for the first two sentences and ink for the rest.
641 Pauline paraphrases a popular saying, included in Francis Grose's (c. 1731–1791) 1790 edition of *A Provincial Glossary; With a Collection of Local Proverbs, and Popular Superstitions*. The proverb is found in the section entitled "Popular Superstitions" and reads: "Happy is the bride that the sun shines on; / Happy is the corpse that the rain rains on" (*A Provincial Glossary; With a Collection of Local Proverbs, and Popular Superstitions* [London: S. Hooper, 1791], p. 44. See https://archive.org/details/provincialglossa00gros Accessed 2 June 2020).
642 The *Oneida* was a steamship built in 1855 by Scott & Sons in Greenock, Scotland. Originally owned by Canada Ocean Steamship Company, it was purchased in 1856 by the Eastern and Australian Royal Mail Company (see www.clydeships.co.uk/view.php?ref=20542 Accessed 2 June 2020). The ship was in service until 1928 when it was burned in a fire near Chile.
643 The words, "you love me not" are written in a heart-shaped circle.
644 The *Simla* was a nineteenth-century steamship. Information provided by the State Library of Australia explains that the ship was built in Glasgow, Scotland, in 1854. The ship was built for the Peninsular and Oriental Steam Navigation Company (see https://collections.slsa.sa.gov.au/resource/PRG+1373/4/12 Accessed 2 June 2020).
645 The *European* was built in 1855 by Scott & Sons in Greenock, Scotland for the European & Columbian Steamship Navigation Company. In 1860, it was purchased for use by the French navy for military purposes. It was in service until 1911 (see www.clydeships.co.uk/ Accessed 2 June 2020).
646 A traditional riddle. The answer to the riddle is the speaker.
647 The *Columbian* was built by William Simons in Glasgow in 1855. It was originally commissioned by the European & Columbian Steamship Navigation Company. The European & Australian Steamship Navigation Company owned it by 1856 and three years later sold it to the Peninsular and Oriental Steam Navigation Company. It was destroyed in 1886 (See www.clydeships.co.uk/ Accessed 2 June 2020).

Image 4 Photographic Portrait of Wilhelm Clairmont by Dr. Székely (photographer). Unknown date.

Source: Visual Materials from the Carl H. Pforzheimer Collection. Photograph.

Credit: The Carl H. Pforzheimer Collection of Shelley and His Circle, The New York Public Library, Astor, Lennox, and Tilden Foundations.

Image 5 Photographic Portrait of Ottilia Clairmont by Dr. Székely (photographer). Unknown date.

Source: Visual Materials from the Carl H. Pforzheimer Collection. Photograph.

Credit: The Carl H. Pforzheimer Collection of Shelley and His Circle, The New York Public Library, Astor, Lennox, and Tilden Foundations.

3

WILHELM CLAIRMONT'S JOURNAL (1861)

SANDS & KENNY'S DIARY AND ALMANAC FOR NEW SOUTH WALES, 1861.*

PUBLISHED BY SANDS AND KENNY GEORGE-STREET SYDNEY

Books to be purchased
Buckler history of the Civilization of England[1]
Mcauleys history[2]
History of the French Revolution
Biograph of distinguished parliamentary men
dito actors
dito lawyers
Machiavelli[3]
Lavater.[4]

List of Australian letters to be delivered-
Commissary General Bishop Malta
    fr. M͏ʳ Mitchell[5]
Mauthner M. H. Weikersheim & C°. Vienna
    M͏ʳ Rawack[6] (verbal)
Bis from Carry.[7]
M͏ͬˢ Howard Williams 18 Cumberland
   Terrace Regents Park London.
    f. M͏ʳ Mitchell 1 parcel
M͏ʳ Firebrace.[8] 24 Gloucestor terrace
   4 George's Road Pimlico S. W.
M͏ͬˢ J. Manning.[9]
Robert Tooth[10] Swift Park Cranbrook
   Kent.
John Croft[11] illeg. near Brighton

Mr Mort Esq.[12] 155 Fenchurchstreet
   London.
Dr Homans letter to his sister
Mrs Buchanan[13] care of
Charles Turner Esqr[14]
Dawlish
Devonshire
England

Mr Paolo Saliba
care of Mss. Joseph Scicluno[15]
       & sons.
  Malta.
In case of instructions for the purchase of an entire about £20 or £25 to be sent in advance he does not expect to go to Berbery before illeg. –

Major Hasell care of Mss. Caloni
&co. Calcutta

   Aunt Claire
alle cure del Signor Cini
496 bis via dei Giraldi
Firence[16]

Forwarded Traps to
~~Hotel de France~~ Office of
   Austrian Lloyd
   Trieste.[17] 4 pieces.

---

1 Camphor box.
1 black trunk
1 hatbox
1 canvassbag.[18]

Madame Clairmont[19]
492 baden
Madame Marie Bácsák
bei Hofrat Bartel
77 Lange Gasse
   Pernßburg[20]
Johann Houdlik

gräfl Ludwig Karolyischen Hofrichter
in Salfa über Stein am anger[21]
promised him to write as to whether I want sheep or not. expects to shear the rams about middle of May. –
Fanny Kraus nunmehr[22]
Mrs Francis Smith
7 Oakley square
N. W. London.

Miss (Ella) Gabrielle Prokesch
Care of Miss Webb.
19 Albert square
Clapham Road
London.
Rittmeister H[illeg.][23]
N^r 140 Troppau[24]

Ths Sterling Begbie Esq.
4 Mansion House Place
London.

Requested Mr Mitchell to send
2 Boxes from Sydney to London
to the care of
Charles P. Schäffer
9B New Broad Street
London.
to be forwarded
pr. Leverson & C°. illeg. Rotterdam
or pr. C Schlossmann & C°. Hamburg.[25]
Difficulties in selecting:[26]

1. the Combination of <u>Length</u> illeg. fineness -is not only now not to be found but is illeg. purposely avoided because it has been found that when attained is speedily degenerates into a loose open wool without either strength or weight –
2. Large frame and excellence of wool are also rarely combined because the thoroughbred bred merino sheep is not large – but there is little doubt that in the <u>good</u> sheep countries of NS.W. their frame would be more developed for the condition of the sheep – the rams excepted, which are fe[27] not as good as illeg. the average conditions of the flocks on a fine saltbush run

1861 1st month   22 TUESDAY [22–343]   **January** [22 to 23][28]

Embarked in Sydney.[29] 3 oclock p.m.
sick after leaving the heads[30]

23 WEDNESDAY [23–342]

Sick more or less all day long.

[24 to 25] **January**   24 THURSDAY [24–341]   1st Month **1861**

More or less sick all day Arrived in Holson's[31] bay at 11 p.m. ran foul of a Buoy after entering the Head.

25 FRIDAY [25–340]

Went on shore at 9 a.m. returned at 8 p.m. saw Library[32] had a Bath & nice dinner.

1861 1st month   26 SATURDAY [26–339]   **January** [2]

Left Melbourne at 9 a.m. Beautiful day steaming down the Bay. Mr J. Manning[33] left at the Head saw Rawdon Green. <u>not</u> sick

---

[27 to 28] **January**   27 Septuages[34] SUNDAY [27–338]   1st Month **1861**

fair wind – muster of crew on deck at 10 a.m. then service read by Captain did not attend –

---

28 MONDAY [28–337]

Sick without vomiting

1861 1st month 29 TUESDAY [29–336] **January** [29 to 30]

Sick headwind – rough –

30 WEDNESDAY [30–335]

fair wind but still sick

[31 to 1] **Jan & Feb** 31 THURSDAY [31–334] 1st & 2nd Month **1861**

Reached King Georges Sound[35] at 5 p.m. Harbour very secure not quite as pittureske[36] as Sydney but pretty. about 150 houses cheerful looking 2 young whalers at anker. and Adelaide[37] steamer waiting for mail – no other ships Resident Magistrate (pompous looking being) came on board.

Feb 1 FRIDAY [32–333]

Went on shore. beautiful walk towards Lady Spencer's farm[38]. talk with Mr Bowden Melbourne radical. returned at 11 a.m. Set sail at 1 p.m. narrow passage between some rocks on which the lighthouse stands. –

1861 2nd month 2 SATURDAY [33–332] **February** [2]

plaid Chess with the Captain and Major Hassal got beaten – in the evening he sang the Wanderer[39] – very <u>nicely</u> for an Englishman.

[3 to 4] **Feb** **3** Sexigesima[40] Sunday [34–331] 2nd Month **1861**

Fair Wind & every prospect of making a splendid passage in another day we shall have the S. E. trade wind to take us right up to Galle.[41] the air begins to feel balmy. Attended service today. had a game of chess. Coast visible on both sides –

---

4 MONDAY [35 to 330]

Arrived at Suez[42] at 6 a.m. sandy beach through which an arm of the sea winds to an eminence on which are situated railway stations 2 hotels post office & bazaar. saw in the latter a man cast out to die. Left Suez for train at 1 p.m. reached Cairo[43] at 6 ½ p.m. desert all the way ~~excepting~~ up to the walls of Cairo where the verdure of the irrigated country forms a beautiful contrast. All the railway stations in the desert are fortified like small castles against the Bedouins[44] –

1861 2nd month   5 TUESDAY [36–329]   **February** [5 to 6]

Left Hotel at 5 a.m. for in a carriage for the citadel and mosque; the Latter is being done up in modern style – the first is a magnificent Building with immense dome – Beautiful view of the Nyle valley Cairo & the pyramides[45] at Sunrise. the illeg. was just about starting for Alexandria[46] – the palace is very fine Left for Alexandria pr. Train at 9 a.m. follow the course of the Nile all the way to Alexandria through a country irrigated & cultivated like a garden. Alexandria more of a European town had much bother about my luggage which I finally shipped for Trieste[47] (4 pieces 1 trunk 1 camphorbox[48] 1 hatbox 1 canvassbag)

---

6 WEDNESDAY [37–328]

Had a ride on a Donkey. expected him to come down every moment Saw Pompey's pillar[49] & Cleopatra's needle.[50] Wanted to buy an amber mouthpiece £ 5.5. too dear – cherrysticks are cheap 2ƒ each but too much bother to carry – the Labyrinth of narrow native streets & bazaars is appalling no wonder they have cholera. the stench is awful – the Pera our boat for Malta[51] cannot start today because part of the Baggage is left behind.

[7 to 8] **February**   7 THURSDAY [38–327]   2nd Month **1861**

Still no prospect of starting – went on shore again.[52]

[14 to 15] **February**   14 THURSDAY [45–320]   2nd Month **1861**

Arrived at Galle[53] early in the morning the tropical vegetation & ancient appearance of Battlements & Buildings give the place a picturesque appearance – there are no old Buildings in Australia. Landed at 9 a.m. got well cheated by the Lascar[54] watermen – all naked – took up quarters at Colemans – went with M^r. Bowden in the evening with a guide – 10 f –

---

15 FRIDAY [46–319]

the Malay servants they have here are capital two little boys called A[illeg.]nyp and Joe – Key – they glide about noiselessly doing everything that is wanted the eastern habit of having to many servants is very seductive –
Went to Cynamon[55] garden saw tea – coffee nutmeg plenty the Cynamon has camphor in its roots and cynamon above it is cut every year for its Bark right off the ground like the illeg.

243

1861 2nd Month   16 SATURDAY [47–318]   **February** [16]

Secured passage pr. Nubia[56] one cabin with M̄ʳ Bedbury Pilke I am afraid we shall be crowded –

I bought a new camphor box today to house all my purchases it cost £ 2 made in China – playd Billiards & lost.

[17 to 18] **Feb**   17 Sunday – 1 in Lent [48–317]   2nd Month **1861**

Got on board in Shingalise[57] canal with Mʳ Bedborough at 3 oclock sailed at 5 p.m. weather fine sea smooth – ship very crowded – great number of Indians and Chinaofficers are on board their scars & mutilated bodies to attest their share in the late wars.[58]

---

18 MONDAY [49–316]

Plaid chess with Mʳ Scott. won. began Wutheringheights[59] able but exaggerated on the whole not much account

1861 2nd Month 19 TUESDAY [50–315] **February** [19 to 20]

Fair weather calm sea but headwind not such speedy progress as pr. Behar.[60]

20 WEDNESDAY [51–314]

Plaid chess with Colonel Heart lost 2games & won 1. He is a strange nervous looking man with a great scar across the forehead and long white beard with a nervous twitching about the mouth.

[21 to 22] **February** 21 THURSDAY [52–313] 2nd Month **1861**

Plaid more chess with Colonel Heart he plays better than I do –

22 FRIDAY [53–312]

Chess. Won 2games from Col. Heart –

1861 2nd Month   23 SATURDAY [54–311]   **February** [23]

Had a talk with one of the Spanish passengers onboard concerning Donkeys. He consulted his friend a Lieult. Col. in the Span.[61] Army who said the best Donkeys were brought from Mancha[62] & Catalonia[63] where they are bred on purpose for copulation with <u>Mares</u>.

[24 to 25] **Feb**   24 SUNDAY – 2 in Lent [55–310]   2nd Month **1861**

Service read by a Scotch minister – i.e. service by Captain & sermon by preacher
Singing very good for an English congregation
Island of Lostra[64] in sight early this morning. nothing but a naked rock – at 12 a. m. Mainland of Africa in sight –

---

25 MONDAY [56–309]

Chess with Colonel Hart & others
no land in sight – they are getting the anker ready for tomorrow.

1861 2nd Month　　　　　26 TUESDAY [57–308]　　　　**February** [26 to 27]

Reached Aden[65] at Sunrise; beautiful morning. it is surrounded by a chain of volcanic rocks rising perpendicularly from the sea & terminating in a sharp razorback. I went on shore with McLeod & Petillo – Bought ostrich feathers and corrals – also a basket & pantherskin – we saw great numbers of camels fetching wood food and even water into the fortress

---

27 WEDNESDAY [58–307]

the most remarkable object are the cantonements[66] sheltered by a chain of rocks like a circumvallation[67] aided only slightly by art
also ancient water tanks, formed by walking up a steep gully in the rocks; they are on a gigantic scale. we leave again at 8 p.m.

[28 to 1] **Feb & Mar**　　　THURSDAY [59–316]　　　2nd & 3rd Mo **1861**

passed Perins the Island at the straights of Babel Manded[68] about which there was some dispute between the English & French. Afterwards Mecca[69] flanked by a high hill a great many mosques.

March 1 FRIDAY [60–305]

finished Valentine Von[70] a very stupid book. although written perhaps with a laudable tendency

1861 3rd Month   2 SATURDAY [61–304]   **March** [2]

Read the report of the Mutiny at Camport. Col Williams who conducted the Inquiry was on board himself – the atrocities committed by these wretches are awful. the fate of the Nana the chief of the Rebellion seems not uncertained but the more than probability is that he died a miserable death in the jungle.[71]

[3 to 4] **March**   3 Sunday – 3 in Lent [62–303]   3rd Month **1861**

We are still going up the ReadSea[72] met the Pottinger[73] today and the Ottaway[74] yesterday both going down the Navigation is so dangerous thus only a narrow track is safe; passed volcanic Island today (Shadmore) coast visible on both sides

4 MONDAY [63–302]

vide[75] Febr 4ʰ

1861 3rd Month   5 TUESDAY [64–301]   **March** [5 to 6]

vide Febry 5 & 6th

6 WEDNESDAY [65–300]

[7 to 8] **March**   7 THURSDAY [66–299]   3rd Month **1861**

No prospect yet of the Pera's[76] starting visited the Marseilles Boat "Valetta" After tiffing[77] went to see Colonel Hart with Willoughby and Thorvold. wanted to see the slavemarket – but they will not show it to Europeans. went on Board for dinner – Band playing in the evening but badly –

8 FRIDAY [67–298]

Started a 6 a.m. smooth sea. chess with Mr Spark & Bill beat both.

1861 3rd Month   9 SATURDAY [68–297]   **March** [9]

Strong Breeze – breakfast here is at 9 p.m.[78] which is a great nuissance. paid chess with Mr Bell & Scott. rough towards evening. –

[10 to 11] **March**   10 SUNDAY – 4 in Lent [69–296]   3rd Month **1861**

Very rough all day in bed nearly all day. no dinner
wind abated towards evening passed the outward bound boat at 6 ½ p.m. fired rockets. as signal "all right"-

---

11 MONDAY [70–295]

White cliffs of Malta[79] in sight at Sunrise – a great many houses & buildings visible – batteries have a very impregnable look frowning down on a ship entering between its walls.
put of up at Dunsfords' Clarence hotel – Delivered my letter to Mr Bishop saw Miss & Mr Bishop Mr Bishop being ill Mr Horn received & instructed my Donkey business for me. Saw fortifications also convent Capuchin church of St. John[80] in the evening theatre Sonambula[81] --

1861 3rd Month   12 TUESDAY [71–294]   **March** [12 to 13]

Inspected the Library got my passport made inquiry at P&O[82] office concerning parcels to Australia also at French office concerning Naples boats. After dinner went with M[r] Saliba & M[r] Bedborough to Cita vechia[83] & several vilages to see Donkeys. they average 13 ½ to 14 hands & 5/1.2 inch girth – Country is beautifully cultivated with dots of stone fences to subdivide and on slopes to prop up the ground – cultivation areas they also grow olives oranges, cactus fruit etc.

---

13 WEDNESDAY [72–293]

Went with M[r] Saliba to Gorzo[84] to inspect Donkeys. saw nothing a./. – Had a frightfully rough passage between rocks and breakers. Goro is even better cultivated then Malta seems better soil – Has beautiful roads. Buildings are all square piles of solid Masonry with hardly any and very small windows – they material they use is splendid but their style of architecture infamous. no doubt it dates from the time where security was more important than comfort –

[1 to 15] **March**   14 THURSDAY [72–292]   3rd Month **1861**

Called on M[r] Bishop & M[r]. Horne
Saw fort San Elmo[85] – very strong in all directions saw palace & armoury – beautiful especially the ancient Tapestry in the Council Chamber. also the historical paintings on the palace and <u>the Modern</u> mosaic works – in the theatre there were selections from Pisano[86] & Sonambula[87] – in the latter interesting young prima Donna "Teroni" 18 years of age handsome and graceful.

---

15 FRIDAY [74–291]

Saw two Barbs[88] and over the water not the true style for Breeding – went with M[r] Bishop to buy Lace for M[rs.] Tooth spent for her £ 10.5.0 [d]. in the evening I wrote all my letters to M[r] Tooth M[rs.] Tooth M[r] Mort. M[r] Saliba & M[r] Mitchell[89]

1861 3rd Month   16 SATURDAY [75–290]   **March** [16]

posted my letters and handed final instructions to Saliba concerning the Donkey. Bought a working table of olive wood for Mamma[90] sent it on to Trieste via Corfu. took leave of M[r] Horne – bought a travelling pouch – 7/ -
In the evening <u>Sonambula</u> – the third time in Malta nevertheless I enjoyed it more than the 2 previous times – the prima Donna is a charming creature, not strikingly beautiful but very interesting. Her great triumph is the final "Ah non giunge."[91] which she has to repeat 2 or 3 times
the Quirinal boat of the Messageries Imperiales[92] by which I was to have left for Naples today did not start because the Boat from Beyrout[93] did not come in – we are to start tomorrow at 11 a.m.

[17 to 18] **March**   17 Sunday – 5 in Lent [76–289]   3rd Month **1861**

Left Malta for Quirinal (Messageries Imperiales) at 12 hr. nice Boat, fair weather. I was however unwell till about 6 oclock p.m. when we got under the Lee of the Island of Sicily[94] – saw Aetna[95] like a dim haze towering above the line of Coast. Saw very little of the Coast although very near to it they have capital beds –

---

18 MONDAY [77–288]

Made Messina[96] at 5 a.m. splendid harbour; with beautiful view up the straights and the snow clad mountains around both in Sicily and Calabria[97] – went on shore breakfasted at Hotel Trinacria[98]; saw cathedral and church[99] at the Nunnery beautiful mosaic work, saw theatre, casino and the ponderous state carriages Went to see the forts battered to pieces by the Sardinians[100] – the latter got splendid positions for their batteries on the eminency commanding the fort. The Bombardment only lasted 4 hours.

1861 3rd Month   19 TUESDAY [78–287]   **March** [19 to 20]

Made Naples[101] at 7 a.m. Unfortunately it was a bad cloudy day Vesuvius[102] enveloped in mist and the Bay not showing to advantage – On the whole I am rather inclined to feel disappointed of Naples; it rained with short intervals all day. Saw the Cathedral,[103] Catacombes[104] – Church of S Maria dei Saryri[105] and Cimetery illeg. this latter well worth seeing – Being St Joseph's day[106] all the National Guard were out in honour of Garibaldi[107] whose name is Joseph – theatre "il Poliato"[108] very stupid splendid ballet principal dancer Signora Boschetti[109] – the Garibaldi hymn was not very warmly received.[110]

---

20 WEDNESDAY [79–286]

Saw Museo Bourbonico[111] too much matter of interest to go into it here – but most of all I was struck with the ancient sculpture Hercole Farnese[112] etc. then Fort San Elmo[113] splendid view of Naples & environs like the View from Salzburg Citadel[114] or Edinburgh castle[115] – saw the prisons for political prisoners in which they were kept without light, air, bed and even necessaries simply on bread and water while the underwent examination
this pris species of torture was intended to make them confess – from such a point of view one must rather rejoice at the Bourbons expulsion[116] in the evening theatro San Carlino[117] – saw Pulicinella[118] Understood little had enjoyed the mirthful faces of all the pretty Italian girls –

[21 to 22] **March**   21 THURSDAY [80–285]   3rd Month **1861**

Made the round through the Grotto of Pausillipe[119] to Bagnoli[120], Puzzuoli,[121] Lake Averno[122] through the arco felice[123] to Cumae[124] thence by Lake Fusaro[125] to Baijac[126] and Misenum[127] Saw all the wonderful ruins on that road including the Via Apia[128] in the evening I went to theatro San Carlo with[129] Il guiramento soso[130] – part of Sensiramide[131] very good – but best of all was the dancing at the Ballet "Meg/qilla"[132] their natural grace and beauty assisted by art and the effects of dress are fascinating beyond expression one in especial is very pretty – would that I could devote illeg. a week to her but there is no time –

---

22 FRIDAY [81–284]

Visited Pompeyi and afterward ascended Vesuvius[133] – unfortunately it was a very unfavorable day. intensely cold where I got up and the wind so strong that I could hardly keep on my legs. the ascent for up the cove which is done on foot is a heavy pull more so than either Tantawanglo[134] or Talbingo[135] and the uncertain footing the lava pieces give you renders the task more difficult. The Crater itself was so full of dense white smoke that one could not see down it – but in the edge there was glowing lava and fumes of Sulphur emanating from small apertures accompanied by occ

1861 3rd Month   23 SATURDAY [82–283]   **March** [23]

sional Explosions – the hotair breathing from these furnace like apertures was rather agreeable on a [hot] cold day and re minded me much of schwedische Öfen[136] – in one of them we roasted some eggs which together with a bottle of Lagrima Christi[137] made afforded a capital dinner. – the most interesting sight are the streams of running Lava – the redhot boiling mass looking like moulten iron runs down majestically in a channels formed through the more ancient Lava. the heat near these currents is very great; the approach to them difficult & dangerous because it is often not easy to distinguish new from old Lava.
Saturday 23rd[138]
Embarked for Civita Vechia[139] after having seen the Palace[140] and the Castel Nuovo[141] the first is splendid – my guide remarked facetiously that the King[142] had lost a "splendid situation"
Had a splendid passage by Nisita Procida Ischia[143] and the Cape Miseno[144] beautiful sunset at sea – saw the Light of Gaeta[145] at in the distance. Chess with Mr. Smyth – beat him.

[24 to 25] **March**   24 Palm Sunday [83–282]   3rd Month **1861**

Arrived at Civita Vechia at 7 a.m. where those vile officials of the pope kept us waiting till 11 ½ a.m. it is fortified and a small but tolerably safe harbour – the annoyance and extortion those vile officials subjected us to is beyond description reached Rome at 3 p.m. went to Hotel de Londres on top of an omnibus. Saw some of the Ruins of Ancient Rome that very evening – At the Tabledhote I met a (without speaking to) a most hand some woman; quite a model of Italian Style perfection of features, lovely figure beautiful complexion elegant though simple dress and dignified manner – [she has] and not <u>above</u> 18 or – 19 she turned out to be – O horror!

---

25 MONDAY [84–281][146]

the <u>wife</u> of an old stupid looking baldheaded snubnosed Piedmontise[147] -

---

Monday 25th[148]
Spent all day in sightseeing – tedious but reliable old guide was most struck with Coliseum. Pantheon, Circus and Baths of Caracalla[149] – the churches though magnificent are more toys in comparison with these grand monuments of antiquity. Saw my beautiful Genoese[150] again at dinner – although seated near her stupid husband I could not initiate a conversation [between] with[151] him or her.

1861 3rd Month   26 TUESDAY [85–280]   **March** [26 to 27]

Went on top of San Peter's,[152] splendid view – the inside of the church <u>surpasses</u> all description the dimensions, together with the elegance of shape and the variety of colour materials and objects produce a wonderful effect. the Vatican[153] is a pile of stupendous excess containing besides the popes palace the Library[154] & Museo[155]. It is enormous Saw also the Muse Capitolio[156] the dying gladiator. the Basilica of San Pavel/Paul[157] – the Island of the Tiber[158] the Jews quarter[159] and the fashionable promenade – At dinner I again saw my [illeg.] Geoess beauty – for the last time I fear. her husband is evidently jealous

---

27 WEDNESDAY [86–279]

A rainy day for leaving – I am not sorry to leave it is a sorry hole – made Civita vechia[160] at 12 pm after some more rain it cleared up – the steamer was so crowded that I had to make up a bed for myself under the table it was a fine moonlight night. although pretty rough I was not sick –

[28 to 29] **March**   28 THURSDAY [87–278]   3rd Month **1861**

Reached Livorno[161] at 5 a.m. Splendid harbour the town two[162] is clean with open streets, no trouble about passeports. the railway drive to Florence[163] along the valley of the Arno is splendid just up at the Hotel New York –
Saw A Claire[164] at Hotel Schneider She has become much older looking She has lost some teeth and lisps as consequence She was affectionate & vivacious She offered to lend me £500 for stocking a farm or £1500 for purchasing Land in a warm climate.[165]

---

29 Good FRIDAY [88–277]

Took my place in the diligence[166] for Bologna;[167] saw the Cathedral.[168] The exterior of which is very splendid – but the interior less so –
Dined with A Claire – rain all day took leave from her at 9 ½ p m supped at the Caffee d'Italia & left pr. diligence for Bologna at 11 p.m. A very dark night with rain now & then.

1861 3rd Month   30 SATURDAY [89–276]   March [30]

Immediately after leaving Florence for Bologna the road ascends the slopes of the Apeninse[169] mountains – and continues a winding zigzag but at an easy gradient up and down across a very wild looking country although cultivated in patches till it descends again into the large plain on the North Side of the Apenines in which Bologna is situated this latter is rather a clean looking town. the trottoirs[170] in all the leading streets are covered in by collonades very ageeable in rainy weather. I had no time to see anything of the town. we arrived at 4 p m I left again pr. rail for Milan[171] via Alexandria[172] at 10 p.m.[173]

[31 to 1] **Mar & Apr**   31 Easter Sun [90–275]   3rd & 4th Mo **1861**

Arrived rather tired at Venice[174] at 11 p.m this evening. having travelled all night & all day – saw Magenta[175] & Solferino[176] also Novarra[177] the Lombard[178] plains are a beautiful country all irrigated and cultivated most carefully Met in the railway a young Austrian officer who had been at siege of Gaeta[179] and got wounded there – he is quite enthusiastic for the queen of Naples[180] – Went from the railwaystation to my hotel "al Vapore" in a gondola never passed through viler darker and more cutthroat looking places in my life – it is all a Labyrinth of narrow passages of water covered here and there by arches

---

April 1 Easter MONDAY [91–274]

A very unfavorable day to see Venice for there was rain and cold I saw the palace of Dogges[181] and some interesting churches but nothing to compare with Rome – I had a guide called Hercule who spoke with French and was a great Radicale in the Evening I made a promenade on the St. Marcus place[182] I left at 10 p m for Trieste had to go by the 3rd Class for want of specie[183]

1861 4th Month   2 Easter TUESDAY [92–273]   **April** [2 to 3]

Had a fine day for my stay at Trieste[184] but rather a long one since I had not money enough to ~~defray all~~ afford a guido. the town has fine broad streets and is full of life & prosperity. the shops look very inviting. the Environs of Triest look very beautiful the Bay is very fine and set off well by the Crescent of Hills to the back of it. I left again by 8 oclock train and managed to illeg. money enough together. for the 2nd class

---

3 Wednesday [93–272]

Beautiful day for my journey through Styria,[185] a most pittoresque looking country but any thing but inviting for agricultural enterprise All the soil I saw even on the alluvial flats is poor & barren looking and full of stones Lots of snow on the Semmering[186] Graz[187] is pretty; the railway[188] over the Semmering magnificent. Arrived in Baden[189] at 5 pm. quite unexpected by dear Mamma.[190]

[4 to 5] **April**   4 THURSDAY [94–271]   4th Month **1861**

Spent this day with dear Mamma and Pauline who arrived in the morning from Vienna went out with Pauline to Weilburg[191] spent a most delightful day. made up my accounts.

---

5 FRIDAY [95–270]

Went to Vienna bought sundry things there. Saw M[r] Smallbones[192] who introduced her to M[r] Schwin Count Carolys[193] manager
In the evening I went to Wieselburg[194] where I found the Schusters[195] delighted to see me.

1861 4th Month 6 SATURDAY [96–269] **April** [6]

Went all over Schusters farm where I saw his beautiful cow illeg. with 220 cows for milking also an artificial apparatus for cooling the milk afterwards we saw the fattening bullocks. 14 were sent off that very day – then I went to Altenburgh[196] where I saw the Zimmermans[197] who were very kind also Pabst[198] and D[r] Moser[199] illeg. Masch.[200] M[rs.] Moser was beautiful she has 3 children. the evening I spent with Zimmermans family [illeg.] afterwards I returned to Wieselburg.

[7 to 8] **April** 7 Sunday – 1 aft Easter [97–268] 4th Month **1861**

Went from Wieselburg to Vienna saw Pauline and M[r] Smallbones returned to Baden in the after noon – spent the evening with Mamma.

---

8 MONDAY [98–267]

Wrote my letters in the morning and my journal made up my acts[201]; Pauline went home i.e to Vienna at 11 a.m. At 3 p.m. Becker[202] & Uncle George[203] arrived. the latter looking very strange in the face as if he had had a severe illness – they were exceedingly amicable at 6 pm we left together pr. train for Oedenburg[204] I put up at the "weisse Rose"[205] was very comfortable –

Oedenburg
1861 4th Month   9 TUESDAY [90–266]   **April** [9 to 10]

Left for Giuer[206] pr stagecoach at 7 a.m. it was a covered Calesch[207] and moderately comfortable fare moderate 2 f 10 kr. traversed a well cultivated country reached Giuer at 12 ½ p.m. dined there and proceeded on a illeg. wagh to Salpy[208] (fare 4 f.[209]) Was received very kindly by illeg. Houdlik who immediately got his carriage out and took me to Gurau the principal sheep station I examined there about 100 Rams till I was quite giddy. They are very good sheep but do not come up to my idea of what is the very best. They are fine and exceedingly equal but neither [illeg.] close enough nor very long in the staple or weighty.

---

10 WEDNESDAY [100–265]

Returned to Gurau [illeg.] to look at some of the best rams again made notes of them and got samples. Saw the other more common sheep. the estate has 4000 acres & 5 farm steads they have a 5 & 7 year course
On my way home he also showed me the Paty farm where I saw the wife of the Verwatter[210] there a very handsome young person and amiable too – a Hungarian. Thence M[r] Houdlik had me taken to Giuer in his carriage where I arrived at 12 m. & had to wait to my disgust till to morrow morning at 8 for the stage coach there being none this afternoon.

[11 to 12] **April**   11 THURSDAY [101–264]   4th Month **1861**

Left Giuer this morning pr. stage coach for Oedenburg. had some political conversation with my companions. everyone has doubts as to the political state of Hungary. the day turned out very fine & warm. I saw M[r] Smallbones place Konitz from a distance M[rs.] Egau being absent from Bernstein I went straight home at Oedenburg I took the railway 3rd Class and illeg. for Baden where I met my dear Missul[211] waiting for me at the railway Afterwards we unpacked my traps[212] Mamma seemed pleased with the work box – wrote a letter to M[r]. Mort.[213]

---

12 FRIDAY [102–263]

Went to Vienna to arrange everything for my departure to Moravia[214] & Bohemia[215] also to get the necessary letters of introduction; got saw Arenstein[216] who gave me a good deal of advice and letters of introduction but did not find any one at home went to the Kärntnertor[217] in the evening with Pauline heard the Profit[218] – after wards we had supper at the 3 illeg. went to Beryrath Hauers[219] but he was not at home.

1861 4th Month   13 SATURDAY [103–262]   **April [13]**

Received several reports from Arensteins on exhibitions of sheep and wool Saw Baron Mundy[220] whose sheep farm is near Brun[221] in Machren[222] made an appointment with him for Tuesday morning. Could not manage it sooner because ~~the~~ his carriage could not be procured sooner –
Saw Mr Rusterschmied[223] who did not give any inviting acts. of the Imperial farms.
Went to Mr Walner to Hitzring[224] in the afternoon and saw the Rambouillet sheep[225] there –

[14 to 15] **April**   14 Sunday- 2 aft Easter [104–261]   4th Month **1861**

Spent all this day getting up accounts writing letters to Grusberg and A. Claire[226] also in reading books & papers furnished me so as to form a plan of operations – Remained at Baden all day – proposing to start tomorrow morning.

---

15 MONDAY [105–260]

Went to Vienna on my way to Brün Saw Schmid. Mr Glamis[227] was not at home – saw Mr. Hauszer[228] about the Thuislands[229]; had dinner with Plin[230] 7 ½ started from Nordbahn[231] for Brün where I arrived at Hotel Pardowitz at 12 midnight.

1861 4th Month 16 TUESDAY [106–259] **April** [16 to 17]

Met Baron Mundy this morning we started for his castle[232] at 8 ½ & arrived there about 11 or 12 – thence we immediately proceeded to look at the sheep. they are very good & figure not too high – Baron Mundys son[233] who formerly was an officer lives here alone with his father – the castle is very large and beautifully renovated the walls are of enormous thickness & all wainscoated it is a charming union of ancient solidity and modern elegance. there is a billiard room & Jagdpalor.[234]

---

17 WEDNESDAY [107–258]

This morning I went with Baron Mundy to see the other sheepstations on which the Maiden Ewes & mothers are kept. of the first some are very eligible we then drove back to the Castle had dinner and went thence back to Brün on the way we passed the famous battle field of Austerlitz[235] the Baron showed me the various positions of the Russians and French also the principal French position on an isolated hill on which the remains of the batteries are still visible this the Russians in vain attempted to storm a chapel[236] marks the place.

[18 to 19] **April** 18 THURSDAY [108–257] 4th Month **1861**

I was the night at Hotel Pardowitz from whence I sallied in the morning to find Baratta[237] I found him in town but not at home. Brün is a very cheerful clean looking town with nice streets and houses and immense industrial establishments there is no appearance of illeg. about it. Saw Baratta who strongly advised me to have nothing to do with farming unless with sufficient capital to enter into sugar manufacturing.
started from Brün pr. Bus at 2. 4 oclock reached Wischau[238] at 8 pm.

---

19 FRIDAY [109–256]

Engaged a coach to go to Hostitz[239] for 9f. reached Hostitz at 12 m. found M[r.] Kraus[240] gone but was very hospitably received by the Burg graf[241] and Inspector. Saw the Schäferin[242]
there is nothing here to suit me. Everybody speaks of poor Charley[243] with great Kindness – the locality and everything else reminds me painfully of him.

1861 4th Month   20 SATURDAY [110–255]   **April** [20]

This morning I went to Schizlawitz[244] where I met Verwalter[245] Hahn from whom I got very interesting information regarding certain moor localities about Laibach[246]; it might lead to a very advantageous purchase – the climate top is very fine. After dinner I went to Littenschitz[247] and saw a fine ram there but the sheep inspector being absent I could not learn whether the ram was for sale and what prices

D[r] Gratechy has a nice daughter (Sophie) she has a nice little figur and very agreable[248] manners she is intelligent and bildsam[249] a face a little countrified with fine grey eyes She plays the piano very tolerably among other things she played Ernets'[250] Elegy and the Standchen[251] I took more than usual interest in her because she was very much attached to Charlie; she & her parents spoke very much of him as did all the people there and at Hostitz.

[21 to 22] **April**   21 SUNDAY – 3 aft Easter [111–254]   4th Month **1861**

I returned to Littenschitz this morning on receipt of a letter from M[r] Kretchy that the Ram N[4] was for sale. Inspected the whole of the sheep farm at the Spanischer Hof[252] and at the further off sheep station – We then had dinner Sophie had played on the piano she looked pleasant and animated. I wonder the poor creatures spirits are not quite crushed – she sees no one all the year round she is said to have a property from her mother of 12000 f – In the evening I found M[r] Fellikyer & Stanzler[253] at Hostitz who gave me a route through Prussia.[254]

22 MONDAY [112–253]

Started for Idannuz[255] which I reached at 8 p.m. went from there with Verwalter Berdnaczdki to the sheep stations – saw then some nice irrigation meadows made by a Hanoverian 80 acres at the rate of 25/ pr acre – thence went to Quadssitz in the afternoon where I was illeg. received very politely by two very pretty daughters of the Verwalter Stiebal who was absent himself.

1861 4th Month   23 TUESDAY [113–252]   **April** [23 to 24]

Saw the Quasinitz sheep stations very fair – after dinner I left Quasinitz for Hallern[256] which I reached at 5 p.m. Having telegraphed to Mama to know whether my letters of 6th for Prussia had arrived yet I returned to the town & took up my quarters at the "Sun."

I was very cold all day and there is an old hag of a housemaid here which makes the weather worse I wrote this evening to Mr Tooth Mamma. A Claire[257] sent & received telegram from Mamma.

---

24 WEDNESDAY [114–251]

Left at 12 m. after having finished my letters reached Troppau[258] at 5 p.m. Went to see M^r & Mrs Helvety (Pepi) met her coming out of her house but did not recognize her for certain she seemed angry for being stared at An hour afterwards I went again and found them at home they were both all full of amiability charming; full of Altenburger[259] reminisces which they left only 12 months ago. He very kindly volunteered to be my Cirrone[260] which I accepted thankfully as he is well connected in the neighborhood

---

[25 to 26] **April**   25 THURSDAY [115–250]   4th Month **1861**

this morning I left early with Mr Helvety for Lipiteri Mr Dudschnickis property, thence to Hoschnitz Darn Princenstion. At the first we were most hospitably received; they are a wonderful family; all the daughters but one married some to Hungarians one to an Austrian and each takes her husbands politics. the unmarried one "Melanie" is rather pretty, very stout – Mrs Dudschuiscki gave me a letter to her daughter Mrs Iony in Hungary I spent the evening with M^r & Mrs Helvety[261]

---

26 FRIDAY [116–249]

Settled my business about the letter of 6th obtained from Mr Schüster 100 fl. then started for Partscendorf[262] pr. rail (station Haudriz) Director Langer turned out to be a regular character a fat stout fellow but no fool, – became quite attached a little bit of a pointer in fixing the price of his rams sat up with him till 12 oclock. Slept all by myself in a great large castle

1861 4th Month   27 SATURDAY [117–248]   April [27]

Left Partchendorf[263] at 3 a m very cold went pr. rail to Schönbrun[264] thence pr. coach to Schönhof[265] situated in a beautiful locality but very cold. illeg. had the goodness to show me all over the sheepfarm which is very fine but no weight of wool.
Afterwards we went to his house his daughter "Louisa" is a strikingly beautiful creature (only 12 years of age) but very tall and well shaped most elegant figure. her eyes were most charming, large, light-blue. her complexion beautifully white. I asked her whether she would come with me to Australia she blushed very much and seemed quite doubtful. She will be beautiful. her hair was long and rich –

[28 to 29] **April**   28 Sunday – 4 aft Easter [118–247]   4th Month **1861**

Wrote to M[r] Mort Left Troppau at 9 a m. made Kuchelna[266] thence Bonitin[267] Rec[d] not very hospitably by illeg. Buchwald who would not give us any dinner. saw the sheep no good; Went on with Helvety to Verottier M[r] [New] Neumauns property who was unfortunately not at home. M[rs] Neuman rec[d] us very kindly

---

29 MONDAY [119–246]

Spent the forenoon very agreably at Ottitz.[268] M[r] alias Lieutenant illeg. Neumann arrived about 12 m. he is very jolly fellow and made all the women/his wife included blush with the very strong things he said. after dinner went to see the Duke of Ratibor's[269] farm could not however see the sheep the dairy cattle are well kept older burger Breed – afterwards saw the jail.

1861 4th & 5th Month   30 TUESDAY [120–245]   **Apr & May** [30 to 1]

It was such bad weather that we could do nothing before dinner plaid first Taroque[270] since many years – it snowed all the forenoon. the climate is very severe here for agriculture. I left Neumans at 4 p.m. went to Ratibor thence at 5 pr. rail to Gogoling[271] thence at 7 ¼ to Oberglogou[272] pr. mail where I arrived at 10 p.m. at a miserable ~~hour~~ [illeg.][273] where the room is cold and the bed too short.

MAY 1 WEDNESDAY [121–244]

Left Oberglobau[274] for Casimir M[r] Pridunitz's place at 7 ½ a.m. he was at Kuchelna[275] – found head Inspector at home – sheep no good returned to Glogau[276] – wrote to M[r] Fellinger about a carriage, went to Churtitz Amtsrath[277] Heller saw the sheep a/. returned to his castle in the evening. his son is a decent young fellow. the old gentleman very deaf. the first decent Electoral flock that I have yet seen.

[2 to 3] **May**   2 THURSDAY [118–247]   5th Month **1861**

As I contemplated purchasing here I stopped one day here to inspect the flock at my leisure I marked 5 rams and 4 Ewes for purchase – [~~illeg.~~] In the afternoon I saw all the old gentleman's prizes for rams I then wrote letters to Mamma A Claire etz. etz. the servant is a queer old stick.

---

3 FRIDAY [123–242]

Started this morning at 1½ from Oderlitz[278] pr. mail for Oppeln[279] cold night reached Oppeln at 6 a.m. wrote to Mamma got my boots mended & started pr Tarnowitzer Bahn[280] for Schwieben[281] where I reached at 2 p.m. M[r] Fellinger was very kind Inspected his sheep in the after noon. they show immense industry & perseverance on his part

1861 5th Month   4 SATURDAY [124–241]   May [4]

this day was bitter cold and rain & snow I feel rather unwell nevertheless went out with Mʳ Fellinger to inspect his farms sheep and above all the drainage which was exceedingly interesting In the evening he gave me all the dates concerning these operations He is a very fine energetic fellow the estate is 8000 morgen[282] of which only 1600 are forest & pastureland there are 4000 sheep and about 50 head of cattle without working bullocks. there is a distillery and a steammill on the place. the soil is indifferent and the climate is worse.

[5 to 6] **May**   5 Rogation[283] Sunday [125–240]   5th Month **1861**

Went to Jastur (Mʳ Bollman's) place from Schurisben[284] – he has an estate of his own and lives there with his family of 3 daughters illeg. not good looking – Mʳˢ Bollman is a nice person – I saw the sheep they are fine but not very a 1 in regard to quantity Spent the evening with them very nice, kind, honest people.

---

6 MONDAY [126–239]

Left Jastur at 6 am. for Oppeln where I was delayed all day in order to see Director Korte it was however quite worth while that I did so as I got very interesting information from him regarding wool etz. etz. Left at 7 ¼ for Ohlau[285] which reached at 8 ¾ put up at the Deutschen Hof[286] Saw Augusta a housemaid complaining of her disappointment in love!

1861 5th Month   **7 TUESDAY [127–238]**   May [7 to 8]

Left Ohlau for Poshhirtz[237] at 7. am. reached at 11. a m. Major v. Naren an eccentric man with wonderfully active imagination and energy of mind he is clever and fond of his own specimens of elocution he treated me to a very nice dinner after which we drove together to Count Behusy's Langendorf[288] where I passed the evening and then went on to the Inn at Bernstadt[289] where I arrived at 10 p.m.

8 WEDNESDAY [128–237]

Left Bernstadt at 8 for Wabusitz proprietor not at home saw sheep coarse but plenty and fine frame went thence to Weidenbach[290] could not see the sheep there because they were out on pasture went on to illeg.; fed horses, then on to Siemenau[291] reached at 8 p.m. infernal road and wretched horses – put up at a decent inn sent a note to Baron Lüttwitz. saw a beautiful Jewish girl the daughter of the Innkeeper with splendid Eyes.

[9 to 10] **May**   9 Holy[292] **THURSDAY [129–236]**   5th Month **1861**

Saw the sheep at Siemenau first not at in point of quantity of wool Old Baron Lüttwitz received me very hospitably introduced me to his daughter in law who was born in Melbourne[293] (a Miss Campbell Simpson) a nice fair creature young apparently of good heart & little head. her companion a Hungarian Miss Saal is a very different creature fine features dark blue eyes with a great deal of expression dark hair she is a little passeé[294] and has false teeth but nevertheless very interesting She plays superbly.

10 FRIDAY [130–235]

Baron Rudolf Lüttwitz a young man of 30 is a very nice fellow, he has been to Australia we rode on & played chess together. the greater part of the day we were in the sheep stable picking a lot for Australia but they are bad and I am afraid going down hill –
He has a splendid stable full of horses in the evening I went to Constadt thence pr. post to Brieg[295] where I arrived at 5 am. Baron Lüttwitz sent me to Constadt in his travelling carriage & four.

1861 5th Month 11 SATURDAY [131–234] **May** [11]

Left Brieg for Breslau[296] at 7. reached the latter at 10 went to the goldene Gans[297] was very tired; slept till 1 table d'hote.[298] – Got letters from M[r] ~~Tooth~~ Mort[299], Habel, Ratchitz[300] and 2 from Mamma & A Claire.
Wrote to ~~Tooth~~ Mort & Mama
took a walk round the tour on the site of the old demolished ramparts. very nice especially that part where the Oder[301] joins it saw the rafts of pine wood like on the Danube. arranged for boxes for the seal for the sheep also for 2 botts of Sulphide of Carbon and an apparatus.
In the evening I went to the theatre saw Aladin die Wunderlampe[302] dancing not a l. Among the actresses frl.[303] Weinn was the best looking a beautiful Brunette with sparkling Eyes acquiline nose and a profusion of brown ringlets a handsome elegant tournure[304] and a most delightful animation on face as well as figure. Among the danseuses frl. Stahl was the best looking.

[12 to 13] **May** 12 SUNDAY – 1 aft Ascen[305] [132–233] 5th Month **1861**

Left pr. Drosckke[306] early at 8 for Mr Lubberts place a fine drive through a well cultivated country on a beautiful spring morning along a chausee[307] studied with fruittrees all in blossom – I found young Lubbert an honest man (apparently) his father illeg. of a Charlatan. at dinner the whole family was together. young Lüb-bert is a son in law of Huwitz. in the evening I went to the theatre frl. Weber and frl. Risker & sang & played both very nicely especially the first. she has a lovely expression of face especially her chin ~~so sharp~~ pointed gives her smile an arch look.

---

13 MONDAY [133–232]

Went to Frankenstein inde illeg.[308] Count Sternberg. Saw nothing worth seeing excepting a find country the railroads are abominably managed this is where they ought to begin with reforms. the villains of Conductors are both stupid and rude In the evening again theatre "Werner" illeg. illeg. – no good all ~~women~~ actresses as ugly as hell – excepting 2 pretty Jewesses near me one of whom turned out to be married – Afterwards Marie.[309]

1861 5th Month   14 TUESDAY [134–231]   **May** [14 to 15]

Started for Liegnitz[310] in the morning at 6 am. went from there to Weisser[311] rode M[r] Frourhold queer old man very rich – has a daughter 14 years of age at school. Wants too much money for his sheep. [illeg.] showed me all about the battle of the Katzbach[312] where the french were. Napoleon was in his own house but had to retreat that night to Liegnitz In the evening I returned to town had a row with the cabman who fetched the police met an enamoured couple at the rail way station and 2 funny prentice Boys Left for Iesswitz at 9 ½ p.m.

---

15 WEDNESDAY [135–230]

Reached Fessnitz at 4 a m. had a sleep in wrapped up in my fur on a bench at the station house; Count Finkenstein close to station – Kindly received there met M[r] Wedel a buyer Finkensteins daughter & niece ugly. but good sort of people. After seeing the sheep there I went to Wirchenblatt[313] where I saw M[r] Fischer; thence to Birtech where I found no one spent the Evening at Count Finkenstein's went to bed early.

[16 to 17] **May**   16 THURSDAY [136–229]   5th Month **1861**

Arrived at Bezhiz[314] a 9 a m. cold and rainy; nevertheless the town with its broad streets and noble buildings produces a pleasant effect. I like the women too who are infinitely superior to Breslau they are tall slim with clear intelligent looking faces. and nicely dressed. In the evening I was in the theatre and met 2 very nice young girls illeg. Johanna the first one quite enchanting so modest and well mannered I wonder how they can allow these young girls to go out by themselves. But there were lots of respectable girls of the same breed – Went to illeg. Linkstraße[315] 44. not at home.
Rendez vous with illeg. for Thursday.

---

17 FRIDAY [137–228]

The whole of this day was spent in letter writing to Mama, Claire Kardorf. Muismer Mort & Tooth[316]. In the evening I heard Trovatore[317] a divine composition. particularly the opening chorus[318] and that song which Phoebe sang – Prima donna frl.[319] Lucca splendid soprano figure not very good nor features but a darling white complexion with jet black hair Italian style exceedingly soft & illeg. expression of eyes.

1861 5th Month   18 SATURDAY [138–227]   May [18]

Ludwigslust[320] is a nice sort of place with lots of shrub parks and nightingales all round it. but the population are all idle villains illeg. soldiers etz living on the bounty of a wretched court – Chaussée to Parchim[321] is splendid all along forests and fields – Parchim is an uninteresting little spot. Innkeeper at Parchim queer old fellow great cheat. had a parasyte friend who praised everything without reference to its merits.

Baron Malrau is a very nice gentlemanly man; also his family; his daughter is not very goodlooking; not generally a virtue of the country girls of North Germany.

[19 to 20] **May**   19 Whit[322] Sunday [139–226]   5th Month **1861**

Left Baron Malrau early went to Passow[323] Weissin[324] Graubow[325] & then pr. mail from Lubz[326] to Ludwiglust. Had dinner at Mr Behr von Regendank said to have 60.000 fl. income he has a very pretty daughter about 18 years of age Mrs Behr (stepmother) is also very young and very amiable. We had dinner on quite a grand scale; there was also a frl. Bulow who had been to West India – for her health! – Mr Kofechlager is a good deal of Hamburg about him; but a jolly fellow – Dr Passow is the best of the lot. quiet and modest unassuming –

---

20 Whit[327] MONDAY [140–225]

Reached Schwerin[328] early this morning was busy writing to M^r. Tooth; had a wretched dinner at the Inn left at 2 p m. for Retchendorf[329] – Is a nice lively town Schwerin clean with chearful streets & handsome buildings the Granddukes castle[330] is particularly handsome – In the evening very well received at Retchandorf nice people especially Mrs Schak; she is fond of riding on horseback saw the sheep was a very cold day – the scenery about the shwerinersee[331] is very fine the lake is very large & deep –

1861 5th Month   21 Whit TUESDAY [141–224]   May [21 to 22]

Passed through a beautiful country & scenery on my way from Retchendorf to Muschow[332] and Güstrow[333] thence pr. stage coach via Teterow[334] and Malchin[335] to Stavenhagen[336] where I arrived at 5 ½. the Meclenburgh post arrangements are good; carriages & roads excellent horses bad – wrote my letter to M[r.] Tooth in the morning & posted same – jaeta est alea[337] – Stavenhagen clean little town but awfully dull; there are some nice looking girls about the streets but they are frightened to look either right or left. all Meclenburgh is a priestridden bigoted hole.

---

22 WEDNESDAY [140–223]

Went early in the morning to New Keutzlin[338] oekonomic rath[339] Maas; a jolly old fellow who formerly lived in Austria his sheep are very good – they are the only real Hostitzer[340] sheep I have seen. He has a queer old character of a sheep master whom he brought from Moravia – the Raths' son is a nice young man his wife & daughter a 1. Left Stavenhagen pr. mail at 5 ½ p.m. reached Brandenburg[341] at 9. p.m Prenzlow[342] at 5 a m. had 2 very nice girls for travelling companions.

[23 to 24] **May**   23 THURSDAY [143–222]   5th Month **1861**

Took a private coach early in the morning and went to illeg. illeg. illeg. he is a douianer[343] püchter – was not at home – his wife rather an unpleasant person but apparently, unconsciously so. The Inspector who showed me the sheep was one of the most ridiculous specimens of Berliner Arogancy I ever witnessed very stupid. Afternoon went to Berlin pr railway had a very pretty vis à vis dark and illeg. but very insinuating her mother & sister were with her. They were on their way to Gräfenberg.[344] Went to the Friedrichs stadt Theater[345] did not see Eunise[346]

---

24 FRIDAY [144–221]

Spent all day at the Thierschau[347] – horrid weather; there were nice animals and also nice machinery exhibited especially a thrashing and wheat cleaning machine with steampower. Here were also nice English bred sheep there.
In the evening I went to Wallner's Sommer[348] Theater they gave Kiselack & seine Nichte[349] a very poor affair, though it seems to create a sensation here – Der beste Witz war: O jütiger Jott wie jros ist doch den Thierjarten[350]!

1861 5th Month   **25 SATURDAY [145–220]**   May [25]

Went again to the Exhibition in the Thier garten[351]; was amused with the Berliner workman describing the use of the thrashing machine: Da sitzst nun ene männlichen Persönlichkeit roft die Früchte des Getreide so, runten um da nun sist wieder e andere Persönlichkeit die lejst's nun so rüber[352]! Saw the King of Prussia also Prince Frederick & both their wives[353] the princes[354] struck me as amiable but as insignificant not to say vulgar looking – Met Count Frikenstein Mr Wedell & Fischer at the Theirschau. – Bought a Tätouris[355] machine. In the evening I saw "Lady Elinor" a most magnificent Ballet with Italian scenery. the costumes and decorations were splendid also the dancing very beautifully arranged but not equal to Italy in point of either beauty or grace. Madmsll[356] Taglioni however has a most beautiful figure & leg and is very graceful – Spent evening with M. Hensel 49 Stromstrasse – Eunice supposed to be Miss Bernhardt[357] Had a call in the evening from Orathekonomie[358] Thaer. Son of the celebrated Thaer – Ach ich schäme mir![359]

[26 to 27] **May**   26 Trinity[360] Sunday [146–219]   5th Month **1861**

Did not get up till 12 at noon. a beautiful warm day. wrote my journal and some letters; had dinner with Maytrand illeg. as bad as it is dear – In the evening I drove to the railway station & thence pr. rail as far as Riseha[361] where I stopped the night. As the Stumme von Portici[362] was being given at Berlin this night I should have much like to have stayed.

27 MONDAY [147–218]

Started early from Risa for Oschatz[363] walked to Sadegasts place on foot he is an uncouth old wretch. returned by 10 o clock train via Coswig[364] to Meissen[365] Had dinner there beim Hieschen[366] took post & went on to Zithain[367] Mr Stiger not being at Home went on to Leutewitz[368] where I saw his Stamm schäferei.[369] He is a very nice straightforward sort of man improving on acquaintance reached Dresden[370] at 8 ½ p.m. beautiful warm summers day.

1861 5th Month 28 TUESDAY [148–217] **May** [28 to 29]

Went through the Grünes Gewölbe[371] in the morning and the royal Gallery of pictures[372] both very beautiful. Dresden is nice lively tours handsome broad streets much adorned by the Elbe[373] running right through the town with its handsome bridges and cheerful looking steamers.
In the evening I saw der Goldbauer von BirchPfeiffer[374] – very stupid no interesting actress but one a frl. Guinau dark handsome fine figure
Left at night travelled all night.

---

29 WEDNESDAY [149–216]

Reached Weissenrode at 5 a m. settled my business there went on in successions to Würchensblatt & Tessitz[375]. spent the evening at the latter place travelled again back all night to Dresden. Took descriptions of the sheep purchased, put capsules on all of them with my seal and branded the Rams T on the horse!

[30 to 31] **May** 30 THURSDAY [150–215] 5th Month **1861**

Reached Dresden at 9 am. slept a little then wrote my letters. – in the evening heard the Trobadour;[376] much worse than at Berlin – the theatre it self is a handsome little building but the actors are 3rd rate and the prices very high – there were large number of very pretty girls (young <u>ladies</u>) in the boxes and galleries which in a measure reconciled me to the ugliness of the actresses.
Leonore[377] was given by ~~one~~ a Petersburg actress; sang well but no comparison with frl Lucca of Berlin either in acting or singing. –

---

31 FRIDAY [151–214]

Left Dresden at 8 reached Wachnitz Dubros place at 9 saw his wife very handsome woman I liked them both very much nice frank unaffected people. they have a beautiful little villa in a beautiful hill on the valley of the Elbe overlooking the surrounding country. I left there at 4 p m. went to Wehlen[378] pr. steamer thence on horseback to Lohmen[379] through the Uttewalde grund[380] to Bastei[381] thence to Rhade thenno[382] pr rail to Konigstein[383] an interesting old fortress stopped at [illeg.] Hauen stein[384] had a flirtation with Nanno the cook
View from Bastei magnificent.

1861 6th Month 1 SATURDAY [152–213] **June** [1]

Started at 1 in the morning for Lobositz[385] view along the Elbe very beautiful especially at Doderbach the frontier station. Reached Perutz[386] at 1 p.m. nice people large castle belonging to Count Thun Hohenstein.[387] Stopped that night there. Saw the sheep & decided to buy through I did not tell them –

[2 to 3] **June** 2 SUNDAY – 1 aft Trin [153–212] 6th Month **1861**

Went to Smečno[388] saw sheep there dined at Verwalters[389] returned after dinner to Schlan[390] thence pr. coach to Brandish[391] then pr. rail to Prague[392] put up at Blauen Stern[393]

---

3 MONDAY [154–211]

In Prague all day writing letters to Perutz – sending money etz. saw Mr Sündermahlers Museum of curiosities. dined with him at the schwarzen Roß[394]

1861 6th Month   4 TUESDAY [155–210]   **June** [4 to 5]

Left Prague pr rail for Brünn[395] thence pr. stagecoach to Wischau[396] put up bei der Stadt Wien[397] (Voseren[398])
very pretty daughter Resi[399]

---

5 WEDNESDAY [156–209]

Reached Littenschitz[400] pr. private coach at 1 p.m. all very amiable sheep not visible

---

[6 to 7] **June**   6 THURSDAY [157–208]   6th Month **1861**

Got my ram N. 4 shorn in the illeg. weighing 12lbs. 12oz. would not let me have N⁰ 30 yearling which I wanted to have – Went to see sheepwash after dinner a nice walk through the woods. Sophie[401] is a nice girl her stepmother unbearable

---

7 FRIDAY [158–207]

Left Littenschitz at 9 a.m. pr coach via Hostitz[402] for Kreuseir[403] thence bus for Hallin[404] – thence rail for Vienna. arrived too late for 8 1/2 train had to wait till 10 reached Baden at 11 p m.

1861 6th Month   8 SATURDAY [159–206]   June [8]

Wrote letters all day relative to delivery of rams – In the afternoon went to Vöslau[405] rain – saw Mrs Mattersdorfer & Mrs Luzzato the latter sang very nicely –

[9 to 10] **June**   9 Sunday – 2 aft Trin [160–205]   6th Month **1861**

More letters – Pauline & Mrs Luzzato came in the afternoon. accompanied them to railway in the evening.

10 MONDAY [161–204]

Went to town early in the morning to post money letters and get money on my letter of 6th returned to Baden at night.

[10 to 11] **October**   10 THURSDAY [283–82]   10th Month **1861**[406]

Wrote to M[r] Tooth Expressed readiness to illeg. sheep purchases for £30 pr. ann or 5 pr. cent commission on purchase money –[407]
     1 pr. trous[408]
     5 shirts
     3 socks
     3 pockthandkchf[409]
     1 flannel shirt

Credit: Unpublished. Text: M.S., Pf. Coll., CL'ANA 0177 (unpublished manuscript, Pforzheimer Collection of Shelley and His Circle, New York Public Library, Astor, Lenox, and Tilden Foundations)

Notes

* Gerald P. Walsh records in the *Australian Journal of Biography* that John Sands (1818–1873) was an engraver and printer (like his father and grandfather before him). His father had worked for *Punch* magazine and his cousin was the poet, Thomas Hood. Sands moved to Sydney for medical reasons and purchased a printing house with Thomas Kenny, his brother-in-law. They named the printing house Sands and Kenny. After Kenny's retirement in 1861, it became Sands and McDougall. As Walsh notes: "By 1870 as stationers, booksellers, printers and account book manufacturers the firm was one of the largest of its kind in Australia and in that year won prizes for printing and book production at the Intercolonial Exhibition in Sydney. Sands printed and published a wide variety of publications, but especially notable were his directories, almanacs, gazetteers and prints" (G. P. Walsh, "Sands, John." *Australian Dictionary of Biography*, http://adb.anu.edu.au/biography/sands-john-4536. Accessed 7 April 2020). An article written on 24 January 1860 and published in the Melbourne

Age (page 5) about Sands and Kenny's Melbourne Directory states: "An octavo volume of 400 closely printed pages is barely adequate to contain the names, addresses, and professional or lending designations of the inhabitants of this city, and of the business portion of its suburbs! . . . We must accept, however, the fact as it stands, and express our obligations to the publishers of this carefully compiled Directory, for having thus mapped out the professional and mercantile divisions of metropolitan society, and accurately registered 'the local habitations and the names' of upwards of 10,000 persons engaged in the pursuit of multifarious callings" (https://trove.nla.gov.au/newspaper/article/154880275?searchTerm=&searchLimits= Accessed 7 April 2020).

Wilhelm writes the names listed below on the first six pages of his diary. For the purposes of space conservation, I have amalgamated the pages into one list.

There are also six initial printed prefatory pages listing the following: the dates and days of each month, including times of sunrise and sunset and the "remarkable days" such as religious holidays and birth or death days of significant historical persons; postage rates and packet rates.

1 Thomas Henry Buckle (1821–1862), author of the three-volume *History of Civilization in England* (1857–1864).
2 Thomas Babington Macaulay (1800–1859), author of *The History of England from the Accession of James the Second* (five volumes, published between 1848 and 1861).
3 The final letter on this name appears to be a "y". Nonetheless it seems likely this refers to Niccolo Machiavelli (1469–1527), Italian statesman and author of *The Prince* (written after 1513 and published after 1527).
4 Johann Kaspar Lavater (1741–1801), Swiss founder of the study of physiognomy. He published his four volume *Physiognomische Fragmente zur Beförderung der Menschenkenntnis und Menschenliebe* [*Essays on Physiognomy*] in 1775–1778. He was also a poet.
5 J.S. Mitchell was a partner in R. and F. Tooth and Company, a brewing and mercantile concern. Brothers Robert, Edwin, and Frederick Tooth were pastoralists in Australia.
6 From *CFL* (I: 352–353): "Graeme Skinner provides bibliographic information on Leopold Ravac (Rawack), a musician who moved to Australia in 1852 and who died in Darlinghurst in 1873 at the age of 54 years. Skinner identifies Rawack as a violinist and merchant. Rawack was apparently one of the organizing committee members of the Sydney University Musical Festival of 1859 and his wife, Amalie Mauthner Rawack, was a Viennese musician who immigrated with him to Australia. Skinner cites the journal of Dr. Karl Scherzer who wrote, 'All the world congratulated the charming, highly educated, but impecunious Miss Mauthner when they heard that she was going to marry a rich merchant from the gold mining district of Australia'. According to Skinner, Amalie Rawack divorced Leopold Rawack in 1861 and returned to Vienna (Graeme Skinner. *A biographical register of Australian colonial musical personnel – R*, *Australharmony*. Web. 26 April 2015. http://sydney.edu.au/paradisec/australharmony/register-R.php)". Accessed again 14 May 2020.
7 Caroline Suttor (1841–1921, and known as Carry), sister of William Henry Suttor, Jr. (Pauline Clairmont's lover).
8 In Australia, Wilhelm worked on a farm called Kameruka. James Manning became manager at Kameruka until the mid-1860s. While at Kameruka, Wilhelm lived with Manning and his wife, Mary Firebrace Manning. After Manning's death in 1887 at his home in Vectis, Double Bay, *The Sydney Morning Herald* of October 27 noted that his wife, the daughter of Major Firebrace, survived him (*The Sydney Morning Herald*. 27 October 1887. National Library of Australia, http://nla.gov.au/nla.news-page13679630, p. 9).
9 In 1852, Australian pastoralists John Edye Manning, James A. L. Manning, William Montagu Manning, Robert Tooth, Edwin Tooth, Thomas Sutcliffe Mort, and John Croft became joint partners in the Twofold Bay Pastoral Association. Wilhelm worked

for the association after the failure of his farm, Kangaroo Hills, in 1856. James Manning was a student in Hohenheim and attended the same institution as Wilhelm had some years earlier. See G. P. Walsh, "Tooth, Edwin (1822–1858)," *Australian Dictionary of Biography*, National Centre of Biography, Australian National University, http://adb.anu.edu.au/biography/tooth-edwin-4944/text7851, published first in hardcopy 1976 Accessed 15 May 2020.

10 Robert Tooth (1821–1893). He and Mitchell co-owned Tooth & Co. after Tooth's brother, Frederick, retired from the alcohol-importing business. Tooth died in England (G. P. Walsh, "'Tooth, Robert [1821–1893]'," *Australian Dictionary of Biography*, National Centre of Biography, Australian National University, http://adb.anu.edu.au/biography/tooth-robert-4731/text7851, published first in hardcopy 1976 Accessed 15 May 2020).

The father of the Tooth brothers, Robert Tooth, lived in Swifts Park (Wilhelm misspells the name), Cranbrook, Kent, in south-east England. See Walsh, "Tooth, Robert."

11 John Croft and Thomas Whistler Smith were importers who owned the firm Smith, Croft & Co. in Sydney, Australia. Smith's father had founded the firm originally as Smith Bros. together with his brother, Henry Gilbert Smith, in 1830. The name was changed to Smith, Croft, & Co. when Croft joined Thomas Smith. Thomas Smith returned to England in 1858 and the company ceased to exist (Vivienne Parsons, 'Smith, Thomas Whistler 1824–1859', *Australian Dictionary of Biography*, National Centre of Biography, Australian National University, http://adb.anu.edu.au/biography/smith-thomas-whistler-2673/text3729, published first in hardcopy 1967 Accessed 15 May 2020).

12 The London address of the Tooth brothers and Thomas Mort's agency was R. & F. Tooth & Mort, 155 Fenchurch Street (see G. P Walsh, "Tooth, Edwin [1822–1858]").

13 From *CFL* (II: 254): "Benjamin Buchanan (1821? – 1912) married Louise Harriet Manning, daughter of Edye Manning (1807–1889). Edye Manning's son and Louise Manning's brother, John Edye Manning, married Caroline Suttor, Willie Suttor's sister. See Niland, John. "Buchanan, Benjamin (1821–1912)", *Australian Dictionary of Biography*. National Centre of Biography, Australian National University. 1969. Web. 10 June 2015. http://adb.anu.edu.au/biography/buchanan-benjamin-3098/text4591 Accessed 14 May 2020.

14 Homans and Turner cannot be identified.

15 Unidentified. Names without endnotes cannot be identified.

16 "Alle cure del Signor Cini" means "care of Mr. Cini" in Italian. "Bis via dei Giraldi, Firence" means "to Giraldi Street, Florence." At this time, Wilhelm's aunt, Claire Clairmont, was living in Florence, Italy. In 1875, she would name her friend, Bartolomeo Cini (1809–1877), as the executor of her will; when he died two years later, she named his son Giovanni. Cini's wife was Catherine Elizabeth Raniera Tighe (1815–1874), known as Nerina. Mary Shelley dedicated her novel *Maurice, or the Fisher's Cot* to Laurette, Nerina's sister, in 1820.

17 Port city in northeast Italy. Österreichischer Lloyd (German for "Austria Lloyd") was a shipping company founded in 1833 and headquartered in Trieste. "Traps" is a colloquial term for luggage.

18 Wilhelm places a bracket to the right of these four items.

19 Antonia Clairmont, Wilhelm's mother, who was living in Baden, a town some 34 kilometers south of Vienna.

20 English translation: Madame Marie Bácsák, c/o Privy Councilor Bartel, 77 Lange Gasse, Pernssburg [Pernsburg]

21 English translation: "Johann Houdlik, judge in the court of Count Ludwig Károly in Salfa, by way of Stein-am-Anger". Stein-am-Anger was the German name for the Hungarian city of Szombathely.

22 German for "now".
23 German for "Cavalry Captain".
24 Nr. is the German for "Number". Troppau is the German name for the Czech city of Opava. See journal entry for 24 April 1861.
25 At this point in the journal, we find an inserted tag from the Galle Face Hotel, Colombo, Ceylon. The tag has a picture of the hotel on it. It has yellowed the paper in which it was preserved. See Wilhelm's journal entry for 3 February 1861.
26 A loose, four-leaf page with numbers and calculations and then these words in Wilhelm's handwriting, beginning with "Difficulties in selecting" was inserted here.
27 Illegible, and written above.
28 I have divided the pages into clusters of dates. Whenever the journal begins a new section of dates with 1861 on the left-hand side of the page, I have started a new section for editorial purposes.
29 Wilhelm left for Alexandria aboard the *Behar*, a passenger liner owned by the Peninsular and Oriental Steam Navigation Company. On 21 January 1861, *The Sydney Morning Herald* announced in a column called "Mails by the *Behar*" that the ship would accept mail for the United Kingdom and other places along the way (such as Malta and Alexandria). See https://trove.nla.gov.au/newspaper/article/13051567 Accessed 8 April 2020. The Melbourne *Age* recorded on 23 January 1861 (page 5) that the Governor-General departed via the *Behar* on 22 January 1861. *The Maitland Mercury and Hunter River General Advertiser* of 24 January 1861 notes the following passengers aboard the P. and O. Company's steamer, *Behar*: "For Southampton: Captain Patullo, Mr. T. Icely, Mr. C. Manning, Mrs. Buchanan. For Marseilles: Messrs. J. McLeod, Wild. For Alexandria: Mr. and Mrs. Pike, Mr. Bedborough, Mr. Clairmont. For Galle: His Excellency Sir William and Lady Denison, Infant, Misses Denison (4), Masters Denison (4). and four servants, Miss Woods." The newspaper also states: "This fine steamship will leave her moorings in Waterview Bay this morning, at eleven o'clock, and after proceeding down the harbour will return to Farm Cove, for the purpose of embarking His Excellency the Governor General. On finally leaving for Melbourne at two p.m., she will be accompanied by the principal portion of the steamers now in harbour, thus affording an opportunity to the public of witnessing his Excellency's departure from these shores" (https://trove.nla.gov.au/newspaper/article/1867994 0?searchTerm=Behar%20passenger%20list%20clairmont&searchLimits= Accessed 8 April 2020). The *Behar* was originally owned by the Cie Franco-Americaine and was known as the *Barcelona*. It weighed 1,603 tons. The P&O Company purchased it in 1858 and named it the *Behar*. In 1874, after its sale to a Japanese company, it became *Niigata Maru*. See www.theshipslist.com/ships/lines/pando.shtml Accessed 18 April 2020.
30 Sydney headlands, at the mouth of the Sydney harbor.
31 Wilhelm means to write "Hobson's Bay." Hobsons Bay is located in Port Phillip, Australia, near to the city of Melbourne. There are some 700 kilometers from Sydney to Melbourne, which is the capital city of Victoria, Australia. It is located in southeast Australia at the north end of Port Phillip Bay. The city was named in 1837 for the British Prime Minister, William Lamb, Viscount Melbourne.
32 The concept of the Melbourne Public Library became a reality in 1853. The first library building was erected in 1856. Today, it is part of the State Library Victoria, the oldest public library system in Australia. See https://guides.slv.vic.gov.au/slvhistory Accessed 8 April 2020.
33 See introductory pages to this journal.
34 Septuagesima, the third Sunday before Lent. Lent begins on Ash Wednesday and lasts until Easter. It is a time of penance and spiritual renewal for Christians.
35 King George Sound is located on the south coast of the state of Western Australia. The city of Albany is located there. It was established as a colonial city in 1826,

three years before Perth. There are about 432 kilometers between Perth and King George Sound.
36 Wilhelm's spelling.
37 Adelaide is the capital of the state of South Australia.
38 The farm of Sir Richard (1779–1839) and Ann (1793–1855) Spencer had been set up as a government farm in 1827. Richard Spencer emigrated from Great Britain to assume the position of Government Resident in Albany in 1833, at which point he purchased the farm. According to Robert Stephens, "On arrival [Spencer] bought Strawberry Hill; to its six cleared acres (2.4 ha) he added 1400 virgin acres (567 ha) and the existing wattle and daub dwelling he enlarged with two-storied additions. Within two years good progress had been made with all his agrarian and livestock plans. The needs of his sheep prompted the purchase of pastures thirty miles (48 km) north-west of Albany on the Hay River. Soon afterwards two-storied additions in granite were made to his homestead . . . His grave, as he wished, overlooked King George Sound. He was survived by his wife, who in spite of a reduced income contrived to maintain great style and gracious hospitality" (*Australian Journal of Biography*. http://adb.anu.edu.au/biography/spencer-sir-richard-2685 Accessed 8 April 2020). Since 1964, the property has been administered by Australia's National Trust.
39 Probably "The Happy Wanderer" (German: "Der fröhliche Wanderer"), written by Florenz Friedrich Sigismund (1788–1857).
40 Sexagesima, the second Sunday before Lent.
41 Galle is a city in Sri Lanka, an island country situated in the Indian Ocean to the south and west of the Bay of Bengal. Sri Lanka was known as Ceylon during its period as a British colony. It achieved its independence in 1948.
42 City in northeast Egypt, located on the Gulf of Suez. The Suez Canal was opened in 1869, facilitating maritime travel and shortening sea voyages.

  Wilhelm makes an error in his journal, which he corrects in his 4 March entry. He mistakenly records the events of 4 March through 6 March in February. Therefore, these three entries should be read instead as occurring on March 4, 5, and 6. He notes this error when he records the events for March 4, 5, and 6 as "vide Febr 4th" and "vide Febry 5 & 6th" later in his journal.
43 Cairo is the capital of Egypt and the largest city in the country. The British assumed control in 1882. However, during Wilhelm's visit, the city was under Ottoman control.
44 Nomadic Arabs who live in the deserts of Northern Africa and the Middle East.
45 Wilhelm's spelling of Nile and pyramids. The three pyramids of Giza are located on the Nile River. The city of Giza is some 5 kilometers southwest of Cairo. Built for three kings of the fourth dynasty (2613 BCE – 2494 BCE), Khufu (Cheops), Khafre, and Menkaure, the pyramids were burial sites.
46 The city of Alexandria (named for Alexander the Great who founded the city in 331 BCE) is located on the Mediterranean Sea in the north of Egypt, some 180 kilometers from Cairo.
47 Northeastern Italian city.
48 Camphor was used to repel moths and other insects and trunks made of camphor were used to transport materials and clothing.
49 A marble column built in 297 CE to commemorate the Roman emperor Diocletian (244 CE – 311 CE). It was originally called Pompey's Pillar due to an incorrect reading of the Greek plaque at the foot of the statue.
50 Three obelisks, known as Cleopatra's Needle, were transferred from Alexandria to Paris, New York, and London in the late 19th century. Cleopatra (69 BCE – 30 BCE) was queen of the Ptolemaic empire from 51 BCE until her death by suicide in 30 BCE.
51 Malta is an island in the Mediterranean Sea, located about 80 kilometers south of Italy.
52 There are no entries for Friday, 8 February through Wednesday, 13 February.
53 See 3 February.

54 Name given to East Indian sailors or military men. The name derives from the Portuguese.
55 Wilhelm's spelling for "cinnamon".
56 The *Nubia* was a P&O (Peninsular and Oriental Steam Navigation Company) ship. The British company was founded in 1836. The *Nubia* was built in 1854. It weighed 2,096 tons, and was sold in 1877 to the London School's Board where it was renamed the *Shaftesbury*. See www.theshipslist.com/ships/lines/pando.shtml Accessed 18 April 2020.
57 Wilhelm references the Singhalese people, the largest ethnic group in Sri Lanka.
58 The British (together with their French compatriots) fought the Chinese from 1856 until 1860 in the Second Anglo-Chinese War. Also known as the Second Opium War, the war pitted the two sets of forces against one another for control of, amongst other issues, the opium trade. The Chinese lost the war and Kowloon Peninsula to the British. Britain controlled India from 1757 until India's independence in 1947. The First Anglo-Chinese War was fought between 1839 and 1842.
59 Emily Brontë's novel, *Wuthering Heights*, published in 1847.
60 See January 22.
61 Spanish
62 La Mancha is a plateau in central Spain. The Castile-La Mancha autonomous region lies north of the region of Madrid.
63 A region in northeastern Spain that has been autonomous since 1979, Catalonia includes the province of Barcelona.
64 Island of El Ikhwa, known as Brothers Islands, situated in the Red Sea, some 67 kilometers from El Qoseir in Eastern Egypt.
65 A city in Yemen, located on the Gulf of Aden.
66 Cantonments: Military quarters for troops.
67 Like a rampart.
68 Perim Island divides the Bab el-Mandeb Straight (a 32 kilometer-wide straight) into two channels. The straight is located between the Arabian Peninsula and Africa and connects the Gulf of Aden and the Indian Ocean with the Red Sea. See www.britannica.com/place/Bab-El-Mandeb-Strait Accessed 17 April 2020.
69 Mecca, the birthplace of Muhammad (who founded Islam) is located in Saudi Arabia and is a holy site for worship.
70 Perhaps *Valentine*, a French novel by George Sand (1804–1876) and written in 1832.
71 In 1857, in Kanpur (a northern Indian town conquered by the British in 1801) and as part of the Indian Mutiny (a first attempt between 1857 and 1859 to achieve independence from the British), British troops were killed by Nana Sahib and his sepoys (Indian troops who had been under British employ). The British exacted a brutal revenge for this massacre. Lieutenant-Colonel Williams led the investigation for the British. Nana Sahib was born circa 1820. After the British defeated him in December 1857, he escaped to the Nepal hills. He died there, possibly in 1859.
72 The Red Sea (1930 kilometers long) runs between the Egyptian city of Suez and the Bab el-Mandeb Straight.
73 Ship named possibly for Eldred Pottinger (1811–1843), a British officer who was known as the "Defender of Herat". The *Pottinger* was a P&O boat that was built in 1846. It weighed 1,401 tons and was scrapped in 1871. See www.theshipslist.com/ships/lines/mm.shtml Accessed 18 April 2020.
74 Another P&O ship, the *Ottawa*, was built in 1853. It was acquired by the P&O company from the Canadian SN Company in 1857 and sold to a company in Hong Kong in 1873. It weighed 1,274 tons. See www.theshipslist.com/ships/lines/mm.shtml Accessed 18 April 2020.
75 Latin for "see". As noted earlier, Wilhelm writes the entries for 4 March – 6 March 6 in February. See details of his March entries in February.

76 Wilhelm's boat for Malta.
77 Word meaning "a slight disagreement".
78 Wilhelm makes an error in designating the time as 9 p.m. instead of 9 a.m.
79 As noted earlier, Malta is an island in the Mediterranean Sea, located about 80 kilometers south of Italy. Malta is one of seven islands in the Maltese archipelago. It is the largest island.
80 The Co-Cathedral of St. John the Baptist in Valletta, Malta, is a Catholic church built by the Knights of Malta between 1572 and 1577. Valletta is the capital city of Malta, an island nation in the Mediterranean Sea. Malta achieved its independence from Britain in 1964. A famous painting in the cathedral is Caravaggio's *The Beheading of St. John the Baptist* (1608). Over 4,00 knights are buried in the church.
81 *La sonnambula* (Italian for *The Sleepwalker*) is an Italian opera Vincenzo Bellini wrote that was first performed in Milan, Italy, in 1831.
82 Peninsular and Oriental Steam Navigation Company, a British company founded in 1837.
83 Mdina, also known as Citta' Veccia, was the capital of Malta before construction on Valletta started in the 16th century.
84 The island of Gozo forms part of the Maltese archipelago and is the second largest of the seven islands. Only Malta, Gozo, and Comino are inhabited.
85 In 1488, a watchtower was built to protect the Maltese harbor. It was named in honor of Erasmus of Formia, a Christian saint known as St. Elmo and who died in 296 CE. St. Elmo is the patron saint of sailors and the weather condition known as St. Elmo's fire, which can happen on ships in thunderstorms, is named for him. He was persecuted by Diocletian and martyred in the city of Formia where he served as Bishop. The Knights of St. John fortified the original watchtower in 1530 due to heightened concerns about Ottoman attacks. During the Great Siege of 1565, St. Elmo Watchtower was one of Malta's important defenses. Since then, it has served as part of the city of Valletta's defenses.
86 Bernado Pisano (his real name was Pagoli, but he was perhaps known as Pisano because he worked for a time in Pisa; 1490–1548), was an Italian composer best known for his madrigals.
87 See 11 March.
88 The Barb horse (or Berber) is a north-African horse.
89 See the introductory pages to this journal.
90 Antonia Clairmont, Wilhelm and Pauline's mother who lived in Austria.
91 The final aria from Bellini's *La sonnambula*: "Ah! non giunge uman pensiero / al contento ond'il son piena" (Italian for: "Human thought cannot conceive of the happiness that fills me").
92 The Messageries nationales was founded in 1851. The French shipping company was later known as the Messageries imperials and then, after 1871, as the Compagnie des messageries maritimes. The *Quirinal* was built in 1857. It weighed 787 tons and was scrapped in 1871. See www.theshipslist.com/ships/lines/mm.shtml Accessed 18 April 2020.
93 Beirut, the capital city of Lebanon today. Under direct Ottoman control from 1865 until 1920, when the French assumed power, Lebanon achieved its independence in 1946.
94 The largest of the Mediterranean islands and an autonomous region of Italy since 1947. Previously under the control of the Bourbons, Sicily was freed by Giuseppe Garibaldi during the Risorgimento in 1860. It became part of the United Kingdom of Italy in 1861.
95 At 3,220 meters, Mount Etna is an active (and Europe's highest) volcano.
96 Port city in the northeast of Sicily.
97 Region in southern Italy.

98   The Grand Hotel Trinacria in Messina was built in 1820 but demolished in 1908 after an earthquake and a resulting fire. Messina itself was severely damaged during the 1908 earthquake and was rebuilt thereafter.
99   The Cathedral and the Church of the Santissima Annunziata dei Catalani in Messina. Rebuilt in 1150–1200 by the Normans on the site of an earlier chapel, the cathedral houses art works salvaged from the 1908 earthquake.
100 Sardinia is another of Italy's Mediterranean islands, the second largest next to Sicily. The Kingdom of Sardinia lasted until 1860 when Sardinia became part of the Kingdom of Italy after the Risorgimento.
101 Third largest of the Italian cities, it became part of the Kingdom of Italy in 1861.
102 Rising above the Bay of Naples, Mount Vesuvius is an active volcano. Its eruption destroyed the city of Pompeii (which was fourteen miles southeast of Naples) in 79 CE.
103 Built between 1200 and 1300, the Duomo di Napoli is dedicated to Saint Januarius who is known in Italian as San Gennaro. Saint Januarius is the patron saint of Naples and one can see a vial supposedly containing his blood in the cathedral. He was martyred during the reign of Diocletian in 305 CE and his feast day is celebrated on 19 September.
104 Catacombs of San Gennaro in Naples. Saint Januarius is buried there. The catacombs have been active since the second century.
105 The Basilica of Santa Maria della Sanità was built between 1602 and 1610. The church was built after a 5–6th century fresco of Mary, the mother of Jesus, was found in the city. Under the basilica are the Catacombe di san Gaudioso. Saint Gaudioso was a Tunisian bishop who died in Naples and who was buried sometime in 451–453 CE in what are now the catacombs of San Gaudioso.
106 March 19 is the Feast of St. Joseph. St. Joseph, husband of Mary, the mother of Jesus, is the patron saint of fathers, travelers, and unborn children.
107 Giuseppe Garibaldi (1807–1882) was the leader of the Risorgimento, the Italian movement for the reunification of Italy. The country was unified in 1861. Giuseppe is the Italian form of Joseph.
108 Gaetano Donizetti (1797–1848) wrote his opera, *Poliuto*, in 1838. He based the story on Pierre Corneille's play, *Polyeucte* (1642), which tells the story of the martyred saint Polyeuctus. *Poliuto* was performed initially in 1848 in Naples in the Teatro San Carlo.
109 Amina Boschetti (1836–1881). She first performed in Teatro alla Scala in Milan and died in Naples. Boschetti was a ballerina, and opera performances in the nineteenth century often included ballet.
110 The words to the national anthem of Italy were written in 1847 by a revolutionary and member of Garibaldi's circle, Goffredo Mameli (1827–1849). Known as "Inno di Mameli," ("Hymn of Mameli") or "Fratelli d'Italia" ("Brothers of Italy"), the work became the national anthem of Italy in 1946. Composer Michele Novaro (1818–1885) wrote the music for it.
111 Known today as the Museo Archeologico Nazionale di Napoli (National Archeological Museum of Naples), the museum was called the Real Museo Borbonico (Royal Bourbon Museum). Bourbon King Charles III (1716–1788) started the collection, which was known as the Farnese collection after his mother, Elisabetta Farnese, whose collections in Rome and Parma he had inherited. Its original purpose was to bring together artefacts from the nearby towns of Pompeii and Herculaneum which an eruption of Mount Vesuvius in 79 CE had destroyed. His son, King Ferdinando I (1751–1825), continued his work in renovating what is now part of the campus of the museum.
112 The *Ercole Farnese* (Italian for "Farnese Hercules") is a statue of Hercules, exhibited at the Museo Archeologico Nazionale di Napoli. The statue is a copy by Glykon of

an older one made by Lysippus, a fourth century BCE Greek sculptor. The *Ercole Farnese* was probably made in the third century CE and is made of marble.
113   Castel Sant'Elmo, a medieval fortress built in the fourteenth century.
114   In Salzburg, Austria.
115   In Edinburgh, Scotland.
116   Kings from the royal house of Bourbon which originated in France. In 1861, Italy threw off its Bourbon yoke and became an independent kingdom.
117   The Teatro di San Carlo was built and named for Bourbon King Charles. It was completed in 1737.
118   Pulcinella is the Italian commedia dell'arte's stock character who originated in the seventeenth century.
119   The Grotto of Posilippo, a 700-meter long tunnel connecting Naples to Posilippo. It was built in the first century CE.
120   One of the quarters of Naples, on the sea.
121   Pozzuoli is a municipality of Naples.
122   Lake Avernus (in Italian: Lago d'Averno) is a lake, about 4 kilometers from Pozzuoli.
123   The Arco Felice (Italian: "The Happy Arch") is an ancient Roman arch on the road to Pozzuoli.
124   About 19 kilometers west of Naples.
125   A lake, about one kilometer from Cumae.
126   Baiae was an ancient Roman town. It is now part of the commune of Bacoli near Naples.
127   A port city located on the gulf of Pozzuoli.
128   The Via Appia was the ancient Roman road connecting Rome to southern Italy.
129   Wilhelm does not write a name here.
130   Italian for "the sworn oath." The opera, *Il guiramento*" (*The Oath*; the first performance was in 1837) was written by Saverio Mercadante (1795–1870) and is based on Victor Hugo's play, *Angelo, tyran de Padoue* (1835).
131   The opera, *Semiramide* (the first performance was in 1823), was written by Gioachino Rossini (1792–1868) and is based on Voltaire's tragic play, *Sémiramus* (1746).
132   Unidentified. The spelling is also unclear.
133   See 19 March.
134   Tantawanglo is a town in the Bega Valley Shire, New South Wales, Australia. Kameruka (where Wilhelm worked while in Australia) is some 19 kilometers from the city of Bega in the Bega Valley Shire. The shire is in the southeast of New South Wales.
135   Talbingo is a small town at the foot of the Snowy Mountains in New South Wales, Australia. Mount Kosciuszko, Australia's highest mountain peak (elevation: 2,228 meters), forms part of the Snowy Mountains.
136   German for "Swedish stoves".
137   The name of a wine, Lacryma Christi (translation: "Tears of Christ"), produced from vineyards on the slopes of Mount Vesuvius. Characters in the works of Nathaniel Hawthorne, Alexander Dumas, and Voltaire have enjoyed this drink.
138   Wilhelm writes in the date by hand.
139   Civitaveccia (Italian for "old city"), a port city on the Tyrrhenian Sea, about 60 kilometers from Rome.
140   The Palazzo Reale di Napoli (Italian for "Royal Palace of Naples") was constructed in the seventeenth century and became the royal residence of Charles III of Spain when he assumed control of the Kingdom of Naples.
141   Castel Nuovo (Italian for "New Castle") is a medieval castle built in 1282 and which served as the residence of the Kings of Naples until 1812. The castle is a museum today.
142   The Kingdom of the Two Sicilies was created in 1816 by the merger of the Kingdom of Naples and the Kingdom of Sicily. Francesco II (Francis II, 1836–1894) was the

monarch in 1860 when Garibaldi and his forces occupied the Kingdom. It was proclaimed a part of a united Italy in 1861.
143 Nisida (Wilhelm spells the island incorrectly), Procida, and Ischia are three of the Phlegraean Islands north of Naples in the Tyrrhenian Sea. Vivara is the fourth island.
144 Capo Miseno (the Italian name for Cape Mesino) is the most northwestern part of the Gulf of Naples. The Capo Miseno lighthouse was built in 1869. Destroyed in the Second World War, the lighthouse was rebuilt in 1954.
145 Gaeta is some 80 kilometers from Naples and has a lighthouse constructed in 1854.
146 The date has been written over by hand.
147 A region in the northwest of Italy. Its capital is Turin.
148 The date has been written over by hand.
149 The Colosseum in Rome, located near the Roman Forum, was a large amphitheater completed in 80 CE. The Colosseum is best known for gladiatorial competitions. The Pantheon is now a church (Basilica di Santa Maria ad Martyres; earlier it was a Roman temple) with an oval opening in the roof. It was built between 113 and 126 CE (it was dedicated during the Emperor Hadrian's reign). The Circus Maximus, located adjacent to the Colosseum, was a stadium used for public games (Italian: "Ludi"). The Baths of Caracalla were named for the Emperor Caracalla, who was instrumental in the construction of the public baths, originally started by his father, Septimius Severus. The baths were built between 211 and 216 CE.
150 Wilhelm misspells "Genovese".
151 Wilhelm writes the word "with" above the elided word "between".
152 Basilica of St. Peter's in the Vatican City. The church was originally built in the 4th century CE. Catholic tradition holds that it was built over St. Peter's burial place.
153 The Vatican City is an independent state fully contained within Rome. The pope lives there in the Papal Palace and is the head of the Holy See which governs the city-state.
154 The Vatican Apostolic Library contains some 1,6 million books and 150, 000 manuscripts.
155 The Vatican holds multiple art collections in various palaces and galleries as well as the Sistine Chapel. Michelangelo's frescoes are in the Sistine Chapel.
156 The Capitoline Museums consist of three buildings. The *Galata Morente* (Italian for "Dying Gladiator") is an ancient Roman model of a lost Greek statue from 331 BCE.
157 The Basilica of St. Paul Outside the Walls, in Rome. It is one of four major basilicas owned by the Holy See and is governed by the Vatican even though it is in Rome. Tradition states that Saint Paul is buried there.
158 Isola Tiberina (Italian for Island of the Tiber) is an island in the Tiber River.
159 Wilhelm could be thinking of two areas in Rome: Trastevere, where many Jews lived during the Roman Republic until the Middle Ages and where Rome's oldest synagogue (dating from 980 CE) was located, or the Jewish Ghetto (Italian: Ghetto di Roma) established in 1555. The ghetto was destroyed in 1888.
160 See 23 March.
161 Known in English as Leghorn, Livorno is a city on the Ligurian Sea. From 1818 onwards, Mary and Percy Shelley spent many summers in Livorno. In 1822, they rented a home (Casa Magni) in Lerici together with their friends, Jane and Edward Williams. Lerici is 72 kilometers from Livorno. Percy Shelley and Edward Williams drowned in 1822 in the Bay of La Spezia near Livorno.
162 Wilhelm's spelling for "too".
163 Capital city of Tuscany, Italy, the city is some 230 kilometers northwest of Rome. The Italian Renaissance started in Florence. In 1861, Tuscany became part of the Kingdom of Italy. Florence was the capital city from 1865 until 1870 when Rome became the capital. The Arno River flows through Florence. Wilhelm's aunt, Claire Clairmont, resided in Florence after 1859.

164 Wilhelm's aunt, Claire Clairmont, who would finance his failed farming enterprise in the Banat. Claire provided admirably for her late brother's children and his widow.
165 In 1871, Claire would provide the money for Wilhelm's purchase of Nikolaihof, a farm in today's Maribor (known as Marburg in German when Wilhelm lived there), Slovenia. The enterprise was unsuccessful and Wilhelm was forced to move his family back to Vienna in 1874. Claire visited Wilhelm, his wife Ottilia, and their two children (Johann Paul was not yet born; see the genealogical table in this edition) at Nikolaihof in September 1871, but she removed to Trieste by November as she found the cold too extreme. Records in the Regional Archives in Maribor (the Pokrajinski arhiv Maribor) state that Mary Jean Clairmont (presumably referring to Mary Jane Clairmont [Claire Clairmont]) purchased the Walcker estate. (The document reads: "Clairmont Mary Jean als Ersteh. der Walcker'schen /: D. Dominikus:/ [illeg.]" Translation by Ann Sherwin: "Clairmont Mary Jean as purchaser of the Walcker (D. Dominikus)." Dr. Dominkusch had originally purchased the farm from Mr. Walcker. Source: Pokrajinski arhiv Maribor (Regional Archives Maribor, Slovenia).
166 Stagecoach.
167 City in northern Italy near the Apennine Mountains, 106 kilometers from Florence.
168 The Cathedral of Saint Peter in Bologna. Built on the site of an older church, the present building dates to the sixteenth and seventeenth centuries.
169 The Apennine Mountains extend through Italy for 1,400 kilometers. Mount Corno is the highest peak (2,912 meters above sea level).
170 French for "pavements".
171 A city in northern Italy and capital of Lombardy province.
172 The city of Alessandria in northwestern Italy.
173 Wilhelm writes the words "10 p.m." in pencil.
174 Island city in northeastern Italy on the Adriatic Sea. The city of 118 separate islands joined by canals and bridges was founded in the seventh century CE and ruled by the doges (dukes).
175 City, 19 kilometers west of Milan. The Battle of Magenta (4 June 1859) led to the ousting of the Austrian army from Magenta by the French.
176 Town in northern Italy, known for the Battle of Solferino (24 June 1859). This was the final battle in the Second War of Italian Independence.
177 Capital city of the Italian province of Novara, 50 kilometers west of Milan.
178 Lombardy is a region in the north of Italy and is characterized by rolling hills and Alpine mountains. Its capital city is Milan. Lombardy is an important agricultural region in Italy, particularly in the area around the Po River.
179 See 23 March. The Siege of Gaeta (November 1860 – February 1861) concluded the war between the Kingdom of the Two Sicilies and the Kingdom of Sardinia. After unification, King Victor Emanuel II of Sardinia was crowned King of the united Italy. Victor Emanuel II was a supporter of Garibaldi's movement for Italian unification and independence.
180 Maria Sophia of Bavaria (1841–1925) married Francesco II in 1859. She was queen of the Kingdom of the Two Sicilies which became part of the Kingdom of Italy in 1861. Her sister, Elisabeth, was married to Franz Joseph I of Austria.
181 Construction on the Palazzo Ducale (Italian for Doges' Palace) began in the fourteenth century on the site of a former palace.
182 St. Mark's Square (in Italian: Piazzo San Marco), the main square in Venice. St. Mark's Basilica stands on the square as does the Doge's Palace.
183 Money.
184 A port-city in northeastern Italy, Trieste was part of the Austro-Hungarian empire until the end of the First World War when it was given to Italy. The city is some 145 kilometers east of Venice and lies on the Adriatic Sea.

185 Styria (Steiermark) is the second largest of the nine states in Federal Austria today. These Länder (Austrian for "states") are Burgenland, Kärnten, Niederösterreich, Oberösterreich, Salzburg, Steiermark, Tirol, Vorarlberg, and Wien.
186 The Semmering Pass is an alpine pass that divides the state of Styria from that of Lower Austria (Niederösterreich).
187 Graz is the capital of the Austrian state of Steiermark (Styria). It is about 155 kilometers south-southwest of Vienna, the country's capital city.
188 The Semmering railroad was built between 1848 and 1854: "The Semmering Railway, constructed between 1848 and 1854 over 41 km of high mountains, is one of the greatest feats of civil engineering during the pioneering phase of railway building. Set against a spectacular mountain landscape, the railway line remains in use today thanks to the quality of its tunnels, viaducts, and other works, and has led to the construction of many recreational buildings along its tracks.

The property Semmering Railway begins at Gloggnitz station, at an altitude of 436 m, reaches its highest point after 29 km over the pass at 895 m above sea level, and ends 12 km further away at the Mürzzuschlag station, 677m above sea level" (https://whc.unesco.org/en/list/785 Accessed 22 April 2020).
189 Baden bei Wein (German for "baths beside Vienna") is the capital of Niederösterreich and is situated some 28 kilometers south of Vienna. The town is best known for its hot springs and thermal baths. Wilhelm's mother, Antonia, moved to the town in 1856 and lived at 241 Baden.
190 Antonia Clairmont, Wilhelm's mother. The widow of his father, Charles Gaulis Clairmont (who was the stepbrother of Mary Shelley and the half-brother of Claire Clairmont), Antonia was of Viennese descent. Charles and Antonia had 7 children. Only Pauline and Wilhelm would survive their mother.
191 Schloss Weilburg (German for "Weilburg Castle") is a castle located in Baden bei Wien. It was built by Archduke Charles, Duke of Teschen (1771–1847) as a wedding gift for his bride, Princess Henriette von Nassau-Weilburg. The castle was demolished in 1964.
192 Paul Anton III, Prince Esterházy (1786–1866) owned an estate in Ödenburg, the German name for Sopron, Hungary. His estate manager was Mr. Smallbones. Peter Love described his meeting with Smallbones in his chapter titled "General Remarks upon Continental Farming" in *The Journal of the Royal Agricultural Society of England* (London: John Murray, 1856), v. 16, pp 160–1: "Mr. Haswell kindly introduced me to Mr. Smallbones, of Deutsch Kreutz, near Odenburg, in Hungary, consulting agent to Prince Esterhazy under whom he occupies an extensive farm, which is a model of what can be done by English ingenuity, industry, and perseverance. Mr. Smallbones is highly thought of in Hungary by both rich and poor" (p. 160).
193 Pauline Clairmont would serve as governess in the home of Countess Károlyi in Rakičan (some 228 kilometers south of Vienna and in Slovenia today). The Countess raised Pauline's daughter, Georgina Hanghegyi, for seven years until 1871 when Pauline took her daughter with her to Florence to reside with Claire Clairmont.
194 Mosonmagyaróvár, a town in northwestern Hungary today, also known as Wieselburg-Ungarisch Altenburg. Until 1939, the city was divided into two towns: Moson (German: Wieselburg) and Magyaróvár (German: Ungarisch Altenburg). The town is about 87 kilometers southeast of Vienna. From *The Clairmont Family Letters*: "In late 1850, Wilhelm began studying at k.k. höheren landwirthschaftlichen Lehranstalt in Ungarisch-Altenburg (Altenburg, Hungary). Altenburg is located in northwestern Hungary about 87 kilometers south-east of Vienna and is known as Mosonmagyaróvár in Hungarian. Today, the academy forms part of the University of West Hungary. While the University of West Hungary is in Sopron (around 90 kilometers south-west of Mosonmagyaróvár), the Faculty of Agricultural and Food Sciences continues to

be located in Mosonmagyaróvár. The educational mission of k.k. höheren landwirthschaftlichen survives in the instruction provided by the Faculty of Agricultural and Food Sciences" (*CFL* I: 94). See "University of Sopron." Web. 22 April 2020. www.uniwest.hu.

195 Unidentified.

196 From 1850, Wilhelm attended k.k. höheren landwirthschaftlichen Lehranstalt in Ungarisch-Altenburg (Altenburg, Hungary). From *The Clairmont Family Letters* I: 102: "Records from the university's register provide information about the courses he studied (such as anatomy and meteorology), the fact that no disciplinary actions were taken against him, and his personal information." The register documents that Wilhelm was born in Vienna on 28 May 1831 and that he was a Catholic. He completed his studies in 1852. In 1865, Professor Hugo Hippolyt Hitschmann, a former student at the school and later a professor, collected information on some 2,000 former students, including Wilhelm. He published this information in *Verzeichniss der Lehrer und Studirenden der erzherzoglichen landwirthschaftlichen Bildungsanstalt und der k. k. höheren landwirthschaftlichen Lehranstalt zu Ungarisch-Altenburg 1818–1848 und 1858–1864* (Ung. Altenberg: Alexander Czéh, 1865 [translation: "Register of Teachers and Students of the Archducal Agricultural Academy and the k. k. Higher Agricultural Academy of Altenburg-Hungary 1818–1845 and 1850–1864]). *Verzeichniss* records Wilhelm's name as 'Wilhelm v Gartlis Clairmont' instead of Gaulis. Hitschmann provides Wilhelm's semester of entry to the college ('1850–51'), his birthdate, place of birth, and his profession (pp. 10–11). Under the column headed 'Gegenwärtig' (German for 'currently'), Wilhelm is listed as a 'Gutspächter bei Temesvár in Ungarn' ('an estate tenant near Temesvar in Hungary'). Professor Hitschmann also collected photographs of the students and the university archive has photographs in its files of Wilhelm and his friend, Rudolf Hauer (Mr. Attila Németh, Secretary of the Alumni Association, University of West Hungary, personal communication: 1 October 2014)." See also the photograph of Wilhelm from the university records in *The Clairmont Family Letters*.

197 This may refer to Mr. Zimmerman, the director of the Hungarian estates of Archduke Albrecht, Duke of Teschen (1817–1895). Antonia referenced this Zimmerman in a letter from Antonia to Wilhelm in 1856. It also might refer to Emil von Zimmermann, who was a student at k.k. höheren landwirthschaftlichen Lehranstalt in 1858–9 (*Verzeichniss* 84–85). Emil von Zimmermann's birthplace was listed in the *Verzeichniss* as Karlburg, Hungary. Karlburg (known today as Rusovce in Bratislava, Slovakia) is 57 kilometers from Mosonmagyaróvár.

198 Professor Heinrich Wilhelm von Pabst was the school director at both Hohenheim and Altenburg when Wilhelm was a student at both institutions. From *The Clairmont Family Letters* I: 102–103: "Professor Hitschmann includes a brief biography in his *Verzeichniss* of Professor Heinrich Wilhelm von Pabst. Hitschmann records that Pabst was born in 1798 in Maar in the Grand Duchy of Hesse and that he held the degree of Doctor of Philosophy. From October 1850 until March 1861, Pabst served as director of the agricultural institute in Altenburg. In 1864, by the time Hitschmann published the *Verzeichniss*, Pabst was serving as an assistant head of a government department and chair of the department of Rural Management (land improvement) in the k. k. Ministry for Trade and National Economy in Vienna. He was an honorary member of many national and international educational associations (p. 4, Prefatory material). Ulrich Fellmeth notes that Pabst implemented 'a new university constitution' while at Hohenheim but that he left the academy due to a dispute with the Württemberg ministry. He published prolifically and made enormous contributions to the field of agricultural sciences. He died in 1868 (Fellmeth, Ulrich. 'Pabst, Heinrich Wilhelm von.' *New German Biography* 19 (1999), p 738 f [Online version]. Web. 16 May 2015.

www.deutsche-biographie.de/ppn116013990.html)." Online version also Accessed 22 April 2020.

In Hohenheim, Germany, Wilhelm was a student for a few months at the Land- und Forstwirtschaftliche Akademie Hohenheim, before beginning his studies in Altenburg.

199 Ignaz Moser was also a professor at k.k. höheren landwirtschaftlichen Lehranstalt. Hitschmann's list includes Moser, whom he records as having the degree of Doctor of Philosophy. Moser was born in 1821 and became a professor at the academy in 1850 (*Verzeichniss*, prefatory material, no page number).

200 Dr. Anton Masch, a professor at k.k. höheren landwirtschaftlichen Lehranstalt. Hitschmann's list of people at the school recorded that Masch was a "med. Dr." and that he was a professor at the academy from October 1850 until 1863. He was born in 1809 (*Verzeichniss*, prefatory material, no page number).

201 Abbreviation for accounts.

202 In a letter to Claire dated 26 December 1863, Antonia stated that Colonel Becker was living in her house in Baden because his sister had passed away. See *CFL* II:45.

203 Georg von Hembyze was Antonia's brother who lived about 63 kilometers south of Vienna in Wiener Neustadt.

204 Ödenburg is the German name for the Hungarian city of Sopron, which is located some 90 kilometers southwest of Mosonmagyaróvár. The Banat region had been part of the Austro-Hungarian Empire since 1718 and the area had been the location for multiple German settlements. Three waves of migration occurred between 1718 and 1787. German-speaking Austrian colonists were encouraged to migrate to the Banat (the Marosch River to the north, the Danube River to the south, the Thiesse River to the west, and the Carpathian mountains to the east formed the region's borders) and were given incentives to farm there. Each town had its own German name (represented here in Wilhelm's journal) and the colonists adhered closely to their own traditions. Many were successful, in spite of the harsh conditions, and Wilhelm aspired to achieve a similar sense of economic success.

205 German for "white rose".

206 Wilhelm misspells this city multiple times in the next few journal entries. He is probably referring to Győr, a city in northwestern Hungary that is today the capital seat of Győr-Moson-Sopron county. There are about 34 kilometers from Mosonmagyaróvár to Győr.

207 A calèche is a covered coach seating two people.

208 Unidentified.

209 Abbreviation for "florin," the currency used in Austria at the time. István Deák notes that the gulden was the currency used in Austria and that the abbreviation "fl" (florins) was used to denote a gulden. Each gulden contained 60 kreuzer. By 1858, all former currencies were replaced with the Österreichische Währung. (*Beyond Nationalism*, New York: Oxford University Press, 1990), p. 115.

210 German for "administrator".

211 Probably a term of affection for Wilhelm's mother, Antonia Clairmont. In a letter dated 29 June 1863 from Bobda in Hungary where he was farming, Wilhelm wrote her, "Nun adiß süßes Missel dein aufrichtiger Sohn" (German for "Now goodbye sweet Missel your faithful son" [*CFL* II: 36]). Bobda is located in western Romania some 90 kilometers north-east of Großbetschkerek. Today, Bobda is part of the commune of Cenei located in Timiş County, Romania. The commune was formed from two small villages, namely Bobda and Cenei.

212 Informal word meaning "baggage".

213 See introductory pages to Wilhelm's journal.

214 Moravia is a region in the Czech Republic today. It became part of the kingdom of Bohemia in the eleventh century.

215 Bohemia is in the Czech Republic today. It was part of the Austro-Hungarian empire until 1918 when it became a province of Czechoslovakia.
216 Unidentified.
217 The Theater am Kärntnertor was a theater in Vienna. It was built in 1709 and demolished in 1870. Today, the Hotel Sacher stands on the site of the former theater.
218 *Le Profète* (French for *The Prophet*) is an opera by Giacomo Meyerbeer first staged in 1849. It tells the story of John of Leiden, a sixteenth-century religious figure.
219 Probably a relative of Wilhelm's friend, Rudolph von Hauer. In his *Verzeichniss*, Professor Hitschmann lists "Rudolf von Ritter Hauer" as one of the students who entered Altenburg in 1850–1. Born in 1830 in Vienna, von Hauer lived in Ciakova after graduation (a town some 34 kilometers south-west of Timişoara in today's Romania, and 50 kilometers south-east of Bobda) and he was listed as a "Gutsbesitzer" (German for "landowner") (*Verzeichniss*, pp. 24–25). Ottilia von Pichler married Wilhelm in 1866. Her sister, Emily von Pichler, married von Hauer.
220 Johann Freiherr von Mundy ("Freiherr" is the German for "Baron"; 1798–1872) owned a large sheep farm in Brünn.
221 Brünn is the German name for the city of Brno, now in the Czech Republic.
222 Wilhelm means to write "Mähren", which is the German for Moravia. Brünn/Brno is located in southwestern Moravia.
223 Unidentified.
224 Hietzing, the thirteenth district of Vienna's twenty-three districts (Wiener Gemeindebezirke). Schloss Schönbrunn (Schönbrunn Palace, the summer palace of the Habsburgs) is located in Hietzing which also includes a section of the Wienerwald (Vienna Woods).
225 Louis XVI was the first to breed these French merino sheep on his estate at Rambouillet, about fifty kilometers from Paris.
226 Wilhelm's aunt, Claire Clairmont.
227 All the names without endnotes in this section are impossible to identify as they appear here for the first time and are not referenced in either Wilhelm's or Pauline's letters or journals.
228 See 12 April.
229 Unidentified.
230 Pauline Clairmont was known as Plin among her family members. Marion Kingston Stocking notes in "Miss Tina and Miss Plin" that Herbert Huscher explained via letter that "in the family she was usually referred to as 'die Ampel' (i.e. a hanging lamp), a further contraction of 'Aunt Plin'" (p. 383, note 4).
231 The Kaiser Ferdinands-Nordbahn was a railway company with lines going from Vienna to Krakow. The lines were known by the name of the the company.
232 Baron von Mundy's father purchased Veveří Castle (some 12 kilometers northwest of Brno) in 1802. His grandson, Jaromír, was born there in 1822. The castle is now owned by the Czech Republic.
233 Jaromír Freiherr von Mundy (1822–1894) served as a military officer and doctor in multiple campaigns. He inaugurated the use of the ambulance service in battle.
234 "Jadg parlor", German for "hunt parlour".
235 The Battle of Austerlitz was fought on 2 December 1805. Napoleon was victorious over a Russian-Austrian coalition, creating peace between France and Austria. Austerlitz is known today as Slavkov u Brna and is located east of Brno.
236 The chapel on Santon Hill, near the site of the battle.
237 Unidentified.
238 Known today as Vyškov, a town in the Czech Republic. Wischau was its German name. There are 34 kilometers between Vyškov and Brno.
239 Hoštice, a town in Moravia. There are six kilometers from Vyškov to Hoštice.

240 In her letter to Claire Clairmont, dated 24 August 1851, Antonia referenced Mr. Kraus: "on the 1st of August Charley begins his new career, in Moravia under the direction of a very able man, a Mr Kraus, where he is instructed in practical farming" (*CFL* I: 114). On 24 October 1851, Antonia expressed her satisfaction with the Kraus family: "With Charley I have every reason to be satisfied also as to the arrangements made for him; Mr Kraus is a very sensible active and kind man, whose letters show the mental attention he pays to his pupils welfare; Mrs Kraus is an amiable woman and very kind to Charley and attentive to his wants; they live in plenty, which is a great thing for a growing lad; as he spends most of his time in the open air, he brings a sharpened appetite home 4 times a day" (*CFL* I: 119). Then on 1 February 1852, she wrote Claire: "also Mr Kraus gives most satisfactory account of him [Charley], he is fond of his business and enters most zealously into it. Mrs Kraus is a kind motherly woman attentive to his comforts and health in cleanliness and good living which is attested by his growth and healthy fresh face" (*CFL* I: 123).
241 Wilhelm means "Burggraf," which translates to the English "Burgrave,", the generic title for a ruler of a castle.
242 German for "the shepherdess" or "the shepherd's wife". Wilhelm probably means the latter.
243 Charley refers to Wilhelm's brother, Charles Gaulis Clairmont, who died in 1856.
244 Unidentified.
245 German for "administrator".
246 Ljubljana, the capital of today's Slovenia, was known as Laibach in German.
247 Litentschitz was the German name for the town of Litenčice in today's Czech Republic. Prior to 1896, the town was known as Littenschitz.
248 Wilhelm's spelling for "figure" and "agreeable".
249 German for "impressionable".
250 Heinrich Wilhelm Ernst (1812–1865), was a composer and violinist who was born in Brno. He composed his "Elegy, Opus 10" between 1829 and 1838.
251 German for "Serenade".
252 German for "Spanish Court".
253 Unidentified.
254 The Hohenzollern Kings ruled Prussia from 1415 until 1918. From 1701, Prussia and Brandenburg were the leading states in the kingdom.
255 Unidentified (Wilhelm's writing is not entirely clear).
256 Unidentified.
257 Claire Clairmont.
258 Troppau is the German name for the city of Opava in the Czech Republic. The city was part of Moravia.
259 Hitschmann does not list Mr. Helvety in his *Verzeigniss* which covered the years 1818–1848 and 1850–1864. Wilhelm obviously knew them from his stay while at school at k.k. höheren landwirthschaftlichen Lehranstalt in Ungarisch-Altenburg.
260 Wilhelm means Chiron, a Centaur best known for his wisdom.
261 All the people Wilhelm mentions are not able to be identified.
262 Partschendorf is the German name for Bartošovice, a city in the Czech Republic today. The city was part of Moravia. It is situated in the area known as the "Kuhländchen" (German for "cow land") due to its excellent agricultural land.
263 Wilhelm's spelling.
264 A city near Ostrava in today's Czech Republic. Ostrava is some five kilometers from Partschendorf. Ostrava is the capital of the Ostrava-City District.
265 The city is known today as Šenov and is located in the Ostrava-City District.
266 German name for the village of Chuchelná.
267 Unidentified.

268 Known as Ocice in Polish, it is near Racibórz (German, "Ratibor"). Ratibor was in Upper Silesia but is now part of Poland. Silesia was a province of the Austro-Hungarian Empire, but it became part of Prussia in 1742. Eastern Silesia was granted to Poland after World War I.
269 Viktor Moritz Carl I (1818–1893) was the Duke of Ratibor. The Duchy of Ratibor (known as the Duchy of Racibórz in Polish) was one of the duchies of Silesia. Wilhelm's search for a farm took him to various villages and towns in Silesia.
270 The card game, Taroky, played in Moravia with four players.
271 A town in southwestern Poland, some 55 kilometers from Racibórz/Ratibor. Wilhelm misspells its name, Gogolin.
272 Wilhelm means to write "Oberglogau." The town is known as "Głogówek" in Polish and is located about ten kilometers from the border with the Czech Republic.
273 Wilhelm writes an illegible word above the word "hour".
274 Wilhelm's spelling for "Oberglogau".
275 The village of Chuchelná.
276 Known as Głogów in Polish, the town is in southwestern Poland.
277 The German word "Amtsrat" means "councilor".
278 Unidentified.
279 Oppeln is the German name for the Polish city of "Opole". It is located in southern Poland.
280 "Bahn" is the German for "train" or "tram". Tarnowitz is known today as Tarnowskie Góry in Polish.
281 Schwieben is the German name for the southern Polish village of Świbie.
282 A unit of measurement for land, corresponding to about 2/3 of an acre to two acres (depending on the country of measurement).
283 Rogation days are days in the Roman Catholic calendar devoted to prayer. The three days before Ascension Day (40 days after Easter) are rogation days. Prayers are said for successful crop production.
284 Unidentified.
285 The town is known as Oława in Polish. It is located in the southwest of the country.
286 Popular name for a hotel or inn, meaning "German Court".
287 Unidentified.
288 German for "long village" ("Langen dorff").
289 German name for the city of Bierutów in southwestern Poland.
290 These are farms Wilhelm visits.
291 Wilhelm misspells the town of Simmenau, a village known today as Szymonków and located in southwestern Poland. Szymonków is 48 kilometers north of Opole (Oppeln).
292 Holy Thursday honors the last supper of Jesus Christ before his crucifixion.
293 Australia.
294 French for "out of fashion".
295 German name for the southwestern Polish town of Brzeg, some 40 kilometers west of Opale.
296 Known in Polish as Wrocław, the city in Western Poland is the largest of the Silesian cities.
297 German for "Golden Goose".
298 French for "host's table".
299 Wilhelm writes the word "Mort" above "Tooth".
300 Unidentified.
301 The Oder River passes through the Czech Republic and forms a border between Germany and Poland as it flows towards the Baltic Sea.
302 German for *Aladdin's Magic Lamp*.
303 Abbreviation for "Fräulein" (German for "Miss").

304 French for "turn".
305 The Feast of the Ascension of Jesus Christ into heaven occurs 39 days after Easter.
306 Unidentified.
307 French for "chaussée" (a "carriageway").
308 Frankenstein in Schlesien (known in Polish as Ząbkowice Śląski) is in southwest Poland today.
309 Perhaps Gaetano Donizetti's opera, *Maria Stuarda* (*Mary Stuart*), first performed in 1835.
310 The southwestern Polish city is known as Legnica today.
311 Probably the name of a farm.
312 The Battle of Katzbach was fought on 26 August 1813 between Napoleon's forces and a combined force of Russians and Prussians. The French were defeated, and Napoleon was forced to retreat. The Katzbach River (Kaczawa in Polish) is located at the site of the battle.
313 Today, the city is known in Polish as Wierzchno. It is located in Western Poland.
314 Besitz (Wilhelm misspells the town's name) is in today's state of Mecklenburg-Vorpommern, one of federal Germany's sixteen Länder (German for "states").
315 German for "Left Street".
316 Kardorf and Muismer are unidentified.
317 *Il Trovatore* (English: *The Troubadour*) is an opera by Giuseppe Verdi that first premiered in 1853.
318 Probably "The Anvil Chorus" ("Coro di Zingari").
319 Abbreviation for "Fräulein" (German for "Miss").
320 Town in northeastern Germany in Mecklenburg-Vorpommern in the district of Ludwigslust-Parchim. Between 1772 and 1776, the Duke of Mecklenburg built a royal palace which can still be visited today. Ludwigslust is named for Christian Ludwig II of Mecklenburg (1683–1756), who built the original hunting lodge in 1724 at the site of the future castle. The town is named for him as Ludwigslust means "Ludwig's joy" in German.
321 Parchim is a town in northeastern Germany in the state of Mecklenburg-Vorpommern. It is the seat of the district of Ludwigslust-Parchim.
322 Whitsunday is also known as Pentecost. It is the seventh Sunday after Easter and marks the day the Holy Spirit descended, fifty days after the Resurrection.
323 Municipality in the district of Ludwigslust-Parchim.
324 Perhaps the Woseriner See, a lake in the district of Ludwigslust-Parchim.
325 Wilhelm misspells Grabow, a town in the district of Ludwigslust-Parchim. Grabow is also the name of the Amt (German for "authority"), a group of municipalities of which the town of Grabow serves as the head.
326 Lübz is a town in the district of Ludwigslust-Parchim. It is also the seat of the Amt of Eldenburg Lübz.
327 Celebrated the day after Pentecost.
328 The capital city of Mecklenburg-Vorpommern, Schwerin is not part of a district.
329 Probably a farm that Wilhelm visited.
330 Schweriner Schloss (German for Schwerin Palace) was renovated between 1845 and 1857 on the site of a former palace. The palace was the residence of the Dukes of Mecklenburg but today is used as the place of assembly for the state of Mecklenburg-Vorpommern.
331 Wilhelm misspells the name of the lake, the Schweriner See. The lake covers an area of about 60 square kilometers and is 52 meters at its deepest point.
332 Muchow is a municipality in the district of Ludwigslust-Parchim.
333 Town in the district of Rostock that lies in the north of the state of Mecklenburg-Vorpommern. Rostock is bordered by the Baltic Sea and Güstrow is the capital of the district. Rostock lies northeast and adjacent to the district of Ludwigslust-Parchim.

334 Town in the district of Rostock.
335 Malchin is a town in the district of Mecklenburgische Seenplatte which is in the southeast of the state of Mecklenburg-Vorpommern.
336 Stavenhagen is in the district of Mecklenburgische Seenplatte. The railway line runs through Stavenhagen to Berlin (Wilhelm's destination). Sections of the railway were built in the mid-nineteenth century.
337 Wilhelm misquotes the Latin phrase, "*Iacta alea est*" ("the die is cast"). Julius Caesar is supposed to have said these words as he crossed the Rubicon River in Northern Italy in 49 BCE.
338 Probably the name of Maas's farm.
339 "Oekonomic" is the German word for "economic" while "Rat" is the German word for "councilor".
340 From the town of Hoštice in Moravia. See journal entry for 19 April.
341 It is possible that Wilhelm refers either to Brandenburg, one of the German federal states, or to the city of Brandenburg an der Havel. The city of Brandenburg an der Havel is about 60 kilometers west of Berlin and the train would have gone there before going to Berlin.
342 Known today as Prenzlau, Prenzlow is 133 kilometers northwest of Brandenburg an der Havel.
343 Misspelling for "douanier," a "custom's official".
344 A town in the state of Bavaria.
345 Wilhelm refers to the town of Friedrichstadt, which is now a neighborhood of Berlin. The Friedrichstadt-Palast is today a theater in Berlin which was built after Wilhelm's visit to Berlin. A theater was built in Friedrichstadt in the eighteenth century
346 Unidentified.
347 German for "animal show".
348 German for "summer".
349 *Kieselack und seine Nichte vom Ballett* (*Kieselack and his Niece of the Ballet*) was a German farcical opera by August Conradi (1821–1873) first produced in 1860.
350 Translation by Ann Sherwin: "The best joke was: O good Lord how big the zoo is!" Sherwin supposes that the humor could be in the pronunciation of the sentence, and she wrote: "The correct spelling would be 'O gütiger Gott, wie groß ist doch der Thiergarten!' But in this quote, every *g* is replaced by a *j* and would be pronounced like English *y*" (Translator's note, 26 October 2018).
351 "Thiergarten" is the German for "zoo".
352 English translation by Ann Sherwin: "A male person sits there now [and] gathers the fruits of the grain this way; down below sits yet another person, who places it over like this". According to Sherwin, and whose translation was confirmed by two colleagues from Berlin, the way in which the story is told conveys its humor, rather than the translation. (Translator's note: 26 October 2018).
353 King Wilhelm Friedrich Ludwig of Prussia (1798–1888) ruled from 1861 until 1888 (from 1871 he was also king of the German empire). His son by his wife, Augusta Marie (1811–1890), was Friedrich Wilhelm Nikolaus Karl (1831–1888) the future King Friedrich III. Friedrich III married Princess Victoria, the eldest daughter of Queen Victoria of Great Britain. Friedrich III died after only 99 days on the throne. His son, Wilhelm II, succeeded him.
354 Pauline means to write "princess", referring thereby to Princess Victoria of England.
355 Possibly a machine to brand cattle.
356 Abbreviation for "mademoiselle" (French for "Miss").
357 Sarah Bernhardt (1844–1923) was a famous French actress.
358 German for "Agronomic Councilman".
359 German for "Oh, I am ashamed!"

360 Trinity Sunday occurs on the first Sunday after Pentecost.
361 Wilhelm misspells Riesa, a city about 40 kilometers north and west of Dresden in the modern German state of Saxony.
362 German for *The Mute Girl of Portici*, an opera written by Daniel Auber and first produced in 1828. The original French title is *La muette de Portici*.
363 Oschatz is about 60 kilometers west of Dresden. Oschatz is about 20 kilometers west of Riesa.
364 Coswig is about 13 kilometers north and west of Dresden in the district of Meissen.
365 The town of Meissen is about 25 kilometers north and west of Dresden and about 9 kilometers north and west of Coswig.
366 "Beim Hieschen" is German for "at the local".
367 Zeithain is in the Meissen district and is a municipality.
368 Leutewitz is a suburb of Dresden.
369 German for "originating sheep farm".
370 Dresden is in the German state of Saxony and serves as its capital city. It was part of East Germany after World War II.
371 German for "Green Vault". In a museum built between 1723 and 1730, August the Strong (1670–1733) began exhibiting his enormous and significant collection of treasures and jewels. Today there are over 3,000 pieces in the museum on exhibit.
372 Probably the Gemäldegalerie Alte Meister (German for "Old Masters Picture Gallery") founded by Augustus of Saxony in the sixteenth century and exhibited in the Zwinger museum in Dresden.
373 River flowing from the Czech Republic through Germany to the North Sea.
374 Charlotte Johanna Birch-Pfeiffer (1799–1868) was a German playwright as well as an actress. She wrote her four-act play, *Der Goldbauer* (English: *The Farmer)*. The word "von" means "by".
375 These three names probably refer to farms Wilhelm visited. No towns he could have been referring to have been identified.
376 Giuseppe Verdi's opera, *Il trovatore* (English: *The Troubadour*) was first produced in 1853.
377 Soprano role in *Il trovatore*.
378 Town on the Elbe River about 23 kilometers south and east of Dresden. Wehlen is in the Sächsische Schweiz-Osterzgebirge district (German for "Saxon Switzerland-Eastern Ore Mountains") in the German state of Saxony.
379 From www.saechsische-schweiz.de/en/region/places/lohmen.html: "The borough of Lohmen spans from the Bastei – the famous view point of Saxon Switzerland – to the romantic rocky world of the Liebethal Grund and the Uttewald Grund" (Accessed 14 May 2020).
380 A famous hiking ravine with a rock arch that has been immortalized in many paintings. German artist, Caspar David Friedrich, painted his *Felsentor im Uttewalder Grund* (German for "Rock Arch in Uttewalder Grund") in 1801. British artist, Joseph Turner, sketched four famous views of the Uttewalder Grund in 1835 (now in the Tate in London): "These are four views of the Uttewalder Grund in Saxon Switzerland. Two of the sketches show the Teufelsküche ('Devil's Kitchen'), looking towards the town of Stadt Wehlen and the view in the opposite direction. The inscriptions "W[...] | OW' and 'Tuforstu[...]' refer to Teufelsküche. See also Tate D31006 – D31007; Turner Bequest CCCVI 62–62a" (Alice Rylance-Watson, '*Four Sketches of the Uttewalder-Grund: The Teufelsküche Looking towards Wehlen; Looking in the Opposite Direction to from the Same Viewpoint 1835* by Joseph Mallord William Turner', catalogue entry, August 2015, in David Blayney Brown (ed.), J.M.W. Turner: *Sketchbooks, Drawings and Watercolours*, Tate Research Publication, August 2017, www.tate.org.uk/art/research-publications/jmw-turner/joseph-mallord-william-turner-four-sketches-of-the-uttewalder-grund-the-teufelskuche-r1186877 Accessed 14 May 2020).

381 Mountain formations in Saxony, about 43 kilometers from Dresden.
382 Kurort Rathen, a spa town in Saxony.
383 Königstein Castle was first referenced in a written document in 1233. Over the course of its history it has served as a castle, a hospital, and a prison. Today it is a tourist attraction in Saxony.
384 Hohnstein is a town with a castle near the Bastei. The original fortress was first built in the thirteenth century. It has served as a castle, a prison camp, a hostel, and now guest house.
385 Known as Lovosice in Czech, the town is in the Czech region of Bohemia.
386 Peruc (in Czech) is a town in the northwestern part of Bohemia.
387 The Thun und Hohenstein family were part of the Austrian nobility. Wilhelm probably refers to Count Leo Thun-Hohenstein (1811–1888).
388 Town in today's Czech Republic, about 38 kilometers north and west of Prague.
389 German for "administrator".
390 Known as Schlan in German, the town's name in Czech is Slaný. It is located about 34 kilometers north and west of Prague.
391 Perhaps the town of Brandýsek, located about 26 kilometers north and west of Prague.
392 Capital city of today's Czech Republic.
393 The name of a hotel (German for "Blue Star").
394 The name of a hotel (German for "Black Steed").
395 See journal entry for 13 April. Brünn is the German name for the city of Brno in the Czech Republic.
396 See journal entry for 18 April. Wischau is the German name for Vyškov, a town in the Czech Republic.
397 German for "at the city of Vienna". Probably the name of an inn in Wischau.
398 Unidentified.
399 Resi is a short form of Theresa.
400 See journal entry for 20 April. Litentschitz was the German name for the town of Litenčice in today's Czech Republic. Prior to 1896, the town was known as Littenschitz.
401 See journal entry from 20 April. Sophie Gratechy was romantically involved with Charles Gaulis (Charley) Clairmont.
402 See journal entry from 19 April.
403 Unidentified.
404 Wilhelm misspells "Hallein", a town in the Austrian federal state of Salzburg.
405 Situated some 35 kilometers south of Vienna, Bad Vöslau is known for its mineral waters.
406 From June 11 until October 10, Wilhelm does not write anything in his journal. However, on September 5, there is a red New South Wales one penny loose postage stamp inserted into the journal. The stamp looks as if it might have been used.
407 On October 13–16, there are four one penny New South Wales stamps. Two appear unused and are still joined. The other two are separated from each other and both appear used. None of the stamps are franked. There are also no more journal entries for the remainder of the year.
408 Wilhelm wrote the following list in pencil on the final lined page of the journal. "Trous." is an abbreviation for trousers.
409 Abbreviation for pocket handkerchief.

Image 6 Photographic Portrait of Walter Gaulis Clairmont. Unknown date.

Source: Visual Materials from the Carl H. Pforzheimer Collection. Photograph.

Credit: The Carl H. Pforzheimer Collection of Shelley and His Circle, The New York Public Library, Astor, Lennox, and Tilden Foundations.

4

"MEINE FUSSREISE IM JULI 1885"

Walter Clairmont's Journal (German transcription and English translation; 1885)

Meine Fussreise im Juli 1885[1]

Die solange ersehnten Ferien waren endlich wieder gekommen. Ich hatte meine sechstes Jahr gottlob mit glücklichem Erfolge zurück gelegt und konnte nun einem angenehmen Zeitraum von zwei Monaten entgegensehen und dies heuer umsomehr, da ich mich durchdie Liebe meines Großpapas in Stand gesetzt sah, die Ferien mit einer netten achttägigen Fußtour zu beginnen.

Am achten Juli verließ ich den in Begleitung meinestreuen Freundes Bleckmann das staubige Wien. In Mürzzuschlag, das der Ausgangspunkt unserer Reise sein sollte, verbrachte ich im Hause meines Cameraden eine Reihe von angenehmen Tagen, für die ich seinen Angehörigen vielen Dank schulde; die Schönheiten des Mürzthales lernte ich genauer kennen; unsere Route wurde festgestellt: Es sollte uns der Weg von Neuberg über das todte Weib nach Maria Zell, von hier über Weichselboden, Wildalpen und der Palfau nach Hieflau führen, darauf Abstecher[2] durchs Gesäuse, von hier über Eisenerz, die Fraumauernhöhle[2] und das Tragößthal nach Leoben, von wo mein Freund in nördlicher, ich in südlicher Richtung zu unseren Angehörigen zurückkehren sollten.

Am 13ten Juli brachen wir auf, voller Unternehmungslust, wie es eben nur Studenten empfinden können, die durch zehn Monate im harten Joch der Schule eingespannt, nun ungebundene Freiheit genießen.

1. Tag. Montag, den 13ten Juli

Vormittag verließen mein Freund und ich das gastlicheHaus in Mürzzuschlag. Schnelleren Fortkommens halber wählten wir die Bahn bis Neuberg. Die Frische des oberen Mürzthales brauch ich wohl nicht besonders erwähnen. Um 10.45 erreichten wir Neuberg; die Rax war inzwischen in unheimliche Nähe betreten. Der Bahnhof liegt abseits vom Ort, dessen eigenthumliche Kirche mir auffiel. Im netten aber theuren Gasthofe zum schwarzen Adler nahmen wir einen kräftigen Inbiss, machten uns ½ 1 auf den Weg; das Wetter war herrlich. Nach und nach entfalteten sich die wirklich ungeheuren Gewerke der alpinen Montan Gesellschaft, welche alle unter der Leitung des Direktor Schmiedhammer stehen. Die gute Straße führt das immer enger werdende Thal der Mürz hinauf, anfangs am linken, nachher am rechten Ufer. Hinter der sog. „Krampen", ein kleines Dorf, gehen die waldigen Berge in nackte Felsen über, südlich das schöne Hocheck. Von weitem schon wird die Nähe Mürzstegs durch ein großes Kreuz auf vorspringendem Kamme verkündet. Mürzsteg liegt in einer Thalerweiterung, die durch Einmünden des Dobereiner Thales gebildet wird; ein kleiner Ort mit einfacher Kirche u. besserem Gasthause, bis zu welchem die Omnibusse von Neuberg führen. Wir erreichten es um ¼ 3 Uhr, hielten uns gar nicht auf, sondern marschierten die Mürz weiter hinauf. Das schon von weitem sichtbare Jagdschlößchen des Kaisers ließen wir rechts liegen; es ist schweizerartig gebaut mit fast keinen Anlagen, dicht dahinter d. i. geg. Nord beginnt dicker Nadelwald, der weiter oben in kahle Felsen, dem gewöhnlichen Jagdterrain des Kaisers, übergeht.

Die Abzweigung übers Niederalpel nach Maria Zell schlugen wir aus und wählten den weiteren aber schöneren Weg über die Frein. Das Mürzthal verliert bis Scheiterboden den alpinen Charakter, aber nach diesem Orte treten die Berge plötzlich zusammen, um nur eine schmale Felsschlucht für die Mürz zu lassen. Der Weg ist in den Berg gearbeitet, hat aber seit dem Unfall der Kaiserin an romantischem verloren, indem der schmale Steig in eine bequeme Straße überging. Den Glanzpunkt dieser Thalenge bildet das „Todte Weib", eine senkrechte Wand, aus der man weiß gar nicht woher, ein milder Gießbach tritt, durch steile Treppen ist es ermöglicht bis zur Austrittsstelle zu gelangen. Vom todten Weib führte früher der Brettersteig ober der grünen Mürz, doch seit oberwähntem Unglücke ist er weggerissen und am rechten Ufer die Straße gebaut. An der Stelle des Unglückes der Kaiserin steht eine Votivtafel.

In einer schwachen halben Stunde erreichten wir nun die „Frein" wo wir im einzigen Gasthaus sogleich Nachtquartier bestellten. Die Frein ist eine Thalerweitung; nördlich gehts gegen Naßwald südl. zum todten Weib, westlich nach Maria Zell. In der Thalsohle liegt nur das Gasthaus, sowie die mit Pfarrhaus combinierte Kirche, die übrigen Hütten sind auf den Gehängen verstreut. Ein bischen streiften wir umher, giengen früh zu Bette, jedoch nicht ohne Kampf, da ein alter Herr durchaus meine Lagerstätte in Beschlag nehmen wollte. Zwar mußte er seine ungerechtfertigte Absicht aufgeben, aber am nächsten Morgen war er, und was viel schlimmer, meine Generalstabskarte, verschwunden, ob aus Rache oder aus Versehen, weiß ich nicht.

2ter Tag. Dienstag, den 14ten Juli

Um 6 Uhr erfolgte der Aufbruch von der lieben Frein. Unser Marschziel war Maria Zell. Der tief liegende Nebel und starke Thau versprachen einen schönen Tag. Bald verließen wir den Weg längs des Fallensteiner Baches und schlugen den kürzeren Steig über den Freinsattel ein, der, allerdings rasch, ins Walde führt, bis man jenseits der Höhe das Salzathal erreicht. Dieses wanderten wir auf staubiger Chaussée abwärts; das Thal hat wenig Reiz. Ein steiler Berg der, vereint mit erdrückender Hitze, uns manchen Seufzer entlockte, ist das letzte Hindernis, dann liegt das geheiligte Maria Zell in voller Ausdehnung vor den Augen des Wanderers. Punkt 9 Uhr kehrten wir ins Gasthaus zum „goldenen Greifen" ein. Um 10 schlugen wir den Weg zur berühmten Kirche ein. Sie ist umgeben von den Wohnungen der Geistlichen, vor dem Hauptportal befinden sich kleine Anlagen, sowie die Statuen Ludwigs [sic] des Großen u Markgf Ludwig von Mähren, zwei bedeutende Freunde der Kirche. Das Schiff selbst ist von bedeutender Höhe, namentl. der Plafond kostbar gearbeitet; im ganzen macht das Innern den Eindruck schrecklicher Überladung; alles hängt voller Opferbilder u dergl. Die Schatzkammer enthält wirklich werthvolle Sachen; so z. B. von der Kaiserin zum Dank für ihre Rettung beim todten Weib eine mit Diamanten besetzte Goldbro[s]che, vom Kaiser sammt Brüdern anläßlich ihres Vaters Tod ein Gemälde, darstellend die Empfängnis des heil. Geistes; in der Mitte steht ein von Markgfn. Ludwig gewidmeter Altar. Vom einfachsten hölzernen Fuß oder Finger bis zum Gold und brillanten protzenden Schmucke ist alles vertreten. Der Nordfront entlang zieht sich der Opferbildergang; die ältesten waren von 1363. Die Besteigung des Mittelthurmes unterließen wir nicht; er ist der höchste (50 Klafter) hat riesiges Uhrwerk und sieben Glocken, darunter, die größte 108 Cntr. Die Aussicht ist lohnend; nach Süden das Salzathal, die Aflenzer und Zeller Staritzen, im Hintergrund die hohe Veitsch; gegen Westen die drei Zellerhüte; im Norden tritt der Ötscher frei entgegen, links davon die Gemeinderechts die Bürgeralm, der Erlafsee ist durch Hügelketten verdeckt. Maria Zell selbst ist in Form eines Dreifußes mit der Kirche im Mittelpunkt gebaut, am Nordrand der Kirche zieht sich eine Reihe von Buden, deren Besitzerinnen nicht müde werden, die Passanten zum Kaufe einzuladen.

Der Nachmittag war einem Besuche des Erla[u]fsee gewidmet. Er ist ca. 5/4 Stunden entfernt, der Weg führt meist im Wald. Der See ist außerordentl. freundl. gelegen. Beiläufig eine bis anderthalb Stunden lang, bildet er die Grenze zwischen N. Ö. und Steiermark. Seine Ufer sind durchwegs bewaldete Höhen; nördl. steigt es direkt zur Gemeindealm an; am westlichen Ende befindet sich eine kleine Wirthschaft eines St. Pöltners. am Nordufer erreichten wir ein Fischerhaus des Lilienfelder Stiftes. Ein Bad wirkte köstlich, der Fischer stellte uns ein Boot zur Verfügung, mit welchem wir das andere Ufer besuchten. Eine Flasche trefflichen Lilienfelders erhöhte unsere Zufriedenheit; um ½ 8 kamen wir nach Maria Zell zurück.

3ter Tag. Mittwoch, den 15ten Juli

Um 4 Uhr fuhr der Postwagen nach Wegscheid ab, in welchem wir zwei Plätze bestellt hatten. Hart genug kam es uns an, die süße Lagerstätte so früh zu verlassen. Nachdem ich in Todesängsten das ganze Gasthaus abgesucht hatte, aber nirgends unsere Schuhe finden konnte, bis mir das verzweifelte Stubenmädchen, das ich aus sanftem Schlummer getrommelt, dazu verhalf, stürmten wir en pleine carrière zur Post, wo wir den Wagen noch glücklich erreichten. Um so langsamer giengs in diesem; kaum konnte ich mich enthalten, so fest einzurücken, wie mein Camerad; daß es mir gelungen ist verdanke ich nur der eisigen Morgenkälte, die mich auf der zweistündigen Fahrt ganz erstarrte. Größeren Ausblick hate ich in Folge des Nebels nicht. Das Gußwerk ist bedeutend, hat mehrere Hochöfen. Wegscheid liegt in weitem Thale. Der warme Caffee daselbst riß mich aus geistiger u. körperlicher Todtheit. Das Gasthaus ist aber so infam theuer, daß uns Schmalhänsen die Haut schauderte, und wir trachteten, nur wieder weiter zu kommen.

Um ¼ 7 brachen wir auf nach Weichselboden. Der Weg über Gußwerk ist zwar bedeutend näher aber ganz ohne Reiz, während wir den schönen „Kastenriegel" passierten. Das Ramerthal marschierten wir in Laubwäldern aufwärts an zahlreichen Köhlereien vorbei. In Serpentinen erreichten wir endlich den sog. „Kastenriegel" eine Thalscheidewand. Die Scenerie geg. Westen ist wildromantisch, während der Riegel geg. Osten sanft abfällt, der Blick geg. Westen zeigt die Aflenzer Staritzen und den herrlichen Hochschwab; während die Straße sich im großen Bogen abwärts senkt, stiegen wir einen schmalen Steig direkt hinunter in die sogenannte „Hölle" mit zahlreichen Sennereien. Die Hölle senkt sich sanft, bis sie plötzlich steil zur vorderen Hölle abfällt. Der Weg macht zahllose Serpentinen, wir wählten die geradeste Luftlinie, indem wir in einer Holzriese zwar etwas halsbrecherisch, aber am schnellsten unter anlangten. Wir erreichten einige Almhütten sowie ein Jagdhaus des Gfn. Meran. Den Abstecher in den ½ St. Südlich gelegenen unteren Ring durften wir natürlich nicht versäumen. Die Felswände bilden nämlich einen kreisförmigen Kessel oder Ring, in welchen man nur von Norden her gelangen kann. Links stürzt ein eiskaltes Wasser den Abhang herab, rechts befindet sich der sog. „obere Ring", der an Großartigkeit den unteren bei weitem übertrifft, doch hat ihn Gf. Meran als beliebter Aufenthaltsort der Gemsen durch Wegsprengung des Zuganges vor Besuchen geschützt. Im September ist die ganze Familie Meran für einige Wochen in ihrem Jagdhäuschen. Die vordere Hölle stiegen wir abwärts und erreichten gerade das Gasthaus Schützenauer, als ein Platzregen los brach. Unser Project den Hochschwab zu besteigen, mußten wir des unverläßlichen Wetters wegen aufgeben. Um 12 Uhr erreichten wir Weichselboden, ein kleiner Ort mit hübscher Lage im Salzathale. Vom Ring bis Weichselboden führt eine Wasserleitung, die auf halb zerfallener Brücke die Salza passiert. Im Salzathale scheint es überhaupt Sitte zu sein, keine Brücke, die der Zahn der Zeit oder die Wuth des Flusses zerstört, wieder aufzubauen; zum öfteren sahen wir noch an den Ufern die letzten Rudimente solcher unglücklicher Passagen.

Nach ein einhalbstündiger Rast, die durch ein frugales Mittagessen versüßt wurde, nahmen wir unseren Weg von neuem auf. Unsere Absicht war, heute noch Wildalpen zu erreichen. Der Weg zieht sich hoch am rechten Salzaufer hin. Gleich hinter Weichselboden verengt sich das Thal, bis die Felsen so nahe treten daß die Straße ein 40–50 Schritte langes Felsentunnel passieren muß, der natürliche Engpaß wurde zu gleich zur Errichtung einer enorm starken Steinwehr benützt, an der die wilde Salza schäumend ihre grünen Fluten bricht. Der Weg bis Wildalpen zieht sich ungemein, das Thal ist meist so eng, um gerade Platz für Fluß und Weg zu lassen. Letzterer ist häufig in Folge der hin u. wieder abstürzenden Gießbäche, fußhoch mit Gerölle bedeckt. Durch Zustoßen des Brunnthales erweitert sich das Salzathal etwas; rechts kommen die nakten Thurauer Almen zum Vorschein, während südlich die ganze Gruppe des Hochschwabs erscheint; ein herrlicher Berg; doch es reute uns nicht, den Aufstieg unterlassen zu haben, da seine Kuppe meist umwölkt war. Nachdem die Straße sich circa 80 Klafter über der rauschenden Salza erhoben, erblickt man schon von weitem Wildalpen, das in einer Krümmung des engen Thales gelegen, sich der Salza entlang zieht. Wir trafen um ¼ 6 ein, nahmen sogleich Betten in Beschlag, und streiften sodann etwas umher. Die Kirche ist hübsch, der Pfarrer ein wüthender Tarokspieler, der Ort ist, seiner reitzenden Lage wegen, stark von Sommergästen besucht. Den Weg nach Eisenerz konnten wir nicht weit verfolgen, suchten aber bei einbrechender Dämmerung die drei Siebenseen auf, damit ich, wie mein Begleiter sagte, mehr zu erzählen hätte. Der halbstündige Abstich war der Mühe werth, den schäumenden Abfluß hinauf führt ein schmaler Pfad.

Der erste See ist der schönste, zwar klein, aber krystallklar und durchsichtig; der zweite, eine Viertelstunde südlicher ist noch kleiner, der dritte daneben am größten. Sie liegen alle reizend; theilweise von Wald, theils von Wiesen umrahmt, gegen die Berge liegt eine Alm, östlich der Grimmstein, südl. die böse Wand u Großberalm[3] sind die bedeutendsten Erhebung in der Nähe der Seen.

Um ¾ 9 suchten wir beide die Lagerstätten auf; wir waren den Tag über ungefähr an 11 Stunden marschiert, dafür aber auch ziemlich mat[s]ch. Das Wetter hatte sich wieder ganz geklärt nur in Wildalpen erhielten wir einen kurzen Strichregen. Unser Auslugen nach Gemsen war immer umsonst, vor Wildalpen sah unsere Phantasie sogar eine auf vorspringendem Felsen stehende Bank für eine Gemse an.

4ter Tag. Donnerstag, den 16ten Juli

Nachdem wir ausgezeichnet geschlafen und uns über den Ärger des Kellners, daß wir ein allgemeinen Schlafsaal um den Preis von 20 Kreutzer in zehn Betten auf einmal schlafen konnten, königlich gefreut hatten, brachen wir um ¾ 8 auf. Den Überstieg nach Eisenerz gaben wir auf, um uns dafür die Palfau anzusehen. Der umwölkte Himmel war uns nur willkommen. Nachdem man hinter Wildalpen eine Thalverengung passiert, wechseln die Scenerien fortwährend. Palfau ist verdeckt durch den kegelartigen Hasenkopf, an einigen Stellen sieht man auch den Hochkahr. Stets am linken Ufer verließen wir dieses vor Palfau mittelst solider Brücke und erreichten rechts eine halbe Stunde vor Palfau ein nettes Gasthaus, in welchem wir auf Anrathen meines ortskundigen Begleiters einkehrten. Wir waren genau drei Stunden gegangen, und ließen es uns jetzt in einer über der Salza liegenden Laube wohl schmecken. – Wir setzten nun unsere Marschroute fest, in dem wir beschlossen nach Besuch der Gamser Grotte und „Noth" in Hieflau zu übernachten. Um 1 Uhr brachen wir denn auf. Der Weg nach Gams ist nicht romantisch, aber die Palfau entzückte mich durch das wirklich Liebliche seiner Lage in dem muldenartig erweiterten Thale, das im Westen und Osten von freundlichen Almen begrenzt ist; der Ort selbst ließen wir rechts liegen; die Salza hat sich im Laufe der Zeit ein 20 bis 30 Klafter tiefes Bett in den Sandboden gerissen. Unseren treuen Begleiter vom Freinsattel verließen wir nun; bei Maria Zell noch ein bescheidenes Bächlein, ist die Salza an dem Punkte, wo wir uns von ihr trennten, schon ein ganz reputierlicher Fluß geworden, der so unschuldiger gewöhnlich ausschaut, doch recht wild werden kann.

Wir zweigten also links ab und erreichten 2.40 Gams, ein kleines Dorf, das sich durch zwei Gärbereien hervorthut. – Nachdem wir durch Gnade des protzigen Wirthes endlich einen Führer bekommen, machten wir uns ¼ 4 zur Besichtigung der sog. „Krausgrotte"; die Grotte liegt hoch, der Aufstieg ein steiler, die Grotte selbst enttäuschte mich etwas; sie bietet nichts großartiges, und sind gerade die größten Tropfsteingebilde abgeschlagen. Alle Sontag wird sie durch Hr. Kraus von Gams aus elektrisch beleuchtet. Der jetzige Eingang liegt gegen Westen; früher mußte man von der Spitze 12 Klafter herunter steigen; betreffs des mineralogischen Theiles, bietet die Grotte nur kleine Tropfsteine, aber schön krystallisierten Gyps. Ein größerer Raum ist zum Tanzplatz hergerichtet; von hier gehts in den sog. Wil[c]zekgang, der sich beiläufig 50 Meter fortsetzt. Besonders schön ist das Elysium, eine Höhle, in welchem die Mischung von krystallisierten Gyps u gelben Kies ein herrliches Blitzern hervorruft. Um ½ 5 verließen wir die Grotte, um sogleich die sog. „Noth" aufzusuchen. So wenig Imposantes erstere bietet, um so großartig ist diese. Das schäumende Wasser hat wirklich seine Noth, durch die Schlucht zu kommen. Die senkrechten Felswände nähern sich auf fünf bis sieben Klafter. Der Brettersteg ist an der Wand angebracht und führt über dem Wildbach. Dieser Engpaß ist ungefähr tausend Schritte lang, hat man ihn völlig durchschritten, so eröffnet sich jenseits wieder ein grünes Thal; die Felsen stehen fast isoliert da. Vollkommen befriedigt kehrten wir nach Gams zurück. Die Jagd gehört hier überall dem Gf. Wil[c]zek; im Gasthaus sahen wir seinen Oberjäger in schön gesticktem Steirer Costüm, ein echtes Alpenkind voller Kraft und Elasticität, der den Weg von Hieflau nach Gams in einer kleinen Stunde zurücklegte, er marschierte heute noch nach Wildalpen, von wo er in der Früh nach Hieflau gegangen war; wir giengen zwar auch tüchtig und fast immer bergab, brauchten aber doch zwei volle Stunden bis Hieflau. Die Straße führt über einen Sattel, von dem man die herrlichste Aussicht auf der Ennsthaler Alpen hat. Bei der Ortschaft Lambach steigt man in steiler Serpentine zur Enns hinab. Über Stärke und Macht derselben, die ich hier zum ersten mal sah, war ich erstaunt; leider hatte ein Regen ihre sonst klaren Fluthen getrübt. Ein herrlicher Abend wirkte erfrischend auf Gemüth und Körper. Nach zweimaligem Überschreiten der Enns langten wir 8 Uhr Abend in Hieflau an. In dem vom gräfl. Wil[c]zek'schen Oberjäger an uns empfohlenen Gasthaus fanden wir treffliche Unterkunft.

Hieflau, ein größerer Markt am rechten Ennsufer, liegt an der rechtwinkligen Krümmung der Enns; es zeichnet sich durch Eisenindustrie aus, und ist des nahen Gesäuses und Eisenerzes wegen beliebter Sommeraufenthalt.

5ter Tag. Freitag, den 17ten Juli

Müdigkeit, herrliche Betten und das Entzücken, nur 10 Kreuzer dafür zahlen zu müssen; machten unseren Schlaf zu einem ausgezeichneten; an ein frühes Aufbrechen war nicht zu denken, wir waren auch gestern wieder circa eilf Stunden gegangen. Für heute war das Gesäuse und Admont festgesetzt.

Unsere Ranzen ließen wir auf der Station, und betraten mit spannender Erwartung das berühmte Gesäuse; von Morgenfrische war leider nichts zu merken, schon um 8 Uhr brannte die Sonne, welche uns heute noch eine gar schwere Stunde bereiten sollte. Die Straße tritt bei der Thalwendung ans linke Ennsufer, verliert sich etwas im Wald, um beim Austritte prachtvolle Aussicht auf die „sausende" Enns und die senkrechten Wände links u. rechts zu gewähren. r. die rothe Zinnödlwand sowie die steile Planspitze l. die herrliche, schneebedeckte Buchalmspitze. Die Straße, für die nur mühsam Platz gewonnen werden kann, schlängelt sich von einem Ufer zum andern. Der Raum für die Bahn hat den Felsen abgerungen werden müssen. Ein schöner Punkt der Chaussée befindet sich beim Austritte des Schienenstrangs aus einem der vielen Tunnels, wobei sie, rechts unter sich die rauschende Enns, diesen kreuzt. – Um 10 Uhr erreichten wir Gstatterboden, eine Oase des Freundlichen in dem schauerlichen Felsengewirr des Gesäuses. Es war uns ein willkommener Rastort. ¾ 11 nahmen wir unseren Marsch wieder auf. Die Buchalmspitze war so nahe gerückt, daß sie mit magnetischer Gewalt die sehnsüchtigen Blicke auf sich zieht. Das Gesäuse erweitert sich ein wenig; die Straße führt am rechten Ufer und passiert mittelst schöner Brücke den Johnsbach, der mit wilder Macht aus dem gleichnamigen, romantischem Thale stürzt. Der Abschluß resp. Beginn des Gesäuses wird durch zwei mächtige Felskegel gebildet, die nur den für Enns und Straße erforderlichen Raum lassen; die Bahn muß auf schöner eiserner Brücke den Fluß, dann einen Tunnel passieren; namentlich auf der Rückfahrt hatte ich dieses imposante Naturthor der Enns bewundert, das viel verheißend die dahinter befindlichen Wunder erschließt. Auf das enge Gesäuse folgte das breite Admonter Thal, welches zwar einen sehr freundlichen Charakter hat, doch ließ die glühende Sonne es uns nicht vollkommen würdigen. Schon vom weitem leuchten die eleganten Thürme Admonts entgegen; aber Tantalusqualen hielten wir aus, bis wir sie erreichten; hofften wir hundertmal nach dieser kleinen Biegung in ihrer Nähe zu sein, so bot sich ebenso oft unseren entsetzten Augen ein neues Stück Weg dar, gerade hinreichend um von frischem gebraten zu werden.

Aber auch das hatte sein Ende; je öfter wir getäuscht wurden, desto wüthender griffen wir, Sonne, Ermüdung und knurrendem Magen zum Trotz, aus. Ein simpler Bauer wies uns an ein Gasthaus „wo in der Regel so junge Herren Studierer einkehren". Er hatte auch in der That für Geldbeutel und Hunger eines Studiosus auf Fußreisen das richtige Verständnis, denn ein Riesenschnitzel mit Kartoffel, Reis, Salat und Compott bekommt nur bei Jerausch in Admont um 30 Kreuzer. Um ½ 2 trafen wir daselbst ein.

Die Lage Admonts ist hübsch, das Ennsthal breit und freundlich, geg Litzen erblickt man den hochgelegenen Wallfahrtsort Fraukirchen[4]; dicht bei Admont liegt auf einem Hügel die Ruine R[e]itzenstein, ein ehemaliges Kloster. Von den schönen Ennsthaler Alpen schaut der Grimmig recht seinem Namen entsprechend herüber, der Pirgas und das Hochthor sind gräßlich zerklüftete Felsmassen, deren unteren Theile durch vorliegende Bergketten verdeckt sind; unser Bekannter aus dem Gesäuse, die Buchalmspitze, guckt auch wieder neugierig hervor.

Der schönste Schmuck Admonts ist das Benediktinerstift. Es wurde 1074 von der heiligen Hemma mit Unterstützung Gebhardts von Salzburg gegründet und mit reichen Besitzungen im Enns- und Paltenthale beschenkt; Benediktiner bezogen es; das Kloster hatte viel zu leiden, circa 1090 wurde es total ausgeplündert, in unserer Zeit 1865 brannte es mit dem Markte nieder, nur die Bibliothek wurde gerettet. Vermöge des Reichthums des Stiftes wurde es wieder ganz neu aufgebaut, nur zwei Trakte blieben unausgeführt, die in nebenstehender Skizze mit punktierten Strichen angedeutet sind. Die Kirche ist doppelthürmig, sehr schlank gebaut, im gothischen Stil, mir fiel namentlich die für eine katholische Kirche ungewöhnliche Prunklosigkeit des Inneren auf, was die Schönheit der steinernen Spitzbögen recht zu Tage treten ließ. An die Kirche schließen sich die Klostergebäude an, welche einen enorm großen Hof umschließen; wir kreuzten ihn, um auch die Bibliothek in Augenschein zu nehmen.

[image][5]

Straße Kirche Klosterhof Bibliothek Klostergarten

Keller

Diese bot mir etwas ganz neues, ich hatte Büchersammlungen in solcher Größe noch nicht gesehen. In drei Sälen untergebracht enthält sie circa 30.000 Bände. Im ersten befinden sich die profanen Schriften, Medicin, Philosophie etc., der zweite Saal umfaßt die verschiedensten Handschriften vom 9ten bis zum 15ten Jahrhundert, der 3te endlich den religiösen Theil. Alle Bände haben gleichen Einband, aber [in] den unteren Kästen befindet sich noch eine Gallerie. Die Ecken der Säle sind geschmückt durch verbronzte Holzschnitzereien, meist aus Thad[d]äus Stammlers[6] Hand. So befinden sich im Mittelsaal die vier letzten Momente im menschlichen Leben: Tod, Gericht, Teufel und Himmel, andere Gestalten sind vier menschl. Eigenschaften: Eitelkeit, Bescheidenheit, Fleiß u. Müssiggang, u. s. w. Der Plafond ist gemalt, der Fußboden aus weißem (von St. Michael), grünen (von Wildalpen) u. grauen Marmor. Eine Platte soll einen Thaler gekostet haben. Die Bibliothek repräsentiert ein ganz hübsches Sümmchen. Was mir besonders auffiel, waren alle Landkarten Steiermarks u. N. Ö. von 1567 und 1668, ferner eine goldene Penduluhr vom 17. Jahrhundert, die dreizehn Monate lang geht, ohne aufgezogen zu werden.

Alle diese Daten verdanke ich einem zu vorkommenden Diener, der uns auch rieth, bei Todesstrafe nicht auf den Klosterkeller zu vergessen, welchen wir sogleich aufsuchten. – Nachdem wir im Fluge einen Thurm bestiegen, giengs im Galopp auf den Bahnhof. Nur zu zweien im Coupé konnten wir das herrliche

Gesäuse noch einmal ungestört genießen. Schneller gieng es wohl, als Vormittag, aber in solcher Windeseile, daß ich fast sagen könnte, wer es nich durchgangen, kennt das Gesäuse nur halb.

Im scharfen Bogen fuhren wir in Hieflau ein, setzten unsere Fahrt gleich bis Eisenerz weiter. Die Bahn u. Straße fuhren in freundlichem Thale, der Erzberg mit seinen unzähligen Schachten schon von weitem sichtbar. Bei den ehemaligen Mutter Brod kehrten wir ein; befriedigt von unseren heutigen Erlebnissen, legten wir uns früh zu Bette, denn für morgen hatten wir einen tüchtigen Marsch vor, der in Wirklichkeit länger war, als wir gemeint.

6ter Tag. Samstag, den 18. Juli

Das Wetter war offenbar der Dritte in unserem Bunde; auch heute erwachten wir bei klarem Morgen.

Eisenerz ist ein größerer Ort, seine bedeutenden Gewerkschaften der Alpinen Montan Gesellschaft geben dem Markte einen ganz großartigen Anstrich. Er liegt in engem Thale am Fuße des durchwühlten Erzberges. Auffallend ist die von Kaiser Rudolph I erbaute Pfarrkirche St. Oswald, die auf einem Vorsprunge des Erzberges gelegen, das ganze Thal bis Münnich beherrscht. Während der Türkenkriege diente sie als sicherer Zufluchtsort. Interessant ist ferner der Schichtthurm, in ebenso dominierenden Lage wie die Kirche; er mußte mit seinen Glocken den Knappen das Zeichen zum Beginne der Schicht (Arbeit) geben. Die Hochöfen und Schachte sind mit der Station durch eine Hundebahn verbunden. Auch eine meteorologische Beobachtungsstation befindet sich in Eisenerz.

Den Vormittag widmeten wir, nachdem wir uns in Ort und Umgebung umgeschaut, einer Besichtigung des Leopoldsteinersees. Den Hinweg wählten wir über die Prossen, ein kleiner Sattel, von dem man einen wunderhübschen Blick auf den See und in das Wildalpener Thal hat, das durch den mächtigen Pfaffenstein abgeschlossen zu sein scheint. Der Leopoldsteiner See hat ächten Alpencharakter; nicht groß, circa 1 Stunde im Umfang können seine meist glatten grünblauen Fluten durch Stürme heftig bewegt werden. Sein Westufer wird durch die unmittelbar aufsteigenden „See Mauern" gebildet, das östliche durch dichtbewaldete Hügel. Er zieht sich in nord-südlicher Richtung und ist gewiß ein lohnender Ausflug von Eisenerz. Beim Rückweg kamen wir über das fürstlich Lichtenstein'sche Sommerschlösschen „Leopoldstein".

Das schöne Eisenerz konnten wir nicht länger genießen, auf einen Besuch des Erzberges mußten wir verzichten; unser Reiseplan war, noch heute durch die Fraumauernhöhle [Frauenmauerhöhle] nach Tragöß zu gelangen, von da den nächsten Tag entweder nach Leoben od. Vordernberg.

Um ½ 1 Nachmittag erschien unser Führer „Anselm Leiss", der Riesenstückchen aus seiner touristischen Praxis erzählte, doch stimmte die That gar wenig mit seinen Worten überein, seine Local Kenntnisse ließen nichts zu wünschen über. Der Weg führt über Trofeng in die Berge hinein, die Prebichlstraße bleibt rechts liegen. Mit der Gsöll Alm hat man den Fuß der Frau[en]mauer, einer hohen Felswand, erreicht, ist jedoch schon bedeutend gestiegen. Schon von weitem erblickt man drei schwarze Flecken, deren mittlerer den Hohleneingang vorstellt. Er ist so in mitten der nackten Wand gelegen, daß es unbegreiflich erscheint, ohne halsbrecherische Kühnheit hinaufzukommen. Es ist aber nicht so schrecklich, als man meinen sollte. Man erreicht den Eingang auf sicheren Serpentinen, nur das letzte Stück bildet eine höchst bedenkliche Stiege. Die Gsöll Alm lag fast senkrecht unter uns; der Nachbarberg ist die Griesmauer, rechts befindet sich das Bärenloch, ein beliebtes Gemsejagdterrain des Kaisers. Nachdem wir uns gehörig abgekühlt betraten wir die wirklich großartige Höhle; unser Führer hohlte seine Fackel heraus, die des scharfen Luftzuges halber fast nicht anbrennen wollte.

Ohne Führer diesen unterirdischen Durchgang zu passieren, möchte ich wohl niemandem rathen, da die unzähligen Seitengänge unfehlbar ein Verirren zu Folge haben müßten. Eine Eigenthümlichkeit dieser Höhle ist ein See, welcher im Sommer eine glatte Eisfläche bietet, im Winter aber offen ist; namentlich prachtvoll sind die mitten im Fließen zu Eis erstarrten Caskaden, die sich in den See stürzen. Den Mittelpunkt der Höhle bildet die sog. Kreutzhalle, eine Erweiterung der Höhle zu unglaublicher Größe und Höhe. Der Zugang zu ihr führt durch die Klamm, eine Felsspalte, die thatsächlich so eng ist, daß wir uns mit Mühe durchwinden konnten, für einen nur halbwegs beleibten Mann wäre dieser Paß ein unüberwindliches Hinderniß. Wir mußten fortwährend steigen, was bei dem Geröll und der mangelhaften Beleuchtung nicht so einfach war.

Drei viertel Stunden marschierten wir in der Höhle; mit Freuden begrüßten wir das Tageslicht; so großartig die Höhle ist, so athmet man doch auf, wieder in der Freiheit zu sein, denn man kann sich einer gewissen Bedrückung nicht erwähren. Der Austritt ist entzückend durch die Aussicht; unter uns liegt die nette Pfarralm. Namentlich schön nimmt sich die Hochschwabgruppe aus. Unser Führer nannte uns alle Spitzen mit Namen; die hervorragendsten waren der Sonnstein, Pribitzkessel, Griesmauer, Hochalm, Aenzer[7] Staritzen etc. isoliert erhebt sich die plumpe Messnerin an derem Nordfuße unser heutiges Marschziel liegt, wir konnten sehen, daß es noch ein hübsches Stückchen war. Während der Führer den Rückweg einschlug, stiegen wir 5 Uhr von dem fast 4700" hohen Ausgang zur Pfarralm herab, wo wir uns mit Milch, wie sie eben nur auf Almen zu haben ist, erquickten. Ohne Weg und Steg jagten wir von hier die Berge hinab ins Tragößthal und marschierten den in der Thalsohle laufenden Pfad abwärts.

Das Tragößthal, oder wie es im oberen Theile eigentlich heißt der Jassinggraben ist von echtem Alpencharakter. Wir durchschritten es in der Abendkühle, welche die Frische der Natur noch mehr zur Geltung brachte. Zu beiden Seiten ist das Thal von hohen Bergen eingeschlossen; prachtvolles Vieh weidet ringsum auf den Almen, ihr melodisches Glockengeläute ist überall hörbar. Nachdem wir ein Jägerhaus passiert, erreichten wir den polypenarmigen Grünsee[8], der seinen Namen vollkommen verdient, denn das Wasser weist vom lichtesten Blattbis zum tiefsten Blaugrün alle Variationen auf. Von hier hat man einen Ausblick auf das eigentliche Tragößthal mit der Ortschaft Oberort, woselbst wir acht Uhr Abend eintraffen und in dem einzigen Gasthause Etschmeier glücklicherweise Unterkunft fanden.

7ter Tag. Sontag, den 19ten Juli

Tragöß oder Oberort eine kleine Ortschaft lehnt sich südlich in die Messnerin, welche sich durch ein natürliches Fenster in der colossalen Felsenwand auszeichnet. Gegen Westen liegt das breite fruchtbare Tragößenthal, das bei Leoben in das Murthal mündet. Oberort besitzt eine alte Kirche. Den Marsch nach Leoben, der wie wir hier erfuhren sieben Stunden erfordert, gaben wir auf, und zogen das nähere Vordernberg vor, um von dort per Bahn ins Murthal zu gelangen. Zu unserer Ehre muß ich sagen, daß wir uns bis jetzt kein einziges mal verirrt hatten, heute am letzten Tag muß uns ein Fehlgehen unterlaufen; wir hielten uns zu lange im Tragößthal, statt der Vordernberger Straße gemäß, unmittelbar hinter der Ortschaft zu steigen. Wir mußten, um unseren Schnitzer gut zu machen einen steilen, sonnigen Schlag hinaufklettern, der unsere Schweißtröpflein zu Strömen anschwellen machte. Die Straße führt über den Hieseleggpass[9], muß aber noch eine Bergkette überschreiten, um direkt nach Vordernberg abzufallen. Wir waren um 8 Uhr früh aufgebrochen erreichten unser Ziel um ½ 12.

Vordernberg, ein ansehnlicher Markt mit 13 Hochöfen u Gewerkschaften der Alpinen Montangesellschaft, ist rings von Hochalpen umgeben. Gegen Nordwest windet sich die Chausée über den Prebichel[10], über welchen man Eisenerz im vier od. fünf Stunden erreicht. Wir speisten und machten uns dann zu dem ½ Stunde südlicher liegenden Bahnhof auf den Weg. Die Fahrt nach Leoben ist hübsch. Ein schöner Punkt ist in Freienstein mit gleichnam. Ruine. Friedau u. Donnawitz sind große Eisenwerke der Alpinen. Um vier Uhr traffen wir in Leoben ein. Unsere angenehme Parthie hatte hier ein Ende. Eine Stunde nachher mußte ich mich von meinem Freunde trennen, der nach Mürzzuschlag zurückkehrte, während ich noch einen Tag bei meinem Onkel verweilte. –

Zum Schlusse muß ich noch meinem lieben Großpapa Dank sagen. Die Tour war nicht nur an und für sich unterhaltend und belehrend, sie wird mir auch eine angenehme Erinnerung für mein ganzes Leben bleiben. Ich hoffe, daß er in diesen Zeilen einen kleinen Beweis meiner Dankbarkeit erblickt, die ich ihm schulde.

Credit: Unpublished. Text: M.S., Pf. Coll., CL'ANA 0063 (unpublished manuscript, Pforzheimer Collection of Shelley and His Circle, New York Public Library, Astor, Lenox, and Tilden Foundations)

Notes

1 Ann Sherwin provided the transcription of the German and the accompanying translation into English. She generally has retained standard nineteenth-century spellings of place names in English (particularly for words with a "th" that are now written with a "t" [for example, "Thal" is now "Tal"]). I have chosen to retain the journal writer's German spelling errors. When the journal writer made an error in a German place name, Sherwin corrected it in the English translation and suggested a correction in the German transcription. For these suggested amendments, Sherwin has placed missing words and/or letters in brackets in the German transcription but has translated the words correctly in the English translation.

2 The correct spelling is Frauenmauerhöhle.
3 Ann Sherwin, translator, was unable to verify this name but suggests Grossberalm.
4 Presumably Frauenberg, See note in the English translation.
5 The journal writer has drawn a sketch using lines and squares to illustrate the locations indicated here.
6 Should be Stammel.
7 The word should read "Aflenzer".
8 The word could be "Grüner See" or "Grünersee". Ann Sherwin chose the latter for the translation.
9 Per Ann Sherwin, translator: "The Hiaslegg is the nearest pass with similar spelling I could find" (Personal Correspondence, 28 September 2018).
10 Probably Präbichl (see note in the English translation).

My Walking Tour in July 1885*

The long-awaited holiday had finally come around again. I had completed my sixth year with great success, praise God, and could now look forward to a pleasant two-month interval – all the more so this year, since, thanks to my grandpapa's love, I was able to begin my holidays with a lovely eight-day walking tour.

On the eighth of July I left dusty Vienna[1] with my faithful friend Bleckmann. In Mürzzuschlag,[2] which was to be the starting point of our trip, I spent several pleasant days at my companion's home, for which I owe his family many thanks. I got to know the beauties of the Mürz Valley in greater detail. We established our route, which would take us from Neuberg[3] via the Todtes Weib[4] to Mariazell[5]; from there via Weichselboden[6], Wildalpen[7], and Palfau[8] to Hieflau[9]; then a detour through the Gesäuse[10]; from there via Eisenerz[11], the Frauenmauerhöhle[12], and the Tragöß Valley[13] to Leoben[14], at which point my friend would head north and I south, back to our families.

We set out on the 13th of July in an adventurous mood, such as only students can feel who have been clamped in the rigid yoke of academia for ten months and now enjoy total freedom.

1st Day. Monday, July 13

In the morning, my friend and I left the house in Mürzzuschlag. To get started sooner, we elected to take the train to Neuberg. I hardly need comment on the freshness of the Upper Mürz Valley. At 10:45 a.m, we arrived at the Neuberg station, which was at the edge of town. Meanwhile we were now incredibly close to the Rax[15]. Neuberg's unusual church caught my eye. After enjoying a hearty lunch at the nice but high-priced Schwarzen Adler[16], we set out at 12:30 in beautiful weather. Little by little the truly enormous operations of the Alpine Montan Steel Corporation[17] became apparent, all under the management of director Schmiedhammer. The good road leads up the ever-narrowing Mürz Valley, first on the left and later the right riverbank. Beyond the little village of Krampen[18] the wooded mountains gradually give way to bare rock, with the beautiful Hocheck[19] to the south. Announcing our proximity to Mürzsteg[20] is a large cross on a prominent ridge already visible in the distance. The small town lies in a widening stretch

312

of valley where the Dobrein flows in, and it has a simple church and a better inn patronized by visitors from Neuberg who come by bus. We arrived there at 2:15 but hiked on up the Mürz without stopping. From a distance we could already see the emperor's hunting lodge[21], and we hiked on past it on our right. It is built in Swiss style, with almost no pleasure ground. The conifer forest begins close behind it to the north, then gradually gives way to bare rock farther up, the emperor's customary hunting terrain.

We decided to forgo the turn-off to Mariazell via the Niederalpl Pass in favor of the longer but more scenic route over the Frein. The Mürz Valley loses its alpine character as one approaches Scheiterboden[22], but after this town the mountains suddenly converge, leaving only a narrow rock chasm for the Mürz. The path is hewn into the mountainside, but it lost some of its romance after the empress's accident[23], when the steep path became a convenient road. The chief attraction of this narrows is the Todtes Weib, a vertical wall from whence a gentle bourn emerges from an unknown source. The point of emergence is accessible via a steep flight of steps. From the Todtes Weib, the plank walkway once led across the green Mürz, but after the aforementioned accident, it was torn out and a road was laid on the right bank. A votive tablet marks the site of the empress's accident.[24]

In just under half an hour we arrived at the Frein, where we immediately booked a night's lodging at the only inn. The Frein is a valley bulge with the Nasswald[25] forest to the north, the Todtes Weib to the south, and Mariazell to the west. There is nothing at the valley floor but the inn and a combined church and parsonage. Other cabins are scattered on the mountain slopes. We ambled around a little, then retired early, though not without a struggle – for an old gentleman was determined to commandeer my bunk. He finally had to give up his unjustified intention, but the next morning both he and – what was worse – my ordnance map had vanished; whether out of revenge or by accident, I don't know.

2nd Day. Tuesday, July 14

At 6:00 a.m. we departed the beloved Frein. Our destination was Mariazell. The low-lying fog and heavy dew promised a beautiful day. We soon left the road along the Fallenstein stream and took the shorter climb over the saddle of the Frein, which leads through forest, albeit quickly, to the Salza[26] valley beyond. We hiked down this slope on a dusty road. The valley holds little charm. A steep mountain, which combined with oppressive heat elicited many a sigh from us, is the final challenge, before the hallowed Mariazell lies in its full expanse before the wayfarer's eyes. At exactly 9:00 we stopped off at the inn Zum Goldenen Greifen[27], then at 10:00 made our way to the famous church.[28] It is surrounded by the homes of the priests. In front of the main entrance are small landscaped areas and statues of Ludwig the Great and Margrave Ludwig[29] [sic] of Moravia, two important benefactors of the church. The nave is of considerable height, and the ceiling, in particular, is luxuriously wrought. On the whole, the interior gives the impression of dreadful ornateness. Sacrificial images and the like hang everywhere. The treasure chamber contains really valuable items: e.g., from the empress[30] as thanks for her rescue at the Todtes Weib, a gold brooch; from the emperor and his brothers on the occasion of their father's death, a painting depicting the Immaculate Conception. In the center is an altar dedicated by Margrave Ludwig[31]. Everything from the simplest wooden foot or finger to the gold and brilliantly ostentatious ornamentation is represented here. The sacrificial image corridor runs along the north side. The oldest images date from 1363. We did not neglect to climb up the middle tower. It is the highest one (50 Austrian klafter[32]), has a huge clockworks and seven bells, the largest of which weighs 108 centner[33]. The view is rewarding: to the south, the Salza Valley, the Aflenzer and Zeller Staritzen[34], and in the background the high Veitsch[35]; to the west, the three Zellerhut peaks[36]. In the north one has an unobstructed view of the Ötscher,[37] with the Gemeindealm[38] left and the Bürgeralm[39] right of it. The lake Erlaufsee[40] is hidden by chains of hills. Mariazell itself is shaped like a tripod, with the church in the center. On the north side of the church is a row of vendor stalls occupied by women who tirelessly invite passers-by to buy.

The afternoon was devoted to visiting Erlaufsee. It is about 5/4 hours[41] away. The path runs mostly through woods. The lake is very nicely situated, about one and a half hours long, and forms the boundary between Lower Austria and Styria. It is bound on all sides by wooded hills. The north bank rises directly to the Gemeindealm; at the west end is a small restaurant run by a St. Pölten resident[42]. On the north bank, we arrived at a fisherman's house belonging to the Lilienfeld Abbey.[43] A watering place looked delightful. The fisherman placed a boat at our disposal, which we took to the opposite shore. A bottle of excellent Lilienfelder[44] added to our satisfaction. At 7:30 we arrived back in Mariazell.

3rd Day. Wednesday, July 15

The mail coach, in which we had reserved two seats, was to leave for Wegscheid[45] at 4 a.m. It was hard enough to get out of that sweet bunk so early. After frantically searching the entire inn, unable to find our shoes anywhere until the poor chambermaid, whom I aroused from peaceful slumber, came to my aid, we raced off to the post office at a gallop, arriving just in time. The ride in the coach went all the more slowly. It was hard for me to resist nodding off as my companion did. That I managed it at all was only thanks to the coldness of the morning, which kept me rigid for the two-hour ride. Because of the fog, I couldn't see much. Gusswerk[46] is impressive and has several blast furnaces. Wegscheid lies in a broad valley. The warm coffee there roused me from my mental and physical torpor. But the prices at the inn were so dreadfully high for our slender means that it made us shudder. We were glad just to move on.

At 6:15 we set out for Weichselboden.[47] While the route through Gusswerk is considerably shorter, it is totally devoid of charm, so we went by way of the beautiful Kastenriegel.[48] We hiked up the Ramerthal Valley through broadleaf forest and passed numerous charcoal burning operations. In a series of switchbacks, we finally reached the Kastenriegel at a crossroads in the valley. The scenery to the west is wild and romantic, while to the east is a gently sloping wall. The Aflenzer Staritzen and the magnificent Hoschschwab[49] are visible in the west. Whereas the road descends in a broad curve, we climbed down by a direct path into the so-called Hölle, a ravine whose name means "netherworld" or "abyss," with its numerous alpine dairies. The ravine starts gently and then drops abruptly to the Vordere[50] Hölle. The road makes countless switchbacks, but we chose the most direct route, through a log flume,[51] which was somewhat hazardous but the fastest way down. We came to several alpine chalets as well as a hunting lodge belonging to the Count of Meran.[52] Naturally we would not think of omitting a side trip to the Lower Ring, about half an hour to the south. Here the rock walls form a circular basin or ring, which can be entered only from the north. An ice-cold waterfall plunges down the left side, and on the right is the so-called Upper Ring, which far surpasses the lower one in grandeur; but because it is a popular habitat for chamois[53], the Count of Meran has protected it from visitors by blasting away the access. Every September the entire Meran family comes to spend a few weeks at its hunting lodge. We climbed down the Vordere Hölle and reached the Schützenauer Inn just as a torrential rain burst forth. Because of the uncertainty of the weather, we had to abandon our plan to climb the Hochschwab. At noon we arrived at Weichselboden, a small town beautifully situated in the Salza[54] Valley. A water conduit runs from the Ring to Weichselboden, crossing the Salza on a half-disintegrated bridge. In the Salza Valley, it seems to be the general practice not to rebuild any bridge that the ravages of time or a raging stream has destroyed. We often saw the last vestiges of such hapless passageways along the banks.

After an hour and a half's rest, sweetened by a frugal noon meal, we took up our journey anew. Our plan was to reach Wildalpen[55] yet today. The path runs high along the right bank of the Salza. Just beyond Weichselboden the valley narrows, the cliffs so close together that the road must pass through a rock tunnel 40–50 paces long, whereas the narrow natural opening was used for the construction of a tremendously strong stone dam to break the green torrents of the Salza's wildwater. The way to Wildalpen is extremely narrow – in most places the valley affords just enough room for river and path. The latter, because of the mountain torrents plummeting at intervals, is often ankle-deep in scree. The Salza Valley broadens somewhat where the Brunn Valley comes in. On the right the open Thurau[56] pastures come into view, while the entire Hochschwab Group appears in the south – a magnificent mountain, but we didn't regret having given up the climb, since its peak was mostly clouded over. Once the road had risen about 80 klafter[57] above the rushing Salza, we could already see Wildalpen in the distance, which lies beside the Salza in a curve of the narrow valley. We arrived at 5:15, reserved beds at once, then walked about for a while. The church is a pretty one, its pastor a passionate Tarok[58] player. The town, because of its charming setting, attracts large numbers of summer visitors. We could not follow the path to Eisenerz[59] very far, but we looked for the three Siebensee[60] lakes as dusk was falling, so that I "would have more to tell," as my companion said. The half-hour trip was well worth the effort. A narrow path leads uphill alongside the foaming outflow.

The first lake is the most beautiful, small but crystal clear. The second, a quarter-hour further south, is even smaller, and the third, right beside it, is the largest. They are all charmingly situated, surrounded partly by forest, partly by meadow. Opposite the mountains is an alpine pasture. The Grimmstein to the east and the Böse Wand and Grossberalm to the south are the most significant elevations in the lake area.

At 8:45 we both headed for our bunks. We had hiked about 11 hours in the course of the day and were thus quite exhausted. The weather had totally cleared up; only in Wildalpen did we get a brief local shower. We had watched for chamois but always in vain. Just outside Wildalpen, our imaginations actually mistook a bench perched on a rock ledge for a chamois.

4th Day. Thursday, July 16

After an excellent night's sleep and a hearty chuckle over the waiter's consternation that for 20 kreutzer[61] we had gotten a communal dormitory room where we could have slept in ten beds at the same time, we set out at 7:45. We decided to forgo the climb over to Eisenerz in favor of a visit to Palfau.[62] The overcast sky was a welcome sight. Once past a narrow stretch of valley beyond Wildalpen, we found that the scenery changed continually. Palfau is hidden by the cone-shaped Hasenkopf,[63] and in a few places the Hochkar[64] can also be seen. Having stayed on the left bank thus far, we left it over a sturdy bridge and came to a nice inn on the right, about half an hour[65] outside Palfau, where we stopped off, on the advice of my companion, who was familiar with the area. We had been hiking exactly three hours and now enjoyed a meal in a bower overlooking the Salza.[66] Here we established our itinerary, which was to visit the grotto and the Noth at Gams,[67] then spend the night in Hieflau.[68] We set out at 1:00. The route to Gams is not romantic, but Palfau captivated me for its really lovely setting in a bulge of the valley, bounded by pleasant alpine pastures to the east and west. We passed by the town itself on our right. Over time, the Salza had cut a bed 20 to 30 fathoms deep into the sandy soil. We now left our faithful escort from the Freinsattel.[69] Still a modest rivulet at Mariazell, the Salza at our point of parting was already a respectable stream, which – innocent though it usually appears – can become quite wild.

We turned off to the left and arrived at 2:40 in Gams, a little village known for its two tanneries. After finally obtaining a printed guide[70] by the grace of the snobbish innkeeper, we set out at 3:15 to visit the so-called Kraus Grotto,[71] situated high up, with a steep access. I was rather disappointed with the grotto itself. It has nothing stupendous to offer, and the largest stalactites and stalagmites are broken off. Every Sunday it is illuminated electrically from Gams by Mr. Kraus.[72] The current entrance faces west, whereas in former times one had to climb down 12 klafter from the summit.[73] As or the mineralogical aspect, the grotto offers only small drip formations, but it does contain beautifully crystallized gypsum, and a larger chamber has been adapted as a dance hall. From there one passes into a corridor called the Wilzekgang, which continues for about fifty meters. Especially beautiful is the Elysium, a cavern in which the mixture of crystallized gypsum and yellow pyrite creates a brilliant sparkling. At 4:30 we left the grotto to visit the Noth, a gorge whose name means "urgency." As little grandeur as the former had to offer, all the greater was the that of the latter. Indeed, the foaming water really did move through the gorge with seeming urgency. The vertical rock walls are only five to seven klafter apart. The plank walkway is attached to the wall and runs along and above the torrent. The narrow passage continues for about a thousand paces, and anyone who walks all the way through emerges into an open green valley, where the rocks stand almost isolated. Completely satisfied, we returned to Gams. Count Wilzek[74] owns all hunting rights in this area. At the inn we saw his chief huntsman in beautifully embroidered Styrian garb, a genuine *Alpenkind*,[75] full of vigor and resilience, who covered the distance from Hieflau to Gams in less than an hour. He would walk back to Wildalpen yet today, where he had started his hike to Hieflau in the early morning. We moved at a brisk pace too, and nearly always downhill, but it took us two full hours to reach Hieflau. The road leads over a saddle, where one has a magnificent view of the Ennsthaler Alps.[76] Near the town of Lambach, one descends via a series of steep switchbacks to the Enns River. Its force and power, which I was seeing here for the first time, amazed me. Unfortunately a rain had roiled its normally clear torrent. A lovely evening had a refreshing effect on body and spirit. After crossing the Enns twice, we arrived in Hieflau at 8:00 p.m. and found excellent lodging at the inn that Count Wilzek's chief huntsman had recommended to us.

Hieflau is a sizeable market town situated on the right bank of the Enns at a right-angled bend. It is known for its iron industry and is a popular summer stopover because of its proximity to the Gesäuse[77] and Eisenerz.[78]

5th Day. Friday, July 17

Fatigue, superb beds, and the delight of only having to pay 10 kreuzers for them – all this made for an excellent night's sleep. An early start was unthinkable, for again we had hiked about eleven hours the day before. Our destinations for today were the Gesäuse[79] and Admont.[80]

We left our knapsacks at the station and entered the famous Gesäuse with the thrill of anticipation. Unfortunately there was no brisk morning air to speak of. By 8:00 the sun was already blazing and would severely test our fortitude later in the day. The road crosses to the left bank of the Enns at the bend in the valley, disappears into the woods for a way, and upon emerging affords a gorgeous view of the rushing "sausende"[81] Enns, the whitewater from which the Gesäuse derives its name, with vertical walls on both sides: on the right, the red Zinnödl[82] and steep Planspitze;[83] on the left, the magnificent snow-covered Buchalmspitze.[84] Making room for the road, which snakes back and forth from one bank to the other, had been an arduous task. Space for the railroad had to be wrested from the rock. A beautiful point on the road is where the tracks emerge from one of the many tunnels and the road crosses them with the rushing Enns below it on the right. – At 10 o'clock we arrived in Gstatterboden[85], a friendly oasis amid the Gesäuse's forbidding maze of rocks and a welcome resting place for us. At 10:45 we resumed our hike. The Buchalmspitze was now so near that it drew wistful gazes with magnetic force. Here the Gesäuse widens a little. The road runs along the right bank and by way of a beautiful bridge crosses the Johnsbach,[86] which tumbles wildly down the romantic valley of the same name. Forming the end or start of the Gesäuse are two massive rock cones, which leave only enough room for the Enns and the road; the railway has to pass the river and then a tunnel by way of a beautiful iron bridge. Especially on the return trip, I had admired this imposing natural gateway on the Enns, which heralds so auspiciously the wonders that lie beyond it. After the narrow Gesäuse comes the broad and very pleasant Admont Valley, but the blistering sun prevented us from fully appreciating it. The elegant towers of Admont[87] beckoned to us from a distance, but we had to endure the torments of Tantalus[88] before we reached them. A hundred times we hoped they would be right around the next little bend, and then, to our dismay, another stretch of road would appear, just enough to be baked afresh.

But this, too, came to an end. The more frequent our delusions, the more furious our stride, despite sun, fatigue, and growling stomachs. A simple peasant directed us to an inn "where young gentleman scholars normally stop." Indeed, he really did have a good grasp of the budget and hunger of students traveling on foot, for only at Jerausch's in Admont could one get a huge cutlet with potatoes, rice, lettuce, and stewed fruit for 30 kreutzer. We arrived there at 1:30 p.m.

Admont is beautifully situated, the Enns Valley broad and inviting; toward Litzen[89] one can glimpse the high-lying pilgrimage site of Fraukirchen[90]; on a hill close to Admont is the ruins of Reitzenstein, a former monastery. Looking out over the beautiful Entailer Alps is the Grimmig,[91] its appearance matching its name. The Pirgas and the Hochthor[92] are dreadfully fissured rock masses, the lower parts of which are hidden behind mountain ridges; and the Buchalmspitze, our friend from the Gesäuse, also peeks out at us curiously.

Admont's most beautiful jewel is the Benedictine Abbey.[93] It was founded by St. Hemma[94] with the support of Gebhardt of Salzburg[95] and endowed with prosperous holdings in the Enns and Palten Valleys[96]. Benedictines moved into it. The abbey endured much affliction. Around 1090 it was totally ransacked; and more recently, in 1865, it burned down along with the market. Only the library was saved. Owing to its considerable wealth, the abbey has been totally rebuilt. Only two sections remain unexecuted, which are indicated in the accompanying sketch by dotted lines[97]. The church is a double-spired, slender structure built in the Gothic style. Especially striking to me was the absence of interior splendor, unusual for a Catholic church, which brought out the beauty of the pointed stone arches. The monastery buildings are attached to the church and surround an enormous courtyard, which we crossed to take a look at the library.

[98]

Road	Church	Monastery Courtyard	Library	Monastery Garden
	Cellar			

This was something totally new to me. I had never seen book collections of such magnitude. The library contains approximately 30,000 volumes, housed in three rooms. In the first are the secular writings, medicine, philosophy, etc.; the second room contains various manuscripts from the 9th to the 15th century; and the third, finally, is the religious section. All volumes have identical bindings, but in the lower cabinets is another gallery. The corners of the rooms are adorned with bronze-plated wood carvings, mostly the work of Thaddäus Stammel[99]. Those in the middle room depict the four last moments of human life: death, judgment, devil, and heaven; other figures depict four human traits: vanity, modesty, diligence, and idleness; etc. The celling is painted, and the floor is of white (from St. Michael[100]), green (from Wildalpen) and gray marble. A slab is said to have cost one thaler. The library represents a tidy little sum. What especially caught my eye were all the maps of Styria and Lower Austria from 1567 and 1668; also a pendulum clock from the 17th century that runs for thirteen months without being wound.

All this information I owe to a forthcoming attendant, who also advised us under penalty of death not to forget the monastery cellar, which we sought out at once. – After also a climbing a tower in haste, we set off for the train station at a gallop. Only when it was just the two of us in the compartment were we able to enjoy the gorgeous Gesäuse again undisturbed. It may have gone faster than in the morning, but at such lightning speed that I could almost say that anyone who has not gone all the way through it knows the Gesäuse only by half.

At the sharp bend we rode into Hieflau, then continued on to Eisenerz. The railway and road led into the pleasant valley, the Erzberg[101] with its countless mine shafts already visible in the distance. We stopped off at the former Mutter Brod.[102] Pleased with our day's experiences, we went to bed early, for we had another strenuous march planned for the morrow, which actually turned out to be longer than we had thought.

6th Day. Saturday, July 18

The weather was apparently on our side; again today we awoke to a clear morning.

Eisenerz is a fairly large town; the substantial operations of the Alpine Montan Steel Corporation[103] give the market town a grandiose face. It lies in a narrow valley at the foot of the heavily burrowed-through Erzberg.[104] A striking feature is the St. Oswald parish church, built by Emperor Rudolph I.[105] It stands on a ledge of the Erzberg that dominates the entire valley as far as Münnich[106]. During the Turkish wars, it served as a safe refuge. Also of interest is the *Schichtturm* or "shift tower," its position as dominant as that of the church. It houses the bell that signals the start of a work shift for the miners. A railway connects the blast furnaces and mine shafts with the train station. There is also a meteorological observation station in Eisenerz.

After looking around in the town and vicinity, we spent the morning on a trip to Leopoldstein Lake.[107] To get there, we chose a route across the Prossen, a small saddle that affords a wonderful view of the lake and the Wildalpen Valley, which appears to end at the mighty Pfaffenstein.[108] The Leopoldstein Lake has a genuine alpine character, not large, about an hour in size[109]; its usually smooth blue-green waters can become very turbulent in storms. The west bank is defined by rock walls that rise directly from the water, while the east bank is bounded by densely wooded hills. The lake runs in a north-south direction. It is certainly worth the trip from Eisenerz. We returned there by way of the royal Lichtensteins' little summer palace "Leopoldstein."[110]

We couldn't stay to enjoy beautiful Eisenerz any longer, and we had to forgo a visit to the Erzberg. Our plan was to get through the Frauenmauerhöhle[111] and reach Tragöss[112] yet today, and to go from there to either Leoben[113] or Vordernberg[114] the next day.

At 12:30 p.m., our guide, Anselm Leiss, appeared. He told us colossal stories from his tourism business. Although reality bore little resemblance to his words, his local knowledge left nothing to be desired. Bypassing the Präbichl[115] road on the right, we went into the mountains via Trofeng.[116] At the Gsöll Alm,[117] having already climbed a significant way, one is only at the foot of the Frauenmauer, a high rock wall. Three black spots are visible in the distance. The middle one is the entrance to the cavern. It is situated so starkly in the middle of the bare wall, that getting to it without risking one's neck appears inconceivable. But it is less frightening than it looks. We approached the entrance via a series of safe switchbacks; only the very last stretch consisted of an alarming flight of steps. The Gsöll Alm now lay below us in a nearly vertical drop. The nearest peak is the Griesmauer,[118] and to the right of it is the Bärenloch,[119] a favorite terrain of the emperor for hunting chamois. After thoroughly cooling off, we entered the cavern, which was truly magnificent. Our guide pulled out his torch, which nearly failed to light because of the sharp draft. Without a guide, this underground corridor is impossible to navigate; I would not advise anyone to try it, because he would surely get lost in the countless side passageways. A unique feature of this cavern is a lake that has a smooth surface of ice in the summer but is open in the winter. Absolutely magnificent are the cascades, which are congealed into ice in mid-flow as they plunge into the lake. The focal point of the cavern is the so-called Kreutzhalle or Cross Hall, where the cave enlarges to an incredible size and height. The access to this chamber leads through the flume, a crevice so narrow that it required great effort for us to wriggle through. For an even moderately stout man, this would be an insurmountable obstacle. We had to climb continually, which was not easy with the scree and inadequate light.

After walking in the cavern for three-quarters of an hour, we were glad to greet the daylight. As magnificent as the cavern is, one still heaves a sigh of relief on being out in the open again, for a certain feeling of oppressiveness inside is inevitable. The view at the exit is delightful. Below us lies the lovely Pfarralm[120], and the beautiful Hochschwab[121] Group is particularly striking. Our guide pointed out every peak by name for us; among the most prominent were the Sonnstein, Pribitzkessel, Griesmauer, Hochalm, and Aflenzer Staritzen. Rising in isolation is the ungainly Messnerin,[122] the north foot of which is our hiking destination for today, and we could see that it was still an appreciable distance away. As the guide started back at 5:00, we climbed down from the nearly 4700"[123] high exit to the Pfarralm, where we refreshed ourselves with milk such as can only be found in alpine pastures. From here, without a marked path, we descended the mountain into the Tragöss Valley,[124] then took the path that led all the way to the valley floor.

The Tragöss Valley – or the Jassinggraben, as it is known in the upper region – has genuine alpine character. We strode through it in the cool of the evening, which enhanced the freshness of the natural world even more. The valley is surrounded by high mountains on both sides. Magnificent cattle graze on the slopes all around, and the melodious tinkle of their bells can be heard everywhere. After passing a hunting lodge, we arrived at the polyp-shaped Grünersee,[125] which certainly lives up to its name, for the water appears in all variations from lightest leaf-green to deepest blue-green. From here one has a view of the actual Tragöss Valley and the town of Oberort.[126] We arrived there at 8:00 p.m. and luckily found accommodation at Etschmeier's, the only inn.

7th Day. Sunday, July 19

Tragöss[127] or Oberort, a small town, faces the Messnerin to the south, which features a natural window in the colossal rock wall. To the west is the broad, fertile Tragöss Valley, which leads into the Murthal[128] at Leoben. Oberort has an old church.[129] The walk to Leoben takes seven hours, we learned here, so we decided to forgo it in favor of the closer Vordernberg, and to go from there into the Murthal by train. To our credit, I must say that we hadn't once gone astray thus far. Of course it would have to be today, our last day, that something would go amiss. We stayed in the Tragöss Valley too long rather than starting our climb directly beyond the town by the Vordernberger Road. To compensate for our blunder, we had to climb a steep, sunny slope, which turned our drops of sweat into rivers. The road leads over the Hieselegg Pass[130] but has to cross another mountain chain before leading straight down to Vordernberg. We had started at 8 in the morning and arrived at our destination at 11:30.

Vordernberg, a respectable market town with 13 blast furnaces and other operations of the Alpine Montan Steel Corporation,[131] is completely surrounded by high Alps. To the northwest is the road winding over the Präbichl,[132] by which one can reach Eisenerz in four or five hours. We dined and then made our way to the railway station half an hour to the south. The ride to Leoben is pretty. One beautiful spot is in Freienstein,[133] with its ruins of the same name. Friedau[134] and Donnawitz[135] are large iron works of the Alpines. At 4:00 we arrived in Leoben. Our lovely trip came to an end here. An hour later, I had to take leave of my friend, who turned back to Mürzzuschlag, while I stayed another day at my uncle's home. —[136]

In conclusion, I must also say thanks to my dear grandpapa. Not only was the tour entertaining and instructive in and of itself, but it will also remain with me as a pleasant memory for the rest of my life. I hope that he finds in these lines a small token of the gratitude I owe him.

Source: Unpublished. Text: M.S., Pf. Coll., CL'ANA 0063 (unpublished manuscript, Pforzheimer Collection of Shelley and His Circle, New York Public Library, Astor, Lenox, and Tilden Foundations

Notes

* The journal writer wrote *Meine Fussreise im Juli 1885* ("My Walking Tour in July 1885") in Kurrent (also known as Kurrentschrift [English: Kurrent script/writing], deutsche Schrift [English: German script] and German cursive), namely the script used before 1911 when it was replaced by Sütterlinschrift (English: Sütterlin writing, named for Ludwig Sütterlin) until 1941, and then deutsche Normalschrift (English: German Normal Writing).

  As indicated in the prefatory material, neither Pauline nor Wilhelm could have written this journal, although Mary Claire Bally-Clairmont suggested that Pauline had. The journal writer credits the sojourn described here as relying on the generosity of his/her "grandpapa." The man Pauline (or Wilhelm) would have called "grandpapa," their step-grandfather William Godwin, died in 1836; it seems unlikely that the 60-year-old Pauline (or the 54-year-old Wilhelm) would have been taking a trip through his largesse almost five decades later. I posit that the writer is the oldest of Wilhelm's three children, Walter Gaulis Clairmont, who would have been a month shy of 17 and old enough (as well as male enough, unlike his closest sibling Alma) to undertake a journey with a friend. The grandfather he refers to is probably his mother's father, Hofrat Johann von Pichler (1799–1890), who was living at the time in Vienna, as Walter's paternal grandfather (Charles Clairmont) had died in 1850.

A transcript of a document Walter Gaulis Clairmont wrote on 3 July 1933 in order to satisfy the National Socialist authorities in Vienna that he had no Jewish ancestors provides further information about his life in Appendix F. Per his account, Walter Clairmont was born in Tuzokrét, in the Banat. He attended the Franz Josef Gymnasium and the University of Agricultural Sciences in Vienna. He graduated from the University of Basel in Basel, Switzerland, with a doctoral degree in Chemistry. He worked in Berlin, Germany, for Agfa, then in Russia, and later in the Neue Augsburger Kattunfabrik (New Augsburg Cotton Mill) in Bavaria. In 1913, he married Frida Zucker. They had no children together. Walter died in 1959 and is buried in the family tomb in Vienna.

1 If Walter Clairmont wrote this journal, he would have indeed been living in Vienna with his family. Wilhelm and Ottilia Clairmont moved to Vienna in 1874 after having lived in the Banat for some years.
2 The editors of *Encyclopedia Britannica* note the following about Mürzzuschlag: "town, east-central Austria, at the junction of the Fröschnitz and Mürz rivers, northeast of Bruck an der Mur. First mentioned in 1227, it was chartered in 1318 and has been an ironworking centre since the 14th century. It has medieval houses and a former Cistercian abbey with a church from 1496 and beautiful cloisters. An Alpine summer and winter resort of the Semmering region, Mürzzuschlag is a noted skiing centre. The town also serves as a market and service centre for the largely rural environs. Pop. (2006) 9, 246" (www.britannica.com/place/Murzzuschlag Accessed 8 March 2020).

Most of the locations this journal references are in the Austrian federal state of Steiermark (Styria). Styria is one of nine federal states and is best known for its recreational activities and its mining industry: "The Erzberg near Eisenerz supplies most of Austria's iron ore and has been mined since Celtic times. Brown coal (lignite) is mined at Fohnsdorf and Köflach and magnesite in the Shale Alps. The state also produces sizable amounts of graphite, talc, gypsum, and salt. Thermoelectricity is generated, and there are hydroelectric plants on the Mur and other rivers. Heavy industry is concentrated in the Mur Valley below Fohnsdorf and in the Mürz Valley. Metal and machine industries, sawmills, automobile development and production, and paper and cellulose industries are important; chemicals, textiles, leather, and food products are also manufactured. Major industrial sites are in Graz, Leoben, Bruck, and Kapfenberg" (www.britannica.com/place/Steiermark Accessed 23 March 2020). Styria comprises some 16, 387 square kilometers.
3 Neuberg an der Mürz is a municipality in the Mürz Valley. It is located in the district of Bruck-Mürzzuschlag.
4 The "Dead Woman" waterfall near Mürzsteg in Styria: "Totes Weib wasserfall or Wasserfall zum Toten Weib is a 40 meters high waterfall south of Frein an der Mürz along the Lahnsattel Bundesstrasse (road 23) in the region Steiermark, Austria . . . The origin of the name Totes weib wasserfall (Wasserfall zum Toten Weib) is unknown . . . The Totes weib wasserfall (Wasserfall zum Toten Weib) is a unique waterfall fed by a natural spring in the Schneealpenstock. The entrance of the source lies south of the Schneealpenstock. The Totes weib wasserfall (Wasserfall zum Toten Weib) can be very powerful. The flow of the spring can vary between 30–300 l/sec" (www.europeanwaterfalls.com/waterfalls/totes-weib-wasserfall/ Accessed 9 March 2020).

5 Small ski town in the north Styrian Alps, some 143 kilometers north of Graz.
6 Located in the municipality of Mariazell in the district of Bruck-Mürzzuschlag.
7 Wildalpen is a municipality in the district of Liezen in Styria.
8 Palfau is part of the municipality of Landl in Styria.
9 Hieflau is part of the municipality of Landl in Styria.
10 Mountain range and national park in the state of Styria.
11 Former mining town, 109 kilometers northwest of Graz. During the Second World War, prisoners from the Mauthausen Concentration Camp subcamp were forced to produce iron ore.
12 Ice caves in Styria, northeast of Eisenerz.
13 In southeast Austria, the Tragoess Valley is known for the Green Lake (German: Grüner See) which is surrounded by the Hochschwab Mountains. The lake rises each summer due to melting snow, and then shrinks again in the winter, illuminating again the submerged summer landscape.
14 On the Mur River, in central Austria, in the state of Styria.
15 Mountain range between the Austrian provinces of Styria and Lower Austria (Niederösterreich). Lower Austria comprises some 19,174 square kilometers. While Vienna lies geographically in the province of Lower Austria, the nation's capital is its own separate political entity. There are nine federal provinces and the city of Vienna serves as one of the nine.
16 German for "Black Eagle".
17 The Austrian-Alpine Montan Company. From the company's website (translation from the German provided on the website): "Founded in 1881 by the merger of Styrian and Carinthian steelworks, with the Leoben-Donawitz center. The location resulted from the proximity of iron ore production on Erzberg (Styria) and Hüttenberg (Carinthia), coal came from nearby lignite mines, hard coal from Bohemia and Moravia. The most important customer[s] for steel was [were]the shipyards on the Austrian Adriatic.

In 1893 Donawitz was the first smelter in Europe to introduce the pig iron ore process in the Siemens Martin furnace; In 1902 the largest blast furnace in Europe at that time (300 tons per day) was built. In 1907 Donawitz owned the largest uniform steel mill in Europe. After 1918 there was a repeated change of ownership; the majority of the shares passed from Italian ownership to German ownership in 1926 (Stinnes and Siemens-Schuckert). In 1938 the Oesterreichisch-Alpine Montangesellschaft was merged with the hut newly founded in Linz to form 'Reichswerke AG Alpine Montanbetriebe, Hermann Göring'. Independent again in 1946, the Oesterreichisch-Alpine Montangesellschaft was nationalized (nationalized industry). New processes, especially the LD [Linz-Donawitz] process, which was put into operation in 1953, and the increased demand let the plant expand. The group's branches were located in Zeltweg, Krieglach and Judenburg, among others. In order to concentrate the Austrian heavy industry, the group was merged with VÖEST AG (VOEST, United Austrian Iron and Steel Works AG) on 1st January 1973 to form VOEST-Alpine AG. After several restructuring[s] of this group in the following decades, the main plant of the former Austrian-Alpine Montan company in Donawitz now belongs to VOEST-ALPINE STAHL AG" ('Oesterreichisch-Alpine Montangesellschaft, AEIOU, in: Austria-Forum, das Wissensnetz, https://austria-forum.org/af/AEIOU/Oesterreichisch-Alpine_Montangesellschaft, March 25, 2016'. Accessed 8 March 2020).
18 In Mürzzuschlag, Styria. The town is part of the Neuberg an der Mürz municipality.
19 Mountain in Styria.
20 Part of Neuberg an der Mürz
21 Emperor Franz Joseph I built this hunting lodge in 1869. Since 1947, the lodge has served as the summer residence of the President of Austria.
22 Bruck-Mürzzuschlag is a district in Styria consisting of nineteen municipalities, including Mariazell, Mürzzuschlag, Neuberg an der Mürz, and Mürzsteg. The following

places mentioned in this journal are all part of the Mürzsteg municipality: Dobrein, Frein an der Mürz, Niederalpl, and Scheiterboden.
23 Empress Elisabeth was married to Franz Joseph I. Their only son, Crown Prince Rudolf, would die in 1889 together with his lover, Mary Vetsera, in a murder-suicide.
24 Lahnsattel Strasse was constructed in 1884 after Empress Elisabeth of Austria had an accident on the original wooden road: "Als Kaiserin Elisabeth mit ihrem Pferd durch eine morsche Brückenplanke brach, wurde mit dem Bau der Straßenverbindung am rechten Ufer begonnen, die 1884 eröffnet wurde und später zur Lahnsattel Straße wurde" (Translation: "When Empress Elisabeth broke through a rotten plank while on her horse, the road connection on the right bank began to be built. It was opened in 1884 and later became Landsattel street"). See https://de.wikipedia.org/w/index.php?title=Totes_Weib&action=edit&section=3 Accessed 9 March 2020.
25 Forest on the northern slope of the Rax.
26 The Salza River and valley today boast whitewater rafting activities. Palfau and Wildalpen are known for whitewater rafting.
27 German for "To the Golden Grasp".
28 Mariazell Basilica (known as Basilica Mariä Geburt, the Basilica of the Virgin Mary's Birth) was built in the seventeenth century after the original fourteenth-century church was burned down in the fifteenth century.
29 According to Ann Sherwin, translator, sources say Heinrich von Mähren (of Moravia); (Personal Correspondence, 28 September 2018).
30 Empress Elisabeth of Austria.
31 Per Ann Sherwin, translator, the reference is probably to Heinrich. Mariazell has a street named for him. (Personal Correspondence, 28 September 2018).
32 Unit of length. Each klafter is about 1,8 meters.
33 Unit of weight.
34 The Hochschwab Alps (German: Hochschwabgruppe) is a mountain range in Styria. The Aflenzer Staritzen and the Zeller Staritzen are part of the range. The following is a description about the mountain trail in Styria: "Aflenzer Staritzen is a 19.5 mile point-to-point trail located near Turnau, Styria, Austria that offers scenic views and is only recommended for very experienced adventurers. The trail is primarily used for hiking, walking, and nature trips" (www.alltrails.com/trail/austria/styria/aflenzer-staritzen?u=i Accessed 14 March 2020). Turnau is a town in the Bruck-Mürzzuschlag district.
35 The tallest mountain in the Mürzsteg Alps.
36 Mountains in the Ybbstal Alps.
37 In the Ybbstal Alps.
38 The Gemeindealpe are peaks near the town of Mitterbach. The highest point has an elevation of 1,626 meters. See www.gemeindealpe.at/ Accessed 14 March 2020.
39 Northern perimeter mountain of the Aflenz Basin.
40 Alpine Lake, about four kilometers from Mariazell.
41 The fraction here seems incorrect.
42 Sankt Pölten is the capital city of the Austrian federal state of Lower Austria.
43 A thirteenth-century Cistercian Abbey, located in Lilienfeld, Styria. The abbey was destroyed in a fire in the nineteenth century but was subsequently rebuilt.
44 The area is known for its vineyards and wine production industry.
45 Wegscheid, a town in Linz, Austria.
46 The word means "foundry". The town is now incorporated into Mariazell. (per Ann Sherwin, Personal Correspondence, 28 September 2018).
47 Town about 15 kilometers southwest of Mariazell.
48 From bergfex.com: "Die Zeller Staritzen im Ortsteil Gußwerk gehören zu einer der schönsten Wanderungen im Mariazeller Land. Zunächst steigen wir zur Vorderen Staritze auf. Von dort aus geht es auf einer wundervollen Almlandschaft auf leichtem Wege zur Hinteren Staritze. Nach einer weiteren kurzen Rast und einer Stärkung auf

der Hütte liegt nun noch der Abstieg zum Kastenriegl vor uns. Von dort aus haben wir nun einen grandiosen Blick in die hintere Höll. Auf leichtem Fußweg gelangen wir dann zurück zum Ausgangspunkt" (Translation from the website: "The Zeller Staritzen in the district of Gußwerk are one of the most beautiful hikes in the Mariazeller Land. First we climb up to the Staritze. From there it is easy on a wonderful alpine landscape to the rear Staritze. After another short rest and a refreshment at the hut, the descent to Kastenriegl is still ahead of us. From there we now have a magnificent view of the back hell. We then return to the starting point on an easy footpath" www.bergfex.at/sommer/steiermark/touren/wanderung/25967,zeller-staritzen/ Accessed 14 March 2020).

49 See journal entry for July 14.
50 German for "near" Hölle. There is also a Hintere ("remote") Hölle.
51 A channel created to transport logs through water.
52 Franz Meran (1839–1891), an Austrian count. His father was Archduke Johann of Austria-Tuscany (son of Grand Duke Leopold of Tuscany), while his mother was the daughter of a postmistress who was later given the title of Baroness. Meran was made a count in 1844 when he was five years old. He had a lodge in Styria.
53 Mountain antelope.
54 See July 14.
55 See introductory section "My Walking Tour in July 1885".
56 Turnau. See July 14.
57 Unit of length, about 1,8 meters.
58 A card game.
59 See introductory section "My Walking Tour in July 1885".
60 Today, a ski resort near Wildalpen.
61 Unit of currency.
62 See introductory section "My Walking Tour in July 1885", and July 14.
63 The word means "rabbit's head" in German.
64 A mountain, known today for its ski slopes. With an elevation of 1,808 meters, it is one of the Austrian federal state of Lower Austria's highest peaks.
65 Ann Sherwin, translator, observes that the writer refers to distance and not time (Personal Correspondence, 28 September 2018).
66 See July 14.
67 The Nothklamm Gorge is between the town of Gams and the Kraushöhle Cave. Gams bei Hieflau (English: Gams at Hieflau) is located today in the municipality of Landl In 1885 (well before the 2015 municipal redistricting of Styria), it was part of the municipality of Liezen.
68 See introductory section "My Walking Tour in July 1885".
69 Literally, the "Frein saddle". See July 14. Topographically, a saddle is the lowest point between two mountain peaks.
70 Per Ann Sherwin, translator: "It says only 'guide,' but since no human guide is mentioned further, I suggest adding this clarification" (Personal Correspondence, 28 September 2018).
71 The Kraushöhle (Kraus Cave) "was the first illuminated show cave in the world and traces of the old illumination system can still be seen today . . . The Kraushöhle Cave is part of UNESCO's Global Geopark Network" (https://gesaeuse.at/en/activity/kraushoehle/ Accessed 15 March 2020). The cave's entrance has been accessible since 1881.
72 The cave is named for Franz Kraus, a Viennese speleologist, who moved to Gams.
73 According to https://gesaeuse.at/en/activity/kraushoehle/, a wooden ladder from 1881 is still extant.
74 Count Johann Nepomuk Wilczek (1837–1922) was an explorer and sponsored the Austro-Hungarian North Pole Expedition in 1872–4. He was president of the Austrian Geographical Society.

75 German for "Alpine child".
76 The Ennstal Alps. The Enns River, which flows through the Alps, is a tributary of the Danube.
77 Mountains where the Enns and Salza Rivers meet. See also introductory section "My Walking Tour in July 1885".
78 See introductory section "My Walking Tour in July 1885".
79 See introductory section "My Walking Tour in July 1885," and July 16. The mountains today boast a host of activities. See https://gesaeuse.at/en/activities-summer/ Accessed 15 March 2020.
80 A town in the Gesäuse. Admont Abbey, founded in 1074, is a feature of this Styrian town.
81 German for "whizzing".
82 The summit of the Zinödl has an elevation of 2,191 meters.
83 A summit in the Gesäuse, its elevation is 2,117 meters.
84 In the Ybbstaler Alps, Lower Austria. Its elevation is 1,483 meters.
85 Styrian town.
86 Since 2015, the town of Johnsbach is part of the municipality of Admont. In the nineteenth century, Johnsbach was its own municipality. The Johnsbach River Basin is located in the Ennstal Alps.
87 The towers of the Benedictine Abbey, Admont Abbey, with its enormous collection of monastic works.
88 Tantalus wronged the Greek gods and was punished, doomed to stand in a pool of water and beneath a fruited tree that retreated ("tantalizing" him) whenever he reached for the fruit to relieve his hunger and thirst.
89 Liezen, a Styrian town, close to Mount Grimming.
90 Probably Frauenberg, a cloister overlooking Admont, described here as a site of pilgrimage (www.stiftadmont.at/kloster/sehenswert/wallfahrtskirche-frauenberg Accessed 15 March 2020).
91 Peak in the Dachstein Mountains. Its elevation is 2,351 meters.
92 The Hochtor is the highest mountain in the Ennstaler Alps. Its elevation is 2,369 meters.
93 Benedictines founded the abbey in 1074. Today, it serves 26 parishes. It has a school and a retirement center in Frauenberg. See www.stiftadmont.at/en/the-abbey Accessed 15 March 2020.
94 Austrian saint, known as Hemma or Emma. Her inheritance helped fund the building of Admont Abbey. She was canonized in 1938. She intercedes on behalf of pregnant women close to giving birth and people afflicted with eye diseases.
95 Eleventh-century Archbishop of Salzburg who was buried in Admont Abbey.
96 Copper and iron mining area during the medieval times.
97 The sketch has two rows of dotted lines.
98 The journal writer has provided a rudimentary sketch using a few lines and squares to represent the different spaces translated here.
99 Josef Thaddäus Stammel was an Austrian sculptor, baptized in Graz in 1695. He worked at the Admont Abbey beginning in 1726 and was responsible for carvings in its impressive library: "The library holds some 70,000 volumes while the Abbey in total owns nearly 200,000 books. The most valuable among these are the more than 1,400 manuscripts (the oldest dating to the 8th century AD) and the 530 incunabula (books printed before 1500)" (www.stiftadmont.at/en/library Accessed 15 March 2020). Stammel died in Admont in 1765: "The Abbey's sculptor Josef Stammel (1695–1765) created the numerous, elaborate limewood carvings in this magnificent space. Particularly striking are the 'Four Last Things'; a group consisting of the oversized figures of Death, Judgement, Heaven and Hell. However, these were carved before the library was built and were only subsequently incorporated, providing a

stark contrast with the Enlightenment-imbued concept of the architect" (www.stiftad mont.at/en/library Accessed 15 March 2020).
100 Sankt Michael in Obersteiermark is located about 50 kilometers from Graz.
101 A mountain peak (elevation 1,076 meters) near the town of Eisenerz. The word itself means "ore mountain". Iron ore has been mined in the area for over 1,000 years.
102 German for "Mother Bread".
103 See July 13.
104 See July 17.
105 Rudolf I (1218–1291), was a German-born Habsburg emperor. He gave the duchies of Austria and Styria to his sons in 1281. Construction on the fortified church began in 1270 when Rudolf laid the foundation stone. In 1470, renovations following gothic architecture commenced. The church was renovated in the early twentieth century, and again in 1993 and 2005. According to accepted stories, Rudolf I laid the foundation stone on the day of the Feast of St. Oswald (February 29). St. Oswald (604–642) was a Northumbrian King who introduced Christianity to Northumbria. Pilgrims believe that prayers to St. Oswald's remains (thought to have been buried in Northumbria) could produce miracles. See www.kirchenburg.at/cms/de/oswaldikirche-eisenerz/zuerst-klein,-dann-oho.html Accessed 16 March 2020.
106 I have been unable to verify a town by this name. The writer probably means Münichtal, which is part of Eisenerz today.
107 Leopoldsteinersee is a lake about 4 kilometers from Eisenerz. The lake was named for Leopoldstein Castle. The lake is fed by the Seebach River as well as many underground springs. It is used for sporting and tourist activities today. See www.bergfex.com/sommer/eisenerz/seen/leopoldsteinersee/ Accessed 16 March 2020.
108 Mountain near Eisenerz.
109 Ann Sherwin (translator) adds the words "hour in size" to render the translation understandable. According to www.bergfex.com/sommer/eisenerz/seen/leopoldsteinersee/, the lake (some 600 meters above sea level) is "1400 meters long and 370 meters wide" (Accessed 16 March 2020).
110 The Principality of Liechtenstein is a small, independent monarchy in central Europe. Its current monarch is Prince Hans Adam II (born 1945). The principality takes its name from the original Liechtenstein family, information about whom was recorded around 1136 and who probably took their name from Liechtenstein Castle in Vienna (www.fuerstenhaus.li/en/history/history-of-the-princely-house/ Accessed 16 March 2020).
111 Literally: Women's Wall Cave. The cave is near Eisenerz. It was first explored in 1820 by miners from Eisenerz. See introductory section "My Walking Tour in July 1885".
112 See introductory section "My Walking Tour in July 1885".
113 See introductory section "My Walking Tour in July 1885". Today, Leoben has about 25,000 citizens and the University (the University of Leoben) is known for its emphasis on teaching mining.
114 Located some 14 kilometers from Leoben and one of Leoben's municipalities.
115 One of the highest mountain roads in Austria.
116 Trofeng is part of the municipality of Eisenerz.
117 The Gsöll Alm (elevation of 1,201 meters) is at the foot of the Frauenmauer. Today, refreshments are available at the trailhead (see www.genussreich.at/gsollalm/ Accessed 17 March 2020).
118 The word means "Semolina".
119 German for "Bear Hole".
120 Pfarreralm is the correct spelling and translates to "Parish pasture".
121 The Hochschwab Massif consists of the Hochschwab peak (the highest peak)
122 Its elevation is 1,835 meters.
123 It is unclear if this is feet or meters.

124 See introductory section "My Walking Tour in July 1885".
125 See introductory section "My Walking Tour in July 1885". The English translation is "Green Lake".
126 Oberort is part of the municipality of Tragöß-Sankt Katharein.
127 I have provided endnotes for all town and mountain names referenced here in the entry for July 18.
128 The Murtal Valley is divided between Styria and Salzburg (another of Austria's nine federal states).
129 Antoniuskapelle, built in the sixteenth century.
130 The correct name is Hiaslegg.
131 See 13 July.
132 Präbichl Sattel, the saddle over the mountain.
133 Sankt Peter-Freienstein is a municipality in Leoben.
134 The service portal of the communal archive of Styria lists Friedau as a town and domination/rule/authority ("Stadt und Herrschaft"), with archival information about the town recorded in the Styrian Provincial Archives. See www.landesarchiv.steiermark.at/cms/beitrag/11682544/77968424/ Accessed 23 March 2020.
135 Donawitz became part of Leoben in 1939.
136 Ottilia Clairmont's brother, Moritz, was an engineer. He owned the family home in Wörthersee, Austria. In a letter to Marion Kingston Stocking written in 2005, Mary Claire Bally-Clairmont indicated that her great-grandmother, Fanny von Pichler, "made many trips and was enchanted of the Wörthersee (lake of Wörther) Austria, about 70 km west Graz, bought there a farmhouse, later changed to a villa (still existing!): her son Moritz took it over. The Clairmonts were often there, as well as Christoph and I for summer holidays. the name of the village is Velden. . . . The villa sold about 26 years ago" (see CL'ANA 0425, unpublished manuscript, Pforzheimer Collection). There are some 103 kilometers between Leoben and Wörthersee.

5

PAULINE CLAIRMONT, THE GOVERNESS OCCUPATION, AND THE GENRE OF LIFE WRITING

The genre of life writing reached a high point in the nineteenth century with women authoring many diaries and letters. Mary Shelley and Claire Clairmont were both prolific letter writers who also recorded their experiences in their respective journals.[1] What Lynn M. Linder calls "an explosion of life writing, including biographies, autobiographies, diaries and letters" in the nineteenth century (Linder 2016: 122) included both commercial efforts and exercises for private enjoyment and contemplation. Many in the former category were accounts of journeys, domestic and foreign, which appealed to armchair travelers (Mary Wollstonecraft, whose *Letters Written during a Short Residence in Sweden, Norway, and Denmark* Joseph Johnson published in 1796, in which Wollstonecraft claimed "to give a just view of the present state of the countries I have passed through, as far as I could obtain information during so short a residence" [*Letters Written during a Short Residence in Sweden, Norway, and Denmark*, Horrocks, ed, 2013: 51], was among those who capitalized on this trend). Pauline Clairmont's journal was in the latter category as she wrote only for herself. Belonging to the genre of life writing, Pauline's journal depicts her everyday experiences in Australia as well as examining and commenting on both her Australian surroundings and her love affair with William Henry Suttor, Junior. This chapter's exploration of Pauline's 1855–57 Australian journal has a twofold purpose. Using Pauline's journal as an example, it explores the nature of nineteenth-century women's life writing, in particular the genre of travel writing in British colonies through the mode of the journal or diary. It also explains the role of educator-governess that Pauline inhabited while in Australia.

Pauline's choice to be an educator facilitated her move to Australia which then enabled her to participate in the life writing genre. Examining her vocational choice allows for reflection on the opportunities available to women at the time. We know that women's education in nineteenth-century Britain was insufficient at best, that professional options were limited for women, and that unmarried women were encouraged to seek new forms of occupation to secure their livelihoods. Jacob Field shows that nearly 25 percent of women over the age of twenty "in reported employment were engaged in domestic service compared to 1.5 per cent of men" (a fact attributed to Leigh Shaw-Taylor and reported in Field

2013: 249), and Sophie McGeevor explains that women who were "regularly employed" (a term taken from the Householder's Schedule for the purposes of conducting census counts from 1851 until 1881; McGeevor 2014: 491) worked in "factories . . . owned and ran shops, inns, workshops, farms" and were "employed in what we would now consider to be the public sector, as school mistresses, or as matrons in institutions such as workhouses and hospitals" (p. 493). Though, as A. James Hammerton notes, in the latter half of the nineteenth century there was a "seemingly infinite range of suggestions [for women] . . . bee-keepers, cashiers, cooks, detectives, domestic pet-rearers, embroiderers, engravers, hairdressers, gardeners, illuminators, journalists, lithographers, masseuses, photographers, prison-warders, wood-carvers" (Hammerton 1979: 41), working women in nineteenth-century Britain were often employed in domestic service. Discriminatory practices prevented women from sharing in educational and professional opportunities, and women were unable to secure many of the jobs Hammerton identifies. Teresa Gerrard and Alexis Weedon point out that some advances were made to assist mid-century working-class women acquire the skills needed to improve their positions. In their study of the education provided by the Huddersfield Female Educational Institute[2] in the 1850s, Gerrard and Weedon observe that while the institute's curriculum was "restricted, gendered, and class-specific" (Gerrard and Weedon 2014: 239), it nevertheless allowed working-class women opportunities to learn "writing, reading and arithmetic, sewing, history, geography, and singing" (p. 239). Examining the library collection of the institute, they show that the collection "reflected the educational purpose of the institute, which was formed from a middle-class understanding of working-class gender roles, and led to a practical and proscriptive curriculum" (p. 258). They conclude that Huddersfield's "working-class women readers" patronized the library and specifically "selected books to aid their chances of employment in domestic service" (p. 258). Margaret Mills explains that "most middle-class women sought paid employment only if it was unavoidable, since leisured women were symbols of the economic success of their male relatives . . . Even intelligent analysts, who advocated reforms in girls' education, remained convinced that a woman's primary function was to support her husband as decoratively as possible" (Mills 2017: 72). Women had few options and brothers were expected to provide a residence for their sisters, clarifies Karen Bourrier, who quotes Valerie Sanders: "it was practically unheard of for young middle-class single women to live alone" (Bourrier 2011: 182). As we know, Pauline originally left Austria to find work in Britain, where teaching was the only job with many openings for middle-class women. Although Pauline had few other ways to earn her living and probably felt compelled to seek employment as an educator, she may not have viewed herself as a typical governess. Instead, she may have considered herself non-conventional in her lifestyle choices and part of the literary Shelley-Godwin circle which opened doors to her.

Pauline was, of course, highly qualified to teach, having been educated by her parents who were both teachers and through the musical instruction we know she received. Her father, Charles Clairmont, wrote to his step-sister, Mary Shelley, in a letter dated 1–23 November 1845 indicating that Pauline "speaks English, French and German almost equally well, and is . . . quite a proficient on the Piano. She is considered one of the best female dilettanti in our capital" (*CC* II: 462). Writing to his half-sister Claire Clairmont on 29 June 1847, Charles deemed Pauline's musical abilities as "positively distinguished" (*CC* II: 482). He later portrayed Pauline's accomplishments in a letter to Claire dated 22 September 1847: "my two eldest girls [Clara and Pauline], without having neglected the usual elements of genteel education, speak and write three languages correctly and fluently besides a little Italian and are excellent musicians, especially Pauline" (*CC* II: 483). Pauline's mother, Antonia Clairmont, told her sister-in-law, Claire Clairmont, in a letter dated 12 December 1839 that she would not send Pauline to England in 1839 "on account of her studies not being finished, especially her music in which she makes astonishing progress; we have this winter taken a first rate master for her at 5. s. per lesson and it would be a pity to break off" (*CFL* I: 2). Her mother's opinion of Pauline's choice to be an educator may indeed have been shaped by love and pride. For example, on 25 April 1850 and prior to Pauline's departure for Britain, Antonia wrote to Claire in which she reflected on Pauline's well-placed contacts and credentials:

> . . . she has the highest recommendations one can have, both with regard to her musical attainments and to the general respectability of herself and family, and some pleasant introductions of the most distinguished kind, one to the duchess of Kent by good kind Count Menzdorf, and another to Lady Flora Macdonald by Miss H. the governess of Archduchess Mary Caroline so that she comes into the immediate neighbourhood of Her Majesty the Queen and can hardly fail of success if her endeavours are equal to her good luck.[3]
>
> (*CFL* I: 80)

In May 1850, Antonia informed Claire that Pauline had made some important contacts while staying with the Austrian ambassador in Berlin on her way to Britain. These contacts, she opined "would be useful to her in her carreer in London" (Antonia's spelling; p. 82). Alluding to Pauline's credentials, Antonia wrote Claire on 22 July 1850, that she thought "it could not be so difficult to find a place for her" (p. 93), although she expressed discontent with Pauline's apparent independence: "to be sure it would be a good thing to have her settled; . . . if she were married, to a good man, capable of guiding her she will turn out well – it was partly her giving lessons, which gave her that feeling of independence and habits of free movements so pernicious in a young female – therefore Emily [Antonia's younger daughter] shall never give lessons, rather gain her livelihood with needlework, and remain under my own eye" (p. 93).

Most working women lacked the resources and the contacts Pauline brought to the job search. Nonetheless, amongst middle-class women, governessing was a common profession at the time that Pauline held it. Kathryn Hughes suggests that there were some 25,000 governesses working in the profession in Great Britain in the mid-nineteenth century (Hughes 2001: xi), a figure that aligns with the 1851 census count that in Britain two percent of "all unmarried women between twenty and forty" self-identified as governesses, given the size of the population at the time (Brandon 2008: 1). Hughes quotes British census numbers from 1861 which showed that 24,770 women entered the governess profession in England and Wales, a few short years after Pauline departed for Australia (Hughes 2001: 22). Recent research illuminates the status of governesses. Mills states that "governessing was one of the few paid occupations open to middle-class women in the nineteenth century" (Mills 2018: 72); however, she observes that the difficulties they encountered were "of immense importance ... Governesses were underpaid, overworked and had no financial security. The sheer numbers of women seeking employment lowered their market value while increasing employers' concerns about educational standards" (p. 72). In her study of British-born women seeking positions in foreign countries between 1862 and 1882, Patricia Clarke considers the "educated" governess who was unable to find a position in Britain (Clarke 1985: 1). Like Charlotte Brontë's fictional Jane Eyre, who secured a job as governess to Adèle Varens, Mr. Rochester's ward, governesses were supposed to be "well-bred and genteel, yet materially they were poor and deprived" (p. 21). Yet, unlike Jane Eyre, Pauline was no orphan, nor was she as impoverished as Jane. As Hughes observes, "becoming a governess was the only acceptable way of earning money open to the increasing number of middle-class women whose birth and education defined them as ladies, yet whose families were unable to support them in leisure" (Hughes 2001: xvi). Hughes notes too that the vocation "remained the only resort for the many middle-class girls who continued to be prepared for the drawing-room but unexpectedly found themselves obliged to support themselves in later life" (p. 196). She writes of governesses at the time that they were "family member[s] who [were] sometimes mistaken for a servant," although Pauline's journal makes it clear this was not an experience she suffered (p. xvi).

Pauline's travel to a foreign country in search of employment was not unusual; Clarke documents that many women became governesses in overseas colonies due to the "lack of opportunity for marriage or for work in the home country" (Clarke 1985: 4). Hughes suggests that governesses sought work in the colonies "to escape the over-supplied domestic market" (Hughes 2001: xv). Foreign job searches became critical in helping women to secure new employment: "a series of philanthropic initiatives between 1840–90 aimed to help single, educated women start a new life, chiefly in Australia and New Zealand" (p. xv). Hammerton documents that the number of women in Great Britain outnumbered men by the middle of the nineteenth century, a fact he attributes to high male infant mortality rates, men's emigration to the colonies, and men's longtime engagement in the navy and the military (Hammerton 1979: 28). As a result, the state encouraged women to go to the colonies. Hughes shows that British governesses were "in demand" in foreign countries throughout Europe and the colonies by "families who wished to provide their offspring with a smattering" of British culture (Hughes 2001, xv). Similarly, Satyasikha Chakraborty affirms that in homes in Indian princely states in the late-nineteenth century, "there was a demand for European women as caregivers – medically trained nurses, nannies who could teach western etiquette and governesses who could teach English. The majority of nurses/governesses were British, although several German, French and occasionally American women also applied and were appointed in princely households" (Chakraborty 2018: 27). As Pauline spoke excellent English, she would have been understood as British, and thus would have appealed to employers seeking to provide English-language instruction to their children. Thus, Pauline's choice of a vocation as an educator-governess aligns itself with the opportunities available to her at the time.

In the early Victorian period Australia would have been an odd choice for a governess, as it was associated with "convict transportation, distress, depravity and prostitution," which, as Hammerton notes, "work[ed] as a deterrent against any system of middle-class emigration in the early-Victorian period" (Hammerton 1979: 46–47). In the 1830s, "The women sought for Australia were domestic and farm servants who would first relieve overworked colonial wives and eventually make wives themselves for the rough convict and settler populations. It was not a world made for Britain's distressed gentlewomen" (p. 54). But by 1853, when Pauline would depart for Australia, the Australian enterprise was touted as superior for British women, part of the "eventual intrusion" of "refined young lad[ies]" "into that world" according to Hammerton (p. 54). As Hammerton asserts, reformers and others saw "female emigration, in various forms, as solutions" to various issues (p. 53). Julia Barst shows how nineteenth-century emigration to Australia "was often encouraged as a solution to a less-than-perfect life in England" and that even before 1851 (when the Australian gold rush began), "attitudes about Australia were shifting: previously viewed as an isolated and dangerous convict dumping ground, the colony was becoming a land of hope and opportunity" (Barst 2011: 201). Barst reveals that women were "encouraged to emigrate to Australia to find domestic work (and husbands)" and that they received financial support from the British government to do so (p. 201). As a result of the gold rush in Australia and settlement in New Zealand, by 1853, according to Hammerton "female emigration [to Australia and New Zealand] assumed a unique importance [in the minds of British colonizers] and prompted a serious discussion on the role of women in the founding of new societies. In the process the issue of female emigration itself became instrumental in revolutionising the appeal of emigration to the middle classes, but more importantly the changes in attitude laid the foundation for more ambitious and enduring ventures to assist educated women to emigrate" (p. 92). Indeed, Hammerton opines, "The history of early-Victorian female emigration is thus partly an account of [Australia's] gradual emergence from this hostile stereotype; it is also an uncharacteristic story of women who were sufficiently courageous to defy the conventions which bound them" (p. 47).

Catherine Bishop and Angela Woollacott discuss women in Australia who sought more political representation in the 1850s. Although employment opportunities were "limited in the colonies," they articulate that as Australia ceased to be a penal colony "various schemes" ensued that "imported single women on free passages, initially to work as domestic servants but also in the hope that they would become wives for the disproportionately high number of single men in the Australian colonies" (Bishop and Woollacott 2016: 86). Many of these women, they argue, became energized by the women's suffragette movements that were prevalent in the United States and Britain, and they sought to achieve economic and political independence. Like these women, Pauline was conscious of defying societal norms that sometimes coded the British woman emigrant as different, possibly poor, troubled, and a figure of contempt by disregarding social stereotypes and traveling to a location in which she could exercise her right to earn her own living.

With the lack of available job prospects in Britain, women looked overseas for employment and the call to improve women's education became allied with helping women get access to these new opportunities. Hughes explains that migration of governesses fits within a broader landscape of social change. As she writes, "It is no coincidence that the governess' 'plight' [meaning the tight job market and the possible poverty they faced in England] and the impulse to relieve it became a catalyst for the most important educational and employment reforms to effect middle-class women during the second half of the nineteenth century" (Hughes 2001: xvi). She suggests that governesses sought work in the colonies "to escape the over-supplied domestic market" and she documents "a series of philanthropic initiatives between 1840–90 aimed to help single, educated women start a new life, chiefly in Australia and New Zealand" (p. xv). Likewise, the thin opportunities for women to become educated in the first half of the century ceded to expansion of women's schools in the second half, notably the 1848 launching of Queen's College, Harley Street under the auspices of Frederick Denison Maurice (1805–1872): "Established as the most progressive of the enterprises of the Governesses' Benevolent Institution, Queen's College both met the immediate needs of the governesses and developed a full-scale experiment in the academic education of young women" (Gordon 1955: 144). (Such advances had their detractors, as evidenced in an 1873 pamphlet stating, "No one denies that providing for the education of girls is a desirable object; but why is it to be done at the expense of the education of boys?" quoted in Fletcher p. 70, from "The Endowed Schools Commission: shall it be continued?" Department of Education and Science Library.) Sheila Fletcher explains that the absence of "adequate education" (Fletcher 2008: 12) made it more difficult for women overall. Yet, even with attempts to correct the situation, women remained woefully undereducated. This lack of advancement in women's education meant that improvements in job opportunities were few.

Scholars have identified the role of the bourgeoning women's movement in this period. Sarah Dredge, for example, documents organizations such as the Owenites in the 1830s and 1840s that aimed to "reconceiv[e society] in order to achieve sexual equality" (Dredge 2006: 134). Dredge explains that feminist concerns included "marriage law reform, professional opportunities, higher education for women, [and] female suffrage" (p. 135), many of which may have driven women to seek employment opportunities in the colonies where sometimes, such as in Australia, women were able to participate in the economy (see Bishop and Woollacott). Pauline wrote her mother from Australia in November 1853 that her "principal object" was "to make money" (*CFL* 1: 161). We know that the Clairmont family had little financial success since the 1850 death of Charles Clairmont, and that Antonia Clairmont relied on the generosity of Claire Clairmont and of her son-in-law, Alexander Knox, for money on which to live. Knox provided financial support which allowed Wilhelm and Pauline the opportunity to travel and, as explained in the introduction to this edition, Claire's legacy from Percy Shelley's will (which she came into after the 1844 death of Sir Timothy Shelley) enabled her to support her brother's family.

Pauline's choice to become an educator parallels that of her aunt, Claire Clairmont, who had also been a governess, but under decidedly different circumstances. As we know, Claire gave birth to her daughter, Allegra, in 1817 but the child's father, Lord Byron, removed his daughter from Claire's care when Allegra was a year old, which British law entitled him to do. Claire never her daughter again, as Allegra died in 1822 while in a convent in Bagnacavallo, in the province of Ravenna, Italy. Claire's position as a governess in Russia was a means of escape from this terrible sadness. Her letters home were largely negative in their comments on the governess profession and on the type of education she was providing. For example, on 29 April 1825 she wrote to Mary Shelley from Moscow, "A [male] tutor is ten thousand times happier than a governess, because boys may jump and play, but girls must be in a perpetual state of etiquette, which constraint spoils their disposition, by forcing it from its natural channel into a narrow space" (*CC* I: 215). Pauline, on the other hand, expressed satisfaction in her letters home. And while the primary factor was probably not having such a profound sense of grief as her aunt had experienced decades earlier, a looser approach to gender may have played a role. For example, one of her pupils was a boy. But she also seems to have been more in accord with her employers in her understanding of her job than her aunt had been. Claire acknowledged that she had tried to instill educational principles contrary to the philosophies espoused by her employers: "I may safely say the Russians and I are always at cross purposes – they pull one way, and I another – they educate a child by making the external work upon the internal, which is, in fact, nothing but an education fit for monkies, and is a mere system of imitation – I want the internal to work upon the external; that is to say, that my pupil should be left at liberty as much as possible, and that her own reason should be the prompter of her actions" (p. 215). As a result, she wrote to Mary Shelley, she had become convinced that she had "the reputation of being the worst governess in all Moscow" (p. 215). Pauline would describe greater success in her chosen vocation. Decades later Pauline wrote to her aunt on 8 July 1853, that she felt she was "likely to be flourishing in a very short time" and she described the Suttors as a "nice agreable family" (Pauline's spelling, *CFL* 1: 153). Her confidence in her achievements shone through her letter: "when I found that my accomplishments were at such a premium I made my conditions accordingly – & I think I shall be very comfortable & happy with my 3 pupils two girls & a boy" (p. 153). She also conveyed to Claire that the city of Bathurst was considered "very comfortable, a horse will be at my disposal & a piano in my own room. Does not all this seem very promising?" (p. 153). On 31 July 1853, she again described the Suttors as "very agreable," noting "they are all kind to me as the day is long. I have 3 children to teach it is true, but every comfort & luxury. They keep a very nice carriage." While the availability of the horse was slightly more equivocal, "I can very often have a horse to ride," she concluded, "In short I am as comfortable & happy as one can be" (Pauline's spelling, pp. 154–155). A letter to her mother dated 22 November 1853 showed similar content: "I am getting on very well comparatively speaking . . . I have been really uncommonly fortunate, and enjoying all the comforts of a well furnished house live with the most generous & agreeable people & receive a salary of £140, which will continue at least I hope for some years till Willy [Pauline's brother, Wilhelm Clairmont] is able to offer you something better" (p. 161). This last sentence likely referred to sending her mother remittances, and the "something better" the possibility that her brother would at some point have more than she. Indeed, she noted that her earnings were "a miserable pittance compared to what any fool of a man can earn," observing, "But I will not grumble" (p. 161). Pauline further remarked on the beautiful surroundings, her "secluded" environment, the relative ease of her charges, and the piano she continued to enjoy playing (p. 161). Even when she was despondent, as her letter to Claire dated 22 and 27 March, 1854 indicated, complaining of the solitary life in Bathurst and her discontent with the people she encountered there, she still conveyed satisfaction in her job: "my only pleasures are books & my piano & it is a good job" (p. 167). In a letter to her sister, Emily Clairmont, dated 8 July 1855, Pauline expressed grief over the death of their sister, Clara Knox, but nonetheless communicated her own material content: "Nun meine beste Emi leb wol, ich wünsch von Herzen dß es dir wol gehe wo du jetzt bist – so gut wie mir denn was äußerliche Umstände betrifft bin ich sehr zufrieden" (*CFL* I: 179–180, translation by Ann Sherwin: "Now, my dearest Emi, farewell. From my heart I wish you well where you are now, as well as I am; for as to external circumstances I am very content").

Even though Pauline did not intentionally sign up with one of the societies that facilitated female emigration to Australia, she became part of the movement to ameliorate the state of education for settlers in British colonies. While she left for Australia in 1853, earlier nineteenth-century colonial administrations had sought to improve education in several colonial outposts, as Jean Gelman Taylor writes in *The Social World of Batavia: European and Eurasians in Colonial Indonesia*. For example, Taylor's investigation of both the Dutch and British colonial occupations of Batavia reveals that for the short British occupation, from 1811 to 1815, various administrators expressed concern over the absence of educational facilities for both men and women. Taylor quotes Major William Thorn, who stated in his *Memoir of the Conquest of Java, with the Subsequent Operations of the British Forces in the Oriental Archipelago* (published in 1815) that "public teachers of any note are not to be found in Batavia . . . and therefore the culture of the youthful mind of either sex is, at the present day, most shamefully neglected" (quoted in Taylor 2009: 102). As a result, Taylor explains, the British sought to "encourage public education" (p. 102). For example, Lieutenant Governor Thomas Stamford Raffles provided books, such as "English spellers, grammars, geography texts, the *Polite Preceptor*, copies of Aesop's fables, and French primers" (p. 102). Likewise, "a consignment of book for adults announced in the *Gazette* in 1814 included 'new novels,' essays on government and literature, prayer books, dictionaries, and 'pamphlets' etc." (p. 102). For the period of British rule in Batavia, the administration tried to reform the state of education in the colony. The vestiges of this first attempt at reform can be found in the years of the later nineteenth century when the ruling Dutch sought to encourage governesses to migrate to Indonesia. Advertisements requesting governesses were abundant and Taylor cites a few such examples. For example, advertisements from *De Locomotief, Samarangsch Handels en Advertentie-Blad* of 27 January 1865 and 21 January 1885 read as follows: "Wanted: a governess, aged between thirty and forty, of the Reformed faith" and "Wanted: a Governess . . . to teach French, Dutch and music" (p. 139). Taylor notes that while "qualified teachers were scarce outside Batavia," "conversational powers and accomplishments were more important than a grounding in arithmetic, for example, and formal qualifications in the teacher" (p. 139). However, despite Taylor's conclusion, Pauline's employers, the Suttor family, strived to provide their children with a much sought-after education by someone whom they considered to be well-educated.

William Henry Suttor (1805–1877) and his wife, Charlotte Augusta Anne Francis Suttor (1817–1879), hired Pauline to teach their twelve-year-old daughter Caroline Suttor (known as Carry, 1841–1921), their fourth child, and her cousin Ruth Amelia Simpson (known as Minna, 1838–1880) on their estate at Brucedale which was situated about 12 kilometers northeast from the town of Bathurst. The third student Pauline referenced in her 8 July 1853 letter was likely George Roxburgh Suttor (1844–1928) the fifth child in the family. The decision to hire Pauline suggests that the Suttor family held a relatively traditional view; other colonizers in Australia were embracing a different approach to promoting educational norms and innovation. For example, in "Periodicals for Schools in Nineteenth Century Australia: Catherine Helen Spence and the *Children's Hour*," Anne Jamison observes that children's literature in Australia during the nineteenth century "embodies the anxieties and the desires of the British colonial enterprise in Australia" (Jamison 2017: 721). She argues that the works of Catherine Helen Spence (1825–1910) for children as well as others are related to the understanding that "the fate of the nation or colony depended on its young citizens receiving a decent education" (p. 722). For Spence, educating Australians meant looking to

Australia instead of to the colonizing country for inspiration and she railed against those who considered England the primary locus of important educational ideas: "Spence's short stories for children actively contributed to the debate over how best to provide Australian children with a moral education, one that would benefit South Australia both politically and economically" (p. 732). Charlotte Suttor, it appears, held a competing ideology and Pauline's employment resulted from the Suttor family's desire to provide a British (or continental)-style education for their children rather than one that supported Australian values.

While Pauline was probably hired due to her excellent credentials, she was quite different from the stereotypical British governess particularly of the first half of the nineteenth century, as she was independent, extremely well-read, musical, and connected to a group as illustrious and literate as the Shelley-Godwin circle. Indeed, Charlotte Suttor's 1853 diary attests to her satisfaction with Pauline and her credentials: "We engaged a lady as governess for Caroline she had just arrived in Sydney, she is highly educated and brought out letters of Introduction to some of the first people here, she is of German birth, her name is Clairmont she is an excellent musician and I hope, and think I shall find her what I wish, she is a most agreeable companion we pay her a high salary, but I hope dear Caroline will reap the advantage of it'" (*Charlotte Augusta Anne Suttor Diaries, 1848–1853*, pp. 228–229; see also Norton and Norton 1993: 139). Suttor's journal includes numerous references to Pauline and her confidence in her. She mentions Pauline beginning to teach her charges, noting that "on the 25th the boys returned to school and Miss Clairmont commenced her duties with Carry and Minna, up to the present time I have had every reason to think most highly of her. She is a most agreeable companion and I feel a very warm attachment to her – I feel sure she is worthy of the serious trust I have reposed in her the education of my dear girls" (*Charlotte Augusta Anne Suttor Diaries 1848–1853*, p. 230). Suttor also records a fall from a horse Pauline experienced, stating that Pauline was "not seriously hurt – although much shaken" (p. 230). Later, Suttor observes that she and Pauline "took a very pleasant walk, the murmurs of the bees amongst the blossoms" on a "beautiful day after the rain, but rather cold for the time of year" (p. 232). On Sunday, October 16, she chronicles that "the children with Miss Clairmont gone to church" (p. 232), showing once again her faith in Pauline. The fact that William Henry and Charlotte Suttor may have named their sixth child, Sarah Pauline, after Pauline (born in November 1853) possibly further emphasizes the strong connection between Pauline and her employers.

The near-equal status Pauline had in the Suttor family's home was unusual. Most governesses to the colony were from poor middle-class families and while Pauline's family suffered financially, she was aware of her excellent social connections. As an emigrant who chose to travel without the backing of an official employment agency, Pauline experienced few of the problems that Clarke describes for most governesses who traveled to Australia. Many governesses attached to an agency (such as the Female Middle Class Emigration Society, founded in 1862 by Maria Rye and Jane Lewin) traveled in second class which caused them significant "physical discomforts" due to "too many passengers to a cabin and [the fact that] any small material comforts, so necessary on a long sea voyage, had to be provided by the passengers themselves" (Clarke 1985: 25). Barst explains that from 1831 the British government sponsored "assisted emigration schemes" which resulted in large numbers of emigrants to Australia (Barst 2011: 203). However, these new arrivals often "endured great hardships such as starvation, abuse, and homelessness" which was countered by philanthropists such as Caroline Chisholm (1808–1877) who provided help (p. 203). As an emigrant who considered herself educated and well-connected, Pauline experienced few such difficulties, and the Suttor family's positive reception to their governess made for a much easier adjustment to Pauline's new station in life. However, some of Pauline's letters home and her journal anticipate many mid- to late-Victorian writings about life in Australia, such as those of Louisa Agnes Geoghegan, whose letters written from Neuarpurr in Western Victoria, Australia, were penned in the 1860s. Clarke identifies Geoghegan's as those of the "first governess to write about life on an isolated station property," "starkly" recording her "shock at the loneliness, isolation, hardships and tragedies of life in the outback" (Clarke 1985: 103). Miss M. A. Oliver was even less, in Clarke's term, "tolerant" of similar conditions when she succeeded Geoghegan in 1871, as Clarke records (p. 108). While Pauline also found life at Brucedale solitary and isolating at times (in a letter to Claire Clairmont, dated 22 and 27 March 1854, she recorded being "literally imprisoned night & day in a house & garden a hundred yards square & as for going to any place beyond a mile it is such an unheard of piece of independence in the eyes of these narrowminded colonists, that the first & only time I attempted a little stroll by myself – terror seized all the inmates of the house when they became aware of my absence" [*CFL* I: 166]), she clearly interacted socially with the Suttor family, particularly with Charlotte Suttor whom she came to regard as a friend. It is likely that Pauline's social class and connections allowed her access to the Suttor family's social circle, which Geoghegan and Oliver would have been unlikely to have experienced.

Turning now to the genre of life writing, we see that Pauline embraced it by penning at least sixteen volumes of it. From the one extant volume, we can infer that her corpus of life writing follows the type of writing both Mary Wollstonecraft and Claire Clairmont practiced. Researchers have described the genre in various ways and have noted its importance to eighteenth- and nineteenth-century studies. For example, Linder argues that nineteenth-century collaborative life writing "highlights the significance of the genre and form of life writing to the construction and representation of identity. Contradictions between texts written for private and social communication on the one hand and those intended for public consumption on the other can reveal tensions between public discourses and the private realities of nineteenth-century men and women" (Linder 2016: 123), while Anne Markey indicates that "another fruitful advance in studies of romanticism is the burgeoning attention being paid to unpublished works written during the period, both by critical analysis of material available only in manuscript form and by first publication of such material (Markey 2014: 559). Amy Culley confirms that life writing "is now established as an essential element of women's authorial experience" (Culley 2015: 2) and she provides an excellent survey of women's life writing in the eighteenth and early nineteenth centuries. Culley shows how the erroneous idea that "the 18th-century autobiographical self was male" allowed for a "shift from autobiography to the more flexible 'life writing'" which has resulted in "a dynamic canon addressing diverse forms such as auto/biographies, memoirs, diaries, journals and letters, by a wider range of authors including women, labouring class writers and slaves and ex-slave amongst others" (Culley 2015: 1). She identifies Mary Wollstonecraft's *Letters Written during a Short Residence in Sweden, Norway, and Denmark*, Dorothy Wordsworth's *Journals* (the *Alfoxden Journal* [1798] and *Grasmere Journals* [1800–1803]), and the writings of Lady Mary Wortley Montagu, Hester Thrale, and Frances Burney[4] as works that helped establish the "emerging canon" which included "the scandalous memoir and spiritual autobiography . . . diaries and letters . . . and Mary Wollstonecraft's travelogue, which was rightfully positioned as a central contribution to self-representation in the Romantic period" (p. 2). In *Reading Autobiography: A Guide For Interpreting Life Narratives*, Smith and Julia Watson define life writing "as a general term for writing that takes a life, one's own or another's, as its subject. Such writing can be biographical, novelistic, historical, or explicitly self-referential and therefore autobiographical" (Smith and Watson 2010: 4). They describe the journal as "a form of life writing that records events and occurrences" (p. 272) and they explain that "journaling is the practice of regular, free life writing" (p. 273). While they acknowledge that there are those critics who "distinguish diary from journal by characterizing the journal as a chronicle of public record that is less intimate than the diary", they observe that others, such as Philippe Lejeune, employ the categories "interchangeably" (p. 273). The diary, they clarify, is a "form of periodic life writing" which "records dailiness in accounts and observations of emotional responses" (p. 266). In discussing the letters written between Anna Jameson (1794–1860) and Ottilie von Goethe (1796–1872), Linda Hughes shows how "collaborative life writing" in the form of letter writing between two friends consists of "an exchange that could only be co-produced by long-time friends, an exchange embodying layered signification that may not be immediately apparent to others. Situating the exchange in a longer sequence of letters and intersecting personal experiences that have been documented, however, renders newly legible the women's shared emotions and the complexity of meaning embedded in their collaborative life writing" (Hugues 2016: 161). As I indicated in *The Kinship Coterie and the Literary Endeavors of the Women in the Shelley Circle*, Mary Shelley and Claire Clairmont participated in a form of coterie dialogue by responding to ideas first explored in Mary Wollstonecraft's writing, thereby anticipating Mikhail Bakhtin's notion of the future answer-word (Joffe 2007: 122). As part of the extended Shelley-Clairmont family, Pauline's writing builds upon the writings of those who came before her. She employs a genre that others in her circle had used to work through their various issues, both ordinary, day-to-day occurrences and internal conflicts. Thus her journal, which she titles "Journal from My Life Book"[5] (ironically using similar language to the genre of life writing and thus anticipating the genre) is filled with interior musings and reflections, much like the journals of Mary Shelley and Claire Clairmont, and contrasts starkly with Wilhelm's, which deals primarily with the daily incidents encountered in his travels or with practical information about his farm-buying enterprise and which does not display the interiority and depth of reflection exhibited in Pauline's 1855–1857 Australian journal. Susan Bassnett's description of gendered differences in travel writing suggest that this contrast was typical for women and men. Bassnett explains that for men, travel writing connects to the naming of foreign spaces – travelers named new places which "became a means of marking ownership, in both physical and intellectual terms" (in *The Cambridge Companion to Travel Writing* 2002: 231). Men therefore appropriated spaces through naming. By contrast, "women travellers had, then, to write about their experiences from within a tradition that denied them a role . . . These women have not been silenced, but have chosen to write about their experiences in full knowledge of the absence of a tradition into which they could insert themselves with any degree of comfort or familiarity" (p. 231). This understanding contextualizes Pauline's choice to keep her writing personal and private; certainly, her intimacy with the Shelleys would have acquainted her with the sometimes punishing reception women could face in seeking a wider audience. Unlike some women travelers who wrote expressly for publication or who later shaped private correspondence into publishable texts, Pauline chose to write for a private audience.

Pauline's sojourn in Australia should have given her ample opportunity to discuss her circumstances with her correspondents. However, only five letters out of the forty-four extant letters she (sometimes together with another family member such as Wilhelm or Antonia) wrote to Claire, Antonia, Wilhelm, and several non-relatives, all of which appear in *The Clairmont Family Letters*, depict her Australian stay. It is likely that many of her other letters have been lost. By contrast thirty-one letters Wilhelm penned while he was in Australia survive (along with 109 others). However, unlike her brother, Pauline was a prolific journal writer. While Wilhelm expressed his thoughts on his Australian enterprise in his letters, Pauline used her journals as a way to document and make sense of her experiences. This likely disparity results from the gendered nature of journal writing. Furthermore, even if we assume that some of Pauline's letters home have been lost or possibly destroyed, Wilhelm's prolific corpus of letter writing – as opposed to the paucity of his journal entries – marks the difference between men's and women's life writing.

Neither sibling had any apparent intention to publish their writing. This assertion becomes clearly apparent from the lack of attempts to revise; what we know of travel writing for publication, for example, provides markers of the private nature of their letters and Pauline's journal. As Smith and Watson record, "in the late eighteenth century [letters] began to be understood as both private correspondence expressing the inner feelings of the writing subject and as public documents to be shared within a literary circle" (Smith and Watson 2010: 273). Eve Tavor Bannet explains that since letters are "an intrinsically fragmentary, discontinuous and miscellaneous form," they were often "altered and adapted" when they were "revised for print publication" (in Pettinger and Youngs, *The Routledge Research Companion to Travel Writing* 2020: 115; 117). Travel letters, she opines, were usually "written, circulated in manuscript, printed, imitated in print and/or belletrised" (p. 117). Bannet identifies "sociable travel letters" as "the kind of travel letter that one wrote to friends and acquaintances while abroad" (p. 117). These travel letters were written "to safeguard relationships and one's place in society and to remind erstwhile companions of the value of their absent friend by once again interesting, informing and entertaining them" (p. 117). Those "sociable travel letters" later revised for publication adhered to specific forms which writers learned from instruction manuals. Bannet gives as examples *The Secretaries* (published in the late seventeenth century and in print until the mid-eighteenth century) and *The Complete Letter–Writer* (1755), both of which advised writers how to present their letters (p. 118). When sociable travel letters were eventually modified for publication, they were frequently edited and significantly altered from the originals. For example, revisions would omit more personal aspects of letters "along with the other party to the correspondence, what was particular to the writer or the writer's friends, and what was merely *fortuitous* about their travels, rather than what was subjective or personal" (emphasis original; p. 121). Bannet describes travel letters as "shape-changers ... frequently revised or extracted for different readerships, different purposes and different outlets, whether by their original authors, or by the author's descendants or by successive editors" (p. 125). Revisions were made, for example, depending on whether the letters formed part of a collection or whether they were printed individually in newspapers or in collections: "Even aside from any alterations made to the letters themselves, changing the location and thus the context of a letter changed its signification" (p. 125). Yet unlike these letters altered for publication purposes, Pauline and Wilhelm seem to have been entirely honest with their recipients in revealing their travel activities, their encounters with various people in different geographic locations, and their feelings towards the cities and locations visited. We note this observation too in Pauline's later letters written to friends and family in the 1880s from various European travel locations. More specifically for their time in Australia, both siblings reflected in their letters, sometimes negatively, their experiences in the Australian outback. They discussed the men and women encountered there, and the mores and traditions by which they were forced to abide. However, unlike Wilhelm's journal which is highly impersonal, Pauline's Australian journal is personal, intimate, truthful, and at times brutally honest in its expressions. Linder asserts that the Victorian journal "served not only as a familial record of domestic life, but also as a chronicle of social, political and national events, thereby positioning an auto/biographical text within the context of a larger – albeit imagined – community" (Linder 2016: 122). Such intimate writing was typical of women's writing at the time. Lynn Mastellotto argues that women's writing participates in a tradition that extends at least as long as from Susanna Moodie's 1852 account of her life in Canada (*Roughing It in the Bush*) to Frances Mayes's 1996 memoir, *Under the Tuscan Sun*. In juxtaposing these works, Mastellotto concludes that in spite of their differences, they are connected "by a common thread – the desire for greater freedom, self-determination and self-expansion that travel often affords women – which leads in both cases to a deliberate act of displacement and a prolonged process of cultural accommodation" (in Pettinger and Youngs *The Routledge Research Companion to Travel Writing* 2020: 61). Pauline's writing shows a similar sense of "cultural accommodation" as she self-displaced from Europe to embrace a new life in Australia. Her journal and letters allow for a deeper assessment of her new circumstances in a way that Wilhelm's journal writing does not.

Pauline's writing can also be classified as a form of travel literature. Texts such as *The Cambridge History of Travel Writing* (2019) and *The Routledge Research Companion to Travel Writing* (2020) document nineteenth-century travel literature without providing a singular definition of the genre. Michael Brennan elucidates the historical lack of consensus about definition and terminology, and the difficulty of affixing parameters. He states, "travel writing is now recognized as a diverse and ever-shifting genre, central to most literary cultures, but one which has never settled (and is unlikely to do so) into a unifying paradigm" (in Pettinger and Youngs, *The Routledge Research Companion to Travel Writing* 2020: 321). Carl Thompson observes that travel writing in the first part of the nineteenth century "remained chiefly focused on the external world, and individual texts typically adopted what now seems a remarkable inclusivity of theme and focus" (in Das and Youngs, *The Cambridge History of Travel Writing* 2019: 112). But, he notes, "it is no easy matter to provide a neat and unproblematic definition, or delimitation, of what counts as travel writing. The term is a very loose generic label, and has always embraced a bewilderingly diverse range of material. This is especially the case as one moves back in time, to consider travel writing in its earliest manifestations" (*Travel Writing* 2011: p. 11). Thompson quotes Jonathan Raban who sees travel writing as a genre that "accommodates the private diary, the essay, the short story, the prose poem, the rough note and polished table talk" (p. 11). Similarly, Nandini Das and Tim Youngs cite Raban and Thompson as well as Patrick Holland, Graham Huggan, and Barbara Korte, who themselves find the genre (in Korte's words) "not easily demarcated" and (per Thompson) "bewildering" (in Das and Youngs, *The Cambridge History of Travel Writing* 2019: 11). They conclude that travel writing "is open to multiple interpretations, each of which will reflect something of the beholder's position" (p. 16). Calling the genre "fluid" and "not fixed," they surmise that "those in the field are akin to travellers regarding the terrain" (p. 16). Thompson describes women travel writers as "a comparatively new phenomenon" in the nineteenth century, observing, "The late eighteenth century witnessed the beginnings of a female tradition in published voyages and travels, but it was not until the 1810s and 1820s that women became a substantial presence in the genre" (p. 113). He states that, like their male counterparts, they "made a significant contribution to the travel writing genre in the Victorian period, although this required them to negotiate the highly constraining norms of femininity that operated in this era ... Many nevertheless produced accounts of their travels, covering the spectrum from largely inconsequential sketches and reminiscences to more substantial interventions in contemporary aesthetic, intellectual and political debates" (*Travel Writing* 2011: 55–56).

Contrasting Wilhelm's journal with Pauline's suggests a difference between women's life writing and men's writing. Journals written by men traveling in European colonies, like Wilhelm's journal, often dealt less with interiority and more with the day-to-day occurrences than women's journals. Likewise "Meine Fussreise im Juli 1885" (see Chapter 4 of this edition), which may have been the work of Walter Clairmont, lacks interior musings and relies almost exclusively on fact-based information. Even though Carl Thompson shows that travel writing allows for a "digressiveness" which "permitted a more detailed portrayal of the interior world of the traveller" and that "the traveller's physical presence at a site will often be a spur for memories, reflections and imaginations that lead far away from the immediate surroundings" (*Travel Writing* 2011: 112), Wilhelm's and Walter's journals show no evidence of their "interior world" or of their interests in politics or current events. Had Wilhelm recorded more in his journal, we might have seen evidence of his political leanings or of his personal thoughts. However, given the paucity of entries, his journal seems merely to reflect on the daily events he experienced as he voyaged from Australia and back to Europe in search of a farm. Only when Wilhelm describes his 1861 encounter with his aunt Claire does he come near to allowing affect to permeate his writing (see his journal entry for 28 March 1861), highlighting once again the differences noted in the Clairmont siblings' respective journals.

Pauline's journal is an important artefact as it aligns with the British interest in colonial travel writing. Multiple texts exist from various British colonial outposts. In a statement that applies to Pauline's writings, Anna Johnston argues that travel is "a powerful trope" in travel writing from Australia during the colonial era, due to the continent's "mix of ancient and contemporary indigenous cultures, and modern settler and migrant cultures" (in Das and Youngs, *The Cambridge History of Travel Writing* 2019: 267). Johnson writes that Australia provided the source for many different genres of travel writing written by "official state-sponsored explorers ... independent adventurers; scientific observers; colonial officials and their families; naval personnel; writers and journalists seeking good 'copy'; and religious travellers" (p. 271). She states that "The colonial world was littered with curious Britons eager for information to use in narratives which they would circulate back home, either in publication or in private circles" (p. 271). Australia became the locus for narratives of exploration Johnston explains, suggesting that "travellers invoked Australia as a new land for exploration, exploitation, and opportunity. Journeys to the interior – from 1817, and from which only some returned – filled newspapers and were transformed into travel accounts" (p. 273). In spite of their private nature, Pauline's descriptions of Australia mimic the types of travel writing produced by those who published as Johnston describes them. As Pauline wrote for her own private audience (her letters were only intended for her family members and her journal was clearly not meant for public viewing), the genres of travel writing and of journal or diary writing are also significant ones to comprehend in the context of Pauline's life-writing. Indeed, these influences shed light on Pauline's life writing.

Cynthia Huff indicates that the travel journal is an example of a diary which fused both travel experiences with daily occurrences at home. She provides an interesting description of the category of "diary writing" when she expounds on the genre as it pertained to nineteenth-century British women. For these women, the diary became the conduit which enabled women to "embrace the flux of life, to store its nuances in a place of safe keeping, so that when the time came they could sift and evaluate the past, whether it was measured by the recurrence of birth and death or by tallying of accounts" (Huff 1985: ix). Studying varying journals that have survived but that, like Pauline's, were not necessarily written for publication, Huff writes that women diarists frequently corrected their diaries as if they expected audiences to read their works. Further, "when the diarists considered a word or a phrase objectionable, they wrote in a foreign language or employed dots and dashes" (p. xix). For example, Huff explains, Lady Marianne Brougham (1785–1865) in her life-writing during her travels in London, Paris, and Italy "crossed through"[6] (p. 3) references to her husband and "frequently use[d] French phrases to refer to unpleasant, unusual, or joyful circumstances, and . . . employ[ed] dots and dashes to express agitation and reserve" (p. 5). Likewise, Eliza Dickenson's (1818 – unknown) nine-volume journal written between 1836 and 1848, partly from India, employed "erasures and the razoring out of pages [which] occur when highly personal events take place" (p. 58). Dorothy Ward's (1874–1960) diary written in 1890 and 1898 "sometimes . . . uses French phrases and designates expletives she does not want to record by dashes for the letters they contain" (p. 88). Similarly, while Pauline wrote predominantly in English, she codeswitched to French and German on many occasions, sometimes writing in these languages for pages, probably, in line with Huff's analysis, to keep information about her relationship with William Henry Suttor from his parents for whom she worked. Huff's analysis supports the contention that Pauline wanted to hide "objectionable" material from future readers. Carol Myers-Scotton posits that "codeswitching of languages offers bilinguals a way to increase their flexibility of expression, going beyond the style-switching of monolinguals" (Myers-Scotton 1993: 1). Pauline's ability to codeswitch allows for such "flexibility" and for the secrecy that writing in a language known only to herself in the household where she was living provided. Her desire to hide her experiences by codeswitching confirms Jenny Davidson's assertion that "life-writers seem to oscillate between contradictory or even incompatible commitments, sometimes occupying a pole of narrative particularity but equally likely to draw a veil of generalization over unflattering particulars in the name of discretion or generosity" (Davidson 2015: 272). For Pauline, codeswitching becomes a way to hide those "unflattering particulars" (p. 272).

Pauline also recorded her attitudes towards the people whom she encountered in Australia, much like Mary Wollstonecraft and Mary Shelley did in their respective writings. Huff observes that travel journals often "reveal the writer's attitude towards foreigners" (Huff 1985: xxi), attitudes which were "quite xenophobic and contrast unfavorably the customs of others with their own" (p. xxii). Huff provides examples from British women's diaries in which the diarist juxtaposes British life with foreign life in order to position British life as superior, such as Lady Edith Lytton's (1842–1936) journal of her 1893 visit to Paris (p. 29). Similarly, Diana Ramsden's (birth and death dates are unknown) 1899–1900 journal written while she was in Queensland, Australia, provides "an account of her impressions and experiences, which contrast with British notions of Queensland" (p. 79). One sees this xenophobia in Mary Wollstonecraft's travel writing, a text with which both Mary Shelley and Claire Clairmont were familiar and presumably Pauline would have read,[7] and also in Mary Shelley's *History of a Six Weeks' Tour* (1817) which included her responses to places she visited and people she met during her travels on the continent with Percy Shelley. For example, in Wollstonecraft's *Letters Written during a Short Residence in Sweden, Norway, and Denmark*, she records her observations about her foreign surroundings. Indeed, Wollstonecraft's host "bluntly" expresses that he found her "a woman of observation" as she "asked him *men's questions*" (Wollstonecraft's emphasis; *Letters Written during a Short Residence in Sweden, Norway, and Denmark*, Horrocks [ed], 2013: 58). On occasions, Wollstonecraft was less than complimentary towards the people she encountered during her Scandinavian travels and reflected negatively on them in her letters. Similarly, Mary Shelley expressed her own xenophobia when she recorded her contempt for some of the people whom she met during her travels in *History of a Six Weeks' Tour*. As such, and in spite of her closeness with the Suttors, Pauline frequently coded herself as superior to the Australians in her letters and journals. For example, in her 22–27 March 1854 letter to Claire, she references the "narrowminded colonists" and the men who "are worse tyrants here than in Europe" (*CFL* I: 166). While she acknowledges that everyone is "very kind & generous," she does position herself as exceptional: "they [those whom she interacts with in Australia] have no sort of refinement no early education no training of any kind no command over their thoughts & feelings no regards for each other, which they most likely do not feel the want of but which grates rather sharply on the strings of my soul" (Pauline's emphasis; p. 167). Ironically, in spite of her feelings of disdain towards the men she encountered ("it is a good job I don't want to marry for I have not seen one man worth having" [p. 167]), Pauline would find love (and the expectation of marriage) with William Suttor.

Finally, as a conclusion, we turn back to Smith and Watson who provide us with two observations about eighteenth- and nineteenth-century life writing that inform Pauline's work. They conclude that in eighteenth-century England, "middle-class women who were sufficiently educated wrote letters . . . and kept diaries . . ., seemingly the marginal forms of marginal subjects that since have been revalued as precise records of everyday life" (Smith and Watson 2010: 116–117), and they explain that nineteenth-century travel narratives frequently "represented acts of female agency in the midst of continuing bourgeois constraints that coded travel as a male activity" (p. 119). In reading both Pauline's and Wilhelm's journals, we see that gendered differences, heightened perhaps by the urgency in Wilhelm's case to acquire a farm in Europe, make for two very different types of journal writing resulting from a brother and sister who all too often wrote to one another and to their family members about pressing concerns. These issues, so interestingly expressed in letter form, are voiced very differently in their individual journals. As this chapter indicates, the genre of life writing and the profession of governess intersected for Pauline as she penned both her letters and her extant journal. Pauline's and Wilhelm's journals are thus significant documents for not only do readers learn more about the siblings' respective lives and the people with whom they interacted but also the manuscripts themselves become important examples of the genre of nineteenth-century life writing.

Notes

1 See *The Letters of Mary Wollstonecraft Shelley* (edited by Betty Bennett, 1980), *The Journals of Mary Shelley, 1814–1844* (edited by Paula Feldman and Diana Scott-Kilvert, 1987), *The Journals of Claire Clairmont* (edited by Marion Kingston Stocking, 1968) and *The Clairmont Correspondence* (edited by Marion Kingston Stocking, 1995).
2 In Huddersfield, West Yorkshire, England, the institute offered classes from 1847 until 1883.
3 Antonia references Queen Victoria (1819–1901; "her Majesty, the Queen") who ruled from 1837–1901. The Duchess of Kent (1786–1861) was Queen Victoria's mother. Count Alexander von Mensdorff-Pouilly (1813–1871) was a diplomat and first cousin to Queen Victoria. Flora Macdonald was a lady-in-waiting to Queen Victoria. Charles Clairmont dedicated his *First Poetical-Reading Book in the English Language* (1845) to Archduchess Mary Caroline (Maria Karoline, 1825–1915), daughter of Archduke Charles and Princess Henrietta. Archduke Charles was the third son of the Holy Roman Emperor Leopold II.
4 Dorothy Wordsworth (1771–1855) was William Wordsworth's sister. She wrote journals and poetry. Lady Mary Wortley Montagu (1689–1762) wrote letters, essays, and poetry; Hester Lynch Piozzi (known as Thrale [1740–1821]) was a Welsh diarist and friend of Samuel Johnson about whom she wrote and whose letters she published; Frances Burney (1752–1840) penned novels such as *Evelina* (1778) and *Cecilia* (1782), as well as numerous letters and journals.
5 In German, "Tagebuch v. m. Lebensbuch".
6 Meaning "crossed out".
7 Claire recorded in her journal that "Shelley reads aloud the Letters from Norway – This is one of my very favorite Books – The language is so (ve) very flowing & Eloquent & it is altogether a beautiful Poem" (*The Journals of Claire Clairmont*, Stocking [ed], 1968: 33).

Bibliography

Bakhtin, M., *The Dialogic Imagination* (Austin: University of Texas Press, 1981).

Barst, J., "Pushing the Envelope: Caroline Chisholm, Colonial Australia, and the transformative power of postal networks," *Prose Studies*, 33:3 (2011), pp. 200–216.

Bishop, C., and A. Woollacott, "The Australian Colonies and the Mid-Nineteenth Century Women's Movement," *Journal of Women's History*, 28:1 (2016), pp. 84–106.

Brandon, R., *Governess: The Life and Times of the Real Jane Eyres* (New York: Walker & Company, 2008).

Bourrier, K., "Dinah Mulock Craik and Benjamin Mulock," *Prose Studies*, 33:3 (2011), pp. 174–187.

Buss, H. and M. Kadar (eds.), *Working in Women's Archives: Researching Women's Private Literature and Archival Documents* (Ontario: Wilfrid Laurier University Press, 2001).

Chakraborty, S., "European Nurses and Governesses in Indian Princely Households: 'Uplifting that impenetrable veil'?" *Journal of Colonialism and Colonial History*, 19:1 (Spring 2018), pp. 25–49.

Civale, S., "Women's Life Writing and Reputation: A Case Study of Mary Darby Robinson," *Romanticism*, 24:2 (2018), pp. 191–202.

Clarke, P., *The Governesses: Letters From the Colonies 1862–1882* (London: Hutchinson, 1985).

Culley, A., "Women's Life Writing in the Long 18th Century: A Critical Survey," *Literature Compass*, 12:1 (2015), pp. 1–11.

Das, N. and T. Youngs (eds.), *The Cambridge History of Travel Writing* (Cambridge: Cambridge University Press, 2019).

Davidson, J., "The 'Minute Particular' in Life-Writing," *Eighteenth – Century Studies*, 48:3 (2015), pp. 263–281.

Davis, G. V. and P. Marsden (eds.), *Towards a Transcultural Future* (Amsterdam: Rodopi, 2005).

Dredge, S., "Opportunism and Accommodation: The *English Woman's Journal* and the British Mid-Nineteenth-Century Women's Movement," *Women's Studies*, 34 (2006), pp. 133–157.

Favret, M., *Romantic Correspondence: Women, Politics, and the Fiction of Letters* (Cambridge: Cambridge University Press, 1993).

Field, J., "Domestic service, gender, and wages in rural England, c. 1700–1860," *The Economic History Review*, 66:1 (2013), pp. 249–272.

Fletcher, S., *Feminists and Bureaucrats: A Study in the Development of Girls' Education in the Nineteenth Century* (Cambridge: Cambridge University Press, 2008).

Gerrard, T. and A. Weedon, "Working-Class Women's Education in Huddersfield: A Case Study of the Female Educational Institute Library, 1856–1857," *Information & Culture*, 49:2 (2014), pp. 234–264.

Gordon, S., "Studies at Queen's College, Harley Street, 1848–1868," *British Journal of Educational Studies*, 3:2 (1955), pp. 144–154.

Hammerton, A. J., *Emigrant Gentlewomen: Genteel Poverty and Female Emigration, 1830–1914* (London: Croom Helm, 1979).

Huff, C., *British Women's Diaries* (New York: Ams Press, 1985).

Hugues, K., *The Victorian Governess* (London: Hambledon and London, 2001).

Hugues, L., "'Given in Outline and No More': The Shared Life Writing of Anna Jameson and Ottilie von Goethe," *Forum for Modern Language Studies*, 52:2 (2016), pp. 160–171.

Hulme, P. and T. Youngs (eds.), *The Cambridge Companion to Travel Writing* (Cambridge: Cambridge University Press, 2002).

Jamison, A., "Periodicals for Schools in Nineteenth-Century Australia: Catherine Helen Spence and the *Children's Hour*," *Victorians Periodicals Review*, 50:4 (Winter 2017), pp. 721–736.

Joffe, S.L. (ed.), *The Clairmont Family Letters, 1839–1889* (London and New York: Routledge, 2017).

Joffe, S.L., *The Kinship Coterie and the Literary Endeavors of the Women in the Shelley Circle* (New York: Peter Lang, 2007).

Kadar, M. (ed.), *Reading Life Writing: An Anthology* (Toronto: Oxford University Press, 1993).

Kauffman, L., *Special Delivery: Epistolary Modes in Modern Fiction* (Chicago: University of Chicago Press, 1992).

Linder, L., "Co-Constructed Selves: Nineteenth-Century Collaborative Life Writing," *Forum for Modern Language Studies*, 52: 2 (2016), pp. 121–129.

Markey, A., "*Selene*: Lady Mount Cashell's Lunar Utopia," *Women's Writing*, 21:4 (2014), pp. 559–574.

McGeevor, S., "How well did the nineteenth century census record women's 'regular' employment in England and Wales? A case study of Hertfordshire in 1851," *The History of the Family*, 19:4 (2014), pp. 489–512.

Mills, M., "Female Education as a Theme in the Novels of Charlotte Brontë," *Brontë Studies*, 43:1 (2018), pp. 71–77.

Myers-Scotton, C., *Duelling Languages: Grammatical Structure in Codeswitching* (New York: Oxford University Press, 1993).

Norton, J., and H. Norton, *Dear William: The Suttors of Brucedale: Principally the Life and Times of William Henry Suttor Senior ("Dear William"), 1805–1877* (Sydney: Suttor Pub. Committee, 1993).

Pettinger, A. and T. Youngs (eds.), *The Routledge Research Companion to Travel Writing* (Abingdon: Routledge, 2020).

Smith, S. and J. Watson (eds.), *Women, Autobiography, Theory: A Reader* (Madison: University of Wisconsin Press, 1998).

Smith, S. and J. Watson, *Reading Autobiography: A Guide for Interpreting Life Narratives* (Minneapolis: University of Minnesota Press, 2010).

Stocking, M. K., "Miss Tina and Miss Plin: The Papers Behind *The Aspern Papers*," in D. Reiman (ed.), *The Evidence of the Imagination* (New York: New York University Press, 1978), pp. 372–384.

Stocking, M. K. (ed.), *The Journals of Claire Clairmont* (Cambridge, MA: Harvard University Press, 1968).

———, *The Clairmont Correspondence: Letters of Claire Clairmont, Charles Clairmont, and Fanny Imlay Godwin* (Baltimore, MD: Johns Hopkins University Press, 1995).

Suttor, C., *Charlotte Augusta Anne Suttor Diaries, 1848–1853* (New South Wales: State Library New South Wales, 1848–1853).

Taylor, J.G., *The Social World of Batavia* (Madison: University of Wisconsin Press, 2009).

Thompson, C., *Travel Writing* (Abingdon: Routledge, 2011).

Wollstonecraft, M., *The Works of Mary Wollstonecraft*, eds. J. Todd and M. Butler (London: Pickering and Chatto, 1989).

———, *Letters Written during a Short Residence in Sweden, Norway, and Denmark*, ed. I. Horrocks (Canada: Broadview Press, 2013).

Wollstonecraft, M., and W. Godwin, *A Short Residence in Sweden And Memoirs of the Author of 'The Rights of Woman'*, ed. R. Holmes (London: Penguin Books, 1987).

Youngs, T., *The Cambridge Introduction to Travel Writing* (New York: Cambridge University Press, 2013).

Image 7 Photographic portrait of Mary Claire Bally-Clairmont, 1987.
Source: Mr. Peter Bally.
Credit: Mr. Peter Bally.

APPENDIX A

The Godwin-Shelley-Clairmont Family Genealogical Table

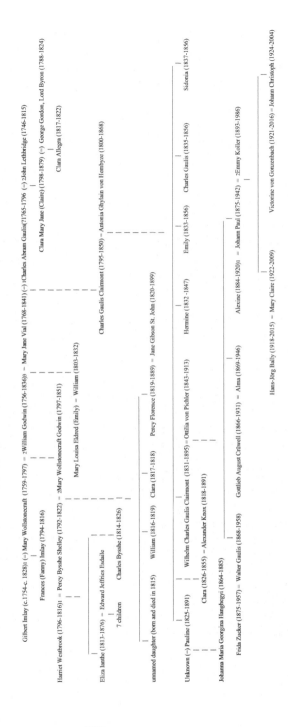

APPENDIX B

Historicizing the Journals: Austria, Australia, and the Banat

Austria, Australia, and the Banat are the three main geographic areas referenced in the journals collected here. This appendix will provide sufficient historic and geographic information to allow for a better understanding of these areas, supplementing the detailed geographical information available in the footnotes to each of the journals. Pauline (Pauline Maria, 1825–1891) and Wilhelm (Wilhelm Charles Gaulis, 1831–1895) were both born in Vienna, Austria, but their lives were filled with sojourns to far-flung places and they both spent years living and working outside of Austria for a variety of reasons. This appendix provides a political and historical context for each of the places in which they resided in order to show the intimate connection between their individual stories and the times in which they lived.

Pauline and Wilhelm's father was Charles Gaulis Clairmont (1795–1850), a British man who had moved to Vienna to teach English where he met their mother, an Austrian and also an English teacher, Antonia Ghylain von Hembyze (1800–1868). She was the daughter of Georg von Hembyze and Anna Schönbigler; he was the son of Mary Jane Godwin and the stepson of William Godwin. Charles and Antonia were married in 1824, and they raised their seven children largely in Vienna, the capital of Habsburg Austria, including, as well as Pauline and Wilhelm, Clara (Maria Johanna Klara Gaulis [later Knox] 1826–1855), Hermine (1832–1847), Emily (1833–1856), Charles Gaulis (Carolus Borromaeus 1835–1856), and Sidonia (1836–1856). Pauline and Wilhelm were aware of their Austro-Anglo heritage and the connections that it brought to them. As members of the Clairmont family, they were linked to the Shelley family through their father and their aunt, Claire Clairmont (1798–1879), who were stepsiblings of Mary Wollstonecraft Shelley (1797–1851). Pauline and Wilhelm knew Mary Shelley and had occasion to spend time with her in England. Furthermore, Pauline and Wilhelm were fluent in both German and English, enabling them to move to English-speaking countries without much difficulty. Charles and Antonia were not wealthy in spite of Charles's teaching position at the Theresianum Ritterakademie and his appointment in 1839 as a faculty member at the Universität Wien (University of Vienna). Charles was also connected to many of the aristocratic families living in Vienna and he supplemented his income through giving English language lessons. In particular, he was the English tutor to the brothers of the

APPENDIX B: HISTORICIZING THE JOURNALS

Habsburg Emperor Franz Joseph I (1830–1916), namely the future Emperor of Mexico (Ferdinand Maximilian, 1832–1867) and Archduke Karl Ludwig (1833–1896), whose son's assassination in 1914 would touch off World War I.[1]

Austria was ascendant in power in the mid-nineteenth century; in December 1848, Emperor Franz Joseph I was crowned both Emperor of Austria and Apostolic King of Hungary. He took the throne after his uncle Emperor Ferdinand I (1793–1875), who had no heirs, abdicated. Hungary was under Habsburg domination until 1867 when the Dual Monarchy (1867–1918) was instituted, thereby giving both Austria and Hungary equal shares in this joint collective enterprise which was known alternatively as the Austro-Hungarian Empire, Austria-Hungary, and the Austro-Hungarian Monarchy. Vienna served as its capital and administrative city and although Austria and Hungary were each ruled by their own prime ministers, the countries were both possessions of the Habsburgs. The Empire would last until 1918. The 1914 deaths in Sarajevo of Archduke Franz Ferdinand (1863–1914), the son of Karl Ludwig and future heir to the throne of the Austro-Hungarian Empire, and his wife, Sophie, Duchess of Hohenberg (1868–1914), would result in a global conflict which terminated in 1918 with the dissolution of the Austro-Hungarian Empire. It was not a time of much success for Charles Clairmont and his family, however. Franz Joseph I had been on his throne for less than two years when Charles Clairmont died at the age of fifty-five, and his widow was forced to rely on her sister-in-law, Claire Clairmont, for money. By 1856, Antonia had lost four of her remaining six children. Only Pauline and Wilhelm would survive their mother.

Three years after their father's death Pauline and Wilhelm departed for Sydney, Australia, primarily to make their fortunes. They perhaps were also fleeing epidemics, such as smallpox and typhus, which were prevalent in the nineteenth century and which would claim three of their siblings by 1856. Pauline spent the majority of her Australian stay working as a governess. Australia traces its colonial ties to 1784 when the British Parliament voted to create a penal colony on the continent. The first ships arrived in 1788 bearing prisoners, in a process that would be repeated for over thirty years. Many of these former prisoners journeyed into New South Wales to find new places on which to farm. By the time Pauline and Wilhelm arrived in New South Wales in 1853, the colony was over sixty years old, with descendants of former prisoners as well as newly arrived immigrants working together. Pauline's governess position was on the Suttor family estate, Brucedale, located some 12 kilometers northeast of Bathurst, New South Wales, which was founded as a town in 1815. While the original inhabitants, the Wiradjuri people, had lived there well before the arrival of the British, colonists created a road in the area by 1815 which then resulted in colonial settlement (Mackaness 1965: 34–62). The Suttor family patriarch, George Suttor (1774–1859) began farming in the area in 1822. Brucedale homestead dates to 1837. In an entry apparently written between 1990 and 2000, The *Australian Heritage Database* notes:

> Brucedale, since its establishment early last century, has been owned by the Suttor family. George Suttor and his wife, Sarah, arrived in New

South Wales in 1800 and settled at Baulkham Hills in 1802. In 1822 the family took up a land grant on the junction of Winburndale Rivulet and Clear Creek north of Bathurst, and the property was named Brucedale. The Suttors' acquisition of this grant was part of the expansion of pastoralism in the area following Governor Macquarie's departure from the colony and the arrival of Governor Brisbane. Third son William Henry Suttor quickly took over the running of the property. William became a major pastoralist and a prominent politician, being a Member of the Legislative Council from 1843 to 1854 and a Member of the Legislative Assembly from 1856 until 1872. Son William Henry junior also was an MLA and MLC and was the author of *Australian Stories Retold* (published 1887) . . . Brucedale Homestead dates from 1837 (the earlier timber and pise house built when the grant was first occupied by the Suttors still stands on the property, a short distance from the present homestead) and is Old Colonial Georgian in style. It is single storey and is constructed of stuccoed sandstock brick. The roof is hipped and clad with iron. Two rear wings form a courtyard which has been covered. A bullnose verandah (built around 1900 to replace the original verandah) runs across the facade of the house and returns down the sides. There are rusticated quoins to the corners of the building and to surrounds to openings, and there are shutters to windows. The front door is four panelled with sidelights and a fanlight. Internally, joinery is cedar and there are decorative plaster ceilings. There is a Georgian marble mantelpiece and other timber mantelpieces, and in the dining room is a built in cedar cupboard. The kitchen is in a separate building at the rear with the dairy and meat house; a breezeway connects this building with the main house. Brick stables and other outbuildings stand on the property ("Brucedale Homestead, Stables and Original Cottage, Peel, NSW, Australia" www.environment.gov.au/cgi-bin/ahdb/search.pl?mode=place_detail;place_id=914 Accessed 17 June 2020)

After her visit to Brucedale in 1982, Jacqueline Voignier-Marshall described the estate as follows:

> I shall never forget arriving on that cool sunny morning in autumn. The gates, so typically Australian, were there in front of us with the name BRUCEDALE. Very excited, we opened them and drove on. The 'dust-road' was long and winding and cattle could be seen grazing in the surrounding landscape. Further on to the right we ascended a hill dotted with beautiful trees which altogether presented a breathtaking spectacle, indeed. A delightful old house appeared, with a spacious veranda around it and a galvinised iron roof which sloped gently down. In evidence also were the original pavement, front door, steps and windows with their wooden shutters
>
> (Voignier-Marshall 1983: 27).

David Suttor, a family Suttor descendant, talks about the rich history of Brucedale in his website, explaining that it is the "oldest family business in Australia". As he writes, "seven generations of the Suttor family have lived and worked on this property," which he observes is "very picturesque" and has a "gently undulating landscape". He describes Bathurst as "the oldest inland city in Australia (population 37,000)," noting, "there are many scenic drives to nearby villages such as O'Connell, Sofala, Hill End, Millthorpe, and Carcoar" (www.brucedale.com.au/ Accessed 19 June 2020).

While Pauline spent four years at Brucedale, Wilhelm worked on many different farms in New South Wales. His letters to Pauline, to his mother Antonia Clairmont, and to his aunt Claire Clairmont tell of his adventures and his reactions to life in Australia.[2] He first worked on the Tala or Kieta Station, some 950 kilometers west of Sydney. In 1855 Wilhelm purchased a farm called Kangaroo Hills with German immigrant Julius Duboc (1829–1903) from William Dangar (1829–1890). However, by 1857, Wilhelm and Duboc had sold their farm back to Dangar as it was unproductive and they could not make the necessary loan payments. Kangaroo Hills is known today as Wongwibinda. It is located about 60 kilometers northeast of Armidale, New South Wales. Wilhelm attributed Kangaroo Hills's failure to the climate which he explained to his mother and aunt was not appropriate for farming sheep. Family historian Owen Wright recorded that Duboc blamed both the climate and the poor wool market at the time (Wright 1985: 73). After his farming enterprise failed, Wilhelm worked for the TwoFold Bay Pastoral Association, a group founded in 1852 by pastoralists John Edye Manning, James A. L. Manning, William Montagu Manning, Robert Tooth, Edwin Tooth, Thomas Sutcliffe Mort, and John Croft. Wilhelm first worked on their sheep run, which was called Cuba, about 631 kilometers southwest of Sydney, near Darlington Point. He then worked on the Association's Kameruka sheep station, an estate that is still a working farm today. Kameruka is located in the south of Australia in the Bega Valley about 500 kilometers from Sydney. The Association ended its partnership in 1860 and Wilhelm went back to Europe in 1861, as his journal in this edition describes.

After his return to Europe, where he briefly spent time with Claire Clairmont in Florence (documented in his journal in this edition), Wilhelm hoped to purchase a farm in the Austrian Empire. His travels across what is now Croatia, the Czech Republic, and Slovenia document his attempts at finding the appropriate homestead. While he was unsuccessful in his purchase, he took advantage of the farming opportunities offered to him in the Austrian Banat and moved there in 1861. The Austrian Banat was a geographical region in Eastern Europe under Habsburg domination from 1718 until its dissolution in 1920 when it was allocated to various European countries. Today, areas of the region are parts of Romania, Serbia, and Hungary. The administrative capital, known as Timişoara in Romanian today and as Temeswar in German when Wilhelm worked there, is now in Romania. Wilhelm's path followed that of many German-speaking immigrants to the Banat who moved there between 1718 and 1787 in three main immigration waves. These migrants had been encouraged by the Habsburgs and given benefits such as "homestead, land, and livestock grants, [and] tax and statute labor (socage) exemptions" (Steigerwald 1985: 3). Many of these migrants achieved economic success, as Wilhelm clearly hoped to do. However, the harsh climate was frequently hostile to farming enterprises. The farms where he worked as a tenant farmer included two in today's Romania, one in Bobda and another called Tuzokrét near today's Ciacova. In 1866, Wilhelm married Ottilia von Pichler, a Viennese, with whom he would have three children. They had two children, Walter and Alma, before departing around 1870 for Belec which is in Croatia today. They then moved to Marburg (Maribor, Slovenia, today) where, by 1871 and with the financial assistance of Claire Clairmont, Wilhelm purchased a farm named Nikolaihof. The introductory chapter to this collection provides more information about Wilhelm and Claire's purchase, which ultimately proved unsuccessful.

By 1874, Wilhelm moved with his family to Vienna where he assumed the role of surveyor of crown properties. Appendix C in this book shows his appointment letter. He and Ottilia and two of their three children and those children's spouses are buried in the Matzleinsdorf cemetery in Vienna (see the photograph of his family tomb in this collection). Pauline died in 1891 in Öblarn, Steiermark (the province of Styria, one of nine Austrian Bundesländer) while walking on the Sonnenburg peak (elevation 1,010 meters) with Wilhelm and Ottilia's younger son, Johann Paul Clairmont (1875–1942). Pauline is buried in Öblarn, a town in the district of Liezen.

Notes

1 Franz Joseph I and Empress Elisabeth's (1837–1898) only son, Archduke Rudolf (1858–1889), killed himself in 1889 in what was assumed to be a suicide pact at his hunting lodge at Mayerling (some 24 kilometers from Vienna) together with his lover, Baroness Marie Alexandrine Vetsera (1871–1889). Franz Ferdinand (1863–1914), Karl Ludwig's son, would become the sole surviving male heir to the Austro-Hungarian throne after the 1896 death of his father.
2 See Wilhelm's letters in *The Clairmont Family Letters: 1839–1889* (edited by Sharon L. Joffe, Routledge, 2017).

Bibliography

Aberle, G., *From the Steppes to the Prairies* (Bismarck, N.D.: Tumbleweed Press, 1981).
Barker, T., *A History of Bathurst* (Bathurst, NSW: Crawford House Press, 1992).
Čerin, B., and F. Vogelnik, *Maribor* (Ljubljana: Cankarjeva zal., 1988).
Engelmann, N., and J. Michels, *The Banat Germans: Die Banater Schwaben* (Bismarck, ND: University of Mary Press, 1987).
Ferry, J., *Colonial Armidale* (St. Lucia: University of Queensland Press, 1999).
Frey, K. S., *The Danube Swabians: A People with Portable Roots* (Belleville, ON: Mika Pub. Co., 1982).
Joffe, S.L. (ed.), *The Clairmont Family Letters, 1839–1889* (London and New York: Routledge, 2017).

Mackaness, G., *Fourteen Journeys Over the Blue Mountains of New South Wales, 1813–1841* (Sydney and Melbourne: Horwitz-Grahame, 1965).

McInherny, F., and T. Schaeffer, *Our Grandchildren Won't Believe it: A Local History of the Wongwibinda, Aberfoyle and Ward's Mistake Sreas* (Armidale, N.S.W.: Historical Group, 2004).

National Center of Biography. *Australian Dictionary of Biography*. Web. http://adb.anu.edu.au/

National Library of Australia. Trove. Newspapers Online. http://nla.gov.au

Norton, J., and H. Norton, *Dear William: The Suttors of Brucedale: Principally the Life and Times of William Henry Suttor Senior ("Dear William"), 1805–1877* (Sydney: Suttor Pub. Committee, 1993).

Paikert, G. C., *The Danube Swabians* (The Hague: Martinus Nijhoff, 1967).

Ryan, B., "Kameruka Estate, New South Wales, 1864–1964", *New Zealand Geographer*, 20:2 (1964), pp. 103–21.

Small, V., *Kameruka* (Bega, NSW: Kameruka Estates, 1989).

Smith, G., *100 Years Peel and District* (Bathurst, NSW: Geoffrey A. Smith, 1998).

Steigerwald, J., *Tracing Romania's Heterogeneous German Minority from its Origins to the Diaspora* (Winona, MN: Translation and Interpretation Service, 1985).

Stocking, M. K., "Miss Tina and Miss Plin: The Papers Behind the Aspern Papers," D. Reiman (ed), *the Evidence of the Imagination* (New York: New York University Press), 1978, pp. 372–384.

Tóth, I. G., *A Concise History of Hungary: The History of Hungary from the Early Middle Ages to the Present* (Budapest: Corvina, 2005).

Tullius, N., A. Leeb, and J. Pharr., "Banat." June 2020. www.dvhh.org/banat/

Vrišer, S., *Maribor* (Motovun: Niro Motovun, 1984).

Voignier-Marshall, J., "Looking for Pauline Clairmont in N.S.W.", *The Byron Society in Australia Newsletter*, 7 (1983), pp. 25–31.

Walker, R. B., *Old New England, A History of the Northern Tablelands of New South Wales, 1818–1900* (Sydney: Sydney University Press, 1966).

Walsh, G., *Pioneering Days: People and Innovations in Australia's Rural Past* (St. Leonards, NSW: Allen & Unwin, 1993).

Wright, O., *Wongwibinda* (Armidale, NSW: University of New England, 1985).

APPENDIX C
Wilhelm Clairmont as an Appraiser

Wilhelm Clairmont returned from Australia in 1861 and searched for a farm to purchase, as this edition of his journal shows. Initially, he spent many years farming as a tenant farmer in the Banat. From 1862, he worked on a farm located in a village called Bobda which today is included in the geographic borders of Romania, close to the city of Timişoara. Pauline resided with Wilhelm at Bobda for two years (1863–1865) before returning to Vienna. From 1866, Wilhelm worked on a farm, Tuzokrét, near Csákova. Known today as Ciacova, the city is located 50 kilometers south-east of Bobda and 34 kilometers south-west of Timişoara. Wilhelm and Rudolf von Hauer, with whom he studied at k.k. höheren landwirthschaftlichen Lehranstalt in Ungarisch-Altenburg (Altenburg, Hungary), married two of the von Pichler sisters (Ottilia and Emily) and both families farmed in the same general area. However, due to extremely harsh farming conditions, Wilhelm moved his family after 1870 to another farm, Belec, in today's Belec, Croatia. By 1871, Wilhelm had purchased Nikolaihof, a farm in Marburg (today's Maribor in Slovenia), a town some 86 kilometers from Belec. Claire Clairmont was instrumental in lending him the money to afford the purchase. By 1874, Wilhelm and his family had relocated to Vienna. The difficulty in making a financial success of Nikolaihof proved too complex and Wilhelm was forced to take a position as a surveyor of Crown properties. The Carl H. Pforzheimer Collection has a document that shows Wilhelm's appointment as an appraiser.

The transcription and translation are provided by Ann Sherwin. Line divisions in the original German correspond to the way in which the document was first written.

Den Wohlgeborenen Herrn Wilhelm Clairmont
Besitzer des Gutes

                                          St. Nikolai
                                          bei Marburg.

s. Angeschlossen beehrt man sich Euer Wohlgeboren
    das von der H. k.k. Statthalterei als Grundlasten
    Ablösungs- und Regulirungs-Landes-Ko'on [Kommission]
    ausgefertigte Ernennungsdekret als Sachver-

ständige aus dem forst- und ökonomischen
Fache zu übersenden.
Bei einer Beruffung zur Dienstleistung wird
Ihnen der vorgeschriebene Eid durch den Leiter
der bezüglichen Ko'on abgenommen werden,
damit Sie nicht deßhalb eine Reise nach Cilli.
zu unternehmen genöthiget sind.
      Kk. Grundl. Ablösend Reg. Loth. Ko'on
       Cilli am. 19. Mai 1873.
        Der Vorsteher.
        Garibaldy

To the Wellborn Mr. Wilhelm Clairmont
owner of the farm St. Nikolai near Marburg

 Attached, I have the honor of sending you [Your Wellborn] the letter of appointment as an expert in the field of forestry and agronomy issued by the imperial royal governor's office as state agency for the relief and regulation of land burdens.

 When you are called on for service, the required oath will be administered to you by the head of the relevant agency, so that you will not need to make a trip to Cilli.[1]

Imperial Royal Agency for the Relief and Regulation of Land Burdens
 Cilli, May 19, 1873
 The Director
 [sig.] Garibaldy

APPENDIX C: WILHELM CLAIRMONT

No. <u>1873</u>.
49
Z. 2352
      An
Herrn Wilhelm Clairmont, Gutszüchter
     in
           St. Nikolai
Nachdem Sie laut Mittheilung des kk. Landesgerichtes Graz von selbem als Sachverständiger des ökonomischen Faches bei Schätzungen der in der steiermärkischen Landtafel einkommenden Realitäten bestellt sind, und jenes Gericht nun hier Ihre hiergerichtliche Beeidigung in der besagten Eigenschaft ersucht hat, so wollen Sie unter Beibringung Ihres Bestattungsdekretes am 1. März 1873 V. M. 11 Uhr wegen Ablegung des Eides in Amtszimmer Nr 3 erscheinen, und beim Herrn kk. Adjunkter Branberger sich melden.
Kk. Bezirksgericht Marburg am 11. Februar 1873.
      Der kk. Landesgerichtsrath:
        [illegible signature]

      To
Mr. Wilhelm Clairmont, agronomist
     in
           St. Nikolai
Now that you have been appointed by the Imperial Royal [I.R.] State Court of Graz, according to a memorandum from that court, as an expert in the field of agronomy for the appraisal of properties being entered in the Styrian[2] Register of Estates, and that court has now requested that you be sworn in at this court in this capacity, you are asked to come to office no. 3 on March 1, 1873, at 11:00 a.m. to take the oath, and to report to I.R. Assistant Branberg, bringing your letter of appointment with you.

I.R. District Court of Marburg, February 11, 1873.
      I. R. District Court Justice
        [illegible signature]

APPENDIX C: WILHELM CLAIRMONT

Notes

1 Cilli refers to today's Celje, the third largest city in Slovenia. There are 47 kilometers from Celje to Maribor.
2 After the First World War, the Duchy of Styria was divided. Austria kept Upper Styria while Lower Styria was assigned to the Kingdom of Serbs, Croats and Slovenes. Today, Lower Styria forms part of Slovenia.

APPENDIX D
Pauline Clairmont's Death Certificate

In 1891, while walking in Öblarn, Styria, with her nephew Johann Paul Clairmont (Wilhelm and Ottilia Clairmont's son), Pauline fell down the mountain to her death. The Viennese newspaper, *Das Vaterland*, reported her death at 67 years of age in its edition of 15 July 1891. Wilhelm was recorded as her brother in the announcement (See http://anno.onb.ac.at/cgi-content/anno?aid=vtl&datum=1891 0715&seite=5). Pauline was buried in Öblarn, a small town near the eastern Austrian Alps in the Austrian state of Styria.

The following is a transcribed and translated copy of her death certificate. Ann Sherwin, translator, has represented the horizontal columns vertically with the English translation side-by-side. The original column titles are only provided in translation and not in the original German.

<u>Diocese: Seckau</u> Death Certificate. <u>State: Styria</u>
No. 113

Year of death: 1891[1]	Buchstäblich: Ein Tausend acht hundert neunzig & eins	Spelled out: one thousand eight hundred ninety-one
Month and day of death	Juli von 6.–7. nachts (sechster bis siebenter)	July in the night of the 6th to 7th (sixth to seventh)
Month and day of burial	Juli 9.	July 9
Place	Walchengraben, Gemeinde Oeblarn, Bezirk Gröbning	Walchengraben, town of Oeblarn, district of Gröbning[2]
House no.	—	—
Name and character of the deceased	Fräulein Clairmont Pauline eheliche Tochter des Herrn Karl Gaulis Clairmont und der Frau Antonia geb. Ghilain von Hembize, geboren in Wien den 27. Juli 1825, ledig, kath. Religion, wohnhaft in Wien, Reisnerstrasse 40.	Miss Pauline Clairmont, legitimate daughter of Mr. Karl Gaulis Clairmont and his wife, Antonia née Gilain von Hembize, born in Vienna on July 27, 1825, single, Catholic, residing in Vienna at Reisnerstrasse 40.
Religion	katholisch	Catholic

APPENDIX D: PAULINE CLAIRMONT

Sex	weiblich	female
Age	65 Jahre	65 years
Illness and cause of death	Stickfluß in Folge Ertrinkens. (abgestürzt bei einer Fußtour in der Walchen)	suffocation as a result of drowning (plunged during a walking tour in the Walchen[3])
Officiating priest	P. Irimbert Scherf... Pfr.	P[ater] Irimbert Scherf...[4], Priest

In witness whereof, the death register here, Vol. II, page 242 and issuance by the parish office. [50 krone stamp]

[seal]   Parish office of Oeblarn   the 9th of July 1891
Parish of Oeblarn   [sig.] P. Irimbert Scherf...
     Priest

Notes

1. The original German for these columns is translated here.
2. Probably Gröbming, a municipality in Liezen. Öblarn and Gröbming are part of the district of Liezen.
3. Ann Sherwin, translator, explains that Walchenbach is a small stream near Öblarn. Therefore, "the Walchen" likely refers the region near the stream (Personal Correspondence, 31 October 2018).
4. Ann Sherwin, translator, noted that the ending on the surname appears different from the ending on the certification below. Therefore, both name endings are omitted (Personal Correspondence, 31 October 2018).

APPENDIX E

Notarized Marriage Certificate of William Godwin and Mary Jane Clairmont

In the 1930s and 1940s, after the National Socialists came to power in Austria, people were asked to provide information (see the words "proof of Aryan descent" in this document) as to their family histories to establish that they were not of Jewish origin. Walter Clairmont and Alma Crüwell-Clairmont wrote testimonies to explain their birth origins (see Appendix F in this edition). Presumably, the following document was also included in the family's file to corroborate that William Godwin and Mary Jane Clairmont (Walter and Alma's great-grandparents) were not Jewish. Clearly seen on the original document is the Reichsadler (the Nazi Imperial Eagle seal). The Carl H. Pforzheimer Collection of Shelley and His Circle has eleven typed and notarized copies of original documents, some dating from the eighteenth century and which were reproduced in the 1930s, in order to examine the family's history (see CL'ANA 0422, unpublished manuscript, Pforzheimer Collection).

The following document was translated from the German by Ann Sherwin.

Page 1

<u>Certified copy of a marriage record</u>[1]
<u>according to the marriage laws in effect from 1836 to 1898.</u>

Registration district of Shoreditsch[2] _____
1801 The marriage took place in St. Leonhard in the parish of St. Leonhard[3] Shoreditsch in the County of London.

Entry no.	1 Date	2 First and last name	3 Age[4]	4 Marital status
3	December 21, 1801	William Godwin, Mary Clairmont	—	widower widow

368

APPENDIX E: MARRIAGE CERTIFICATE

	5 Character or occupation	6 Place of residence at time of marriage	7 Father's first and last name	8 Father's character or occupation
	—	this parish this parish	—	—

The marriage was performed in the parish church in accordance with the rites and rules of the – _____ – of – _____ – or after proclamation by me, Joseph Rose, Pastor.

This marriage between us: William Godwin, Mary Clairmont took place in our presence: James Marshal, George Limming[5]

I, Francis Edward Birch, Vicar of Shoreditsch in the County

of London hereby certify that this is a faithful copy of entry no. 3 in the marriage register of said church.
  In witness thereof, my signature on Sept. 12, 1927.
                                        F. E. Birch, Vicar m. p.[6]
For proof of Aryan descent, therefore exempt from stamp duty
  I certify under oath that the foregoing translation agrees with the English original._____
  The printed instructions for the registrar were not translated._____
  Vienna, on the sixth of September one thousand nine hundred thirty-eight.___
L.S.[7] Dr. Josef Wagner-Löffler, notary public m.p._____
This copy, for proof of Aryan descent and therefore exempt from stamp duty, agrees completely with the translation before me, which is attached to the English original.
Vienna, on the eighth of September one thousand nine hundred thirty-eight.___
  Fee for copy and inspection, RM 1.20   Dr. Josef Wagner-Löffler m.p.
                                        Notary Public
Seal: Dr. Josef Wagner-Löffler, notary public, court interpreter for English, Wien-Margarethen.
                        . . . oOo. . .

Compared and found to agree completely with the original before me. ---- Vienna, on the fifth of November one thousand nine hundred forty._____

Fee for inspection, RM 1.08
[seal]   [signature]
Dr. Josef Hofbauer   DrHofbauer
Notary in Vienna   Notary

Notes

1. Ann Sherwin translated the German document into English. The 1927 copy of the Godwins' English-language marriage certificate was translated into German in 1938, probably at the request of the Nazi authorities. The 1938 translated document was then certified to be an original copy in 1940. Therefore, Ann Sherwin's English translation provided here is of a document that was translated into German from the original English.
2. The original spelling was "Shoreditch" but the German translator in 1940 spelled it as "Shoreditsch".
3. The translated German document shows that the letter "h" in the original word "Leonhard" was deleted in both representations of the word. Undoubtably the translator struck the letter after the spelling was authenticated.
4. According to Ann Sherwin, translator, the German word "Spalten" indicates the number of the column. However, the information on the second page actually shows that it is the entry number (Translator's note, 31 October 2018).
5. These four typed names would have been actual signatures in the original. However, they are not designated as such in the German translation.
6. Abbreviation for "manu propria," Latin for "[signed] with one's own hand".
7. Abbreviation for "locus sigilli," Latin for "seal" or "place to which seal is affixed".

APPENDIX F
The Testimonies of Alma Crüwell-Clairmont and Walter Clairmont

After the annexation of Austria by the National Socialists in 1938, pernicious anti-Semitic regulations were enacted. As in Germany, Jews were forced out of their professions, they were herded into ghettos, their property was confiscated, and they were ultimately sent to concentration camps. Of Austria's pre-war Jewish population of 185, 000, the United States Holocaust Memorial Museum estimates that 65, 459 people were killed in concentration camps (representing 35% of the Jewish population of the country) while Yad Vashem (Israel's Holocaust Museum) puts the figure at 50, 000 (27% of Austria's Jewish population. See www.jewishvirtuallibrary.org/estimated-number-of-jews-killed-in-the-final-solution Accessed 18 May 2020).

Similar to their German counterparts, Austrians frequently had to demonstrate that their families were not of Jewish descent. Churches issued baptism certificates and people completed Aryan certificates ("Ariernachweis") to prove the absence of Jewish ancestors. Wilhelm and Ottilia's children, Alma Crüwell-Clairmont and Walter Clairmont, likely wrote these testimonies with the purpose of receiving Aryan certificates.

Alma Crüwell-Clairmont's testimony is translated first. Ann Sherwin, translator, provided the English translations.

Origins of the Clairmont Family[1]

Our grandfather, Carl Gaulis Clairmont, according to the baptismal certificate in my possession, was born June 4, 1795, in Bristol, England, son of Charles Gaulis Clairmont and of Mary Jane Devereux, daughter of Andreas Peter Devereux.

After the early death of his father, his mother married the well-known English author and scholar William Godwin, in whose house our grandfather and his sister Claire grew up. Because their stepsister Mary Godwin was the wife of the poet Shelley, they developed close relations with the literary circle around Shelley and Byron. Indeed, the name of Claire Clairmont, through her love for Byron and the friendship that tied her to Shelley, is not unknown in the history of English literature.

Our grandfather came to Vienna in the 19th century, at the start of the 1820s, and soon earned a name for himself here as an English language instructor. He was a professor at the Theresianum and at the university for many years and published textbooks in the English language that were very well known and widely used in their day. In 1824 he married <u>Antonia Ghislain d'Hembyse</u>, a Viennese woman descended from an old Walloon family. Her mother, our great-grandmother, was a <u>Schönbichler</u>.

I have in my possession the authentic copy of a renewal letter signed by Empress Maria Theresia in 1764 affirming the nobility of the Ghislain d'Hembyse family, which had been temporarily forgotten after the family's emigration to Austria in 1650 but is proven as far back as the 14th century.

Charles G. <u>Clairmont</u> died on February 2, 1852, in Vienna. Since the closing of the [General] Währinger Cemetery*[2], his headstone now lies in our vault at the Matzleinsdorf Protestant Cemetery.

Among the children issuing from his marriage, most of whom died young, was my father, <u>Wilhelm Gaulis Clairmont</u>, born May 26, 1831. Christened Catholic, like his mother, in St. Michael's Church,[3] he was raised with the Scots and in Melk; but after his agricultural education in Altenburg and a lengthy stay in England and Australia, where he worked many years as a sheep breeder, he converted to his father's Anglican faith in 1866 before his marriage. In 1874 he took up permanent residency in Vienna again, where my brother, <u>Paul Clairmont</u>, was also born and completed his middle school and university studies, and where the family life generally unfolded.

Our mother, <u>Ottilie von Pichler</u>, born in 1843, was the daughter of Johann Pichler, a civil servant in the Ministry of Commerce. The latter was descended from a lower-middle-class family, but of best German race, from Plan bei Marienbad, Bohemia. His wife, our maternal grandmother, Fanny von <u>Horstig</u>, was the daughter of Consistorial Councilor Horstig, a Protestant pastor, Herder's successor in Bückeburg. In the family from which his wife, our great-grandmother, a <u>d'Engelbronner d'Aubigny</u>. is descended, family traditions and worship were practiced with utmost devotion. These lines trace back to Holland, by way of Kassel and France, to Huguenots.

Thus our family stock represents a strong mix of good German, Roman, and English blood and contains not a drop of Semitic blood, as malevolent rumors would have it. The brunette features that Paul Clairmont, his brother Walter, and I share are first and foremost a dominant traits inherited from the Walloon-Belgian race, family characteristics that that can also be observed in the last female representatives of this family, two Ghislain d'Hembyse ladies living in Linz.

Testimony of Walter Clairmont:

3 June 1933[4]

Origins of the Clairmont Family

My grandfather, Charles Gaulis Clairmont, was born June 4, 1795, in the St. Nicolas parish on Bridge Street in Bristol, England, son of the knight Charles

Gaulis Clairmont and of Mary Jane Devereux, daughter of Andreas Peter Devereux. After the early death of our great-grandfather, our great-grandmother married the well-known English author and scholar William Godwin in 1801, in St. Mildred's Church in London, and our grandfather and his sister Jane, later called Claire, grew up in Godwin's house. Because their stepsister Mary Godwin was the wife of the famous English poet Shelley, they developed close relations with the Shelley and Byron families. Mention of my grandfather's friendship with Shelley can be found in any history of English literature.

My grandfather came to Vienna in 1820 and soon earned a name for himself here as an instructor of the English language. He was a professor at the Theresianum and at the university for many years and published textbooks in the English language that were very well known and widely used in their day. In 1824 he married Antonia Ghislain d'Hembyse, a Viennese woman descended from an old Walloon family. Her mother, our great-grandmother, was born a Schönbichler.

In my sister's possession in Vienna is the authentic copy of a renewal letter signed by Empress Maria Theresia affirming the nobility of the Ghislain d'Hembyse family, which had been temporarily forgotten after the family's emigration to Austria in 1650 but is proven as far back as the 14th century. Most of the men of this family were officers in the Austrian army.

My grandfather died in Vienna on February 2, 1852. After the closing of the Währinger Cemetery, his headstone now lies in our vault at the Matzleinsdorf Protestant Cemetery.

Issuing from his marriage, among other children, most of whom died young, was our father, <u>Wilhelm Gaulis Clairmont</u>, born May 26, 1831. Christened Catholic, like his mother, in St. Michael's Church, he was raised with the Scots and in Melk. He enjoyed an agricultural education at the renowned academies in Altenburg and Hohenheim. As a young man he spent many years in Australia as a sheep breeder, returning to Austria in 1864, where he purchased a farm in the Banat and was married in 1866 in the Protestant community of Liebling in the Banat. In 1874 he took up permanent residency in Vienna again, where he[5] worked as an agricultural consultant for the Lord Marshal's Office[6]. He died on December 26, 1895, in Vienna.

His wife, my mother, Ottilie von Pichler, born January 22, 1843, in Vienna and baptized Catholic, was the daughter of Hofrat[7] Johann Pichler, later ennobled, undersecretary of the Imperial Royal Ministry of Commerce in Vienna, from his marriage to Fanny Horstig. Grandfather Pichler was descended from a modest Catholic family of best German stock from Plan bei Marienbad, where he was born in 1799. He died in Vienna in 1890 after a distinguished career in civil service. My Grandmother Pichler was the daughter of Consistorial Councilor and Court Chaplain Horstig, Herder's successor. She was born in 1805 in Bückeburg and married Grandfather Pichler in the Catholic church in St. Oswald bei Graz. My great-grandmother, wife of Consistorial Councilor Horstig, was born a Baroness d'Aubigny from Holland. My great-grandfather acquired the Miltenburg Castle as a retreat and died there in 1853. The Horstigs were ennobled to "von

Horstig d'Aubigny" and were a good Bavarian family. Rudolf von Horstig, who lives in Würzburg today as the university's chief building inspector, is a nephew of my grandmother, sister of Mrs. Frida Maria von Grafenstein's mother.

I was born on August 3, 1868, on Tuzokrét, my father's farm in the Banat, and was baptized Protestant on August 30, 1868, in the Swabian enclave of Liebling. I studied in Vienna at the Franz Josef Gymnasium and University of Agricultural Sciences, was assistant in the Archducal Dominion of Bellye[8] for two years, but then changed careers; studied chemistry at the University of Basel, received my doctorate there on the basis of a dissertation on "Cretone" in 1893, worked for Agfa in Berlin as a chemist two years, then in a [textile-]printing factory in Russia seven years. Since 1903 I have been manager of the Neue Augsburger Kattunfabrik.[9] I acquired Bavarian citizenship in 1910 and was mustered out to the militia in 1911. On June 5, 1913, I married my wife, Frida née Zucker, in the Budapest Protestant church.

My wife Frida is the daughter of Johann Zucker from his marriage to Maria née Pfeifer. He was born March 13[10], 1837, and baptized Catholic in Jauernigg-Johannesberg, Administrative District of Freiwalden, in Austrian Silesia.

Father Zucker comes from a simple, modest Catholic family. His father was a prince-diocesan civil servant. His biography appears in the enclosed article, page 270 of "Ehrenhalle des politischen Bezirk Freiwalden"[11], in which good friends placed a memorial to this honorable man.[12]

My wife's mother, maiden name Pfeifer, was born in 1853 to Protestant parents and baptized Protestant. Her father, Julius Pfeifer, came from the Burgenland and was a senior railroad official. Her mother's maiden name was Deutelmoser, and the latter's mother was a sister of my Grandmother Horstig. The Deutelmosers themselves are an Austrian family, whose head, Hofrat Deutelmoser, is chief of the Austrian airship fleet today.

Notes

1 Alma Crüwell-Clairmont wrote this testimony. Although undated, it appears that Alma Crüwell-Clairmont's note was written first and that Walter Clairmont took information directly from it to compose his own testimony. As Marion Kingston Stocking confirms, Alma and Walter severed connections over Alma's support for the National Socialist regime in Austria. Stocking recounted that Walter Clairmont "had opposed the Nazi regime, and profound differences had caused him some years before to cease communication with his sister Alma" ("Miss Tina and Miss Plin," p. 373).

2 The star symbol points the reader to a handwritten margin note. The German reads as follows: "Der anschließende jüdische Friedhof blieb erhalten, auch bezeichnend für die Wiener Verhältnisse und die Richtung der roten Gemeinde Wien" (English translation: The adjacent Jewish cemetery was preserved, also indicative of the Viennese situation and the orientation of Red Vienna). Vienna was known as "Rotes Wien" (Red Vienna) from 1918 to 1934 when the Social Democrats held power in the city. Communal housing projects were instituted and socialist policies governed the city. As some of the city's leaders were of Jewish origin, Red Vienna was often the locus for anti-Semitic sentiments.

3 Alma begins the second page here.

APPENDIX F: THE TESTIMONIES

4 It is unclear as to why Walter Clairmont dated this testimony 1933 as the National Socialists only came to power in 1938.
5 Page 2 begins here.
6 The German word is "Obersthofmarschallamt" which means "Lord Marshal's Office".
7 German for "court counselor" or "advisory counselor".
8 Bilje in Croatia today.
9 English translation: "New Augsburg Cotton Mill".
10 There is an overstrike of two typewriter keys, 3 and 4.
11 The original word "Bezirk" is incorrect. It should be "Bezirks". The title translates as "Hall of Fame for the Administrative District of Freiwalden".
12 Page 3 begins here.

APPENDIX G
Rosalie, Lady Mander's Letters to Alma Crüwell-Clairmont

Rosalie, Lady Mander (1905–1988) was a prolific writer who authored books on Shelley-circle participants such as William Godwin, Mary Shelley, Claire Clairmont, and Edward John Trelawny. She was born Rosalie Glynn Grylls in Cornwall, a county in the southwest of England, and received her degrees from Queen's College, London, and Lady Margaret Hall, Oxford University. She married a member of the British parliament, Sir Geoffrey Mander (1882–1962), and the couple had two children, John Geoffrey Grylls Mander (1932–1978) and Anthea Loveday Veronica Mander (1945–2004). In 1939, John Murray published Mander's book, *Claire Clairmont: Mother of Byron's Allegra*, under the name R. Glynn Grylls. The fourteen letters below to Alma Crüwell-Clairmont about the Shelley-Clairmont family history were part of her research process. They were bequeathed to the Carl H. Pforzheimer Collection of Shelley and His Circle by Mary Claire Bally-Clairmont and Christoph Clairmont in their 1997–1998 gift. They are printed here for the first time, Mander's grandson, Christopher David Lahr, having granted me permission to transcribe and edit them. Their references to Pauline Clairmont, Georgina Hanghegyi, Claire Clairmont, Percy Bysshe Shelley, and Lord Byron are likely to interest the reader as they add additional detail to our understanding of the lives of these Shelley-circle participants. Mander thanks Crüwell-Clairmont and identifies Crüwell-Clairmont's connection to the circle in her "Author's Acknowledgments": "I am also indebted to Frau Alma Crüwell, granddaughter of Charles Clairmont, for sending me information with regard to Claire's later life" (Mander 1936: 226).

The fourteen letters transcribed here are all identified by a particular call number that begins with the word CL'ANA, followed by a number. As I explained in the "Editorial Standards and Practices" and in my edited collection, *The Clairmont Family Letters: 1839–1889*, the Pforzheimer Collection has assigned each letter has a call number. The Clairmont family papers were designated by "Clairmontana," a call number system that identified documents pertaining to Claire Clairmont. Every letter reproduced here has a unique number that begins with CL'ANA. In this edition, as in my previous edition of the letters, the words "Unpublished. Text: M. S. Pf. Coll." follow each CL'ANA number. These words explain that the letter has not been previously published, and that the manuscript is located in the Carl H. Pforzheimer Collection of Shelley and His Circle, The New York Public Library, Astor, Lenox and Tilden Foundations.

The letters were typewritten on Mander's personal stationary except as mentioned in the endnotes, and some second pages of Mander's stationery repeated the address block instead of being plain.

APPENDIX G: ROSALIE, LADY MANDER'S LETTERS

Telephone
25 Tettenhall
Telegrams
Mander, Wightwick,
Wolverhampton.

Wightwick Manor,
Wolverhampton.[1]
October 24th. 1937

Dear Madam Cruwell,
I am answering your kind letter without delay in order to show you how much I appreicate[2] your writing so fully and also so frankly. I shall be very pleased to send you a copy of my "Mary Shelley" when it is published;[3] there has been some delay as there is a lot to correct in the proofs as it is a book very <u>documenté</u>[4]. I was very fortunate in having had access to manuscripts of the Shelley family which had not been printed before so I quite understand what are the feelings of the descendants of these people! You will appreciate, I am sure, that in my book on Mary, I have taken <u>her</u> point of view about Claire; the Byron incident is only treated as an 'incident', but I do stress how tiresome it was for Mary always to have Claire living with her![5] This would apply equally to any other woman, although as Claire had a rather vivid personality, clashes were even more likely. I have, however, tried to bring out the courage in Claire's character; the way she went back to her work after the death of Allegra and the cheerful way she faced life in Russia; her letters of this period show her to great advantage beside Mary. Curiously enough when she came into the Shelley money, she 'let go' and her letters became complaining and irritable!

I entirely agree with you about "Ariel"; I have tried to show what I think of it by classing it with two other books known to be third-rate, below a little line in my bibliography. The others are "Last Links" by William Graham, which I expect you know as it is supposed to be an interview with Claire in old age in Florence and makes her say some ridiculous things, and the other is 'The Romantic Life of Shelley' by Francis Gribble. The title will tell you enough. I think it is not possible for the Latin mind to understand the curious altruism of which the Anglo-Saxon is at times capable; Maurois deals excellently with Byron whom he can perfectly understand, but Shelley is beyond his grasp.[6]

I have a Russian Journal of Claire's for Dec 1825 and Jan 1826,[7] but it is disappointingly bald. I should, of course, be intensely interested to see yours and the portrait. I do hope I may be able to come to Vienna again next year and have the pleasure of meeting you. Yours sincerely,

Rosalie Mander

Unpublished. Text: M.S., Pf. Coll., CL'ANA 0008

APPENDIX G: ROSALIE, LADY MANDER'S LETTERS

> 4. Barton Street, Westminster.
> Whitehall 1747.
>
> Nov. 16th 1937

Dear Mrs Cruwell,
Thank you very much for your letter. I am only answering shortly in order to express my interest in what you tell me. The <u>dossier</u> is a curious document; did you also see the anonymous letter with it? Because this is full of inaccuracies (like saying that Clairmont was son of Godwin and Mary Wollstonecraft) and therefore it is not surprising that the police have got the 'wrong end of the stick' about Mrs. Clairmont.

Do you know anything about his second name Gaulis? It does not sound to me English at all and I wondered if it was a translation, like Carl for Charles.[8] I should be glad to know if you can tell me.

I hope to send you the book at Christmas and also copies of the letters I have from Claire with accounts of her brother's family. In my other letter by 'the incident' I meant to refer to Claire's <u>liaison</u> with Byron.

With kindest regards and very many thanks for your expressions of interest and sympathy

> Yours sincerely,
> Rosalie Mander.

I send copies of the letters now; they are only extracts I am afraid as the originals are in Scotland where I copied from them. Others are quoted in full in my book.[9]

Unpublished. Text: M.S., Pf. Coll., CL'ANA 0009

Telephone
25 Tettenhall
Telegrams
Mander, Wightwick,
Wolverhampton.

Wightwick Manor,
Wolverhampton.
February 20th. 1938

Dear Frau Cruwell,

Thank you very much for your letter which I was very honoured to receive. I feel very unworthy when I consider that in a foreign language you are able to write so easily and to exercise such an independent judgement. You are quite right about Claire's portrait by Miss Curran[10] and I certainly made a silly slip (which so far none of our critics here have noticed! though there have been others which have not escaped them) as I had in mind that it was the portrait of Mary and of William[11] that were lost. Of course, I know the portrait of Claire and very bad I think it is! It gives no idea of the vivacity that I am sure was her principal charm; it is a pity that she has not some of the lightness of which there is too much in the Shelley portrait by Miss Curran.[12]

I regret more every day that I was not able to see you when we were in Vienna. I only hope that events will not make it impossible to pay a visit some other time.[13] I had planned, as far as possible, to be there perhaps in the summer. The present position with my book is that I have[14] nearly finished the second part which comes up to the deaths of Allegra and Shelley.[15] I then have to do a lot of reading to get the 'local colour' for her life in Vienna and then in Russia. Will you be so good as to help me with Vienna? It would be delightful if it turned out to be possible to meet and to go through it together and for me to see your diaries, if you will be so kind as to allow me. I may say directly that if you happen to come across some good old[16] print of Vienna in 1822[17] which shows a characteristic part of the town and, if possible, some people also in it, I should be extremely glad if you would acquire it for me and send it to me with details of any expense involved. We have friends at the Legation, Mr and Mrs Mack,[18] who forwarded the <u>dossier</u> and would no doubt take charge of anything else if there is difficulty with ordinary postage. I do not know if I told you that my husband is a member of Parliament. Our time is therefore by no means always our own.

With kindest regards,

Yours sincerely,
Rosalie Mander.

Unpublished. Text: M.S., Pf. Coll., CL'ANA 0010

(1

Telephone
Finchfield 61025
Telegrams
Mander, Wightwick,
Wolverhampton.

Wightwick Manor,
Wolverhampton.
March 6th. 1938.[19]

Dear Frau Cruwell,
I must apologise for writing to you again so soon, for I am sure that you must have many present-day cares and interests and not much time to devote to what happened so long ago when Claire Clairmont walked in such a different world! I hope you will forgive my bothering you, but I am having to hurry on with my book much sooner than I intended as there is another one coming out in the autumn which is going to deal with her relations with Byron. My publisher wishes me to finish my book quickly so that he can decide whether to bring it out before or after this other book. Of course, mine will be from the point of view of Claire and sympathetic to her. I am just coming to[20] the part where she leaves Italy for Vienna and I have been reading many contemporary travels to get some idea of what the town was then like. I shall get an Austrian friend in London to read it for me, but in case you happen to know, I should be most grateful if you could tell me if you know whereabouts Biber Bastei[21] was. It is her first address. Would it be near the Graben?[22] And am I right in supposing that where the fortifications were, is now the Ring?[23]

If you would be willing for me to see and make use of the Journal in your possession, would you prefer me to wait until[24] I can get to Vienna or would you be willing for anyone to make a copy for me? No doubt there would be some scholar (such as the Baroness Hofrat found for the Dossier copying) who could undertake it and I could defray any expense involved. Does Claire give any description of Moscow in your Journal? the one that I have is little more than a record of daily visits except for an account of a child's death where the parents behave exactly as they would in Tchekov;[25] Claire could be so very witty that it is disappointing that she does not make more comments on the Russians.
    I have never heard from your brother in Zurich but I presume that he leaves Claire matters[26] to you and has no other papers of his own. Did I telllyou[27] that a new letter I have found from Claire in old age says that "Paula" had a very good offer of marriage from an Austrian cavalry officer and that she would not stand in her way, but evidently "Paula" decided to put her duty first;[28] I cannot understand in the Dossier how Charles Clairmont says that he never knew Shelley and that he died in Switzerland. This shows there must be other

inaccuracies. I am quite sure for instance, that Mrs Godwin never went over to Vienna.

I do hope that I am not putting you to a lot of trouble.
With kindest regards,
Yours sincerely,
Rosalie Mander.

Unpublished. Text: M.S., Pf. Coll., CL'ANA 0011

APPENDIX G: ROSALIE, LADY MANDER'S LETTERS

Telephone
25 Tettenhall
Telegrams
Mander, Wightwick,
Wolverhampton.

                                                                   Wightwick Manor,
                                                                   Wolverhampton.
                                                                   April 3 rd. 1938

My dear Frau Cruwell,
I am simply overwhelmed with delight at the prints; it is most kind of you to have sent them – and such charming ones. How did you find the actual Biber Bastion?[29] It is extremely good as it combines a view of the town. I do not know which I like the most and do wish the publisher would let me use them all. . . . but whether he does or not, I shall have the pleasure of them framed in a series on my wall. I had looked at a few prints that there were in the British Museum, of Vienna while I was searching for something of Moscow (for there is no one <u>there</u> to help me! as you may imagine. . . . I rather wish Claire had not travelled so much!) and I came across one of The Graben which I should have used if I had not received these. I chose this because it seems to me that the Plague memorial[30] there might well be called the 'quintessence of Baroque' and is a sort of test whether the Austrian baroque appeals to you or not. But you have even included the Graben in this series![31] so the collection is beyond my most helpful dreams. Thank you so very much.

    You said that you thought you had an explanation of why Charles Clairmont said that he did not know Shelley. I should be very interested to know what is your interpretation of it. How dull a heroine can appear in a Police report! This is poor Claire with all her adventures, still you and, at times, animated and beautiful . . . 'Klara Clairmont, aged 24, spinster, of London, daughter of a book-seller.'[32] I was very surprised of what you told me of Knox marrying Cleary; what happened? as the Dictionary of National Biography gives quite a different wife and there is no reference to the incident in any letters that I have seen here.[33]

    Did you tell me that you had the little book on Allegra by Countess Origo[34] (an American married to an Italian Count). I should so much like to send it to you if you do not possess it.

    With very, very many thanks; I am most grateful to you for your great kindness,
    Yours sincerely,
    Rosalie Mander.

P.S. The dresses of the period are so delightful – I should love to include Paradies Garten for that.[35]

Unpublished. Text: M.S., Pf. Coll., CL'ANA 0012

APPENDIX G: ROSALIE, LADY MANDER'S LETTERS

Telephone
Finchfield 61025
Telegrams
Mander, Wightwick,
Wolverhampton.

Wightwick Manor,
Wolverhampton.
April 21 st. 1938

Dear Frau Crüwell,
Thank you for the printed address from the Anglo-Austrian Society which I found very interesting. I notice that the stamps on your envelope is are[36] already changed!

I thought you would be interested to hear that I have now been told of a descendant in Florence of Madame Mason, the Lady Mountcashell[37] who was so friendly with Claire, and I understand that she has a lot of letters written in old age. They should be very interesting. I wish I could charter a private aeroplane and visit all the places where there are these Shelley connections – and the descendants of their friends. Did you know why Paula left her Aunt? I notice, by the way, that in letters Claire refers to her as Pauline and not Paula, but then she was fond of changing names! Charles must have moved about a lot in Vienna; there is an English Guide-book of 1839 which refers to him and he is then living at Wallnerstrasse, 267.[38]

It is a constant delight to look at those prints of Vienna; they are simply charming – it was most kind of you to part with them once you had found them.

Yours sincerely,
Rosalie Mander.

Unpublished. Text: M.S., Pf. Coll., CL'ANA 0013

4. Barton Street, Westminster.
Whitehall 1747.

[39] as from,
Wightwick Manor,
Wolverhampton.

May 8th. 1938,
Dear Frau Crüwell,

I really must resist the temptation to 'bombard' you with letters and questions (particularly in my hand-writing! which I am always told is very difficult) but in case you are on the way to writing to me about any other Clairmont matter, I wonder if you[40] can tell me when Claire died and where she is buried.[41] That book by Wm Graham that is so unreliable says her grave was at Trespiano[42], but this is contradicted by a magazine of 1893 which says Rania d'Antella, 3 miles out of Florence. An Italian correspondent of mine (descendant of Emilia Viviani[43], whose Life she wrote last year in Italian) has very kindly looked for me, but found no trace!

Do you possess the charming little book[44], "Allegra" by Countess Origo? With kindest regards, Yours sincerely, Rosalie Mander.

Unpublished. Text: M.S., Pf. Coll., CL'ANA 0014

Telephone
Finchfield 61025
Telegrams
Mander, Wightwick,
Wolverhampton.

Wightwick Manor,
Wolverhampton.
May 21 st. 1938

Dear Frau Cruwell,

I hasten to acknowledge your letter with its very interesting enclosures; it was most kind of you to copy them out as I know what a lot of time that sort of thing takes and particularly when it has to be translated. You have evidently inherited your great-Aunt's talent for languages! It is interesting that curious reference to the Cinis in Florence, because those are the same people that I am now trying to get into touch with; Signora Farini-Cini is the descendant of Mrs Masons daughter, Nerina.[45] I had drawn from imagination a picture of Claire in old age very much like that which your letters confirm; I think she must have been the first of the 'maiden-Aunts' – a typically English phenomenon who travel from pension to pension in Italy or on the French Riviera[46] and are something of a trial to their younger relations; I told you, did I not, of her letter which someone here showed me, to a friend about an offer of marriage which Pauline received from an Austrian colonel but which Claire rather obviously hopes she will not accept as it would mean leaving Italy for Austria . . . she says that the girl must decide for herself, but I fear she probably persuaded her against it![47]

I have told my bookshop to send you a copy of "Allegra," which I am sure you will agree is a charming little book. The authoress, an American married to an Italian Count now possesses that miniature of Allegra which Byron consented to send Claire. I have also asked them to send you "Last Links" by William Graham, but there may be some delay in obtaining it as it is an old book. I may say it was completely discredited the moment it appeared here, so do not take any notice of what it says, but you may find it interesting and certainly ought to know about it.

It is curious to think of all the other people who were in Florence when Claire was an old lady . . . the Brownings, Walter Savage Lander (who one day threw his dinner at kind Mrs Browning; a 'savage' man, I fear!) A.H. Clough[48] . . . . one wishes she could have met them, but I suppose she would have thought them xxxxxx pygmie[49]s compared to the giants she had known.[50]

Thank you so much; I will write when I hear from the Cinis.
Yours sincerely,
Rosalie Mander.

Unpublished. Text: M.S., Pf. Coll., CL'ANA 0015

Telephone
Finchfield 61025
Telegrams
Mander, Wightwick,
Wolverhampton.

                                                          Wightwick Manor,
                                                          Wolverhampton.
                                                          May 28 th. 1938

Dear Frau Cruwell,

    Thank you very much for your most interesting postcard. I will write to my Florence correspondents for information about the cemetery of the Antella; it may have been moved, as you suggest, or it may be a familiar name for one of the other two where she was supposed to have been buried. Trespiano or Bagno à Ripoli.[51]

    I am afraid there will be some delay in sending you a copy of the xxxxxxxx[52] Graham book as it is out of print and we have to look for a second hand copy.

    With very many thanks,
            Yours sincerely,
                Rosalie Mander.

Unpublished. Text: M.S., Pf. Coll., CL'ANA 0016

APPENDIX G: ROSALIE, LADY MANDER'S LETTERS

Telephone
Finchfield 61025
Telegrams
Mander, Wightwick,
Wolverhampton.

Wightwick Manor,
Wolverhampton.
4 th June, 1938.

Dear Frau Cruwell,
It is most kind of you to have copied out the letter for me; I know what a time that sort of thing takes, and in your case, it has to be translated as well. Or does it Not? I meant to ask you earlier if the Clairmonts all spoke English and German equally easily and used both in their home. This is a delightfully 'human' letter and I am much amused at the Cini girl's flirtation! with her future husband, I presume.

I have now found a reference to 'the Antella'; apparently the full name is Campo Santo della Misericordia de Ste. Maria d'Antella. S. E. and it is at Bagno a Ripoli about three miles out of Florence. I am hoping to hear more about it and perhaps get a picture from some of my correspondents, or from the Anglo-Italian Institute which I have heard of out there.

The miniature is not reproduced in 'Allegra', because, much to the Countess Origo's disappointment, she was not able to acquire it in time. She bought it in America later and now has it. It was sold by Paula to Mr. Buxton Forman and dispersed with his collection.[53]

But I have made one discovery this week about which I was going to write to you in any case. I have found that portrait of Claire by Miss Curran which has been reproduced several times. It has just been given by Colonel Edgcumbe (whose father had it from Trelwany)[54] to Newstead Abbey[55] which is Byron's old home and has now been preserved as a Byron[56] museum.. It is a much more attractive picture than the old reproductions show, much 'lighter' as the hair is escaping in little curls, and the colouring is delicate. I have arranged with a photographer there to make copies and will certainly send you one, if you would like it.

I have also met during the last fortnight a descendant of Trelawny, a grandson of 'Zella',[57] and he showed me a new letter from Trelawny very much approving of that portrait of himself by Millais. I daresay you have seen reproductions; it is called The North West Passage[58] and shows and old man sitting huddled up in a chair and a very young girl at his feet. A biographer of Trelawny's, Mr. Massingham, had commented that the old Pirate would not have liked to be shown so bent and aged, but apparently he approved. I like Trelawny' in[59] contrast to Byron, for his faults were not those of meanness or sentimentality and hypocrisy whatever they may have been. I agree with Mrs. Gisborne[60] (did you notice the note in my book?) that Claire would have done best to marry Peacock;[61] he had common sense enough for the lot of them.

Thank you so very much again for this letter – and for your letter. It is such a pleasure to correspond with you, and I do hope I am not taking up too much of your time.

Yours very sincerely,
Rosalie Mander.

Unpublished. Text: M.S., Pf. Coll., CL'ANA 0017

APPENDIX G: ROSALIE, LADY MANDER'S LETTERS

Telephone
Finchfield 61025
Telegrams
Mander, Wightwick,
Wolverhampton.

Wightwick Manor,
Wolverhampton.
July 11 th 1938.

Dear Frau Crüwell,

Under separate cover I am sending you a copy of the Claire portrait and some of her letters to Bartolomeo Cini who married Nerina Mason. The portrait has been done in brown tones as the artist assured me that it would in that case be perfectly safe for travelling. I have also another letter to Cini to send you when it has been typed. Thank you for the information about Georgina: you will see from one of the letters why I wanted it. The fact that she was no relation makes a rather interesting new point, it shows Claire keeping up something of Shelley's quixotry![62]

I agree with you entirely about her relationship with Byron and have said much what you say in several places in the book. "She was emotional from the head and not from the heart", and she was anxious to 'show off' her friendship with him much more than to have the relationship that followed. She says as much herself in one letter to Byron that I am quoting, and I entirely believe her – in spite of the theories of some psychologist s[63], not unknown to Vienna!

I must also tell you that the British Institute in Florence has proved most serviceable as they sent out someone to the Antella and she has sent me a description of the grave and a rubbing of the actual stone. Where Graham got his idea of Ripoli from and his story of the inscription is quite amazing, and he says in that letter in the book that a British Consul, Connaghi, told him.

-2-[64]

Perhaps I should ask the British Institute if there is any possibility of the grave having been altered or transferred. Had you heard of the inscription before?

With renewed thanks for all your help and interest. It has been delightful writing a book with someone so interested following its course. It has now gone to the publisher whose verdict I await. I suggest sending certain chapters to you, if I may, before publication, but it was urgent for him to have a look at it as soon as possible. I hear of yet another American on the track, but Mr. Buxton Forman is very kindly protecting my interests over the Journals in the British Museum. This American has not communicated with me at all; the other three have retired!

Yours sincerely,
Rosalie Mander.

Unpublished. Text: M.S., Pf. Coll., CL'ANA 0018

APPENDIX G: ROSALIE, LADY MANDER'S LETTERS

from Lady Mander[65]

Telephone
Finchfield 61025
Telegrams
Mander, Wightwick,
Wolverhampton.

Wightwick Manor,
Wolverhampton.
August 28 th, 1938

Dear Frau Crüwell,
    This is to be just a short note in answer to yours. The name about whom I would like more particulars if you have them is Mrs Mason, the Lady Mountcashel who is the Cini's ancestress.[66]
    I have heard from someone at Newstead Abbey who is finding out about making a water colour of Claire and will let me know further particulars as soon as possible.
    I have written about the death certificate, but have had no answer as yet. I will send you the Vienna chapters for your criticism, if I may, also to see if any references to the family are[67] incorrect or not desirable. This will be in about two weeks.[68]

Yours sincerely,
Rosalie Mander.

Illeg. Allegra by
<u>Iris d'Origo</u>
Illeg. I"ve
In illeg. illeg. character?   Edward Dōwden
Portr.t Cl.Cl. von Mrs Curran   The life of
Trelawny, illeg.   Percy B
Illeg Bŭxton   Shelley
Forman

<u>Emilio Biode</u>
La figlia di Lord Byron[69]

Unpublished. Text: M.S., Pf. Coll., CL'ANA 0019

APPENDIX G: ROSALIE, LADY MANDER'S LETTERS

Telephone
Finchfield 61025
Telegrams
Mander, Wightwick,
Wolverhampton.

Wightwick Manor,
Wolverhampton.

Dear Frau Crüwell,

I am writing this note in haste as I feel sure that if you do not already know, you will be as interested as I am to hear that both Charles Clairmont and his wife published English school books. Two are in the British Museum; perhaps you could find them and others in Vienna.

(English and German title page)
(1)   First Poetical Reading Book etc.
       by Charles Gaulis Clairmont
            Vienna
       Braumuller and Seidel. 1845
(2)   and with the same publisher, but all in German except for English dedication to Imperial and Royal Highness The Most Illustrious Priness[70], Mary Caroline, Archduchess of Austira[71] etc. by Antonia Clairmont.[72]

I[73] should be very interested to know if you have heard of these. Evidently Gaulis' is his English name; there is an idea that his father may have been a Huguenot emigré.[74]

Yours sincerely,
Rosalie Mander.

P. S. I send you a card with the actual German title.[75]

Unpublished. Text: M.S., Pf. Coll., CL'ANA 0020

392

Telephone
Finchfield 61025
Telegrams
Mander, Wightwick,
Wolverhampton.

Wightwick Manor,
Wolverhampton.
<u>August 16th</u>[76]

Dear Frau Crüwell,

    I was just about to send these snapshots when your letter arrived; I am glad you will be able to show them to your brother[77] at the same time as he is also interested. They were taken for me by Signora Farini-Cini, whose kindness is really very great as she has made several visits to the Antella. She wondered if the grave was originally in the present position[78] or if it had been moved. The only record of the burial seems to be the name written in a book as shown in the snapshot,[79] but I will get the British Institute to have an authorised certificate made from it. I am also asking the Newstead Abbey photographer about the portrait – would your brother like a coloured reproduction? The colours are very pleasing although the canvas is so worn & a little torn in parts. If you know anything more about M^rs. Mason I should[80] be very glad to send details to the Cinis

  – With kindest regards, Rosalie Mander.

Telephone[81]
Finchfield 61025
Telegrams
Mander, Wightwick,
Wolverhampton.

> Wightwick Manor,
> Wolverhampton.

P.S. I see I have not answered your question about my name. Grylls was my maiden name; a very old Cornish one that we can trace back to the Conqueror.[82] There are few of my family unfortunately in Cornwall now. I can connect my Pedigree with that of Trelawny. which is, perhaps, why I have tried to give as good a character as possible to the old ruffian!

I would love to come to Vienna, but there are reasons that I never leave my husband for more than an odd night. I very much hope we may be able to plan our annual tour abroad this year to be near Vienna so that I at least might come over and meet you.

Unpublished. Text: M.S., Pf. Coll., CL'ANA 0021

Notes

1 The address on Mander's stationery was printed in blue ink. The telephone and telegram information on the left side of the paper was printed on the diagonal and in uppercase letters. I have standardized all capitalization. All of the letters include Mander's own handwritten signature.
   Wolverhampton is in West Midlands county in west-central England. Since 1937, Wightwick Manor has been part of the National Trust.
2 Mander's spelling.
3 Oxford University Press published *Mary Shelley: A Biography* in 1938.
4 French for "documented".
5 See the Introduction to this edition for more information about Claire Clairmont and Byron.
6 The books mentioned here are *Ariel, ou la Vie de Shelley* by André Maurois (1923; the English translation was published in 1924); *Last Links with Byron, Shelley and Keats* by William Graham (1898); *The Romantic Life of Shelley and the Sequel* by Francis Henry Gribble (1911); *Byron* by André Maurois (1930).
7 Harvard University Press published *The Journals of Claire Clairmont* in 1968. Marion Kingston Stocking and David Stocking edited them.
8 See the Introduction to this edition for more information about Charles Clairmont's paternity.
9 Mander handwrote this final section.
10 See this edition for a copy of Amelia Curran's 1819 portrait of Claire Clairmont.
11 Amelia Curran (1775–1847) painted the portrait of William Shelley (1816–1819), Mary and Percy's son, in Rome in 1819. The painting is now in the Carl H. Pforzheimer Collection of Shelley and His Circle.
12 Curran painted Percy Shelley in 1816. Her painting now hangs in the National Portrait Gallery in London.
13 The pending war and the rise of National Socialism in Austria.

14 Mander began a new page after the word "have" on a new sheet of stationery.
15 Allegra died in 1822 in a convent in Bagnacavallo, Italy. Shelley drowned in 1822 aboard the *Don Juan* in the Gulf of La Spezia near Livorno in Italy when the vessel overturned in a storm. His friend Edward Williams who was traveling with him died as well.
16 Mander wrote the word "old" by hand.
17 Mander typed the number "9" for the date but then changed it to an "8".
18 Probably Sir William Henry Bradshaw Mack (1894–1974), who later became the British ambassador to Austria after the Second World War.
19 Mander wrote the date in ink. She also numbered the pages of this letter.
20 Mander began a new page here. In addition to the address, the handwritten number 2 appears at the top of the second page.
21 *The Clairmont Correspondence* includes a letter from Claire Clairmont to Lady Mount Cashell (see footnote 2, letter of 21 April 1938), dated c. 24 September 1822 and written from 37 Biber Bastei, Vienna (see *CC* I: 199). Mander records in *Claire Clairmont: Mother of Byron's Allegra* that "Charles lived in a big block of flats built up against the Biber Bastion, one of the ramparts whose name is still preserved in the Bibergasse that runs parallel to the Stubenring" (1939: 167).
22 A commercial street in the First District (Innere Stadt) in Vienna today. Originally, it was a ditch (Graben" means "ditch" in German).
23 The Ringstrasse is a road that circles Vienna's Innere Stadt.
24 Page 3 begins here. The handwritten number 3 also appears at the top of the third page.
25 Russian writer, Anton Chekhov (1860–1904).
26 Page 4 begins here and includes a handwritten number 4.
27 A typographical error.
28 On 25 December 1869, Claire Clairmont wrote a letter to Edward John Trelawny in which she told him about Pauline's marriage proposal: "My niece during and after her Mother's sickness and death was very much assisted by an elderly Austrian retired Major – he wishes to marry her; he cannot leave Austria or he would lose his pension . . . I have told Pauline to do exactly what she thinks will be best for her happiness. I will give no advice or take any responsibility on myself in her affairs" (*CC* II: 602).
29 See letter of 6 March. Mander wrote the English for the Biber Bastei.
30 The Pestsäule (German for "Plague Column") was completed in 1694 on the Graben to commemorate the Great Plague of 1679.
31 Mander began a new page here. In *Claire Clairmont: Mother of Byron's Allegra*, Mander includes two pictures that Crüwell-Clairmont sent to her. One of these she describes thus: "Vienna in 1822 . . . the Stefansdom with its one tower that springs straight from the earth to heaven and forever lacks its twin: the apex of the city as it is the landmark for miles around." She labels the other: "The Graben, Vienna. Claire must have visited the shops in the Graben and gazed sceptically at the Plague memorial that stands there, the quintessence of Austrian baroque" (1939: after 173). In her acknowledgment page, Mander thanks Crüwell-Clairmont for "the old prints of Vienna which I have been able to reproduce" (1939: 226).
32 In 1822, the Austrian authorities ordered Claire (who was visiting her brother) and Charles Clairmont to leave Vienna under suspicion of dissident behavior. Their connections to Godwin and Shelley likely played a role in the order. They were, however, exonerated, and permitted to stay.
33 See the Introduction to this edition for more information about Clara Clairmont's marriage to Alexander Knox.
34 Dame Iris Margaret Origo (1902–1988) wrote *Allegra* in 1935. In *Claire Clairmont: Mother of Byron's Allegra*, Mander thanked "the Marchesa Origo, author of *Allegra* (Hogarth Press, 1935)" who "most generously allowed me to reproduce the miniature

35 Mander wrote this postscript by hand and at the top of the second page of this letter. The words "Paradies Garten" are German for "Paradise Garden". In *Claire Clairmont: Mother of Byron's Allegra,* Mander identified Paradies Garten as "a popular pleasure outside the walls" of Vienna (1939: 166).
36 Mander wrote the word "are" in pen and above the elided "is".
37 A former pupil of Mary Wollstonecraft, Lady Margaret Mount Cashell (born Margaret King, 1773–1835) was a close friend of both Mary Shelley and Claire Clairmont. She acquired her title from her marriage to Stephen Moore, Lord Mount Cashell with whom she had seven children. She left Cashell for George William Tighe (1776–1837). She called herself Mrs. Mason after Wollstonecraft's character in Wollstonecraft's *Original Stories from Real Life* (1791) who provided instruction for her two students, Mary and Caroline. Lady Mount Cashell had two daughters with Tighe, Lauretta (1809–1880) and Nerina (1815–1874). Mary Shelley wrote her story, *Maurice, or the Fisher's Cot* (1820), for the couple's older daughter, Lauretta. The manuscript was published in 1998, after having been found in 1997 in Italy. The younger of the couple's two daughters, Nerina, married Bartolomeo Cini (1809–1877), Claire's friend whom she named executor of her will.
38 *Picture of Vienna Containing a Historical Sketch of the Metropolis of Austria* (1844) records that Charles Clairmont lived at 267 Wallnerstrasse (Vienna: Braumüller and Seidel, 1844) p. 111.
39 Mander handwrote this letter on two pages.
40 Page 2 begins here.
41 Claire was buried in the Camposanto della Misericordia di Santa Maria all'Antella (Cemetery of the Mercy of Saint Maria all'Antella) in Florence, Italy. Her bones were later dug up, buried under the pavement, and a plaque now marks her name.
42 The Cimitero di Trespiano (Trespiano Cemetery) is located near Florence.
43 Percy Shelley dedicated his 1821 poem, "Epipsychidion" to Teresa Viviani (Emilia).
44 Mander wrote these final words on the side of the page.
45 See letter of 21 April.
46 Mander repeated this idea in *Claire Clairmont: Mother of Byron's Allegra* (1939: 210).
47 See letter of 6 March.
48 Mander referenced British poets Robert (1812–1889) and Elizabeth Barrett (1806–1861) Browning, Walter Savage Lander (1775–1864) and Arthur Hugh Clough (1819–1861).
49 Mander elided the original word with six letter "x"s and wrote the word "pygmies" above the elided letters.
50 Mander duplicated these words in *Claire Clairmont: Mother of Byron's Allegra* (1939: 194).
51 Both in Florence, Italy.
52 Mander typed eight letter "x"s over an illegible word.
53 Harry Buxton Forman (1842–1917) was a biographer and his subjects included Percy Shelley and John Keats. He also collected items pertaining to the Romantic writers. Forman and Thomas James Wise (1859–1937) forged many documents between 1886 and 1916. See letter of 3 April 1938,
54 Edward John Trelawny (1792–1881), author and friend of Claire Clairmont and the Shelleys. He published *Recollections of the Last Days of Shelley and Byron* in 1858. He is buried beside Percy Shelley in Rome.
55 See a copy of the portrait in this edition. Newstead Abbey in Nottinghamshire was Byron's home.
56 Page 2 begins here.

APPENDIX G: ROSALIE, LADY MANDER'S LETTERS

57 Trelawny's daughter, Zella (1826 – c. 1907).
58 Sir John Everett Millais's painting *The North-West Passage* which he completed in 1874. It now hangs in the Tate Britain in London.
59 Mander originally typed "Trelawny's" but she handwrote "in" above the "s".
60 Maria Gisborne (1770–1836), friend of Mary Wollstonecraft and of Mary and Percy Shelley. Godwin proposed to her after Wollstonecraft's 1797 death, but she refused him.
61 Thomas Love Peacock (1785–1866), author and friend of Percy Shelley.
62 Georgina Hanghegyi (1864–1885), Pauline Clairmont's daughter. See the Introduction to this edition for more information about her life. As Pauline's daughter, Georgina was Claire's great-niece and step-great-niece to Mary Shelley. Her paternity is unknown.
63 Mander's spelling. She likely referred here to psychologists like Sigmund Freud and Carl Gustave Jung.
64 Mander began her second page here.
65 These words are written in pencil at the top of the page, above the address.
66 See letter of 21 April.
67 The second page begins here.
68 Mander handwrote this final sentence.
69 These final words were written in pencil, probably by Crüwell-Clairmont. She referenced the portrait of Claire Clairmont by Amelia Curran ("Portr.t Cl.C. von Mrs Curran) and Edward Dowden's (1843–1913) *The Life of Percy Bysshe Shelley* (1886). *Allegra, La Figlia di Byron* is the Italian title for Origo's *Allegra*.
70 Typographical error.
71 Typographical error.
72 See the Introduction to this edition for more information about Charles and Antonia Clairmont as writers. It was Charles, not Antonia, who dedicated his book to the Archduchess of Austria.
73 Page 2 begins here.
74 See the Introduction to this edition for more information about Charles Clairmont's father. The Huguenots were Protestants, originally from France.
75 Mander handwrote the postscript.
76 Mander handwrote this letter instead of typing it.
77 Walter Clairmont.
78 Page 2 begins here.
79 The Carl H. Pforzheimer Collection of Shelley and His Circle has these photographs in its collection.
80 Mander wrote these final words on the side of the letter.
81 Mander typed this final page. She began typing on a new sheet of paper with the address printed on it.
82 William the Conqueror, from Normandy, conquered the British Isles in 1066.

INDEX

Note: Page numbers followed by "n" indicate a note on the corresponding page.

A *see* Bowler, Adelaide Agnes Henrietta
AB *see* Bowler, Adelaide Agnes Henrietta
Abercrombie, John 49, 90, 209n82
Ad *see* Bowler, Adelaide Agnes Henrietta
Addy *see* Bowler, Adelaide Agnes Henrietta
Admont 319, 320
Admont Valley 319
Aflenzer 314
Aflenzer Staritzen 315, 323
Agfa 374
Albert, Prince of Saxe-Coburg-Gotha 227n460
Alfred, Lord Tennyson *see* Tennyson, Alfred, Lord
Alighieri, Dante 231n573
Alloway Bank 67, 69, 123, 137, 212n151, 223n382
Alpine Montan Steel Corporation 312, 322, 324
Anton, Paul III, Prince Esterházy 287n193
Apollo 94, 215n236
Arden, Jane 3
Aryan descent, proof of 16, 368, 371
Atkins, John 210n89
Aubigny, Fanny Horstig d' *see* Pichler, Fanny von (née von Horstig)
Austerlitz, Battle of 261, 290n236
Australia viii, xvii, xviii, 1, 12, 13, 20, 21, 24n7, 199n1, 200–201n2, 201n4, 202n21, 206n60, 209n83, 224n394, 225n406, 229n514, 243, 276n1, 277n9, 279n33, 332, 335, 336, 337, 342, 344, 346, 348, 355, 358, 373; Adelaide 241, 280n38; Albany 279n36, 280n40; as a source for governess 336; Bathurst ix, 50, 71, 200n2, 201n3, 212n152, 212n156, 213n163, 218n257, 220n288, 339, 359; historical background 357; Hobson's bay 239, 279n32; King Georges Sound 241, 279n36; Melbourne 239–240, 267, 279n32, 279n33, 292n294; Melbourne Public Library 239, 279n33; New South Wales 201n3, 233n623, 284n135, 284n136, 296n407, 296n408, 357–358, 359, 367; pastoralism 277n6, 277n10; Port Philip 278n32; Queensland 349; Sydney 50, 209n82, 223n385, 224n391, 239, 278n12, 357; Tantawanglo 253, 284n135; Talbingo 253, 284n136; women emigration to Australia 336
Australian Tales Retold: and, Sketches of Country Life 21, 224n388
Austria 24n9, 356, 359, 368, 374; Austrian Banat 356, 359, 374; Austro-Hungarian monarchy 357; Baden bei Wein 22, 257, 259, 260, 287n190; Burgenland 374; Carinthia 24n9; Graz 257, 287n188; Hallein 275, 296n405; historical background 357; Kaiser Ferdinands-Nordbahn railway 260, 290n232; Liezen 360, 367; Styria 287n186, 365n2; Vienna 23, 258–260, 286n166, 290n225, 356, 362, 373–374; Vöslau 276, 296n406; Weilburg 257, 287n192
Austro-Hungarian Empire 357

B *see* Blair, Mr.
B, Miss *see* Bowler, Adelaide Agnes Henrietta 59,
B, Mr. *see* Bowler, Ernest Ulysses
Baden 22

INDEX

Bacon, Francis, Sir 52, 210n90
Bácsák, Marie 237, 278n21
Bakhtin, Mikhail 343
Bally-Clairmont, Mary Claire 2, 14, 15, 16, 22, 24n9, 25n11, 323n1, 199n1, 208n67, 219n287, 376
Bally-Clairmont, Mary Claire family tree 24n6, 24n7
Bally, Claus 2, 15
Bally, Hans-Jörg 2, 15
Bally, Peter 2, 15
Bally, Sylvia 15
Banat 22, 362
Bannet, Eve Tabor 345
Bärenloch 322
Baron Verulam *see* Bacon, Francis, Sir
Barst, Julia 336
Basilica of St. Peter's 255, 285n153
Batavia 340
Bathurst 50, 71, 83, 108, 125
Baulkham Hills 137, 223n385
Beachy Head 195, 233n616
Beadon, Robert 24n3
Beaulier, Konstantin Bouhelier 10
Becker, Colonel 258, 289n203
Bedborough, Mr. 251
Beethoven, Ludwig van 138, 224n399
Behar steamer 239–242, 245, 279n30
Belec 362
Benedictine Abbey 320
Benedictine library 320
Benedictines 320
Bennett, Betty 6
Bernhardt, Sarah 272, 294n358
Berry, Alexander 20–21
Beyond Nationalism 200n1
Bidder, B. 232n584
BirchPfeiffer, Goldbauer von 273
Bishop, Catherine 336
Bishop, Mr. & Miss 236, 250, 251
Blacket, Edmund 213n163
Blackman, James 213n163
Blackwoods Edinburgh Magazine 231n572
Blair, Mr. 22, 209n83, 219n287, 223n377
Bleckmann 312
Blood, Fanny 2
Bode, Annie Isabel Jane 223n362
Bode, Frederick Robert 131, 223n36
Bohemia 372; *see also* Czech Republic
Boleyn, Anne 228n499
Bollman, Mr. 266
Boree Creek 127, 222n352

Böse Wand 316
Botting, Eileen 4
Bourrier, Karen 333
Bowler, Adelaide Agnes Henrietta 21, 67, 114, 201n6, 203n22, 204n44, 208n72, 209n79, 214n188, 215n205, 217n255, 219n281, 228n502, 229n524; (A in Pauline Clairmont's journal) 35, 36, 65; (AB in Pauline Clairmont's journal) 106; (Ad. in Pauline Clairmont's journal) 107, 108, 114; (Addy in Pauline Clairmont's journal) 77; (Miss B. in Pauline Clairmont's journal) 59, 76
Bowler, Adolphus Charley Robert (D. Bowler) 72, 201n6, 214n169
Bowler, Ernest Ulysses 131, 201n6, 203n27, 217n256; (E in Pauline Clairmont's journal) 36, 38, 64, 65; (Mr. B in Pauline Clairmont's journal) 100
Bowler, John 201n6
Bowler, Julia Francis Nina 217n253
Bowman, William 83, 215n203
Breillat, Mr. and Mrs. (M.B. in Pauline Clairmont's journal) 154, 227n442, 227n450, 229n524, 230n542
British Critic of 1796 3
British Women's Diaries 349
Brontë, Charlotte 335
Brontë, Emily 281n60
Brougham, Marianne, Lady 348
Brougham, Lord 212n161
Broughton, William Grant 213n163
Brown, Mrs (Mrs. B in Pauline Clairmont's journal) 169, 170, 174, 225n400, 229n505, 230n528, 230n542, 231n560
Brucedale homestead 21, 49, 51, 65, 67, 132, 137, 157, 181, 182, 199n1, 200n2, 201n3, 210n86, 222n33, 357
Buchalmspitze 319, 320
Buchanan, Benjamin 236, 278n14
Buckle, Thomas Henry 236, 277n2
Bürgeralm 314
Burne-Jones, Edward Coley 213n163
Burney, Francis 343, 350n4
Burns, Robert 143, 221n322, 226n412, 232n583
Byron, Clara Allegra 7, 338, 378, 383, 395n15
Byron, Lord 7–8, 19, 20, 152, 184, 205n57, 216n232, 217n248, 227n439, 231n564, 371, 373, 338, 378, 394n6

INDEX

Cambridge History of Travel Writing 346
Cape Horn 229n514
Carl H. Pforzheimer Collection of Shelley and His Circle 2, 14, 15, 24n9, 26, 362, 368, 376, 377, 394n11
"Cattle Muster on the Plains, A" 21
Caroly, Count (Countess Károlyi in Rakičan) 257, 287n194
Catacombes of San Genaro 253, 283n105
Catherine of Aragon 228n499
Catholic Church 320
Cecilia 350n4
Chakraborty, Satyasikha 336
"Charge of the Light Brigade" 219n287
Charles, Archduke 350n3
Charlotte Augusta Anne Suttor Diaries 341
Chisholm, Caroline 342
Christianity 16
Church of S Maria dei Saryri (Basilica of Santa Maria della Sanità) 253, 283n106
Churtitz, Amtsrath 265, 292n278
Cini, Bartolomeo 278n17, 390
Cini, Giovanni 237, 278n17
Claire Clairmont: Mother of Byron's Allegra 376, 395n21, 395n34
Clairmont, Alma Pauline 10, 14, 15, 16, 17, 22, 199n1, 325n1, 360, 368, 371, 374, 376
Clairmontana 376
Clairmont, Antonia (née von Hembyze) 1, 9, 11, 12, 22, 24n1, 208n67, 221n313, 223n369, 229n370, 232n587, 278n20, 282n91, 287n190, 289n203, 291n241, 334, 356, 357, 372, 373; (M) 92; (Mamma in Wilhelm Clairmont's journal) 252, 257, 258, 263, 265, 268, 269, 282n91, 287n191, 359; (Missul) 259, 289n212; Belgian roots 10; with cancer 13; children 10, 11, 13, 357; as English teacher 9; *Erste Schritte zur Erlernung der englischen Sprache, für Kinder von sechs bis zehn Jahren* "First Steps to Learning the English Language, for Children ages six to ten" 9, 24n6; as writer 9, 10
Clairmont, Charles Abram Gaulis 371
Clairmont, Charles (Carl) Gaulis 1, 3, 4, 5, 8, 9, 24n1, 24n6, 334, 350n3, 356, 371, 376, 381; children 10; death 11–12, 357; as English tutor 9, 356–367; *First Poetical-Reading Book, Being an Impressive Collection of the Most Interesting Pieces in Verse in the English Language* 9, 350n3, 392; Kollonitz 12; liberalism 10; parents 9; political views 10; *Reine Grundlehre der Englischen Sprache* "Basics of English Language" 9; in Vienna 10; *Vollständige Englische Sprachlehre: die Syntaxis in 30 Lectionen eingetheilt* "Complete English Grammar: Syntax in 30 Lessons" 9; as writer 9; *see also* Clairmont, Antonia (née von Hembyze)
Clairmont, Charles Gaulis (Charley), Jr. 1, 10, 11, 21, 170, 206n57, 210n98, 216n227, 220n293, 223n368, 261, 291n241, 291n244, 356
Clairmont, Christoph *see* Clairmont, Johann Christoph
Clairmont, Clara Mary Jane (Claire) 1, 3, 5, 6, 7, 8, 19, 200n2, 202n21, 222n335, 332, 356, 359, 362, 371, 373, 378; (Aunt Claire, as mentioned in Wilhelm Clairemont's letters) 255, 260, 263, 265, 268, 269, 278n17, 285n164, 285n165, 285n166, 289n203, 290n227, 291n241, 359; 1819 portrait 388, 394n10; estates 13; generosity to relatives 1, 8, 10, 11, 12, 357; husband 7–8; parents 4–5; Russian journal 378; Shelleys 7–9; *see also* Byron, Lord
Clairmont Correspondence, The 395n21
Clairmont diaries 18
Clairmont, Emily 10, 11, 26n14, 207n66, 207n67, 208n68, 216n227, 216n238; (Emmy in Pauline Clairmont's journal) 21, 208n67, 216n238, 217n242, 220n293, 339, 356; (Emy in Pauline Clairmont's journal) 45, (Emi in Pauline Clairmont's journal) 97; (Goldlosi in Pauline Clairmont's journal) 109
Clairmont family vii, x, 1, 11, 204n57, 206n58, 208n65, 356, 371, 372; papers x, 2, 14, 17, 24n7, 376; stock 16, 372; table 355; tomb viii, 15, 22, 23, 24n8, 26n14; *see also* Shelley- Clairmont family history
Clairmont Family Letters: 1839–1889, The ix, x, xii, 1, 2, 3, 13, 22, 23,, 24n4 200n1, 287n195, 288n197, 343, 344, 360, 376
Clairmont Family Journals: 1855–1885, The 22, 23
Clairmont, Frida (née Zucker) 15, 17–18, 374

400

INDEX

Clairmont, Hermine (Mina) 10, 356
Clairmont, Johann Christoph (Christoph) 2, 14, 15, 22, 24n9, 219n287, 376
Clairmont, Johann Paul 14, 16, 23, 24n8, 360, 366, 372
Clairmont, Maria Johanna Klara Gaulis (née Clara Knox) 1, 11, 24n1, 200n2, 204n57, 207n63, 207n65, 207n66, 208n68, 211n128, 214n192, 216n228, 217n242, 220n294, 232n581, 233n620, 339, 356; reference of death 44, 45; (Clari, in Pauline Clairmont's Journal) 9; (Dohl in Pauline Clairmont's Journal) 95, 97, 109
Clairmont, Mary Jane *see* Vial, Mary Jane (Mary Jane Godwin; Mrs. G)
Clairmont, Ottilia (Ottilie) 1, 14, 15, 17, 24n1, 24n8, 26n14, 286n166, 289n220, 360, 362, 372, 373
Clairmont, Paul *see* Clairmont, Johann Paul
Clairmont, Pauline Maria (Plin) 1, 3, 9, 11, 12, 15, 16, 18, 21, 25n10, 32, 200n2, 224n388, 31n289, 257, 258, 276, 287n192, 287n194, 290n231, 324n1, 325n1, 332, 356; on Adelaide Bowler 35–36, 65, 106, 114, 204n55; Australian journal (1855–1857) 32, 344, 346; in Austria 257, 287n192; in Bobda, Romania 362; brothers 42, 99; with Clarkson and James Osborne 157–196; daughter 17, 19, 202n18; death 5, 22–23, 360, 366; death certificate 366–367; death of sisters 92, 97; describing the Suttors 339; in England 20; with Ernest Bowler 38; feminist thoughts/inequality of men and women 339; in Florence, Italy 19; on God/religion 159, 162; as governess 12, 19, 20, 21, 341, 357; on hope 111; in Hungary 17; on jealousy 53, 57, 102; journals 15, 16–17, 18–19, 20, 21; linguist 20; on love 58, 102, 120; on marriage 61–62, 69–70; pianist 20, 22, 210n86; pregnancy 19; in Romania 13; romantic interests 53, 88, 90, 152–157; as teacher 20, 22; *Waterloo* vessel 22
Clairmont, Sidonia (Sidi) 10, 11, 21, 92, 208n67, 216n227, 217n242, 356
Clairmont, Walter Gaulis 2, 3, 14–18, 199n1, 325n1, 360, 368, 371, 374

Clairmont, Wilhelm Charles Gaulis 1, 2, 3, 9–15, 21, 24n1, 24n8, 26n14, 95, 201n3, 202n18, 203n21, 204n55, 210n98, 214n191, 216n237, 218n256, 224n394, 233n626, 236, 324n1, 325n1, 339, 356; Altenburgh 258, 288n197, 289n199, 372; as an appraiser 362, 363, 364, 373; in Australia 12, 357; in *Behar* steamer 239; books to be purchased 236; education 372; journal 13, 235, 276–277n1; religion 372; in Romania 13, in Slovenia 13; surveyor of crown properties 14, 360; in Vienna, Austria 14, 258, 360, 362, 372; wife 1, 14, 15, 17, 360; (Willy in Pauline Clairmont's journal) 72, 97, 145, 149; *see also* farm/farming
Clairmont-von Gonzenbach, Victorine 2, 15
CL'ANA 376, 378, 379, 380, 382, 383, 384, 386, 387, 389, 390, 391, 392, 394
Clarke, Patricia 335
codeswitching 348
Columbian, steamship 234n648
"Comin Thro' the Rye" 232n583
Complete Letter–Writer, The 345
Coodgee Bay 139
Corsica 23
Cotton, Alfred John 223n362
Croatia 359, 362, 375n8
Croft, John 236, 278n12, 359
Cross Hall 323
Crüwell-Clairmont, Alma *see* Clairmont, Alma Pauline
Crüwell, Gottlieb August 15, 26n14
Cully, Amy 343
Cultural Heritage Unit of Municipal Department – 7 for Culture in Vienna 23
Cumberland, St. 142, 225n411
Curran, Amelia 380, 394n10, 394n11, 394n12
"Curse of Minerva, The" 215n217
Cyclopedia of Popular Songs 2 232n584
Czech Republic 359; Bavaria 294n345; Brandenburg 271, 294n342; Brandish (Brandýsek) 274, 296n392; Brünn (Brno) 260, 275, 290n222, 290n223, 290n237; Gräfenberg 271; Hostitz (Hoštice) 261, 271, 275, 290n240, 294n341; Kulchena (Chuchelná) 264, 265, 291n267, 292n276; Litentschitz (Litenčice) 262, 275, 290n248, 296n401; Lobositz (Lovosice) 274, 296n386; Moravia 259,

401

261, 263, 289n215, 289n216, 290n223, 290n240, 291n263, 292n271; Oder 267, 292n302; Partschendorf (Bartošovice) 263, 291n263; Perutz (Peruc) 274, 296n387; Plan bei Marienbad 372, 373; Prague 274, 275; Prenzlow 271, 294n343; Schlan 274, 296n391; Schönbrun (Ostrava) 263, 291n265; Schönhof (Šenov) 263, 291n266; Smečno 274; Troppau (Opava) 263, 291n259; Veveří Castle 261, 28n233; Wischau 261, 275, 290n239

Dangar, William 359
Dargin, Eveleen 212n142
Darvall, John Bayley, Sir 184, 231n564
Das, Nandini 346
David, King 87, 215n214
Davidson, Jenny 348
Deák, István 289n210
Dear William: The Suttors of Brucedale 201n3, 203n41
Democritus 47, 208n69
Denison, William Thomas, Sir 233n623
Denlinger, Elizabeth 10
Deutelmosers 374
Deutelmoser, Hofrat 374
Devereux, Mary Jane *see* Vial, Mary Jane (Mary Jane Godwin; Mrs. G)
Devereux, Andreas Peter 371
Devonshire 24n6
Dickenson, Eliza 348
Dietrichstien, Prosekau-Lestic, Count 9
Diverty/Deverty 148, 153, 226n432, 227n443
Divine Comedy, The 231n573
Dobrein 313
Dohl *see* Clairmont, Maria Johanna Klara (née Clara Knox)
Dominikusch, Dr. 13, 14, 286n166
Dominion of Bellye, Archducal 374
Don Juan 186, 231n573
Donnawitz 324
Drathshmid, Frederic 207n67
Dredge, Sarah 337
Drysdale 158, 161, 225n400, 228n478, 228n490
Duboc, Julius 359
Du Plessis, Armand-Jean 232n594

E *see* Bowler, Ernest Ulysses
Egypt: Alexandria 243, 280n47; Cairo 242, 243, 280n44; Cleopatra's Needle 243, 280n51; Island of Lostra (Brothers Islands) 246, 281n65; Nile River 243, 280n46; Pompey's Pillar 243, 280n50; Red Sea 248, 281n73; Suez Canal 242, 280n43
Eissner, Frau von 17
Eisenerz 312, 316, 317, 318, 321, 322, 324
Elba 23
Elisabeth, Empress 286n181, 327n24, 327n25, 327n31, 360
Elysium 317
Emanuel II, Victor, King of Sardinia 286n180
Emmy/Emy/Emi *see* Clairmont, Emily
England 20, 21, 156, 196, 228n499
English Woman's Journal 337
Enns River 318, 319
Enns Valley 319, 320
Ennsthaler 318
Entailer Alps 319
Erlaufsee lake 314
Ernst, Heinrich Wilhelm 262, 291n251
Erste Schritte zur Erlernung der englischen Sprache, für Kinder von sechs bis zehn Jahren ("First Steps to Learning the English Language, for Children ages six to ten") 9, 24n6
Erzberg 322
Eskeles, Baron 9
An Essay on the Principle of Population as It Affects the Future Improvement of Society, with Remarks on the Speculations of Mr. Godwin, M. Condorcet, and Other Writers 222n341
Etschmeier 323
European, The 234n646
Evangelischer Friedhof Matzleinsdorf 24n8
Evelina 350n4

Fallenstein 314
Farini-Cini, Signora 386, 393
farm/farming 12–14, 24n7, 273, 286n165, 360; Banat 356, 362, 373, 374; Bobda 362; New Keutzlin 271, 294n339; Nikolaihof 13, 286n166, 360, 362; Kameruka 277n9; Kangaroo Hills 278n10, 359; Lady Spencer's farm 241, 280n39; Retchendorf 270, 271, 293n330; Schusters 257, 258, 287n196; Weisser 269, 293n312

INDEX

Fellinger, Mr. 265, 266
Female Middle Class Emigration Society 341
Ferdinand, Franz 9
Ferdinand I 357
Fieber, Marianne 14
Field, Jacob 332
Firebrace, Major 236, 277n9
First Poetical-Reading Book, Being an Impressive Collection of the Most Interesting Pieces in Verse in the English Language 9, 350n3, 392
"First Steps to Learning the English Language, for Children ages six to ten" 9, 24n6
Fletcher, Sheila 337
"For the Sake O' Somebody" (poem) 119, 221n322
Francesco II 286n181
Francis, Henry 108, 225n405, 220n288
Francis, Ruth Grosvenor 141, 144, 220n288, 225n405
Frankenstein, Or the Modern Prometheus 3, 6, 24n2
Franz Josef Gymnasium 374
Fraukirchen 319
Frauenmauer 322
Frauenmauerhöhle 312, 322
Freienstein 324
Frein 313, 314
Freinsattel 317
Friedau 324
Friedrich III (Friedrich Wilhelm Nikolaus Karl, Prince) 272, 294n354

G (Pauline's suitor) 60, 87, 211n119
Gams 317, 318
Garibaldi 286n180
Garrison, James 17–18
Gebhardt 320
Gemeindealm 314
General Währing Cemetery in Vienna 12, 373
Germany: Bastei 271, 298n382; Berlin 272; Bezhiz (Besitz) 269, 293n315; Coswig 272, 298n365; Dresden 272, 273, 298n371; Elbe 273, 298n379; Gemäldegalerie Alte Meister 273; Graubow (Grabow) 270, 293n326; Grünes Gewölbe 273, 298n372; Güstrow 271, 293n334; Hauen stein (Hohnstein) 271, 298n385; Konigstein Castle 271, 298n384; Leutewitz 272, 298n369; Lohmen 271, 298n380; Ludwigslust 270, 293n321; Malchin 271, 294n335; Meissen 272, 298n366; Muchow 271, 293n333; Oschatz 272, 298n364; Parchim 270, 293n322; Passow 270 Lübz 270, 293n327; Rhade thenno (Kurort Rathen) 271, 298n383; Risa (Riesa) 298n362; Schwerin 270, 293n329; Schweriner See 270, 293n332; Stavenhagen 271, 294n335; Teterow 271, 294n335; Uttewalde grund 271, 298n381; Wehlen 273, 298n379; Weissin (Woseriner See) 270, 293n325; Würzburg 374; Zithain (Zethain) 272, 298n368
Goethe, Ottilie von 343
Geoghegan, Louisa Agnes 342
Geonese (Genovese) 254, 255, 285n151
Gesäuse 312, 318, 319, 320
Ghislain d'Hembyse family 373
Godwin, Mary Louisa Eldred 5
Godwin, Mary *see* Shelley, Mary
Godwin, Mary Wollstonecraft *see* Shelley, Mary
Godwin, William 1, 3, 15, 324, 356, 368, 371, 373; *Memoirs of the Author of a Vindication of the Rights of Woman* (1798) 3, 4
Godwin, William Jr. 4–5
Goldlosi *see* Clairmont, Emily
Görlich, Ernst Joseph 9, 10
Gouldesbury, Francis Elphistone 120, 221n325
Grafenstein, Frida Maria von 374
Graham, William 378
Grassaltowitsch, Princess (née Esterhazy) 9
Gratechy, Dr. 262
Gratechy, Sophie 262
Greycliffe 224n391
Gribble, Francis Henry 378, 394n6
Griesmauer 322, 323
Grimmig 319
Grimmstein 316
Grossberalm 316
Grünersee 323
Grylls, Glynn R. 376
G.S., Mrs. *see* Johnston, Jane (Mrs. G.S.)
Gsöll Alm 322
Gstatterboden 319
Gump, Baron 9
Gusswerk 315

INDEX

Habsburgs 360
Hammerton, A. James 333, 335
Hamilton's Universal Tune Book: A Collection of the Melodies of All Nations 230n549
Hanghegyi, Georgina (Johanna Maria), 19, 22, 202n18, 203n38, 287n194
Hasenkopf 317
Hassall, Rowland 213n163
Hassall, Thomas 213n163
Hauer, Emily von *see* Pichler, Emily
Hauer, Rudolf von 14, 289n220, 362
Hawkins, Emily Jane 222n360
Heller 265
Helvety, Mr. & Mrs. 263, 264, 291n260, 291n262
Hembyze, Antonia Ghylain von *see* Clairmont, Antonia (née von Hembyze)
Hembyze, Georg von 10, 258, 289n204, 356
Henrietta, Princess 350n3
Henry VIII 163, 228n499
Hiawatha 111, 220n301
Hieflau 312, 317, 318, 321
Hieselegg Pass 324
Hindle, Maurice 7
History of a Six Weeks' Tour 6, 349
Hitschmann, Hugo Hippolyt 14
Hochalm 323
Hochkar 317
Hocheck 312
Hochschwab 323
Hochthor 320
Hoeveler, Diane Long 20
Holland 372, 373
Holland, Patrick 346
Hölle 315
Holmes, Richard 4
Holy Trinity, The 229n517
Hood, Thomas 276n1
Horn (Horne), Mr. 250, 251
Horstig, Court Chaplain 372, 373
Horstig, Fanny von *see* Pichler, Fanny von (née von Horstig)
Horstig, Rudolf von
Hoschschwab 315
Houdlik, Johann 259, 278n21
Huff, Cynthia 348
Huggan, Graham 346
Hughes, Kathryn 335
Hughes, Linda 343
Hungary 22, 359; Altenburgh 258, 263, 288n197, 288n199, 290n260, 372; Giuer (Győr) 259, 289n207; Ödenburg 258, 289n205; Wieselburg 257, 258, 287n195
Hunt, Marianne 5–6
Husband, P. 17, 18
Huscher, Herbert 12, 15, 22, 25n10, 202n18, 290n231
Hutton, Howard 190, 192, 232n582, 233n601

Imlay, Fanny 3, 6–7
Imlay, Gilbert 3
Immaculate Conception 314
Inferno 231n573
Inquiries Concerning the Intellectual Powers and the Investigation of Truth 209n82
Iony, Mrs. 263
Iriquois Confederacy 220n301
Italy 278n17; Apennine Mountains 256, 286n168, 286n170; Bologna 255, 256, 286n168; Calabria 252, 282n98; Cape Miseno 254, 283n145; Castel Nuovo 254, 284n142; Civita Vechia 254, 255, 284n140; Florence 255, 278n17, 285n164, 359; Gaeta 256, 286n180; Grand Hotel Trinacria 252, 283n99; Kingdom of the Two Sicilies 254, 284n143, 286n180, 286n181; Light of Gaeta 254, 285n146; Livorno 255, 285n162; Lombard plains 256, 286n179; Magenta 256, 286n176; Malrau, Baron 270; Messina 252, 282n97, 283n100; Milan 256, 286n172; Mt. Corno 256, 286n170; Mt. Etna (Aetna) 252, 282n96; Mt. Vesuvius 253, 283n103; Mundy, Baron 260, 261, 289n221, 290n233, 290n234; Mundy, Jaromír Freiherr von 290n234; Naples 253, 283n102, 283n103; Museo Bourbonico 253, 283n112; Nisita Procida Ischia 254, 285n144; Novarra 256, 286n178; Palazzo Reale di Napoli 254, 284n141; Pompeii (Pompeyi) 253, 283n103; Sardinia 252, 283n101; Sicily 252, 282n95; Solferino 256, 286n177; Trieste 256, 257, 286n166, 286n185; Tuscany 285n164; Venice 256, 286n175

James, Henry 19–20, 25n11
Jamison, Anne 340
Jane Eyre (character) 335
Jassinggraben 323

INDEX

Jastur 266
Jewish origins, disproving 16, 368, 371
Joffe, Sharon L. 12, 19, 72, 76, 80, 81, 113, 129, 154, 160, 162, 168, 206n57, 219n266
Johnsbach 319
Johnson, Robert, Esquire 94, 216n233
Johnson, Joseph 332
Johnson, Samuel 350n4
Johnston, Anna 347
Johnston, Jane 223n376, 226n435
Joseph, Franz I (Kaiser Franz Joseph I) 9, 206n57, 357, 360
"Journal From My Life Book Continuation VIII" 199n1, 343
Journals of Claire Clairmont, The 394n7

K *see* Knox, Alexander
Karl, Franz, Archduke 9
Kameruka 277n9
Kangaroo Hills 216n240, 278n10, 359; *see also* farms/farming
Károly (Károlyi), Countess xvii, 19, 22, 202n18, 287n194
Kastenriegel 315
"Katty Darling" (song) 158, 228n474
Katzbach, Battle of the 269, 293n313
Kelso Holy Trinity Church 71, 213n163
Kenny, Thomas 276n1
King, Margaret (Lady Mount Cashell) 391, 395n21, 396n37
Kinship Coterie and the Literary Endeavors of the Women in the Shelley Circle, The 343
Knox, Alexander 11, 12, 69, 200n2, 205n57, 206n60, 207n63, 212n157, 338; (K) 44
Knox, Clara *see* Clairmont, Maria Johanna Klara (née Clara Knox)
Koller, Emmie 14
Kollonitz, Mrs. 12, 206n57
Korte, Barbara 346
Kozlow, Elizabeth 4
Krampen 312
Kraus, Mr. 261, 291n241
Kraus Grotto 317
Kretchy, Mr. 262
Kreutzhalle 323

Lahr, Christopher David 376
Lambach 318
"Lament of Tasso, The" 186, 231n571
Langer, Director 263

Lavater, Johann Kaspar 236, 277n5
Lebanon, Beirut (Beyrout) 252, 282n94
Lee, Ray E. 17–18
Lee, William 212n156, 234n639
Legislative Assembly 215n203
Leiss, Anselm 322
Lejeune, Philippe 343
Leoben 312, 322, 324
Leopoldstein Lake 322
Lessons 3, 24n2
Lethbridge, John 5
Letters Written during a Short Residence in Sweden, Norway, and Denmark 332, 343, 349
Lewin, Jane 341
Lichtenstein 322
Life of Lord Byron, The 217n248
Life of William Wilberforce, The 228n483
life writing 332, 342, 343
Lilienfeld Abbey 314
"Lines Written by a Celebrated Authoress on the Burial of the Daughter of a Celebrated Author" (1834) 8
Litzen 319
Lizard Lighthouse 194, 233n612
Locksley Hall 219n287
London 12, 368, 373
Long Creek 34
Longfellow, Henry Wadsworth 220n301
Lord Verulam *see* Bacon, Francis, Sir
Lottie *see* Suttor, Charlotte Augusta Anna Francis
"Lotus-eaters, The" 224n393
"Love Lies Bleeding" 132, 223n364
"Love of the Angels, The" 99, 217n248
Lower Ring 315
Lubbert, Mr. 268
Ludwig, Christian II of Mecklenburg 270, 293n321
Ludwig, Karl, 9, 206n57, 357, 360
Ludwig, Margrave 314
Ludwig, Michael 23
Ludwig the Great 314
Ludwig, Wilhelm Friedrich, King of Prussia *see* Wilhelm I (Ludwig, Wilhelm Friedrich, King of Prussia)
Lüttwitz, Rudolf, Baron 267
Lynder, Linn M. 332

Macaulay, Thomas Babington 277n3
Macbeth 221n317
MacDonald, Flora 350n3

INDEX

Machiavelli, Niccolo 236, 277n4
Mack, William Henry Bradshaw, Sir 395n18
Mackenzie, Henry Douglas 217n253
Maitland Mercury and Hunter River General Advertiser, The 218n257, 279n30
Malta 236, 243, 250, 280n52, 282n77, 282n80; Citta' Veccia (Cita vechia) 251, 282n84; Co-Cathedral of St. John the Baptist 250, 282n81; Gorzo (Island of Gozo) 251, 282n85; Mdina 282n84; San Elmo (St. Elmo Watchtower) 251, 282n86
Malthus, Thomas Robert 124, 222n341
Mander, Geoffrey 376
Mander, Anthea Loveday Veronica 376
Mander, John Geoffrey Grylls 376
Mander, Rosalie 376, 377; book about Mary Shelley 378; *Claire Clairmont: Mother of Byron's Allegra* 376
Manfred 215n223
Manly Beach 147, 226n428
Manning, James A. L. 236, 240, 277n9, 278n10, 359
Manning, John Edye 277n9, 278n14, 359
Manning, Mary Firebrace 236, 277n9
Manning, William Montagu 359
Mariazell 312, 313, 314, 317
Markey, Anne 342
Marsden, Samuel 213n163
Martin, Georges 152, 226n438
Mary Caroline, Archduchess 350n3
Mary Shelley: A Biography 394n3
Masch, Anton 258, 289n201
Massé, Marsel 152, 153, 155, 156, 226n438
Matzleinsdorf Protestant Cemetery 12, 360, 372, 373
Maurice 278n17
Maurice, Frederick Denison 337
Maurois, André 378
Maximilian, Ferdinand, Archduke 9, 357
Maximilian, Ferdinand, Emperor 206n57
Mayes, Frances 346
McDougall, Sands and 276–277n1
McGeevor, Sophie 333
Memoir of the Conquest of Java, with the Subsequent Operations of the British Forces in the Oriental Archipelago 340
Mensdorff-Pouilly, Alexander von, Count 350n3
Meran, Count of 315

Messageries Shipping 252, 282n93
Messnerin 323, 324
Metamorphoses 232n595
Mills, Margaret 333
Miss B *see* Bowler, Adelaide Agnes Henrietta
"Miss Tina and Miss Plin: The Papers Behind *The Aspern Papers*" 15, 16, 18, 19–20, 25n10, 202n18, 207n62, 290n231
Mitchell, J.S. 236, 238, 251, 277n6
Montagu, Mary Wortley, Lady 343, 350n4
Moodie, Susanna 346
Moore, Thomas 99, 102, 216n232, 217n248, 219n263
Moravia 23, 314
Morris, Augustus 218n257
Mort, Thomas Sutcliffe (Mort, Mr.) 251, 259, 264, 268, 269, 359
Moser, Ignaz 258, 289n200
Mount Cashell, Lady 395n21
Murray, John 376
Murthal 324
Mürz Valley 312, 313
Mürzsteg 312
Mürzzuschlag 312, 324
Myers-Scotton, Carol 348

Napier, Francis 141, 144, 145, 148, 225n406, 226n425
Naso, Publius Ovidius 232n595
Nasswald 313
National Advocate, The 212n152
National Socialists 15, 368, 371, 374
Navy Surgeon: Or, Practical System Of Surgery. With A Dissertation On Cold and Hot Mineral Springs; And Physical Observations On The Coast of Guiney, The 210n89
Neue Augsburger Kattunfabrik 374
Neuberg 312, 313
New Zealand 335
Nice 23
Niederalpl Pass 313
Norton, Judith 203n41
Noth 317
Nubia ship 244, 281n57

Oberort 323, 324
"Ode to the West Wind" 223n375
Oliver, M. A. 342
Oneida steamship 234n643

INDEX

Opie, Amelia Anderson 215n208
Orange 91, 216n224
"Original Correspondence – Shelley and Byron" 17, 20
Origo, Iris Margaret, Dame 395n34
Osborne, George 188, 232n576
Osborne, Harry 161, 228n489
Osborne, James 157, 227n472, 229n510, 230n531, 230n534; (O in Pauline Clairmont's journal) 158; (James O in Pauline Clairmont's journal) 164, (J in Pauline Clairmont's journal) 171, (J.O. in Pauline Clairmont's journal) 170, 174, 175
Ötscher 314
Ottitz (Ocice) 292n269
Owenites 338

Pabst, Heinrich Wilhelm von 258, 288–289n200
Palfau 317
Palten Valley 320
Parker, Frederic 72, 214n168, 218n256
Parker, James 218n256
Parker, Langloh 217n256, 220n296; (L.P.) 100
Parramatta 145, 226n419
Pasquale 19
Pavlovna, Anna, Grand Duchess of Russia 232n577
Penrith 121, 221n330
"Periodicals for Schools in Nineteenth Century Australia: Catherine Helen Spence and the *Children's Hour*" 340
Pfaffenstein 322
Pfarralm 323
Pfeifer, Maria *see* Zucker, Marie (née Maria Pfeifer)
Pfeifer, Julius 374
Pforzheimer Collection *see* Carl H. Pforzheimer Collection of Shelley and His Circle
Philosophy of the Moral Feelings, The 209n82
Pichler, Emily von 14, 289n220, 362
Pichler, Fanny von (née von Horstig) 14, 372, 373
Pichler, Johann Franz Hofrath von 14, 325n1, 372, 373
Pichler, Mortiz von 24n9
Pichler, Ottilia von *see* Clairmont, Ottilia (Ottilie)
Picture of Vienna 200n1
Piozzi, Hester Lynch 350n4

Piper, John, Captain 212n151
Piper, Sarah Anne 114, 221n304
Piper, Thomas (TP) 218n256, 220n296, 221n304
Pirgas 320
Planspitze 319
Plin *see* Clairmont, Pauline Maria (Plin)
Plutarch 224n390
Poe, Edgar Allan 221n308
Poland: Bernstadt 267, 292n290; Breslau (Wrocław) 268, 269, 292n297; Brieg (Brzeg) 267, 292n296; Frankenstein 268, 293n309; Glogau (Głogów) 292n277; Gogoling (Gogolin) 265, 292n272; Liegnitz (Legnica) 269, 293n311; Oberglogau (Głogówek) 265, 292n273, 292n275; Ohlau (Olawa) 266, 292n286; Oppeln (Opole) 265, 266, 292n280; Ottitz (Ocice) 264, 292n270; Ratibor (Racibórz) 264, 265, 292n270; Schwieben (Świbie) 265, 292n281; Silesia 264, 292n270, 374; Tarnowitzer Bahn 265, 292n281; Wirchenblatt (Wierzchno) 269, 293n314
Präbichl 322, 324
Pribitzkessel 323
Prossen 322
Provincial Glossary; With a Collection of Local Proverbs, and Popular Superstitions, A 234n642
Prussia 262, 291n255
Punch magazine 276n1
Pyramul 34, 201n8

Quarm, Anne 232n584
Queen's College 337
Quirinal boat 252, 282n93

Raffles, Thomas Stamford, Lieutenant Governor 340
Raitt, Francis Mary Jane 201n6
Ramerthal Valley 315
Rawack (Ravac), Amalie Mauthner 233n626, 277n7
Rawack (Ravac), Leopold 233n626, 236, 277n7
"Raven, The" 221n308
Rax 312
Reading Autobiography: A Guide For Interpreting Life Narratives 343
Recollections of the Last Days of Shelley and Byron 205n57

INDEX

Redall, Mr. and Mrs. 157, 189, 225n400, 227n458
Regendank, Behr von 270
Reiman, Donald H. 2
Reine Grundlehre der Englischen Sprache "Basics of English Language" 9
Reitzenstein 319
Rivals, The 230n552
Robinson, Charles 6, 20
Rochester 335
Romania 13, 359; Bobda 360, 362; Tuzokrét 360
Rome: Coliseum 254, 285n150; Pantheon 254, 285n150; Circus Maximus 254, 285n150; Baths of Caracalla 254, 285n150; Ruins of Ancient Rome 254
Romantic Life of Shelley, The 378
Roquelle 153, 227n445
Roughing It in the Bush 346
Routledge Research Companion to Travel Writing, The 345, 346
Rudolf, Archduke 360
Rudolph I, Emperor 322
Rye, Maria 341
Ryper, Astrid 23

Saal Miss 267
Sahib, Nana 248, 281n72
Saliba, Mr. 251, 252
Salza 316
Salza Valley 314, 315, 316
Salzburg 320
Sanders, Valerie 333
Sands & Kenny's Diary and Almanac for New South Wales 235, 276n1
Sands, and McDougall 276–277n1
Sands, John 276n1
Sardinia, Kingdom of 286n180
Saudi Arabia: Bab el- Mandeb Straight 247, 281n70; Mecca 247, 281n70; Perim Island 247, 281n70
Schak, Mrs. 270
Scheiterboden 313
Schmiedhammer 312
Schönbigler (Schönbichler), Anna 10, 24n6, 356, 372, 373
Schüster, Mr. 263
Schwarzen Adler 312
Schwin, Mr. 257
Schützenauer Inn 315
Secretaries, The 345
Sedley, Amelia 232n576

Serbia 359
"Serpent that is Shut Out From Paradise, The" 48, 208n73
Shakespeare, William 221n302, 221n317
Shaw-Taylor, Leigh 332
Shelley family 1, 356
Shelley, Charles Bysshe 6
Shelley-Clairmont family history 3, 23, 344, 354, 356, 376
Shelley, Eliza Ianthe (Esdaile) 6
Shelley, Jane Shelley, Lady 6, 7, 11, 205n57
Shelley, Mary 1, 3, 5, 11, 20, 205n57, 216n227, 278n17, 285n162, 332, 334, 356, 371, 373, 396n37; 1859 *Shelley Memorials* 6; *Frankenstein, Or the Modern Prometheus* 3, 6; death 11; *History of a Six Weeks' Tour* 6; *Mary Shelley: A Biography* 394n3; *Maurice, or the Fisher's Cot* 278n17; *see also* Shelley, Percy Bysshe
Shelley papers *see* "Original Correspondence – Shelley and Byron"
Shelley, Percy Bysshe 5, 6, 208n73, 285n162, 338, 356, 371, 373; *History of a Six Weeks' Tour* 6; painting by Curran 394n12
Shelley, Percy Florence 11, 48, 205n57, 285n162
Shelley, Timothy, Sir 10, 334
Shelley, William 394n11
Sheridan, Richard Brinsley 230n552
Sherwin, Ann 10, 13, 15, 32, 34, 36–41, 46–48, 53, 54, 55, 65, 66, 73, 95–97, 108, 109, 116, 117, 193, 199n1, 203n29, 207n66, 208n68, 220n291, 286n166, 294n353, 362, 366, 367, 370n1
Siebensee lake 316
Silsbee, Edward Augustus 19, 20
Simla, steamship 234n645
Simpson, Campbell 267
Simpson, Ruth Amelia 340
Sketches of Country Life 21
Slovenia 359; Celje 365n1; Laibach (Ljubljana) 262, 291n247; Marburg (Maribor) 13, 206n57, 286n166, 360
Smallbones, Mr. 257, 258, 259, 287n193
Smith, Thomas Whistler 278n12
sociable travel letters 345
Social World of Batavia: European and Eurasians in Colonial Indonesia, The 339
Society for Textual Scholarship 2

INDEX

Sofala 34, 38, 94, 200n2, 201n4, 212n149
"Song" 84, 215n208
"Song of Hiawatha, The" 220n301
Sonnenburg peak 360
Sonnstein 323
Sophia, Maria of Bavaria 286n181
Sophie of Bavaria, Archduchess 9, 12
Sophie, Duchess of Hohenberg 357
Southey, Robert 4
Spain: Catalonia 246, 281n64; Mancha 246, 281n63
Spence, Catherine Helen 340–341
Spencer, Ann, Lady 241, 280n39
Spencer, Richard, Sir 241, 280n39
Sri Lanka: Galle 242, 243, 280n42; Galle Face Hotel, Colombo, Ceylon 279n26; Singhalese canal 244; Singhalese people 281n58
State Library Victoria 279n33
Stafford, Vicki Parslow 5
Stammel, Thaddäus 320
St. Clair, William 4
Steiermark 23
Stiebal, Verwalter 262
Stocking, David 394n7
Stocking, Marion Kingston 2, 9, 10, 15, 16, 17, 18, 19, 20, 22, 24n7, 24n9, 25n10, 25n11, 199n1, 290n231, 374, 394n7
St. Michael's Church 320, 372, 373
St. Mildred's Church 373
St. Oswald bei Graz 373
Stow, Catherine Eliza 217n256
St. Pancras Churchyard
St. Pölten 314
Styria 23, 314, 320
Sunstein, Emily 4
Suttor, Andrew Johnston (An.) 149, 226n435
Suttor, Caroline Elizabeth (Carry) 66, 209n77, 277n8, 278n14, 340; (Carry in Pauline Clairmont's journal) 49, 59, 88, 103, 115; (C in Pauline Clairmont's journal) 65
Suttor, Charlotte Augusta Anne Francis 21, 73, 201n12, 209n76, 210n91, 211n117, 214n173, 218n258, 220n288, 340; (C in Pauline Clairmont's journal) 53, 210n102; (Mrs. Suttor in Pauline Clairmont's journal) 49, 83, 122, 168; (Mrs. S in Pauline Clairmont's journal) 66, 71, 75, 98: her thoughts on Pauline 341

Suttor, Charlotte Augusta Anna 203n40, 215n204
Suttor, David 200n2, 359
Suttor, Dora Henrietta 201n6
Suttor, Elizabeth 216n230, 218n257; (Mrs. K in Pauline Clairmont's journal) 93; (Mrs. Kerr in Pauline Clairmont's journal) 100
Suttor, Emilie Henrietta 209n75, 211n110, 214n186; (E in Pauline Clairmont's journal) 76; (Emily in Pauline Clairmont's journal) 59
Suttor family 12, 220n288, 357
Suttor, Florence Adelaide 84, 215n205
Suttor, Francis Bathurst 212n147, 222n360; (F in Pauline Clairmont's journal) 66; (Frank in Pauline Clairmont's journal) 130
Suttor, George 21, 201n3, 357
Suttor, George Roxburgh 203n35, 204n43, 208n71, 212n142; (G in Pauline Clairmont's journal) 38, 39, 41, 47, 88, 90, 112
Suttor, Grace Agnes 201n6
Suttor, Herbert Cochrane 201n3, 209n75, 215n204; (Herby in Pauline Clairmont's journal) 49; (H in Pauline Clairmont's journal) 83
Suttor, Horace Melbourne 212n151
Suttor, Isabel Adelaide 201n6
Suttor, John Bligh 201n3, 201n6, 217n253
Suttor, Julia Nina Sofala 217n253
Suttor, Kathleen Francis 201n6
Suttor, Lilliane 201n6
Suttor, Maria 100, 217n256
Suttor, Mary Anne Grosvenor Francis 201n12, 204n54, 212n153, 215n206, 218n258; (Mary in Pauline Clairmont's journal) 68, (Mrs. T in Pauline Clairmont's journal) 33 (Ms TS in Pauline Clairmont's journal) 43, 84, (Mrs. Ch S in Pauline Clairmont's journal) 100
Suttor, Norman Lachlan 212n151
Suttor, Sarah 357
Suttor, Sarah Pauline 341
Suttor, Sarah Cordelia 203n41; (Mrs. Beverley in Pauline Clairmont's journal) 40
Suttor, Thomas Charles 201n12
Suttor, Una Leonora 201n6
Suttor, William Beverley 204n41

INDEX

Suttor, William Henry 21, 210n91, 211n138, 212n151, 214n181, 215n205, 234n639, 340; (Mr. S in Pauline Clairmont's journal) 53; (Mr. Suttor in Pauline Clairmont's journal) 76; (W.H.S in Pauline Clairmont's journal) 163

Suttor, William Henry, Jr. (Willie) 21, 23, 99, 201n3, 201n6, 202n20, 203n26, 203n30, 216n237, 224n388, 332 (W in Pauline Clairmont's journal) 37, 72, 90, 100, 101, 105, 106, 121, 132; (William Henry Suttor the younger in Pauline Clairmont's journal) 212n151; *Australian Stories Retold* 21; "A Cattle Muster on the Plains" 21; *Memoirs* 21; *Sketches of Country Life* 21; "Van Dieman's Land Ghouls, The" 21; Mr. Blair 21

Switzerland 381

Sydney 50, 66, 67, 97, 117, 154, 175, 190, 239, 279n30

Sydney Almanac and General Calendar 209n83

Sydney Morning Herald, The 200n2, 209n83, 279n30

Sydney Harbour 138, 224n396

Szombathely (Stein-am-Anger) 278n22

Tala (Kieta) Station 359
Tantalus 319
Tarok 316
Taylor, Jean Gelman 339
Tennyson, Alfred, Lord 21–22, 107, 138, 210n83, 219n287, 224n397
Teresa, Gerrard 333
Thackeray, William Makepeace 226n416
Theresia, Empress Maria 10, 372, 373
Theresianum Ritterakademie 9, 356, 371, 373
Thompson, Carl 347
Thorn, Major William 339
Thrale, Hester 341
Thun-Hohenstein, Count 274, 296n388
Tighe, Catherine Elizabeth Raniera (Nerina) 278n17
Tighe, Laurette 278n17
Toché, Paul 162, 226n421, 226n438; (Tochet in Pauline Clairmont's Journal) 145, 148, 152, 153; (T in Pauline Clairmont's Journal) 155; (Paul T. in Pauline Clairmont's Journal) 157
Todd, Janet 5, 6

Todtes Weib 312, 313, 314
Tooth, Robert 236, 251, 263, 268, 270, 271, 277n10, 277n11, 359
Tooth, Edwin 359
Tragöß Valley 312, 323, 324
Tragöss 322, 324
travel journals 348–349
travel literature 346
travel writing 332, 346, 347; difference between men and women's writings 344, 347–348, 350
Trelawny, Edward John 8, 205n57, 388
Trofeng 322
Trollope, Frances 8
Tucker, Evelyn 17
Turkish war 322
Turner, Joseph Mallord William 298n381
TwoFold Bay Pastoral Association 216n240, 359

Under the Tuscan Sun 346
Universität Wien (University of Vienna) 9, 356
University of Basel 374

"Van Dieman's Land Ghouls, The" 21
Vanity Fair 144, 188, 226n416, 231n563, 232n576
Varens, Adèle 335
Vatican City 255, 285n154
Vaughan Williams Memorial Library 232n584
Veitsch 314
Vetsera, Marie Alexandrine, Baroness 360
Vial, Mary Jane (Mary Jane Godwin; Mrs. G) 5, 6, 9, 24n6, 356, 368, 371
Victoria, Princess 294n354, 294n355
Victoria, Queen 222n336, 224n388, 227n460, 294n354, 350n3
Vienna 10, 12, 14, 23, 258, 259, 260, 286n166, 290n225, 312, 325n1, 362, 371, 373, 374, 381, 395n22
Viktor I, Moritz Carl (Duke of Ratibor) 264, 292n270
Voignier-Marshall, Jacqueline 358
Vollständige Englische Sprachlehre: die Syntaxis in 30 Lectionen eingetheilt "Complete English Grammar: Syntax in 30 Lessons" 9
Vordernberg 322, 324
Vordere Hölle 315

Walcker Estate 13, 14, 286n166
Walla Walla (Wallawa) 132, 223n366
Walpole, Horace 3
Walsh, Gerald P. 276n1
Wandering Willie 119, 221n323
Ward, Dorothy 348
Warren, Alexander 97, 217n243
Waterloo vessel 22, 224n400, 227n459
Weedon, Alexis 333
Wegscheid 315
Weichselboden 312, 315, 316
Westbrook, Harriet 6, 7
Wilberforce, Samuel 159, 228n483
Wilberforce, William 228n483
Wildalpen 312, 315, 316, 317, 318, 320
Wildalpen valley 322
Wilhelm I (Ludwig, Wilhelm Friedrich, King of Prussia) 272, 294n354
Wilhelm II 294n354
Wilkerson, Christine 4
William II 232n577
Williams, Edward Ellerker 209n73, 285n162, 395n15
Williams, Howard 236
Williams, Jane 285n162
Wilson, John 231n572
Wilzek, Count 317, 318
Wilzekgang 317
Wiradjuri people 357
Wollstonecraft, Edward 20
Wollstonecraft, Elizabeth 20
Wollstonecraft, Mary 1, 3, 332, 343, 396n37; Wollstonecraft's educational philosophy 3; *Lessons* 3, 24n2; *Maria, Or The Wrongs of Woman* [1798]) 3; *Mary, A Fiction* [1788] 3; *A Vindication of the Rights of Woman* (1792) 3; *Letters Written during a Short Residence in Sweden, Norway, and Denmark* (1795) 3
Wongwibinda *see* Kangaroo Hills
Woollacott, Angela 336
Wooloomooloo 141, 225n404
Wordsworth, Dorothy 343
Wordsworth, William 223n364, 350n4
World War I 357, 365n2
Wright, Owen 359
Wuthering Heights 244, 281n60
Wyagdon 34, 59, 65, 84, 91, 100, 115, 201n3, 228n480

Yemen: Aden 247, 281n66
Young, Captain 158, 228n480, (Cpt Y in Pauline Clairmont's Journal) 174
Youngs, Tim 346

Zdaunek 23
Zeller Staritzen 314
Zellerhut peaks 314
Zimmerman, Emil von 258, 288n198
Zinnödl 319
Zucker, Frida *see* Clairmont, Frida (née Zucker)
Zucker, Johann 374
Zucker, Marie (née Maria Pfeifer) 374
Zum Goldenen Greifen 314

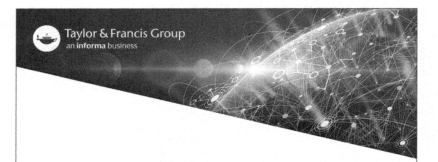

Taylor & Francis eBooks

www.taylorfrancis.com

A single destination for eBooks from Taylor & Francis with increased functionality and an improved user experience to meet the needs of our customers.

90,000+ eBooks of award-winning academic content in Humanities, Social Science, Science, Technology, Engineering, and Medical written by a global network of editors and authors.

TAYLOR & FRANCIS EBOOKS OFFERS:

- A streamlined experience for our library customers
- A single point of discovery for all of our eBook content
- Improved search and discovery of content at both book and chapter level

REQUEST A FREE TRIAL
support@taylorfrancis.com